AMERICAN
SOLUTIONS
WITHOUT
SACRIFICE

AN END TO SPECIAL INTERESTS
A RETURN TO AMERICAN MIDDLE-CLASS INTERSESTS

★ ★ ★ ★ ★ ★ ★

RONALD A. DRUM

(For ordering information call 1-800-879-4214)

PITBULL PRESS * PALM BEACH

Certain of the names, characters, places, and incidents either are the product of the author's imagination or are used fictitiously. Any resemblance to events or persons, living or dead, is entirely coincidental.

Although the author and publisher has exhaustively researched all sources to ensure the accuracy and completeness of the information contained in this book, we assume no responsibility for errors, inaccuracies, omissions or any other inconsistency herein. Any slights against people or organizations are unintentional. Readers should consult their government representative at the local and national level, or their attorney, or accountant for specific applications to any data or suggestions in this book.

American Solutions Without Sacrifice. Copyright © 1996 by Ronald A. Drum. Printed and bound in the United States of America. All rights reserved. No part of this book may be reproduced in any form or by any electronic or mechanical means including information storage and retrieval systems without permission in writing from the publisher, except buy a reviewer, who may quote brief passages in a review. Published by Pitbull Press. First edition.

Library of Congress Cataloging in Publication Data:

Drum, Ronald A.
        American Solutions Without Sacrifice: an End To Special Interests-A Return To American Middle-Class Interests / Ronald A. Drum — First Edition, First Printing.

        LCCN   96-092594 (1996)

        ISBN   0-9654025-0-9 (1996)

        96-092594
        CIP

Copyright © 1996 by Ronald A. Drum

Edited by Kandace Phillips, Andrea Rodriguez, and Sandra Pekar.
Typeset by Kandace Phillips

Price: U.S. $15.95

PITBULL is a tradename and trademark belonging to Pitbull Publishing.

FOREWORD

On June 27, 1991, I sent a letter to Representative John M. Dingell (D-MI) regarding the state of the nation as I saw it from my own perspective then. A copy of this letter was sent to every member of the U.S. House of Representatives, every member of the U.S. Senate, the Governor of every state, and to every major newspaper and major media talk show in the United States. Over 40% of the elected officials who were sent copies of this letter responded. Some of these responses were mere courtesies, and others were very passionate in their agreement with what I suggested might be a *solution for creating 30 million, high-wage, quality jobs in the United States* during the decade of the 1990s. A few of these letters have been included in Appendix B of this book. This letter created *no* change in America, and was probably forgotten by most of its recipients within moments after they had signed their impassioned response letters to me. I should also remark that there were no responses from anyone in the media, except from the L.A. Times, the editor advising me that they do not publish manuscripts. I presume this was because the June 27, 1991 letter to Congressman Dingell was not a thirty-second-sound-bite.

It was this June 27, 1991 letter to Congressman Dingell and those *so quickly* forgotten, yet impassioned responses from so many of our elected officials that I received in 1991, that inspired me to go directly to you, the American people, with some of the *solutions* presented in that letter, and *solutions* in other letters I have been writing to Washington over the years.

In the year 2000, I hope that I will not be looking back and saying, in my next book, that you too, after possibly being impassioned to restore the American Dream and some of the solutions that you agree with in Chapters 19 and 20, that you too, did nothing.

Ronald A. Drum

******

Greater than the tread of mighty armies is an idea whose time has come.

Victor Hugo

PROLOGUE

THE BOOK OF PSALMS
BOOK ONE
PSALM 1

Blessed is the man
 Who walks not in the counsel
  of the ungodly,
 nor stands in the path of
  sinners,
Nor sits in the seat of the scornful;
But his delight is in the law
  of the Lord,
And in His law he meditates
  day and night.
He shall be like a tree
  Planted by the rivers of
  water,
That brings forth its fruit in
  its season,
Whose leaf also shall not
  wither;
And whatever he does shall
  prosper.

The ungodly are not so,
But are like the chaff
  which the wind drives
  away.
Therefore the ungodly
  shall not stand in the
  judgment,
Nor sinners in the
  congregation of the
  righteous.

For the Lord knows the way
  of the righteous,
But the way of the ungodly
  shall perish.

CONTENTS

1 | Numbers Can Be Scary!

The National Debt

Have you ever tried to write down the number *five trillion*? Perhaps just to see how it looks, or how many zeros it has? Or maybe you wanted to get a feel for this *America's National Debt* relative to your weekly take home pay? Well, I attempted to write it down and had a real problem just figuring out how many zeros were involved. After a few tries, I think I finally got the right amount of zeros.

5,000,000,000,000

When I put in the dollar sign and two decimal places, the magnitude of *America's National Debt* became a nightmare.

$5,000,000,000,000.00

If you look at the National Debt in the context of how many new American millionaires could be created from this $5 trillion, the answer would be an astounding 5,000,000 new American millionaires. Now, this would take a whole bunch of those poor people and homeless right out of poverty. It would result in one helluva **bang** to the consumer retail industry, the housing industry, and all of the four professions cited in this book, vis-à-vis the trickle-down-effect. The unfortunate fact is it's a *debt, not a surplus,* and, therefore, we won't be making any more new American millionaires.

Now, we have another problem. The $5,000,000,000.00 is the amount that our government admits owing at the end of June 1996. Now, the shock-waves begin! Like you, and probably 266 million other Americans, I keep saying to myself, "It ain't got nothing to do with me. — I didn't borrow it; I didn't spend it; I don't owe it; and I sure didn't guarantee it."

Then I tried to rationalize a work-out to put this whole debt thinking in calmer perspective. What if it were the *mortgage* on a five trillion dollar house I might have had the insanity to buy? How much a month in interest and principal would it cost to pay it off in thirty years? Using today's best mortgage interest rate, 8.29%, blew-up my computer when I put in the variables, so I worked it out by hand. After a couple of hours, I figured the monthly payments. Now you're asking: "So what did it come to?" An astronomical $37.7 billion per month, or just over $1.25 billion per day! Now, I'm convinced - those 535 maniacs in Congress are not just crazy, but also suicidal.

The good news is this only comes to a monthly contribution for each American man, woman, and child of $141.77 a month for 30 years. This presumes, of course, that all 266 million of us are willing, and more importantly, able to contribute that $141.77 per month. How do you tell someone on Social Security that he or she has to pay back $141.77 a month to pay down the National Debt? How many kids in this country get a weekly allowance large enough so he or she can ante-up his or her $141.77 each month?

Then I thought about all of those single-parent-families, those on welfare, the homeless — and the working-poor. It doesn't seem fair to expect any contributions from these folks since the Republicans have already contracted-away even their subsistence moneys, which will probably result in their mass starvation before the year 2010 - long before this debt can be repaid.

It wasn't long before I concluded that only one fifth of us could afford to contribute. With this realization, the monthly mortgage payment for those of us left came to $708.85 a month. What your government does not include in this $5 trillion National Debt number are those off-balance sheet obligations, such as Bob Dole's and his wife's federal pensions, and don't forget those other vested obligations, such as the federal pensions due our public servants (all those present and past U.S. Congressmen and U.S. Senators); state and local government debt; unfunded future Baby Boomers Social Security benefits, etc., etc.? If all of the aforementioned off-balance sheet items were added to the known $5 trillion National Debt, the *real* National Debt would exceed $20 trillion, with each of us being burdened to the tune of $2,835.40 per month for the next 30 years! That's the equivalent of each of us giving up four brand new, leased 560SL Mercedes Benzs. Certainly, this is not part of that ***American Way*** you've been anxiously using to excuse all malfeasance of your elected representatives over the past thirty years!

It was when I arrived at the $20 trillion National Debt number that I became absolutely certain none of this was any of my business and decided I was going to retire to Ireland. I was also absolutely convinced those 535 maniacs playing ***politics*** and ***money madness*** in the U.S. House of Representatives and U.S. Senate were completely out-of-their-minds, or as they say in California: "Must've been smoking some bad-rope in the back rooms over there in Washington, D.C.!" — Something I, too, had long ago concluded, but had put in the denial quadrant of my brain. This, along with such other *inside-the-beltway-scandals*, i.e. Senator Orrin Hatch's and Arlen Specter's disgraceful orchestration of the televised Clarence Thomas-Anita Hill U.S. Senate Judicial Committee Hearings in 1991; Watergate in 1973; Iran-Contra in 1988; Filegate in 1996; Whitewater-gate in 1995; and Hillarygate in 1992-199?.

So what if the National Debt doesn't get paid?

Then I read the morning's newspaper. Front page news: 101 American Billionaires. I think, "Nobody makes this kind of money without a little larceny!" So, I think lawyer-like: A little *financial eminent domain*. We'll have the government confiscate *one billion dollars* a piece from these high-flyers for the public well being to reduce the National Debt. Bingo! The National Debt drops One Hundred and One Billion Dollars and only a few of our billionaires are left without at least a hundred or so million dollars in accrued interest in their sundry and other usually hidden Swiss Bank accounts!

Now only $4,899,000,000,000.00 of the National Debt to go.

I'm still short, so I think CPA-like: What about those other 2,000,000 or so American Millionaires — probably just as dishonest as their more successful billionaire brothers! Bingo! I think: The big money; volume matters, that is with a little more confiscation, vis-à-vis a little more *financial eminent domain* and we now have an astonishing $2,000,000,000,000 ($2 trillion) in newly collected taxes, and we're now down to having the National Debt at:

$2,089,000,000,000

We would have certainly shown all those greedy American Millionaires and Billionaires (many of whom have never worked for their wealth, but received it through theft or inheritance) what it's like to live in the real world. No doubt what some of you are now thinking! Those of you, who recently fell out of the middle-class (due to corporate cutbacks, technology, and under-employment opportunities) are thinking, "America in less than 250 years, has completed its Second Revolution, ridding itself of its First Aristocracy!" Many of them (Billionaires and Millionaires) are now being forced to join the ranks of the homeless, camped out on the streets, and for those more inventive, "networking" themselves alongside you, flipping hamburgers and pizza for $6 an hour, as their kids now attend the same public schools as your kids. Even you bemoan their fate, but finally, in the depths of your own mind you know the *level-playing-field* envisioned in 1991 by former President George Bush has finally been realized. America has now joined the ranks, as a full fledged member, of that group we refer to as Third World Nations.

Back To The Brutal Reality of America's National Debt

After going through the above exercise, it struck me how few Americans have even the vaguest idea of the awesome *numbers* that will ultimately impact everyone of us, and once known, may very well scare many of them (you) to death!

So, I started to put some numbers together using some older editions, as well as the most current edition of <u>Statistical Abstracts of the United States — The National Data Book</u>, compiled by the U.S. Department of Commerce. The other *numbers* that you will see in the following sections of this chapter have been obtained with the help of the Palm Beach County Library Reference Desk, who researched for numerous hours providing me with information necessary to send some shivers up and down your spine. No doubt the stress of seeing these numbers had significant impact on them. Since I began this book, I have noticed over fifty percent of the research staff has changed.

Over the years, the U.S. Commerce Department's table formats have changed, and therefore I had to — in several instances — interpolate the data to have it make any sense at all, not that the magnitude of the numbers alone could ever really make any sense to any human being still of sane mind.

I projected certain *future numbers* based on both current and historical growth rates, and then had them compared to several of the other *official estimator's* guesses, as well as other *guesstimator's* projections.

As a result of all of these efforts, there developed the section below of "Startling Facts & Figures."

STARTLING FACTS & FIGURES

A. The U. S. National Debt: (1945-1996)

B. The Nation's State and Local Government Debt: (1980-1995)

C. The Nation's Consumer Debt: (1960-1995)

D. The Nation's Home Mortgage Debt: (1980-1994)

E. Assets and Liabilities of Individuals in the U.S.: (1980-1994)

F. Unemployment in America: (1929-1995)

G. The Population Explosion Nightmare: (1650-2100)

H. The World's Vehicles & Automobiles: (1980-2014)

I. Who is Investing in America? (1950-1994)

J. Gross Private Domestic Investment: (1970-1994)

K. Growth in U.S. Social Security Expenditures: (1960-1995)

L. Mergers and Acquisitions — Summary: (1969-1994)

M. Bankruptcies Petitions Filed: (1905-1996)

N. The U.S. Trade Deficit: (1960-1995)

O. Family Values & Other Related Quality of Life Statistics: (1990s)

Now, I am certain your curiosity is fully whetted, so go take a quick peek at the below sections that interest you most, but first put your bookmark here so you can come right back to this spot and see what I found so Stephen King-ish about all of these *numbers.*

A. The U.S. National Debt: (1945-1996)

It is completely understandable if you are sufficiently shook-up and perhaps even angered after reading the beginning of this chapter. You might very well suspect there was malfeasance of office by every member of the U.S. Congress and the White House during at least the past twenty-five years. What is most shocking about the 1980s decade is that the National Debt nearly quadrupled, while the population of the United States, during this same period, only increased by 10%. Since Clinton's watch began in 1992, in less than four years, another trillion dollars has been added to the National Debt, a 25% increase. The population during this same period has grown just over 4.8%. With these correlations, every one of you should be a proponent of birth control and euthanasia. Perhaps there was economic motive behind the three *not guilty* verdicts in the Dr. Kevorkian cases.

"Are you any better off than you were four years ago?" That is what President Ronald Reagan said in 1980, when he ran against Jimmy Carter! Now you have had eight years of Ronald Reagan, four years of George Bush, and almost four years of Bill Clinton, and between the three of them, during their three successive 'watches,' your National Debt has grown from $980 billion to $5 trillion! Remember, all three of these 'watches' were being watched-over by your elected U.S. House of Representatives and U.S. Senate, under the "separation of powers doctrine" set forth by our nation's forefathers in our U.S. Constitution.

Now, it's time for some personal reflection. Are you any better off than you were sixteen years ago when Ronald Reagan was first elected? Or eight years ago when George Bush was elected? Or four years ago when Bill Clinton was elected? Would Dole or Clinton dare ask these three questions of you prior to your going to vote in the 1996 presidential election? But, then, it's not bad for everyone! The Bill Gateses, the Ted Turners, the Rupert Murdochs, and a few others, including every member of the U.S. House of Representatives and U.S. Senate are certainly far better off; compared with 90% of the rest of you, who are now, not only worse off, but have lost most of your hope of ever having a higher standard-of-living, much less keeping the one you have now.

B. The Nation's State and Local Government Debt: (1980-1995)

What most of America's "best informed" are completely unaware of, is that while our federal government was quadrupling our National Debt, America's state and local governments were collectively tripling their aggregate state and local government debts, between 1980 and 1995, to $1.163 trillion. This borrowing occurred over the same 1980s decade, and part of the 1990s, while those 537 maniacs in Washington D.C. were also going *bonkers*. Now, I ask all of you good citizens — are your local towns, cities, or states $633 billion improved over what they were twelve years ago? Are you aware that this $633 billion increase alone over this twelve year period, exceeds all state and local government debt outstanding for the period 1750 through 1960, cumulatively? Again, remember, that for us to pay-off the $5 trillion National Debt over thirty years was going to cost you and me $141.77 per month, that was, if everyone in the nation was able to ante-up — or $708.85 per month, if only 20% of us are in a position to afford it. Now, if you go with the 20% of us being able to afford to pay, you can add on $164.88 per month for the next 30 years to pay-off the malfeasance of your state and local elected representatives. Finally, are you any longer perplexed as to why anybody would want to bother being an elected public servant at the state or local level? Well, now you have your answer. There's just a lot of *pie* out there to be divvied-up amongst these alleged public-service-oriented individuals. Maybe now you understand why all of your current elected officials no longer refer to themselves as *public servants*. This term has virtually been dropped even by the media when referring to those people elected and employed in the public sector.

C. The Nation's Consumer Debt: (1960-1995)

A lot of Americans along with their federal, state, and local elected officials were themselves reaching into their future incomes to finance their personal indulgences of the 1980s. The difference here, of course, is you were borrowing and spending your "own" money and not someone else's as were your "elected representatives" signing your name to IOUs that you were obligated to pay, without either your permission, pleasure, or knowledge. All-in-all, given (1) the record number of "bankruptcies" (See Section M. below), (2) the doubling of the nation's consumer debt over the 1980s decade, and (3) the $70 billion added in home equity loans during this period, all of you and many of our foreign friends will have to conclude that we Americans during the past 15 years had one helluva party? In 1980, consumer installment debt was a mere $298.2 billion; at the end of March 1996, American consumer installment debt more than tripled to $1.046 trillion. The $298.2 billion owed in 1980, and this $1.046 trillion were more than twenty times the consumer installment debt than at the end of the so called "*wild and willie*" 1960s. Sort of makes you wonder how wild the 1960s really were!

D. The Nation's Home Mortgage Debt: (1980-1994)

In 1980, there was $1.480 trillion in home mortgage debt and just under $60 billion in home equity loans in the U.S. At the end of 1994 these figures rose to $4.416 trillion and $258 billion, respectively, an aggregate rise of over $3.157 trillion during this fourteen year period.

There are a lot of strange smelling fish in these **numbers**. If the Federal Reserve Board is correct in its calculation that there are truly $900 billion in government secured (insured) mortgages, and another $3.77 trillion in uninsured residential mortgages out there, it would seem that private mortgage companies, insurance companies, savings and loans, and the commercial banking sector must have gone into a lending frenzy during this same period, but using your savings, your C.D.s, and maybe some of your universal life fully paid-up life insurance premiums.

The next time you hear that the foreclosure rate on residential property is increasing, or that more U.S. jobs are being **outsourced** to Mexico and Bangladesh, think about this $4.416 trillion mortgage debt that is held by the aforementioned institutions, $900 billion of which is guaranteed by the United States Government vis-à-vis the V.A., Fannie Mae, Freddie Mac, and Ginnie Mae. Just think of all these aforementioned government agencies as being synonymous with you, the U.S. Taxpayer. It's the other uninsured $4.416 trillion home mortgage portfolio that rightfully should keep many a banker and insurance company executive awake each night.

E. Assets and Liabilities of Individuals in the U.S.: (1980-1994)

Now, here is where we get down to the real truth. All along most of you have been saying you're not better off than you were four years ago, eight years ago, or sixteen years ago. But according to the U.S. Department of Commerce, you should be almost three times better off than you were in 1980, because the total of all Americans' assets increased two-and-a-half times while all of your total liabilities (your credit card balances, your mortgages, and your auto loans) only increased 2.37

times during this sixteen-year period. One could argue that you should be at least two-and-a-half times better off in 1996 than you were in 1980, regardless of this new debt. After all, isn't the true measure of pleasure the wealth you enjoy, a reflection of your assets regardless of the debt attached to it? Those enjoyable assets rose $6 trillion between 1980 and 1996. If you, like me, can't find this $6 trillion in additional wealth, perhaps you should go back to Sections A. and B. and re-examine how far our federal and state governments have gone into debt to improve our standard-of-living. Maybe it's just a case of America's *top-two-percenters,* we'll soon be talking about, who are the real recipients of 98% of all of the **new assets** created since 1980, and you, the rest of America are the ones who got 98% of all the **new debt** created since 1980.

F. Unemployment in America: (1929-1996)

Since I was unable to find unemployment statistics in any one source (i.e. Statistical Abstracts of the United States 1995 only showed selected unemployment statistics going back as far as 1991), I thought it would be interesting to see, even with all of the hocus-pocus played with the unemployment statistics by both the Department of Labor and the Department of Commerce, how the rate of unemployment looked for the period 1929 through 1995. Since the end of the Great Depression in 1938, where unemployment crested at 19.0%, the trend-line looked good until 1975, when again unemployment seemed to take the upper-hand, rising to 8.5%. Since 1975, except in 1989, and again in 1996, when unemployment reached fourteen-year and eighteen-year lows of approximately 5.3%; other than these two lows, unemployment has remained at least 6.1%; reaching a high of 9.7% in 1982.

I don't believe it takes a *brain surgeon* to understand the cause for the dramatic improvement in the low unemployment rate achieved by the Clinton Administration. Who do you know who isn't required to work two jobs, whether or not his or her spouse or roommate is also working? Now that American workers are priced so low (i.e. in my region, I personally know of two Chiropractors and one MBA flipping hamburgers for around $6 an hour), and their productivity so high, it is no wonder we have such a low unemployment rate.

Remember folks, the term "productivity" is not merely a function affected by new technology or increased efficiency, but more importantly, affected by how *cheaply* the resulting product or service can be produced.

Believe it or not, it is *your continual reduction in wages* which has resulted in America's continual rising level of productivity over the past two years, notwithstanding either technology or the efficiency of those MNCs moving all of their manufacturing plants overseas. Now, it certainly matters that our government defines *increased productivity* simply as *more output per labor hour for lower cost*. Think about this, when you hear about future gains in U.S. *increased productivity.* Won't *maximum productivity* of the American worker be realized when global competition forces his or her wages down to $.20 per hour, or less? Isn't this where we must ultimately go to succeed in the global market? Unfortunately, our *maximization of U.S. productivity* in the global market comes at a stiff price — A Third World standard-of-living and eighty hours of work each week for every man, woman and child in America!

Although the above example is extreme, and hopefully unlikely, we should all consider what the *real measure* of our American standard-of-living is — for us it is our **under-employment** rate, and **not** our **unemployment** rate that matters. It's simply a matter of how many of our former ambitious fellow citizens are now literally working to eat, to feed their children, or just to keep a roof over their heads. How many of you are worried today that you will not be able to make that next mortgage payment? Conversely, how many of you out there today are secure in your current employment, not fearing that tomorrow your company will "downsize" you out, and that you too, will be competing to apply your talents at a fast food counter for a job just long enough to get past this period of "low," yes, I said "low" unemployment. Keep dreaming! If you, and the rest of your peers, don't get it yet, this **under-employment** is permanent, and although you don't like Pat Buchanan for a lot of good reasons, at least he was honest when he spoke about all of Reagan's, Bush's and Clinton's free-trade propaganda, telling you that NAFTA and GATT, like a vacuum cleaner would be sucking jobs out of America; and that you, the American worker, might well be competing in the world's "global-labor-market" at between $.20/hour and $.80/hour.

G. The Population Explosion Nightmare: (1650-2100)

Many of you, who are below thirty and reading this book have probably never heard of Thomas Robert Malthus (1766-1834). Those of you who were alive and in school in the 1930s, are probably very familiar with Malthusian economic theories on over-population. Many of Malthus' economic theories sound very much like they were the basis for Newt Gingrich's 1994 Contract with America. Malthus propounded, among other theories, the following:

1. Population increases would occur at a "geometric" rate (2,4,8,16,32), and if allowed to go unchecked, would overtake the food supply which grows at, what Malthus believed, was an "arithmetic" rate (2,4,6,8,10). In the early 1830s, it was obvious that Malthus did not foresee the possibility of the American Farmer, nor the American ingenuity that would evolve in the 1900s improving crop yield 500% or more per worker, per acre; nor the advent of industrialized corporate farming, as well as the new drugs and other advances in medicine that are now prolonging life everywhere, regardless of the

quality of this service to its sometimes non-curable comatose American citizens with substantial assets, and also subsidized by Medicare, both being paid over to the American medical profession. Factors change, world leaders continue to remain in denial, new-contra-theorists are hatched weekly, but in the long-run, I suspect Malthus' theories will prevail.

2. War, famine, and plague were, according to Malthus, positive checks on the world's population growth. Needless to say, it is not difficult to determine how Malthus would have reacted to the aforementioned continual flow of Medicare and other entitlements, new drugs, and genetic engineering. His position would most definitely have been no funding of Medicare, no funding of Medicaid, no Social Security, no welfare, and no funding of genetic engineering, except if it resulted in fewer people of superior ability with lesser appetites for food consumption.

3. The world's upper-classes should resist any and all welfare measures — and any re-distribution of the wealth through taxation or the inevitable unproductive consequences that result from government welfare spending. Haven't you heard some of this in Newt Gingrich's 1994 Contract with America.

4. Unemployment is endemic to capitalism — its consequence of misery, a natural phenomena associated with over-population created by excessive reproduction in the lower-classes. Obviously in the early nineteenth century, Malthus was ignorant of such things as George Bush's New World Order, GATT, or NAFTA, but certainly he would've approved of each, his own economic theory having its foundation based on laissez-faire capitalism.

5. Since the world's upper-classes would inevitably, as a consequence of not redistributing its wealth through either taxation of itself or subsequent spending on welfare measures, Malthus concluded that "unproductive consumption" by the upper-classes should be encouraged as the means to keep the economy in balance. Now, doesn't this ring true with Newt Gingrich's 1994 Contract with America!

With the exception of some comments I've currently added, much of this information comes from lecture notes taken during my undergraduate studies at New York University. I am certain that present-day economic texts do not differ significantly in their discussion of Malthusian Theory. Of note, there is a striking resemblance between much of Malthusian Theory and the past and current policies of the Reagan, Bush, and now, the Clinton Administrations.

POPULATION PROJECTIONS**ACTUAL AND ESTIMATED

YEAR	U.S. POPULATION	WORLD POPULATION
1980	226,542,199	4.457 billion
1990	248,718,291	5.296 billion
2000	275,005,000	6.169 billion
2020	324,668,000	10.000 billion
2050	391,000,000	23.000 billion

The population projections on the previous page should also be of great importance to each and every person who now inhabits the earth, especially if you already feel the world has become a rather small place. Imagine, if you will, the population of the world doubling within twenty-five years; quadrupling in the next fifty-five years to 23 billion human beings, well in the range of kids today, fifteen years or younger. Some environmental pessimists suggest there might not even be sufficient oxygen to support the projected human population and its expected voracious consumption demands on Planet Earth by the year 2050.

H. The World's Vehicles & Automobiles: (1980-2014)

in 1994, there were approximately 450,000,000 motor vehicles allegedly registered and operating world-wide, and approximately 196,000,000 of these were in the United States. In 1994, world production of motor vehicles approximated 49,693,000, with 24.7% and 20.9% of this total being produced in the U.S. and Japan, respectively. In 1950, the U.S. produced 75.7% of the world's motor vehicles, as opposed to 24.7% in 1994. During the 1977 gasoline shortage, the United States had a total of 151 million motor vehicles, and the world, only 260 million motor vehicles, a little more than half the vehicles that exist today. One can only imagine the turmoil should there be another gasoline shortage, especially in the year 2014 when there are expected to be in excess of *one (1) billion motor vehicles world-wide*.

Automobiles are still one of America's largest exports, approximately five million new automobiles being produced and exported in 1995 and an additional two million used automobiles being exported to Third World Nations in the same year. Just imagine if the U.S. still produced 75.7% of the world's automobiles as it did in 1950! Do you think anybody would be unemployed in America?

I. Who is Investing in America? (1950-1994)

Most of the foreign direct investment into the U.S. over the past twenty years was used to purchase American commercial real estate and "already" existing plants and factories or to invest in U.S. Treasury Obligations (that's how we finance our National Debt). Most of the U.S. direct investment abroad was used to build "new" plants and factories by American Multinational Corporations (MNCs)! If you want to know where twenty million American jobs were relocated, all you really have to do is trace the $2.349 trillion that has been invested abroad, and you will have your answer. Don't expect anyone in the present Administration or in the past Bush or Reagan Administrations to agree with this analysis — to them it's only the efficient allocation of resources, and not American jobs, nor America's standard-of-living, nor our overall national well-being.

J. Gross Private Domestic Investment: (1970-1994)

I include this particular section to avoid the future argument of "bias" that will certainly be directed against me by every Democrat, Republican, and Independent politician in the United States today. They will argue the 1980s saw direct investment by Americans in the United States of $4.2 trillion versus $2.4 trillion that was invested by Americans overseas. I would have no argument with this, except that the majority of this domestic investment can be seen as one flies over our American cities and sees the majority of this $4.2 trillion invested in non-manufacturing Skyscrapers built to house America's new 'global' service industries and shopping centers, built for the convenience of what was hoped to be the everlasting voracious American consumer. Can you figure out what these exportable service industries are going to be besides the transfer and sale of what little technology we have left that hasn't been stolen by the rest of our G7 allies and Iran?

Well, folks, I finally found some hard core data that will blow even the most indifferent of your minds. I will ask many times in this book: Where are all the new jobs being created in the United States? We've got the answer! It was put out by the U.S. Bureau of the Census and was entitled, Fastest Growing Occupations: 1992 to 2005. Guess what folks! If you really want to raise your standard-of-living, you better start learning how to clean bed pans. Here's the list in order of growth:

AMERICAN OCCUPATION GROWTH RANKING

RANK	OCCUPATION	AGR*
1.	Home Health Aids	138%
2.	Human Service Workers	137%
3.	Personal and Home Care Aids	130%
4.	Computer Engineers & Scientists	112%
5.	Systems Analysts	109%
6.	Physical Therapy Assistants	92%

7.	Physical Therapists	88%
8.	Paralegals	86%
9.	Occupational Therapy Assistants	78%
10.	Electronic Pagination Systems Workers	78%

* Annual Growth Rate

Given what I've seen of American education, and also the rather abrupt decline in demand in 1996 for computer engineers, scientists, and systems analysts (whose successes only reduce the demand for additional employment in their occupations), America's hope of survival and improvement in it's standard-of-living appears to be tied to the **bedpan**, the demand for rehabilitative therapy, and home care services for Americans by other Americans. Obviously, as the nation becomes poorer and poorer, and the balance of the middle-class slips further and further into poverty, these allegedly wonderfully new *opportunities* that Messrs. Reagan, Bush, and Clinton created, will evaporate as quickly as American jobs were sucked out of the U.S. by Messrs. Reagan, Bush, and Clinton's giant NAFTA and GATT vacuum cleaners. If you miss my point, think of the proposed congressional major reductions in Medicare and Medicaid growth.

K. Growth in U.S. Social Security Expenditures: (1960-1995)

YEAR	SOCIAL SECURITY	MEDICARE	VETERANS BENEFITS
1960	$ 11,602,000,000	N/A	$ 5,441,000,000
1970	$ 30,270,000,000	$ 5,907,000,000	$ 8,679,000,000
1980	$118,547,000,000	$ 32,090,000,000	$21,185,000,000
1990	$248,623,000,000	$ 98,102,000,000	$29,112,000,000
1995	$336,149,000,000	$157,288,000,000	$38,392,000,000

For those of you who continually wonder what is meant by the "entitlement programs" that both the Administration and the Congress were talking about the 1990s, and are now talking about in this election year, it is primarily the Medicare and Social Security expenditures listed above and further described below. In 1992, entitlement expenditures approximated 61.6% of total government outlays and 57.1% of total federal outlays. In 1995, these entitlement expenditures approximated 63.5% of total government outlays and 61.6% of total federal outlays. Looking at the above chart of selected expenditures, you can get a feel for the horrific growth in these expenditures. Either our poor, elderly, and unfortunate are being a lot better treated in the 1990s than they were in the 1960s or a lot of people and sundry professionals have gotten their hands into what has become an enormous cookie jar. I remind you again, the population in 1960 was just over 180 million Americans, in 1996 there are 266 million Americans. This represents a 48% increase in population and yet we see almost a 3000% increase in Social Security and Medicare spending. Before you reach any conclusions, I suggest you finish reading this chapter and Chapters Fifteen, Nineteen, and Twenty.

There is more bad news down the road. Not only from the growth of these entitlement programs, but from the decline of future tax revenues derived from future generations of Americans who will be required to fund these social programs won't be there. The same elected officials who promise to expand these entitlements in election years, are simultaneously allowing the export overseas of the best of American jobs, and thus, denying those future generations of Americans to earn sufficient wages to carry the cost of these same future entitlement burdens.

Simply put, our elected officials are burning both ends of the candle, which has resulted in America being placed in the financial-vise — exploding entitlement expenditures on one side, and no money to pay for them on the other side. Compounding this problem, is the failure of our elected representatives to adopt a meaningful and effective National Health Care Program, which might well reduce the cost of America's most expensive entitlement programs by as much as 20%. Of course, this would *only* be possible, as later elaborated on, if there were significant criminal laws in place to restrain the greed in the medical care profession, **a tough goal**, given the size and enormous lobbying and PAC power of the Medical Insurance Industry in Washington, D.C. and in every one or our state capitals.

L. Mergers and Acquisitions — Summary: (1969-1994)

Throughout this book there is continual reference made to the "M&A Gang." These M&A gangsters to whom I refer have been around America in force since the 1900s, but did not come into real vogue until the mid-1960s when their composition changed from the singular Robber Baron to the multiple professional combinations of lawyers, CPAs, Raiders, Commercial Bankers, and the Investment Bankers, the majority of whom reside in and around Wall Street.

The U.S. Commerce Department analyzes the effects of the M&A Gangs by breaking down their attacks on fifteen separate American industry sectors, which include, among others, manufacturing, agriculture, mining, construction, trans-portation, and public utilities. All fifteen separate American industries are individually analyzed, and thus, if you wanted to know the total damage inflicted by these M&A Gangs, you would have to add up all of the destruction in all of the sectors. Of the 1501 mergers and acquisitions in 1989, almost 42% were solely in America's manufacturing sector. Of the total merger and acquisitions completed in 1989, 542 of these represented foreigners acquiring U.S. Companies with a total value of $53.1

billion. On the other hand, Americans, in 1989, acquired 256 foreign companies with a total value of $15.1 billion.

During the entire decade of the 1980s, there were 29,027 U.S. mergers and acquisitions valued at almost $1.3 trillion. This compares with 4,789 such transaction in the 1950s, 12,579 in the 1960s, and 18,361 in the 1970s. In 1990, there were 4,239 mergers & acquisitions valued at $205 billion; in 1991 there were 346 mergers & acquisitions valued at $141 billion; and in 1992 there were 3,502 mergers & acquisitions valued at 125 billion. Obviously, there are currently slim pickings for the M&A Gangs after the rampages of the 1980s and 1990s. Supporting this fact, are the declining incomes in the 1990s of the legal and CPA professions, who were major benefactors of this destruction of America.

The mergers and acquisitions prior to the early 1970s were of a vastly different character than those that occurred in the period 1972 through today — different in that it was generally the *acquiring company* that conceived the idea of a particular merger or acquisition, and not a Raider, investment banker, lawyer, or CPA. Most pre-1972 mergers and acquisitions were based on certain genuine industrial or economic *efficiencies* or *objectives*, as opposed to the post- 1972 mergers and acquisitions that were motivated by the humongous profits and fees relating to the insidious efforts of the M&A Gangs to break up companies, and then sell the sum of the parts for two or three times more than they had paid for the company as a whole. This new financial profit factor being the *new-age-american-economic-objective*, regardless of the economic efficiencies or objectives achieved by the targeted American Industry or Business.

M. Bankruptcy Petitions Filed: (1905-1996)

As you might recall from Section G of this Chapter, America's population increased slightly more than 10% between the period 1980 and 1990, whereas the number of bankruptcies filed during this same period rose almost 300%.

If you look back at the Sections involving our National Debt, State and Local Government Debt, Mortgage Debt, and Consumer Debt it should be obvious that the picture is not going to be getting any better in the near future, unless some drastic steps are taken to foster America's economic growth. I also suspect that the improvements of 1991 and 1992 in the American consumer debt picture observed by Alan Greenspan, Chairman of the Federal Reserve Bank, through his continual pointing to the reduction in overall consumer debt was not so much a 'pay-down' of consumer debt, but rather a result of the large number of bankruptcy 'write-offs' occurring during this same two year period in the United States. The comparative statistics set forth below for the period 1985-1996 supports this allegation..

In 1985, 364,536 bankruptcies were filed in the U.S. This number rose to 561,278 in 1987, to 594,567 in 1988, to 642,993 in 1989, to 725,484 in 1990, to 880,399 in 1991, to 972,490 in 1992, and then dropped back to 918,734 in 1993, and even lower in 1994, to 845,257. Increases in filings again occurred in 1995, with 881,399 bankruptcies being filed. It is estimated that in 1996, the number of bankruptcy filings will approach 1,050,000. The first four months of 1996 represents the largest four month rate of increase in filings since 1986, and also represents the largest four month rate for total bankruptcies ever filed in the United States. Based upon consumer installment debt outstanding as of March 1996 at an all time record high of $1.045 trillion, and with American jobs and industries shrinking, there is no question that future bankruptcies will continue at these new historic record levels.

N. The U.S. Trade Deficit (1960-1995)

In order to understand the true meaning of the U.S. Trade Deficit, you must look to both *exports* and *imports*. "Exports" are reflective of "jobs" created by goods manufactured in the U.S. and exported overseas; and "imports" are reflective of the "jobs" lost in the U.S. where goods are manufactured overseas for consumption by Americans.

According to the former Bush Administration, $1 billion in exports results in the creation of 20 thousand new jobs, and thus, it would take $1 trillion in new exports to create the 20 million jobs which Mr. Bush promised he would create during his Administration. Mr. Clinton and the gurus in his Administration claim that since taking office they have created 10 million new American jobs by June of 1996. I showed you where the growth jobs are in America in Section J of this chapter. The majority of these jobs certainly weren't in the high-tech, high-export market you hear Mr. Clinton speak of or that you heard Messrs. Bush or Reagan talk about between 1980 and 1992. It is because of all this political double-talk that it is important to always keep in mind the difference between **under-employment** and **unemployment** which will be emphasized and re-emphasized throughout this book.

Although there have been some advances made in America's upper economic strata, especially in the employment areas of computer technology and genetic engineering and research where good paying jobs have been created, there is very little else to cheer about for the 90% of Americans who need, but will never have, the opportunity to become a job-holder in these two elite technological groups. This is primarily due to their varying, and often deplorable, levels of education, and more importantly, because of the scarcity of these jobs which will become scarcer, the greater the success these new occupations have.

This squares with the fact that the most the U.S. has ever exported (1994) in manufactured goods outside of its borders came to only $502.8 billion. The promise, which I like to refer to as the "Big Lie" in the Bush formula, was that this $502.8 billion in exports was only $62 billion in increased exports. This should have resulted in an additional 1,240,000 new

American jobs over the two years after Mr. Bush left office, and far short of the 18,000,000 new export-created jobs he had projected being created during his 1992 election campaign. The truth in 1992 was that American unemployment was at record highs because even with the rather modest increase in jobs from exports, hundreds of thousands of American blue-collar manufacturing jobs of ordinary Americans were still being exported to Mexico and other low-cost job markets. The estimates of the growth of the high-tech, high-pay new jobs were never realized in the numbers estimated by the Bush Administration because they just weren't there. One also has to wonder what "goods" Mr. Bush was contemplating would amount to $1 trillion in "new" American exports?

So, let's take a careful look at the underlying data that Mr. Bush, during his watch, used in support of the "Big Lie," or "Fast-Track," the accelerator of the NAFTA deal. Here, Mr. Bush and Carla Hill, the U.S. Trade Representative at the time, were saying that the "Fast-Track" of NAFTA would result in a $6.4 trillion "megamarket" of 363 Million consumers. To the always 'greedy' American ear, this sounded spectacular — even fabulous — and perhaps even a trip back to the alleged glorious days of the Reagan 1980s. Let's remove some of the 'spin' for those 'greedy' Boobus Americanus who were blinded by this fifteen-second 'megabuck' sound-bite, and put these factors into the equation:

- Of the 363 million consumer market, 253 million are Americans. Canadians represent a mere 27 million, and Mexicans, 83 million. That means almost 70% of this megamarket is already a free market to America (us)!

- The 1991, per capita income of Americans was $22,400; the Canadians were close with $21,980, and the Mexicans were at a meager $3,400. Do you think its the Canadians who are going to be buying all of America's "new" export goods? Guess again?

- The 1991 American manufacturing wage was $16.02 per hour, the Canadians were second at $14.77, and the Mexicans were a distant and shameful third at $1.80 per hour — approximately one-tenth of the American hourly manufacturing wage! How many Cadillacs, or for that matter Sunbirds, do you think are going to be sold in Mexico?

- Finally, for those of you who are not yet convinced, look at the three countries' GDPs (U.S. $5.7 Trillion, Canada, $500 Billion, and Mexico $300 Billion) — the U.S. represents 87.7% of the this 'megamarket's' buying power, Canada 7.7%, and Mexico 4.6%. Does it still sound to you like a 'new' $6.4 Trillion consumer 'megamarket?'

So, you may all now wish to ask Mr. Bush, where are the Mexicans and Canadians, the alleged source of America's new "export trade" through "Fast Track NAFTA" going to raise $1 trillion, or even half of this, to purchase all of America's new allegedly competitive products? Or, is it the service industries, i.e., such thugs as our investment advisors and stock brokers, or was he referring to the selling of advice by our lawyers and CPAs that our North American trading partners were going to be importing from us? I don't think our neighbors to the North or South will be fooled into allowing these services into their countries. I want all of you readers of this book to keep this in mind when you read Chapter Thirteen - The Free Trade Myth and the two Chapters that are dedicated to CPAs and the Legal Profession.

It is also important to know that up until the 1980s the United States always had a trade surplus. But, since Reagan of the early 1980s, the United States has had a continuing and explosive Trade Deficit. In 1987, the U.S. Trade Deficit peaked at $152.5 billion. It is fairly safe to say that the combined Trade Deficits of the 1980s wiped out all U.S. Trade Surpluses of the previous 200 years. In 1988, 1991, and 1992, some improvement was seen as the Trade Deficit was reduced to $118.5 billion, $65.3 billion, and $84.5 billion, respectively. But, the Trade Deficit again exploded in 1993 and 1994 to $115.6 billion and $151.1 billion, respectively. In 1995, the U.S. Trade Deficit slacked back to $111 billion. This data implies one of three things: (1) Foreign goods are superior or cheaper to American goods and thus, American jobs are still being exported out of America; or (2) The decline to $111 billion in 1995 reflects a decline in America's disposable income and the American wallet can no longer afford the imports of the past which is contradicted by the rise in imports of almost $178 billion between 1990 and 1994; or (3) The Reagan, Bush, and Clinton Administrations have lied to us with regard to their assessment of the effects of GATT and NAFTA, that these treaties would result in tremendous growth in American *exports*, which only grew over the 1990 to 1994 period by $119 billion, far less than the growth of $168 billion in American *imports* over this same period. Conclusion: The America's export of its jobs during 1990-1994 continues at an alarming rate of no less than 395,000 jobs per year based on the net Trade Deficit of $69 billion during this four year period when measured by George Bush's formula of $1 billion in exports resulting in 20,000 new or lost American jobs.

O. FAMILY VALUES AND OTHER AMERICAN QUALITY OF LIFE STATISTICS

Like many of you, I search out other people's solutions to the problems facing America vis-à-vis the plethora of current T.V. news shows. For the past six months, I have been jotting down statistics quoted by famous Americans that have appeared on several of these shows. The following compilation of alleged facts, is probably reliable, or at least as reliable as the other data set forth in this book that has been garnered from U.S. government sources. During the first six months of 1996, there were positive facts, negative facts, and a lot of contradictory facts. I suggest this is due to many of our famous Americans, especially those in politics, attempting to put the most favorable "spin" on the facts that serve their interests. The facts I jotted down are as follows:

- Conservative talk radio and T.V. host Armstrong Williams is heard nationally by more than ten million listeners.

- Conservative talk radio and T.V. host Rush Limbaugh is heard nationally by more than thirty million listeners.

- $650 million was lost by the cellular telephone industry in 1995 as a result of theft (cloning) of services by cellular telephone pirates.

- 80% of the American population no longer reflects membership in what is described as the nuclear family (Ozzie & Harriet Nelson of 1950's fame).

- In thirty years America has gone from having 17% to 37% of its children living apart from their natural fathers.

- 95% of Americans pray.

- 66 2/3% of Americans are members of a Church or Synagogue.

- 75% of Americans who marry, get married in a church.

- Over 50% of American marriages end in divorce.

- In 1995, $400 billion was stolen by dishonest U.S. telemarketers.

- 53% of black men between the ages of 21 and 34 are unemployed.

- In the entire history of the United States there have only been two black people elected to the U.S. Senate.

- There has never been a black CEO, President, or Chairman of the Board of a Fortune 500 company.

- In 1995, black people made $6.00 to every white person's $10.00 wage in America.

- In 1965, black people made $6.10 to every white person's $10.00 wage in America.

- In 1960, one-third of black women worked in the U.S. Labor Force as domestics.

- In 1990, college educated black women earned 10% more than their white women contemporaries of the same age and education.

- 87% of Afro-Americans in 1940 were below the poverty line.

- 30% of Afro-Americans in the U.S. were below the poverty line in 1970.

- 30% of Afro-Americans in 1995 still remained below the poverty line.

- Black families make about $26,000.00 a year, whereas white families make about $28,000.00 per year.

- In 1995, Black families in America have net worths of, on average $4,000.00 whereas white families have $44,000.00 of net worth on average.

- $5 trillion has been spent on the war on poverty since 1965.

- In the past twenty years 80% of those in the middle-class have had their standard-of-living decline.

- 25% of the children in this country work and live in poverty.

- Since 1988, the opportunity for Americans to change class (class mobility) has declined 75%, with more people involuntarily falling out of the middle-class than ever before.

- America has created 28 million jobs since 1980, 8.5 million of these jobs being created after 1991.

- Since 1980, 97% of all increases in income has gone to the top 20% of Americans, and the remaining bottom 80% have had their income increase by 3%.

- The United States has been the most productive and competitive nation in the world for the two years of 1994 and 1995.

- With regard to income distribution, 20% will always be at the bottom, 20% at the top, and 60% will always be in the middle (this is a clear example of political rhetoric, i.e. does this structure look like a pear, an orange, or a mushroom, the head being the top two percenters?).

- 60% of all jobs created in the U.S. in the last ten years were created by small businesses employing fewer than seven employees (author's comment: 90% of all small businesses fail within their first five years of operation).

- One out of every four jobs that exists today wasn't around in 1980 (author's comment: conversely three out of eight jobs that were in the United States in 1980 are in Mexico and other foreign countries today).

- $500 billion will be required to bail out the S&L crooks of the 1980s.

- In 1995, only 11 to 12% of the American work force were Union members.

- More Generation X-ers (those in their twenties) believe in UFOs than believe that Social Security will be around in the year 2040 (author's comment: probably the year 2021 would be more realistic).

- The $380 billion in U.S. taxes going to the poverty industry is paid 80% to those who run the industry (the administrators, social workers, etc.), with 20% going to the poor.

- The head of Nike Shoes made more money than all of the Nike employees in Indonesia who produced 19 million pairs of Nike sneakers in 1995.

- In 1995, corporate welfare (U.S. taxpayer dollars directly or indirectly given to U.S. corporations) was estimated to be $140 billion a year.

- In Scandinavia, less than 1% of children live in poverty.

- The United States remained the richest nation in the world in 1995 (author's comment: everything is relative, one can only imagine how much more badly the rest of the world is doing).

- American pension funds have in their control $4 trillion.

- Over the past twenty years, as a result of treaties like NAFTA and GATT, Americans have suddenly come into competition with a billion new workers in the rest of the world.

- America's productivity growth rate in the 1960s and 1970s was 4% a year. Since 1980, American productivity growth has averaged 1% a year.

- People earning the minimum wage in the United States earn half the poverty level.

- The bottom 90% of American people, in terms of wealth are equal to the top 1% of the American people.

- In 1979, there were only ten CEOs in America who made $1 million or more per year.

- In 1995, there are no less than 700 CEOs making between $1 million and $221 million per year.

- With a negative GNP and a 25% unemployment rate during the Depression years of the 1930s, both crime and illegitimacy were less than 10% per capita of what they are today.

- In 1995, it is estimated there are 3 million cocaine addicts in the United States.

- In 1995, it is estimated that there are 250,000 youths annually joined gangs.

- In 1994, over half of America's public school teachers sent their children to private schools.

- In the last general election in 1994, more people voted in fourteen states for "term limitations" than voted in the national elections.

- 25% of all the equities in the stock market today are owned by pensions and retirement funds.

COMPOSITE DICTIONARY

Gross Domestic Product (GDP): GDP differs from Gross National Product (GNP), in that it only measures the country's total output of goods and services, giving no consideration to investment by foreign investors.

Gross National Product (GNP): The total value of goods and services produced in the U.S. economy over a specified period of time, usually one year. The GNP growth rate is the measure of how well the economy performed over the specified period. GNP includes all consumer and government purchases, private domestic and foreign investments in the U.S., and the total value of exports. The term "Real GNP" is the inflation-adjusted version of GNP.

Home Equity Loan: A concept of consumer borrowing that took hold "en mass" during the later part of the 1970s and exploded through most of the 1980s. Essentially the loan is a credit line offered by banks and brokerage firms allowing homeowners to borrow against the built-up equity in their home. The credit line is secured by whatever value the homeowner has in his or her home at the time the credit line is established, thus all mortgages that remain open on the property prior to the creation of this home equity loan remain superior to this new line of credit. The home equity loan itself may be looked at as a revolving-credit-line "second mortgage."

Most important is to put Home Equity Loans in perspective as they relate to the American debt picture. So let's look at some facts. Residential long-term mortgage loans on family homes in the United States in 1960 amounted to $139.1 Billion; by 1970, this number rose to $292.2 Billion; in 1980 these loans amounted to $950.3 Billion; and by 1990 these same type residential mortgage loans had reached $2.38 Trillion. From almost being an unknown borrowing method in the decade of the 1970s, home equity loans grew by 1990 to over $70 billion; this representing almost half the total amount of all long-term mortgage loans for residential property in 1960. Essentially this $70 billion, applying the "money-multiplier-effect," and assuming a constant 20% bank reserve requirement, added $350 billion of money supply into the American economy in the 1980s decade. Many commentators have concluded that this is a further example of American's mortgaging their futures to satisfy their voracious appetites for consumption in the 1980s.

Indexing: An arithmetic process of relating one economic variable to a second economic variable, usually inflation, so that each variable "adjusts" with the other so as to remain in the same or equal relationship. Federal income taxes were recently indexed to inflation to prevent what is known as "bracket creep."

Mortgage: A debt instrument usually associated with real estate by which the borrower (mortgagor-homeowner) gives the lender (mortgagee-the bank) a lien on the real property as security for the re-payment of the loan used to purchase the property. The borrower is said to own the property and have full use of the property; the lien is removed when the obligation is fully paid.

The most common mortgages offered by lenders today are the Conventional Mortgage, the Adjustable Rate Mortgage (ARM), and the Variable Rate Mortgage (VRM).

Conventional Mortgages are generally of fixed-terms of fifteen, twenty-five, or thirty-years, and require a monthly fixed principal and a interest payment over their term. Adjustable Rate Mortgages differ in that the interest rate may be changed at specific times over the life of the loan in accordance with an established index such as the Federal Funds Rate, or the U.S. Treasury Bill Rate. Variable Rate Mortgages differ from both conventional and ARM mortgages in that the interest rate may be adjusted on a six month basis over the term of the loan, generally with the interest rate increases restricted to no more than 1/2% per year, with a 2 1/2% maximum increase (cap) over the life of the mortgage.

Tax Deed: The deed given at a "tax-sale" upon a sale of real property made for non-payment of real estate taxes to convey the title of the property to the real property's new purchaser. The Tax Deed does not imply that the property is free and clear of all other liens, mortgages, etc.

Tax Title: The "title" by which one holds land which he or she purchased at a tax sale.

Trust Deed: A conveyance of real estate to a third party (usually a bank) as security for a loan outstanding against real property. A Trust Deed is commonly used in several states in place of a mortgage in that it allows a more efficient conveyance of the property to the lender if the property owner fails to pay his obligation on the property.

Zero-Based Budgeting: A budgeting concept that caught on with great popularity in the mid-1970s which required that all federal budgets should be started at "zero" each year, as opposed to what had been appropriated in the previous year or years.

2 | Getting a Handle on the Problems!

This book is not an attempt at scholarly endeavor, nor is it bound in the protocols of form, footnote, or even good grammar, but it does have a didactic (educational) purpose — its objective is to teach you about your government and the American economy; how they work, and how they have combined to exclude you from the political and governing process of America, and the once-upon-a-time, **American Dream.**

There is very little pleasantry or humor in this book: No sex, drugs, or rock n' roll. Serious problems never lend themselves to this treatment, especially when serious solutions are sought. Once you have a full grasp of the problems, you will be given a firm grasp on the solutions that will assist you in taking back America so that it again serves your needs. More importantly, you will know what **you**, and the **rest of us** have to do to solve the problems that are bringing all of us, and America to its knees.

Before you had read Chapter One of this book most of you knew there were many things *wrong* with the America of today. You also knew there were many things *right* with America or else you would have already been off to greener pastures. The vast majority of Americans and foreigners alike, despite America's decline, agree that America still offers the greatest hope and potential for prosperity than any other country in the world. That's why you remain an American, damned with all of your arrogance, pride, and sporadic demonstrations of patriotism. That's why you still get *goose-bumps* when you hear the ***Star-Spangled Banner***, or when you see one of our young American athletes win an Olympic Gold Medal. But for those of you middle-class American's today, this is just ***not*** good enough.

You know America is on very tenuous ground. The America you've known for years has changed. You also have changed. You hear the media referring to a **new lean and mean America**, in a **new lean and mean world**, but you want it back the way it was promised to you. The way it was suppose to be for you, for your children, and for your grandchildren. But all you ever hear about are America's insurmountable and pressing problems without any apparent solutions except the tightening of your belt and the **lowering** of your standard-of-living!

This book will help you put a lasso around these pressing problems, and show how you can be a part of taking America back from those who have looted and plundered its wealth for the last twenty-five years while telling you it was necessary for the preservation of your American freedoms and liberties. You will no longer be fooled by those who have robbed you, your children, and your grandchildren of your rightful American heritage under the pretense of preserving American democracy, the very system they have used to facilitate the demise of your American standard-of-living..

The Myth of Democracy in American Self-Government

Most of you know there's something very wrong with your government and the direction America's moral tide and social order is heading, but feel impotent to change it. At home, in the office, and even at the mall you hear the dissatisfaction. Damn Bill Clinton! Damn the Congress! Damn the ACLU! Damn the Right Wing Republicans! And &#$% all those Liberal Democrats who put half the country on welfare!

Then you hear the *rationalizations of surrender*: We elected them, so we're stuck with them. So what if every promise they've made before every election is reneged on! That's what politics is all about. Lies, lies, and more lies — and then the next election rolls around. Some of us (even you) actually change parties and vote for the *candidate-of-change*. Whether someone new is miraculously elected, or the incumbent survives, there is still <u>no change</u>; just the same bunch of cats in a slightly different uniforms!

Seeing no difference at all, year after year, slowly destroys your desire to vote. Soon the only segment of the American electorate voting are those with a 'special interest': Gray Panthers, state and local government employees, the Gay Community, the Pro-Choicers and Pro-Lifers, and, of course, the Lawyers, Doctors, and CPAs.

Who do these groups vote for? — Whoever their PAC money or other contributions helped put on the ballot. Even in the rare event, where one seemingly political misanthrope does sneak by the barred-turnstiles of the America's two party political system, and does get himself or herself elected, we can be sure that either *seniority rules* of the particular state, local, or federal legislature he or she enters, or the *party rules* will quickly neuter, or smother any ambitions he or she initially had for change. He or she will either *get along*, *not make waves*, and become a *team player* or will be lost forever in the sub-cellar of the Capitol Building on a sub-committee studying the mating habits of purple penguins on Parker's Peak in the South Pole.

For the ordinary citizen who hasn't the time nor the inclination to schmooze at the unpublicized local meetings held in the little-known now smoke-free rooms of the Democrat and Republican party's Political wards and cells in every county across this country, the voting process is as useless as a thong-bikini to a naked Boris Yeltsin.

These same frustrations trickle down to, and are manifested in, voter apathy during every state, local, and federal election; the vast majority of independent Americans not voting for someone in particular, but, if they vote at all, voting to register their protest against the greater of the two evils on the ballot before them.

Unfortunately, the American voter is right. His or her vote, after the mandates of the back-rooms (the wards and cells) have been forged into the Democrat and Republican *party platforms*; and after the hundreds of millions of dollars have been spent on the thousands of fifteen-second sound bites; and after the *money* or *votes* of the *special interest groups* have confirmed both parties' political agendas along with their desired government spending objectives, why confirm their agendas with your meaningless vote? All we can do from that point on is sit back and watch the grid-lock — our alleged American *representative democracy* again being paralyzed for two-more-years, four-more-years, or six-more-years, while another trillion or so dollars are annually divvied-up from the U.S. Treasury, or borrowed elsewhere to take care of the *special interest groups*, who then, in turn, assure the re-election of those very incumbents they initially had bought into both the U.S. Senate and the U.S. House of Representatives.

What is this *representative government* and *representative democracy* that our politicians, news media, and educational institutions flaunt in front of us under this often seemingly illusive concept of <u>democratic self-government</u>?

Partly, it's the confusion of rhetoric; and partly, it's the over use of certain words. For example, the word *free* attached to almost any other *word* makes *both words* immediately and completely palatable to all Americans; i.e. free-trade, free-markets, free speech, free press, etc., etc., etc., and even free-love, until a lot of American fathers of a lot of American daughters caught on to the moral bankruptcy of this *American-Animal-House-Type* marketing ploy. How is it then, with all this *free rhetoric*, most of us sense our *real freedoms*, as well as our hope, and economic opportunities are steadily being stripped away?

Then there's the respite that occurs every four years; the primary and campaign season is over and you're tuned in for four days to the Republican or Democratic National Convention. New hope! Another Ronald Reagan, George Bush or Bill Clinton has gone over the top and is now on his way with his wife and family to the Convention Hall from his observation booth located in the restaurant in Macy's Cellar, or some other vogue watering hole, where the wonderfully American marching-band music is played to the rhythm of the tons of flickering aluminum reflectors dumped from the heavens amongst a half-a-million red, white, and blue balloons so important to this almost malignant right of passage. In all of us, for the moment, there is a sense of reborn hope. For almost 20 minutes of national T.V. coverage, we all feel the same goose-bumps.

In 1992, it was Hillary, Chelsea, and Bill Clinton, an American family making their way into Madison Square Garden, not to accept the Democratic Party nomination which has just been bestowed, but to deliver a simple ***thank you***, and a well rehearsed strategy photo op. For a moment we forget that it was the "Democrat Majority" of the Congress, the party that Bill Clinton will soon lead as its Presidential Nominee; the same party that stood by as Ronald Reagan and George Bush permitted the lootings of America's S&Ls, the raiding of American Industry by the Mergers & Acquisition Gangs of Wall Street, along with the destruction of America's middle-class and its hard-earned standard-of-living. We only think of a new beginning, as ***hope,*** for a moment, again springs eternal!

As soon as you turn off the T.V., you again ask: "Will a new man at the top ever make a difference?" You answer: "Probably not!" It certainly wasn't you who gave him the nomination to run for President; it was the ***special interest groups*** that brought him to this point in his career, and it is to those ***special interest groups*** that he owes his allegiance. And yet you still want there to be change, but this will not occur . . . .

Not unless you and the rest of America demands fundamental change in the way these alleged public servants are elected, paid, and recalled when they themselves become the richest wards of the state. . . . . Not unless you and the rest of America take a few moments to learn about, and then demand change in our representative system of self-government that again and again disen-franchises you, the American Citizen. ... Not unless you and the rest of America get a better handle on how American Capitalism has become the enriching tool of the few, and demand change in our present system of American Capitalism that should have its focus on maintaining America's and your standard-of-living. There will be no change ever unless you and the rest of America demand change in the free-wheeling, self-indulgent forces that have woven the ***moral fabric*** over the past thirty years, forces which have permitted some to hoard ***kingly fortunes***, destroying America with drugs, and poisoning the entire nation's ***moral values*** with ***pornography*** and ***violence glorification*** under the amorality guise of ***criminal free speech***, posing as what was once defined by our forefathers as ***political free speech***.

No longer can America's weakened, and now fragile, social infrastructure tolerate further indifference and lootings of its morals, its financial institutions, its industries, or its national Treasury as its alleged ***representative government*** both benefits from, and supports America's ***top-two-percenters***' abuse of American Capitalism and their lewd and lascivious destruction of our moral fabric that has occurred over the past fifty years.

If you are one of those people who profited from the decline of America, this book is not for you. Nor is it recommended for the ungodly pseudo-heroes of the 1980s, the Phil Donahues or Howard Sterns, who, for a few TV or radio ratings and its derivative wealth, profited greatly, aiding and abetting the collapse of America's values and morals under the guise of enlightenment.

For those of you who seek to be a part of the restoration of America and its values, this book is MUST reading.

Overview

This book is broken down into Twenty Chapters as set forth in its Table of Contents. Most Chapters have their own unique Spin-Glossaries and Composite Dictionary sections. The Glossaries are unorthodox, the author putting his own "spin" on those glossary terms to give the reader a clearer view of each "term's" esoteric or cryptic meaning. All concepts in this book are presented in such a manner, hopefully to be didactic and informative — "brutal frankness" has not been spared.

By the time you have completed this book, there is no doubt you will see where you fit in America's future, and how you can change American Capitalism, American Government, and American Morality so that your life in America might be seen in the context of hope and opportunity as was once depicted as the "American Dream," rather than what most of us presently perceive as the "American Nightmare."

A Quick Primer On The Learning Process

The first step that anyone should take when seeking to learn a subject is to establish a mental framework, or overview of the universe of knowledge sought to be to mastered. One method used by many successful high school and college students is to first analyze the "Table of Contents" and "Index" of each course's subject textbook.

Upon completing this task, the student immediately has a clear idea of the beginning and end of the subject matter's universe, a feel for the learning flow, and usually a plan of attack to make the learning process more expedient and enjoyable. It is then that the student can begin an efficient learning process, knowing both where the course material begins and where it will finally end.

It is in this light that the framework or outline entitled "The Key Institutions of America" is presented in Appendix C. The major institution of America, and sub-institutions presented are those that make America work, or in some instances, now keep it from working. Inevitably, there will be disagreement with the outline. Some of you will argue for a separate 'Institutional Classification' for — i.e. 'American Political Institutions' with subheadings 'Democratic' and 'Republican' Parties; others will argue that the outline is not as comprehensive or detailed as it might be; or that some of America's major institutions have been left out (i.e. The U.S. Postal Service; The Cruise Ship Industry) and so on. Still others will argue that Doctors, Lawyers, and CPAs, based on their present numeric size and power, should be included in either a 'Government' category, or individually, as separate 'Financial Institutions.'

Here again, this is only a general outline of America's major machine parts being presented to provide a framework so that you will have a feel for the day-to-day economic, political, and social forces simultaneously at work in America. The one thing I am certain of, is that if you return to this outline, or imaginary "Table of Contents" in Appendix C, once you have completed this book, you will have an even greater appreciation for the parts of this great 'American Machine', the complexity of all of its parts, and how it affects you, your economy, your government, and ultimately, your present and future standard of living.

Imagine all of the listed categories and sub-categories in Appendix C that you have just reviewed. And those you, yourself have identified as being overlooked, interacting with one another, directly or indirectly. Think about the interdependencies of one industry on another, or several others, and the numerous interdependencies between government, business and industry that exists presently in the United States. Think about these categories and sub-categories in the context of the global economy of the Twenty First Century - - all of these parts in continuous motion, twenty-four hours a day, seven days-a-week - making up our national and international trade and commerce, and their impact on our social, moral, and economic well being!

Now that you have been through this mind-boggling, perpetually moving machine parts list in Appendix C "Table of Contents," it's time to look through Appendix D entitled "The Illusory Index" of this same imaginary book to get a grasp on how America's Institutions interface and interrelate with one another. Many of the Index subheadings are presented as declarative statements, others should arouse in you a question, and other subheadings are stated as direct questions. Most of the answers to the questions posed will be found in the Glossary and Definitions sections which have been included in the chapters that follow.

Several Chapters of this book will deal directly with many of the listed Institutions or Sub-Institutions that are currently out-of-synch with the needs of Americans or are just simply out-of-control. These Institutions and Sub-Institutions will be examined and scrutinized based upon how most of us ordinary John and Mary Does either participate in their *motion dynamics*, observe them from a distance, or how we are, or have become their victims.

Now that we have our "Table of Contents" and The Illusory "Index" for our *America*, we must take a look at the esoteric language, the so-called *buzz words* of economists, business, and government. These *buzz words* must be defined and examined, so we (the ordinary Mary & John Doe's of America) are all on the same wavelength, or succinctly said, on the same side of that next line drawn in the sand.

In this regard, you may first want to quickly breeze through each Chapter's Spin Glossary and Dictionary Sections. This will get you quickly-in-tune with where this book is going, and will clarify certain things for many of you immediately.

- AUTHOR'S REVERSE "SPIN" GLOSSARY -

American Dream:
<u>What they say it means:</u> To some hard-working Americans it was the proverbial "Home in the suburbs, two kids, two cars in the garage, a career with potential, and an annual three week vacation." To others, it was becoming a rock n' roll or famous movie star, or sports hero. To others, the American Dream meant unlimited money, power, sex, drugs, and a large enough stereo system to entertain (or annoy) the whole City of New York.

Contrary to what you hear, there really is no one single American Dream, and in the 1980s and 1990s it had little to do with "making it through hard work."

<u>What it really means:</u> The abstract concept used mostly in election years to describe what the incumbent has taken away, and what his opponent will restore, in an unending cycle of unfulfilled illusory promises. It works well because of its generic quality, and 'nationalistic connotation.'

American Way [The]:
<u>What they say it means:</u> A term commonly used by many Americans to describe the conduct of their fellow citizen's immorality, dishonesty and out right thievery. The term, as used, is not one of commendation, nor condemnation, but rather one that seems to have its roots in commiseration — i.e. the other guy's integrity, honor, veracity, etc. are in the same 'crapper' that mine are in.

<u>What it really means:</u> The ultimate cop-out, as Americans sink deeper-and-deeper into the seemingly warm and comfortable waters of its own "Made-in-America" cesspool.

Boobus Americanus:
<u>What they say it means:</u> A term believed to be coined by a sportscaster named Gabby Bell (WJNO Radio-West Palm Beach, Florida),

which he uses to reference American middle-class sports-fans, who anxiously pay anywhere from $20 to $1,000 to view a sporting event. Mr. Bell finds it overtly amusing that these Americans are simultaneously complaining about the high prices of their tickets, while simultaneously applauding the multi-million dollar pay raises achieved by a whole host of mediocre athletes, which he never fails to remind his listeners will result in even higher priced tickets the following year. (See also "American Way" above.)

What it really means: The unique American human sub-species that evolved between 1969 and 1992, and that might very well some day dominate on the Earth until the "Second Coming."

Bundling:

What they say it means: The political process and technique of grouping several "issues" under one banner (i.e. for the Republicans — ProLife, favorable capital-gains-tax-treatment for the wealthy, strong law enforcement, and "no-job-quotas") to achieve that political party's agenda on all issues, which if presented singularly would be opposed to what the majority of citizens would want. (See also Two Party System)

What it really means: Within the backrooms of Congress the term "bundling" refers to that process of getting more money to candidates than is allowed under federal election law, the primary method being the particular "Fund Raising Group" instead of depositing contributions received by it, merely endorses the "check" and contributes it directly to the candidate's campaign fund. "Fund Raising Groups" say these questionable contributions should *not* count towards their contribution limit of $17,500 to each Senatorial Candidate, or paying that Senatorial Candidate's bills (depending on population of that Candidate's state — $100,000 in Wyoming to $1.2 million in California) since the "checks" never actually enter the Fund Raiser's bank account. Although the FEC (the Federal Election Commission) established new "bundling" rules prior to the 1988 election, these practices were rampant then, and continue even today.

Capitalism:

What they say it means: An economic system in which the "private ownership" of property exists, as opposed to the "government ownership" of all property; an economic system where the income from property or capital (meaning factories, machines, and other man-made tools in the production process) accrues to the individual or firms that accumulated it and/or own it; where individuals and firms are free to compete with others for their own profit and economic gain; and where the profit motive is the most fundamental aspect of the system's economic objective.

__What it really means:__ Circa America 1980-1992: An economic system where the private ownership of property by the "top-two-percenters" is guaranteed by the government; the income from that property accrues to whoever has political control over the government that protects that property; and where the social order requires that all individuals who are neither connected with wealth, nor talented in such a manner that can be exploited by those with wealth, remain in the lowest economic-class best suited to their skills and abilities as determined by the government — and this regardless of how much wealth is achieved by those primarily in the top 2% of the system's economic strata, or the deterioration of the standard-of-living for everyone else not in the top 2%. Earl Butz, a former member of President Richard Nixon's cabinet exemplified those 2% of Americans best when he indicated that those in the lower strata are essentially happiest when kept barefoot, in warm surroundings, while dancing to the beat of some form of Neanderthal era music.

Democracy:

__What they say it means:__ A form of government where sovereign power resides, and is exercised by the whole body of free citizens, directly or indirectly, through a system of representation.

__What it really means:__ Circa U.S. 1996 — A system of representative government (representing the nation's well funded "special interest groups") where the predominant political two parties, first "divvie-up" (vis-à-vis the biannual, quadrennial, and hexennial November election process) for their party hacks, the seats in the United States Senate and House of Representatives, and the Presidency by nominating or locking-in their "own-party-representative-insiders" on the ballots; then, and thereafter, until the next election, divide the electorate (the people) by continually diverting their focus on such issues as Abortion, Civil Rights, Affirmative Action (job quotas), Willie Horton, and other sundry and miscellaneous "fears," as they precede "quietly" and "unashamedly" to divide up the U.S. Treasury while simultaneously restructuring the United State Supreme Court with their "political representatives" (Justices) for life tenures, as further "insurance" that their agendas and those of their "special interest" constituents will remain a force long after they're gone and are drawing princely government pensions and other government retirement "perks."

Depression:

__What they say it means:__ Commonly known as the "D" word, it is never referred to directly by anyone either in government or business directly. Economists stoically define the "D" word as the period of the "business cycle" when production is lowest, unemployment highest, consumer confidence at its worst, optimism in long-term remission, and prices at their lowest. The "poor" refer to it as **starvation**, the middle-class masses refer to it as **severe economic hardship**, and the wealthy **deny its existence**.

What it really means: Capitalism has again failed in its endeavor at "efficiently allocating resources" due to factors beyond its "control," and government has again failed to prevent another major "looting" of the nation's wealth.

Investment:

What they say it means: The purchase or acquisition of something (i.e. stocks, bonds, mutual fund shares, real property, annuities, collectibles, baseball cards, coins, gold, to name a few) where there is an expectation of earnings or appreciation, or both.

What it really means: With the exception of those limited funds that are invested in research and development, property, plant, and equipment, there is little, if any, real investment in America today. The term "investment" as applied to the purchase of existing stocks or bonds, coins, stamps, mutual funds, do not create any new productive assets that create jobs, produce goods, or add real growth to any of the infrastructure elements of the economy (i.e. new homes, factories, laboratories, education facilities, commercial buildings, roads, railroads, airlines, bridges, etc).

Given the Judaic-Christian foundation of America, one can only imagine what might happen to Wall Street, if the day-to-day trading of stocks, bonds, options, futures, and all of the other investment vehicles was simply redefined as ordinary "gambling," and put on the same level as "Gambler's Anonymous" vices like "horse playing" or spending a lifetime at the "dog track." Some commentators insist that it is the "confusion" surrounding the term "investment" that has resulted in America's failure to invest both in its Industrial Infrastructure (PP&E) and the National Infrastructure of roads, bridges, and transportation systems, etc. The two concepts of "investment" can also be simply defined as: (1) "Financial Investments": the purchase of existing stocks, bonds, and other property which, upon analysis, promises in the long-term "minimal" safety of principal and a "nominal" return; and (2) "Economic Investments": defined as the creation of new or added means of production that includes property, plant, equipment, labor education, training & development, research & development, and which in the long-term promises "greater" safety of principal and "maximization" of return, not just in money, but in an improved real quality of life for all those in the nation. So you ask why haven't we Americans caught on? The answer. We just don't like the risk, nor trust our government to protect our industries as the Japanese, the British, the Germans, and others, protect their industries, which is simply a failure of national leadership, an inevitable condition brought on by the natural insulation created by our present system of "representative government," and the carrot chasing all of American society has succumbed for a faster return on *Wall Street* than *Main Street*.

Laissez-Faire:

What they say it means: Principally an economic doctrine or concept that concludes interference by government in business and economic affairs should be kept at a minimum. The Wealth Of Nations, written by Adam Smith in 1776, described Laissez-Faire economics in terms of the "invisible hand." It was this "invisible hand," according to Adam Smith, that would provide the optimum "allocation of resources" resulting in the maximum benefit for all, if businessmen were free to it pursue profitable opportunities as they saw them.

What it really means: It does not seem that the "invisible hand" that Adam Smith spoke of was the same "invisible hand" of Alan Greenspan, who has a difficult time keeping his "invisible hand" out of manipulating both the money supply and interest rates in the United States. Neither could Adam Smith have been referring to Ronald Reagan or George Bush, whose "invisible hands" have sent to the Congress the largest spending budgets in the history of the United States between 1980s and 1992.

Merger & Acquisition Gangs ["M&A Gangs"]

What they say it means: No one really says what this "M&A Gang" thing really means. They don't say what it means anywhere! They just pretend these "Thugs" don't exist, and never did! Just like the Mafia didn't ever exist. After all, what could possibly be immoral, unethical, or illegal in the eyes of any good Republican Administration when it comes to a few good American Billionaires making a few more Billions, especially when it results in a weakening of (1) the economic and political power of the "middle-working-classes" of America, (2) the "damned corrupt" labor unions, and (3) the "lazy" poor; even if it coincidentally results in the destruction of America's Industrial Infrastructure? After all, what can better improve efficiency and profitability than paying someone $70 a week for an eighty-hour work week, as opposed to $400 a week for a forty-hour work week, especially when you're also able to simultaneously achieve your foremost political objectives: creating a true "American Aristocracy." Global Republican thinking: workers can always be found, replaced, and soon will either be genetically engineered, or be stored on "floppy disks" — Global Republican Theology: it is the "free-market architects" of American Capitalism that are irreplaceable, and truly in "scarce supply!"

What it really means: A rhetorical question is best served by either a rhetorical answer, or no answer at all.

Raider:

What they say it means: An individual, or group of individuals, or a corporate investor whose intention it is to acquire a sufficient percentage of stock of a corporation to exercise a controlling interest. The Raider then usually assumes the role of CEO and installs his own management group. Under the Williams Act (1968), raiders who accumulate 5% or more of the outstanding stock in the "target company" have to make "public disclosure" of this fact and their future intentions regarding the "target company" to the SEC.

What it really means: The "Raider" was originally the vilest member of the M&A Gang, which includes, amongst others, the Investment Banker, a major law firm or two, a major CPA firm, and usually a compendium of commercial bankers required to finance the initial acquisition of stock. Pre-1990 financial theory held that the "capitalist" objectives of the "raider" and his M&A Gang was to streamline American Industry and Business, making it more efficient and globally competitive. If you still believe this, you still believe "Fast-Track" is going to create 2,000,000 new jobs in the U.S. The evidence proves otherwise; all one has to do is drive through America's former steel, textile, machine tool manufacturing industrial centers amongst others, or research the devastation inflicted on America's retail industry to understand the true implications of the M&A Gangs streamlining of America.

Recession:

What they say it means: Recession has been defined as the economic circumstance of your neighbor being out of work; as opposed to a depression, which exists when both you and your neighbor are out of work. Many economist define recession as a down-turn in economic activity as evidenced by at least two consecutive quarters of decline in the nation's Gross National Product. Most Americans define recession as a mild form of depression, where optimism as to the future is lacking, and neither job security, nor the potential for growth is anywhere on the horizon.

What it really means: A decline in the standard-of-living felt by approximately 60% of America's middle-class as a result of Ronald Reagan holding office for eight-years; and for approximately 80% of America's middle- class as a result of George Bush holding office for four-years.

Reaganomics:

What they say it means: Most commentators define Reaganomics as a general collection of Supply-side economic based principles (a no tax, massive wealth-creation economic system, thus resulting in new investment and new jobs) combined with a general collection of conservative, "free-market" policies favored by President Reagan and his Administration.

What it really means: There can be no argument that Reaganomics resulted in a tripling of the National Debt, a decline in middle-class America's standard-of-living, and "economic division" in the country that may take decades to rectify. For those who believed that Reagan and his Reaganomics were responsible for the end of the Cold War, one need only to have traveled the USSR in the early 1980s to understand that Communism was already a victim of its own economic policies, and near collapse. Mr. Reagan and his policies had very little, if anything to do with the collapse of Communism, but everything to do with the "economic dilapidation" America suffers today. And you still wonder why he quickly disappeared into the sunset in 1988? Out of sight, out of mind — and perhaps Boobus Americanus might yet blame this whole "mess" on George Bush!

Rhetoric:

What they say it means: The term as used here refers to "political rhetoric," the language art form developed by the unique breed of American political handlers for exploiting the English language (i.e. "spin" control) so well that those listening believe it to be either directly from the Gospel, or an absolute truth, derived therefrom.

What it really means: The things our politicians tell us, and the things we only want to hear as we remain isolated in our collective American "denial": there is no "bad news," and even if there "was," we still don't want to hear it!" That is, not until it knocks us completely off our feet — so right now it doesn't really matter that the National Debt has exploded to $5 Trillion; and it matters even less that the standard-of-living for the bottom 40% of the population has dropped into Third-World poverty. And it doesn't matter that our elected representatives for the last sixteen years have sold America out to any *special interest group* that would buy a hot lunch for them at Washington's Grill Club.

Supply-Side Economics:

What they say it means: A theory of economics championed in the late 1970s by nationally known economist and professor of economics, Arthur Laffer, who contended that drastic reductions in both taxation and in tax rates would stimulate investment by corporations and wealthy individuals in property, plant, and equipment for the benefit of the entire society.

What it really means: The rich got richer, the poor got poorer, and both U.S. Corporations and Wealthy Americans found more money to invest in overseas property, plant and equipment, as opposed to investment in the American Industrial Infrastructure. Prior to the late 1970s, Supply-side economics was obviously unknown to most Americans, and hopefully it, along with Arthur Laffer, will become equally unknown to future Americans.

Trickle-Down Economic Theory:

What they say it means: Trickle-down economic theory is essentially the "middle-classes" synonym for Supply-side economic theory. It holds that if business and wealthy individuals are allowed to flourish (i.e. not taxed at all) there will follow a natural "trickling-down" of some of their wealth to the middle and lower economic classes, who naturally benefit by the increased economic activity both business and the wealthier members of society will be free to create.

What it really means: The Latin expression "res ipsa loquitur" is best applied here: "The thing speaks for itself."

COMPOSITE DICTIONARY

Bill of Rights: The first Ten Amendment to the U.S. Constitution. The most often referred to Amendments in the Bill of Rights are: the First Amendment, which protects the freedoms of religion, press, speech, assembly, and the right to petition the government for grievances; the Fourth Amendment which protects citizens, their homes, their papers, and their effects against "unreasonable searches and seizures," and requires "probable cause" for required court-issued search and arrest warrants; the Fifth Amendment which protects against: self-incrimination, double jeopardy, the deprivation of life, liberty, or property without due process of law, the taking of private property for public use without just compensation (the government's power of eminent domain), and "indictment" without benefit of a grand jury hearing for capital or otherwise infamous crimes; the Sixth Amendment guarantees the right of a speedy and public trial by an impartial jury, the right to confront witnesses, the right of the accused to bring favorable witnesses to his defense, and the right to legal counsel; the Eighth Amendment protects against excessive bail, fines, as well as "cruel and unusual punishment" by either state or federal governments.

Constitution (U.S.): The written instrument agreed upon by the people of the United States as the absolute rule of law, interaction, and decision for all branches and officers of the government in respect to all points of freedoms, rules, restrictions, and covenants covered by it, which must control until changed by the authority which established it (i.e. by amendment) and in opposition to which any act or ordinance of any of the federal, state, or local governments or officers thereof is null and void. The United States Constitution and ratified Treaties of the United States are the supreme law of the land. On September 17, 1787, the Constitution was approved unanimously by those present at the Constitutional Convention. Ratification of the Constitution by the states was completed on May 29, 1790.

Corporate Democracy: The assumption by America's Corporate Boards of Directors and Corporate Management that they have the unfettered "right" to "loot" the company and its pension plans by selling the company, acquiring other companies, merging the company, acquiring the company for themselves with the company's money, or merely taking the company's money simply by vote or proclamation.

Do-gooder: A term that once had excellent moral connotation until the Republican "Spin Doctors" decided to make persons in this group a part of the "Big Bad Liberal Spending Wolf" species — the term "do-gooder" suddenly becoming a part of the "wimp" world-of-words — that lumps together all those Americans not "tough enough" to see hardship inflicted on the poor and those incapable of functioning in George Bush's tough new world order that emerged in the 1990s — "Democrat Liberals" are those *do-gooders* who supported such programs as Aids to Families with Dependent Children (AFDC), Head-Start Programs, Food Stamps, etc.

Economic Class-The Upper Class: The *top-two-percenters*. The top 2% of the economic strata of the United States as measured by their composite income, existing wealth, and exercise of power.

Economic Class-The Gentry Middle-Class: Generally speaking the next 8% of the economic strata of the U.S. just below the economic upper-class (2%), who are either lawyers, doctors, dentist, Certified Public Accounts, and the upper echelons of American Corporate Management who have generally accumulated less than five-million-dollars or less and whose jobs and earning power are protected by professional licenses, the autocratic exercise over the confidential matters of business and state, or membership in the appropriate organizations and institutions.

Economic Class-The "Necessary" Middle-Class: This group includes those sandwiched-in the economic strata representing the 11th percentile and the 22nd percentile, but who rarely have the "goods" to ever rise into the top 10% of the country's economic strata. This group includes those persons with excellent technical expertise, special (generally unlicensed) academic or organizational skills, and those of superior intelligence who are able to maintain existing economic facilities, and sometimes create new ones. The "necessary middle-class" is the "foundation or bedrock" of the two economic classes above it, and generally possess wealth in excess of $300,000, but under $1,000,000.

Economic Class-The Slipping Lower Middle-Class: This group is characterized by those Americans who are presently employed, but who go home each night unsure of whether they will be employed tomorrow. This group also includes those professionals that were unable to attain the status of the "gentry middle-class." The slipping lower middle-class represents approximately 48% of America's population (the 23rd to the 30th percentile); they live in the suburbs usually thirty-miles from the location of their employment, their spouses are generally required to work full time, and their combined household income does not exceed $70,000; their net family worth never exceeds $300,000, which includes their home and all other personal assets.

Economic Class-The Working Poor: This group comprises approximately 20% (the lower 29th to the lower 11th percentile) of the economic strata and economically represents those persons with less than $50,000 of net worth and less that $30,000 per year in total household income. Both adult members of these households always hold full-time positions in jobs generally considered to be blue-collar or clerical. Another characteristic of this class is that they average approximately 3.4 children per household. If they are fortunate to own their own home (in many cases a "prefab" home or a "trailer"), generally having a value of between $15,000 and $50,000 upon which there usually exists an 80% loan-to-value mortgage.

Economic Class-The Non-Working Poor: This class includes all of those person who are unemployed and who are surviving on various federal, state, and local entitlement or welfare programs, and make up the lower 10th percentile to the lower 3rd percentile of America's economic strata. Generally, these persons have a zero net worth. A vast majority of families in this category are those defined as single parent families and teenaged-mother headed families.

Economic Class-The Homeless: This group comprises the lowest 2% of American citizens on the economic scale. These persons are usually unemployed, but in some instances do on occasion earn the minimum wage, but are still unable to afford even the most meager of shelters. Citizens in this group have been eliminated from all government entitlement programs because they either have no children, are not sufficiently physically disabled, or are not "criminally" insane, although many in this group did spend major segments of their earlier lives institutionalized, being put back into society during the entitlement program cost-cutting decade of the 1980s.

Indifference Curves: A micro-economic theory which quantifies one's indifference towards various combinations of different things. For example, imagine an upper right quadrant graph, the X axis representing different amounts of "apples" in left-to-right ascending order, and the Y axis representing different amounts of "pears" in bottom-to-top ascending order — an individual's indifference to any given combination of "apples and pears" might be shown as the coordinates representing his or her different combined preferences for both — i.e. he or she might accept thirty pears for six apples or twenty-two pears for eight apples or perhaps even twelve pears for twelve apples. The concept here is to show that there are compromises and alternatives with respect to most attitudes, consumption preferences, and the relationship between "sacrifice" and "goal attainment." This will be an important concept to keep in mind as you read Chapters Nineteen and Twenty of this book.

Keynesian Economics: Essentially the theories of Great Britain's most famous economist John Maynard Keynes (1883-1946) of which the primary theory is that "national income" is the key factor in bringing a nation's economy into equilibrium, rather than changes in price as is argued by the classical (Micro-Economic) school of thought. Keynesian Economics is considered to be synonymous with "fiscal policy" (the taxing and spending levers of the central or federal government).

Laissez-Faire Capitalism (also known as "Pure Capitalism"): Located on the absolute "right" side of the political and economic spectrum, and primarily espoused by the "top-two-percenters" (2% of the economic wealthiest), who have both the necessary wealth and power to best exploit this form of economic system, it is defined as that economic system where individuals and groups are left absolutely free of any government regulation, and thus able to make those economic choices which they feel are most appropriate with respect to the needs and desires of their own specific personal objectives. On the absolute "left" side of this spectrum, rests socialism and communism, which in theory holds that the sum of free economic choices by individuals and groups can never result in either the fairness or efficiency of allocating a nation's resources. Between these "left" and "right" extremes exists an unlimited number of ways of attempting to achieve the economic objective espoused by each of the extremes; specifically the "efficient allocation of the nation's and world's scarce resources," and to do it in such a matter which will not destroy the source of wealth, Planet Earth and its ecology.

Liberal: A "hate" term used by Republicans to define all members of the Democratic Party, especially when the Democrat is either up for election or re-election. The term engenders those who support big government and large spending on the public welfare. It generally includes those who take a broad-minded approach to abortion, civil liberties, but who are also anti-death penalty, pro-gun control. "Conservative" is the exact opposite of "liberal." See "bundling" and "do-gooder" above.

Liberty: Exemption from extraneous control. Freedom from all restraints except those that are justly imposed by law or under conditions essential to the equal enjoyment of the same rights by others. Liberty is the absence of arbitrary restraints, not immunity from reasonable regulation and prohibitions imposed in the interest of the whole community. Liberty is *not* synonymous with democracy; liberty implying freedoms, and democracy meaning "representative government."

Optimist: One who adheres to the doctrine that this world is the best possible world and as a matter of outlook, puts the most favorable construction upon actions and happenings, and anticipates the best possible outcome.

Pessimist: One who is inclined to emphasize the adverse aspect, conditions, and possibility of both future and present events, and thus lives with the expectations of the worst possible outcome. Those that adhere to the doctrine of pessimism, generally believe that evil overpowers both good and happiness.

Polarization: Synonymous with "divisiveness." A political tactic of both Republican and Democratic Parties to divide the population along opposing political lines where compromises are made difficult or impossible. Issues such as race, abortion, and job quotas are some of the common polarization tactics used by both political parties to obscure real issues.

Right of Privacy: The right to be let alone; the right of a person to be free from unwanted publicity. The "term" Right of Privacy is a "generic" term encompassing various rights recognized to be inherent in the concept of ordered personal liberty — such rights prevent or restrain governmental interference in "intimate" personal relationships or activities, freedoms of the individual to make fundamental choices involving himself or herself, his or her family, and his or her relationships with others. The right of an individual to withhold himself and his property from public scrutiny, if he so chooses, so far as its assertion is consistent with the same consensual collective right of <u>all</u> others. It is the duty of society to protect the individual's "right of privacy" when they are violated by others who are motivated by curiosity, gain, or malice (i.e. Slander, Defamation, Stalking Laws, etc.). The "right of privacy" is not a "right" specifically enumerated in the U.S. Constitution, although most believe it to be an "implied" right.

Spin: An attempt to cast a bad political situation in the most favorable of lights. More formally, the term "spin" is known as "spin control." Spin control is primarily used by the elected officials and government appointees to disguise bad news in the cloak of irrelevant facts and rhetoric. Some economist in the country have applied a "spin equation" to this practice. It is said if government is delivering good news, divide it by two; if government is espousing bad news multiply it by four to assess its true gravity.

Spin Doctor: A credential generally applied to such experts as Alan Greenspan, Chairmen of the Federal Reserve Board, Richard Darman under President Bush, Director of Office of Management of the Budget, Gen. Kelly, Pentagon spokesmen during the Persian Gulf War, and countless others who have successfully cast a bad situation in a most favorable light, or made small or irrelevant matters, bigger-than-life itself, or vice-versa, as they buried important national issues in fifteen second inconsequential sound bites.

States' Rights: According to the Constitution, states' rights are those powers not specifically delegated to the Federal Government. During the mid-20th Century, it was said to be the "code word" for the broad national opposition to "civil rights."

Three Branches of Government: (Separation of Powers Doctrine) The three branches of U.S. Government are the Executive, Legislative, and Judicial. It is generally thought these "three branches" were envisioned by the "founding fathers" in theory to create a "system of checks and balances" to minimize possible abuses believed inherent in government. The three branches of America's federal government are described below.

<u>The Executive Branch:</u>

The Executive Branch is comprised of the President, the Vice-President, the President's Cabinet that includes the Secretary of Defense, Treasury, Department of the Interior, Agriculture, Commerce, Labor, Housing and Urban Development, Transportation, Energy, Education, and Veterans Affairs. Also included in the President's Cabinet is the U.S. Attorney General, who heads up the U.S. Justice Department.

The following Executive Agencies are also apart of the Executive Branch of Government: the Central Intelligent Agency (CIA); Federal Bureau of Investigation (FBI); the Federal Reserve System; the Federal Trade Commission (FTC); the Environmental Protection Agency (EPA); the Federal Communications Commission (FCC); the National Aeronautics and Space Administration (NASA); the Securities & Exchange Commission (SEC); and the Office of the Surgeon General of the United States.

The Executive Office of the President includes his principle advisers who are: the White House Chief of Staff; the Director, Office of Management and Budget; the National Security Adviser; Director, Office of Drug Control Policy (the alleged "Drug Czar"); the U.S. Trade Representative; the Chairman, Counsel of Economic Advisers; and the U.S. Ambassador to the United Nations.

Other departments and agencies that are also under the Executive Branch of Government include: the Department of Agriculture; the Department of Commerce; the Department of Defense; the Department of the Air Force; the Department of the Army; the Department of the Navy; the Department of Education; the Department of Energy; the Department of Health and Human Services; the Department of Housing and Urban Development; the Department of the Interior; the Department of Justice; the Department of Labor; the Department of State; the Department of Transportation; the Department of the Treasury; the Department of Veterans Affairs; and over one hundred supposedly independent agencies, the most prominent of which are the American Red Cross, Amtrak, the Commission on Civil Rights, the Commodity Futures Trading Commission, the Consumer Product Safety Commission, the Equal Employment Opportunity Commission, the Environmental Protection Agency, the Farm Credit Administration, the Federal Communications Commission (FCC), Freddie Mac, the Federal Labor Relations Authority, the Federal Maritime Commission, the Federal Mine Safety and Health Review Commission, Fannie Mae, the Federal Reserve System, the Federal Trade Commission (FTC), the General Services Administration, the Government Printing Office, the Interstate Commerce Commission, the World Bank, the International Monetary Fund (IMF), the Legal Services Corporation, the National Commission on Aids, the National Endowment for the Arts, the National Labor Relationship Board (NLRB), the National Transportation Safety Board, the Nuclear Regulatory Commission, OSHA, the Office of Personnel Management, the Peace Corps, the Pension Benefit Guaranty Corporation, the Postal Rate Commission, the Resolution Trust Corporation (RTC), the Selective Service System, the Small Business Administration (SBA), the Smithsonian Institute, the Tennessee Valley Authority (TVA), the U.S. Information Agency, the

Voice of America, the U.S. International Trade Commission, the U.S. Postal Service, and the U.S. Sentencing Commission, amongst others.

Of curiosity to many of you may be the Department of the Treasury. Within this Department are the Internal Revenue Service (IRS), the Bureau of Alcohol, Tobacco, and Firearms (ATF), the U.S. Customs Service, the U.S. Secret Service, the Bureau of Engraving and Printing, the Office of Thrift Supervision (OTS), and the Controller of the Currency.

The Legislative Branch:

The Legislative Branch consists of the U.S. Senate and the U.S. House of Representatives. The U.S. Senate has 100 members, two from each state, who are always elected for partially overlapping terms of six-years each. The U.S. House of Representatives consists of 435 members, each member representing approximately 500,000 citizens from their respective congressional districts. All members of the House are elected every two-years. Much of the business of Congress in done in "committee" and "subcommittee." When Congress is in session, literally dozens of committee and subcommittee hearings and meetings are held daily. There are fifteen Standing Committees in the Senate and twenty-one Standing Committees in the House of Representatives. There are four Select Committees in the Senate and five Select Committees in the House; there are also four Joint Committees of Congress: The Joint Economic Committee, the Joint Committee on Taxation, the Committee on the Library, and the Joint Committee on Printing. Also noteworthy is the fact that there are approximately 107 Senate Subcommittees for both the fifteen Senate Standing Committees and four Select Committees, and 243 Subcommittees in the House of Representatives underlying their twenty-one Standing Committees and five Select Committees.

Some of the better known Senate Standing Committees are: the Committee on Appropriations; the Committee on Banking, Housing and Urban Affairs; the Committees on Armed Services; the Committee of Foreign Relations; and the Committed on the Judiciary headed up by U.S. Sen. Joe Biden (D-Del.), notorious for their handling of the disgraceful Clarence Thomas vs. Anita Hill hearings in 1991.

Some of the more prominent Standing Committees of the House are: the Committee on Appropriations; the Committee on Banking, Finance, and Urban Affairs headed by U.S. Congressman Henry Gonzalez (Texas); the Committee on Energy and Commerce, headed by Congressman John Dingell (D-Mich.); and the Committee on Ways and Means, headed by Congressman Dan Rostenkowski (D-Ill.). Also included in the Legislative Branch is the sometimes heroic independent Congressional Agency known as the General Accounting Office (GAO) which was established in 1921, and which reviews federal government financial transactions, expenditures of appropriations of Federal Agencies and reports them directly to the Congress. Of all federal agencies, the General Accounting Office is thought to be the most unblemished and uncorrupted agency within American Government.

The Judicial Branch of Government:

Article III of the Constitution states: "The Judicial power of the United States shall be vested in one Supreme Court, and in such inferior courts as the Congress may from time to time ordain and establish." All Federal Judges, including Supreme Court Justices, Court of Appeals Judges, and Federal District Court Judges are appointed by the President and confirmed by the Senate for life terms. They can be removed only through passage of a bill of impeachment by the House of Representatives and then, only after being found guilty at a formal impeachment trial by the Senate.

The U.S. Court of Appeals includes eleven geographical circuits plus the District of Columbia and a roving "Federal Circuit." Each circuit Court of Appeals is headed by a chief judge and comprises between six and twenty-six judges who meet usually in three-judge panels to review decisions of lower courts in their federal circuits. Should an important case arise within the circuit, larger panels are formed; and in rare cases all judges may join "en bank" to hear an appeal. Salaries for Supreme Court Justices and Circuit Court Judges exceed $100,000 per year. Congress has established Federal District Courts in every state, the District of Columbia, and in U.S. Territories. Each state has at least one such court and the larger states are divided into as many as four sub-districts. The Federal District Court is the trial court and they are divided into civil and criminal divisions. The annual salary of a Federal District Court Judge is approximately $90,000 per year.

Somewhat paralleling the Federal Judiciary is the State Court System. Although each States System differs slightly all are basically setup with "inferior" courts which are the courts of original jurisdiction (trial courts) and appeals courts. Some states also divide their lower courts geographically by counties, cities, towns, or villages. These courts usually have jurisdiction only within their own local borders, and jurisdiction over violations of local ordinances or disputes involving limited dollar amounts. Several states also have specialized local courts handling certain matters such as probate, juvenile offenders, domestic relations, traffic offenses, etc. Many jurisdictions also have small claims courts where injured parties can bring actions without a lawyer. Every state has a state Supreme

Court (usually known as such, except in New York, where the lowest state courts are known as "Supreme Courts"), which parallels the role of the U.S. Supreme Court at the state court level.

As one would expect, almost 100% of the judges in the U.S. are or were lawyers. What may surprise most of you is that two-hundred-and-fifty-one (251) members of Congress are also lawyers. Fifty-nine (59) lawyers are in the Senate and one-hundred-and-ninety-two (192) lawyers are in the House of Representatives. Perhaps from this we should conclude that it is the "legal profession" that is the most significant and powerful "special interest group" in both America and in the U.S. government.

Third World Country: Those countries or nations economically under-developed that were neither politically tied directly to the West or the USSR. These nations have no middle-class and the average annual worker's wage is between 5% and 10% of the average American worker's annual wage. Today many economist believe that the former nations that comprised the USSR, and perhaps even the U.S. will inevitably become part of the Third World.

Too-Big-To-Fail: A concept coined in the very late 1980s or early 1990s to emphasize the importance of not allowing anyone of America's largest fifteen commercial banks to go under (fail); the consequence of which it is theorized by many economists and financial gurus, would have such impact on the U.S. Treasury and the U.S. Taxpayer that it might even bring down the entire financial and economic system of the United States. In essence what is being said is: If a bank such as Citibank or Bank of America fails, such failure might result in the collapse of the entire American economy. Thus the government will do everything in its power, including going "bankrupt" with it to prevent its failure. So much for the "efficient allocation of resources" and "free-market" theories of American capitalism.

Quid Pro Quo (Latin): The literal translation is: Something for something; and as used by contract lawyers, it refers to the "consideration" requirement for a valid contract.

Reaganomics: A general collection of conservative, free market "economic policies" centered around the concept of supply-side economics as favored by President Ronald Reagan and his Administration. (See also Glossary Section-Reaganomics) Are you better off after the eight years of Reaganomics practiced between 1981 and 1988?

3

American Unemployment and Under-employment

Year after year newspaper headlines seem to herald the problems of some far off land.

- *AT&T To Cut 54,000 Middle Managers*
- *Sizzler To Close 480 Restaurants, 4800 Jobs Lost*
- *Chemical & Chase Banks To Combine - 20,000 to be Laid-off in Re-organization*
- *Hewlett Packard to Cut 2,000 More Workers*
- *Unisys Corporation Losses at 3 Billion - Restructuring Will Permanently Eliminate 10,000 Jobs*
- *IBM To Cut 60,000 Jobs Over Next Two Years*
- *Continental Airlines Lays Off 890 Employees as Part of Troubled Carrier's Efforts to Cut Costs*
- *GM Announces Permanent Plant Closing Over Next Two Years and Will Cut 70,000 Jobs as Plants are Closed*
- *Florida Power and Light Company to Eliminate 1,500 Jobs*
- *Scott Paper to Cut 20,000 Jobs in New Consolidation*
- *Digital Equipment to Lay-Off 20,000 Employees*
- *Sears to Fire 50,000 Employees*
- *Philip Morris Lays Off 14,000 to Cut Expenses*
- *Boeing to Lay-Off 28,000 Blue-Collar Workers*
- *Nynex Lays Off 16,800 Employees After Consolidating Computer Division*
- *McDonald Douglas to Lay-Off 17,000 Employees*
- *GTE Corp. Lays Off 17,000 in Downsizing Operations*
- *Delta Airlines Cuts Back 15,000 Personnel*

The list goes on and on. Day after day, week after week. Defense contractors, decimated by the end of the Cold War are projecting lay-offs of over 300,000 Americans by 1998. State and local government lay-offs are expected to exceed 290,000 in the fifty states by 1998. Between 1992 and 1996, the federal government, to reduce the national annual deficit, had cut federal civilian employment by 100,000 and will further cut U.S. military forces by an additional 40,000 through the year 2000.

In 1992, State Governors of half the states requested an emergency $15 billion for immediate assistance from the Federal Government in order to continue to provide necessary services, such as police, Medicaid, etc. Since 1992, these requests have become the norm, and when these requests are denied, state and local services are simply cut back. Then we read in the newspaper that such-and-such city or county no longer has sufficient funds to keep its fire department or police force employed. In some instances, some local towns have even had their water utilities shut down.

During the early 1990s the Bush Administration refused to acknowledge the "R-word" (the Recession word), insisting the economy was either in a robust recovery or the recession itself was non-existent. The Clinton Administration, continuing the 1980s Republican drive toward making America part of the Global Economy, completed the execution of NAFTA and GATT, accelerating the American workers' escalation into decline to a third-world standard-of-living.

It wasn't until the latter part of 1991 that Bush finally admitted that the country had been in recession for almost two years, when the U.S. Commerce Department announced that as a result of certain "statistical errors" total "lost jobs" due to the "now existent" recession had been understated by 700,000 jobs. This brought the total number of permanently lost jobs in the United States for this part of the 1990-1992 recession to 2.2 million, somewhat contrasting with the promised creation of 30 million new jobs by George Bush at the beginning of his 1988 Presidential Campaign.

The Clinton Administration has allegedly created over 10 million new jobs since 1992, but most Americans in 1996 feel more hopeless and deprived of future opportunity than ever before. Unfortunately, the vast majority of these jobs pay thirty to forty percent less in buying power than those jobs lost prior to George Bush's 1992 Recession, and have few if any fringe benefits such as employee medical insurance or pension plans. As pointed out before, and evidencing this reality, is the Clinton Administration's own estimate that in 1996 there are 41,000,000 now not covered by medical insurance, 4,000,000 more than in 1992.

In 1996, there is no greater evidence that the country's economic infrastructure is in serious trouble, than the Dow Jones Industrial's doubling in value since 1992 while simultaneously, corruption in government and racism are the primary focus of the media and the political powers that be. This, of course, is the usual technique for our politicians in Washington to keep Boobus Americanus' eyes off the ball. After all, who can focus on Wall Street's setting the stage for another depression, or the nation's unemployment and under-employment when such issues as Hillarygate and racial civil war are the major threats on the horizon requiring every citizen to purchase of an AK-47 Assault Rifle to feel safe.

Making the latest U.S. unemployment and under-employment data even more horrific than during any previous period are the following realities:

1. The Cold War has ended and there will probably be no excuse to jump start the economy as did President Reagan in the early 1980s. The need for a large military build-up of equipment, bases, and military manpower seems no longer a necessity to the ordinary American since the threat of Communism has seemingly ended along with the "economic benefits" and "deficit spending" that accompanied it.

2. American-owned factories that once provided millions of jobs for middle-class American are now located in Taiwan, China, Mexico, and other areas where the labor is cheap, environmental protection laws minimal, governmental regulation nonexistent, and where the weather is warmer. What incentive is there for American Business to return these industrial factories to American soil? The old American industrial plants should not be confused with the influx of Japanese and European assembly plants built in America since 1990. These assembly plants represent low skill assembly jobs where Americans are generally paid half of the wages of their predecessor skilled American auto workers of the 1960s and 1970s.

3. There exists little, if any, American leadership, either in government or business that is concerned with America's past or present standard-of-living, especially if maintaining that past or present standard-of-living is of any cost to them. Or as Mike Royko, the New York Times columnist once said describing the thinking of America's emerging political leaders and billionaire class: "No need to make any changes so long as my belly is full."

It's just not manufacturing jobs that have left and are leaving America. The so-called "service" industry jobs are also making their exodus out of America, as was reported to the great dismay of the 1992-1996 high school graduating classes. As early as October 6, 1991, Miami Herald writer Greg Fields wrote as follows:

"U.S. service firms, following a trend set by manufacturers, are moving functions such as data-entry by computer-keyboard operators, telemarketing and the processing of insurance claims and airline tickets offshore, frequently to the Caribbean. These so-called "back-office" jobs, in fact, are becoming an economic gain for the long-suffering Caribbean Basin.

Technology deserves much of the credit. Fiber optic phone lines, worldwide computer networks and satellite communication systems are making the modern office a possibility in even the most remote island outpost."

Now, with the aforementioned factors in mind, the most important questions confronting us as Americans are:

1. What are we going to do with the present twenty-five million unemployed, under-employed, and yes, homeless Americans who are so inadequately trained in manufacturing technologies that just about any foreign $ .60-per- hour-or-less worker has, or will soon easily replace Americans in these manufacturing jobs?

2. What are we going to do with those "service" sector Americans lurking in America's back-offices, soon to be displaced by Caribbean Basin and other foreign workers earning one forth the American wage?

3. What are the myths, the "Government Spins," and the "realities" of this continual erosion and disappearance of American jobs and what, if anything, is anyone doing about it in your representative government?

The President, his economic advisers, and the majority of U.S. economists would have us believe that this dilemma has to do with the more efficient use of world resources and the re-training of the American work force to enable Americans to effectively compete. But today, American workers are not competing with the Japanese and the Germans, but are now, competing with child labor in such places as India, Pakistan, Bangladesh, Indonesia, etc. How does this "global worker competition argument" square when, in some instances, these child workers, and sometimes adult workers in these foreign nations, earn as little as $.20 per hour ($16.00 per week for an 80-hour week). It is no wonder these workers are now taking ten thousand jobs each month from American workers previously paid $600.00 a week.

The Reagan, Bush, and Clinton Administrations have oft repeated that it's a consequence of the new "free trade" practices emerging in the new "global economy" of the "new world order." These are the new "buzz words" of the 1990s. No less than death to Pat Buchanan and Ross Perot for being anti-NAFTA & GATT, the two trade treaties most responsible for the relocation of American middle-class jobs exported overseas by America's very own insatiable profit hungry Multi-National Corporations

(MNCs), who outsource American jobs through a sophisticated system of secretive multi-level international bidding and penurious labor sub-contracting techniques.

The Administration's propaganda line used to further its "free trade" policy resulting from the PAC *payoffs* of the MNCs relies on several arguments: ■ First, the notion that by creating economic well being, for example, in Mexico, will enable U.S. Companies to manufacture and export their allegedly "other more superior complex American products" and "superior American services," to Mexico, Pakistan, Bangladesh and other third world nations. ■ Second, Americans will be able to purchase the very products made overseas for a fraction of what they cost to make in the USA. ■ Third, the best high-paying jobs requiring the most superior technical skills will be retained in America allowing Americans to improve their standard-of-living beyond anything realized in the past. ■ Lastly, it's (the Global economy) inevitable anyway, so there's nothing much to stop it! Now, you have to wonder if these Harvard, Yale, and other Ivy League policy makers have ever had any direct contact with Boobus Americanus or other American Citizens comprising the lower 98% class-structure of Americans beneath them? You have to wonder whether or not these *top upper-class two-percenters* ever watch COPS, THE SIMPSONS, or any other T.V. shows that unashamedly characterize the real majority of Americans today? The result: Every American, including Boobus Americanus, THE SIMPSONS, and the rest of the bottom 98% must become experts on computers and learn new skills so that America might create new industries and new superior complex products and services in order to have something to sell both here and abroad.

How is this new creativity to be accomplished? The Administration's answer is: Through the development of small business in America!

No country in the world has better propagandized, nor glorified the 100,000 or less citizen entrepreneurs of their nation, who have succeeded in getting beyond the five year, one-hundred-hour-work-week to achieve a modicum of success in the "small business" sector of its economy than the U.S. government. According to the Republican Party and the present Administration, Small Business will again rise and save the day for America. If you believe this, read no more. If you have trouble swallowing this fiction, read on.

There is no doubt that "small business" plays a significant role in moving the U.S. economy. The average Small Business requires anywhere from $10,000 to $500,000 of investment to get off the ground. The vast majority of these small businesses include barber shops, car dealerships, small retail boutique shops, small restaurants, small store-front accounting and bookkeeping services, and a whole variety of other retail and service oriented businesses. It would be difficult at best to identify even 2% of America's new "small businesses" that are manufacturing-oriented.

Of course, not all is grim! We **cannot** overlook those businesses of the past that have started out and have become the **giant players** in the American economy, such as, the software development businesses (Microsoft), the computer manufacturing clone business, the small movie production company, the fast-food franchising business, and the single label record recording studio, amongst a few others. Besides these winners, there has really been <u>no</u> other major successful growth industry with global trading or export potential to come out of the "small business" sector in the past ten years. Obviously, there are also the McDonald's, the Dunkin' Donuts, the Burger Kings, and all of the other franchise operations that made many Americans millionaires during the early and mid-seventies have now reached domestic maturation. Major avenues remain for these franchise operations to license their operations overseas, which was begun long ago, but this does not and will not put Americans to work, nor does it create very many "new" jobs in American Industry.

What does all this mean for Boobus Americanus, THE SIMPSONS, and the remainder of the dwindling middle-class of Americans, and for those who have never had the opportunity to attain this status?

What are the real issues affecting America's ability to grow and compete in this allegedly new and demanding "global economy?"

Besides those few businesses or industries noted above, has anyone figured out what America's other new superior "services and products" are going to be, much less exported to third world nations, to fully employ the already 25 million displaced American workers and the 5 million that will be inevitably added each year to this unwieldy herd of under-employeds, unemployeds, and hopeless loads of homeless? Some of the solutions put forth by American policy makers are the very myths and contrasting realities set forth below.

The Myths

I. The Mexicans, Eastern Europeans, and the Third World's workers are getting rich and will soon be buying the yet-to-be developed "new" American superior technological products and services. The Japanese, the Germans, and the rest of Western Europe will also see the light and become super-consumers of these same American products and services. (Do any of you watch the CNBC Financial News Network?)

II. American entrepreneurs and workers will be able to create new industries and services to sell to our alleged trading partners described in Myth (I) above.

III. The Small Business sector of the American economy will create thirty million, and more jobs, as needed, that will keep America out of any recession.

The Realities

I. The wealthiest 2% of Americans and the 2% elite of our trading partners will continue to become richer and richer.

II. Twenty-five million Americans are unemployed or under-employed already requiring some form of partial or full public assistance. These existing unemployed and underemployed twenty-five million Americans are no longer part of the U.S. tax base and no longer carry their share of the country's tax burden. Their ranks will grow by five million or more each year, if something isn't done.

III. The American Consumer, the Administration's acknowledged driving force of the American economy, has had its purchasing power shriveled by approximately 20%. The remaining consumer base remains terrorized by a President and Congress that appear eager to sell their fellow Americans into slavery for a larger piece of what they view as the international "free trade" pie to make the "top-two-percenters" and some of their relatives and friends even richer than they are already. (Does anyone wonder why we no longer hear about demand-pull inflation?)

IV. Has anyone reading this book ever read a "Que Book?" These are computer application instruction books published by the Que Corporation. The average length of each book is 800 pages explaining software sold by such companies as Microsoft, Inc., Lotus, etc. Neither the Que Book nor the software they describe create any new American products or services; it's the software and the Que Books that are the "new" high-tech American products and services. That's all there seems to be on America's creative horizon! Of course, there's always hope that perhaps the U.S. Commerce Department is holding back a little something in this election year? Maybe there are some "new" surprise products and services requiring the employment of American workers that they will unveil in late October just before the next presidential election. Frankly, I'm not holding my breath.

V. Ninety percent of all new "small businesses" in the United States fail in the first five years of their existence. It is the number of "small business" entrepreneurial men and women who have begged, borrowed, and in some cases even stolen, who have helped keep some of the cash-flows alive in this country during the past fifteen years. It is that marginal incremental contribution by these entrepreneurs that has kept this country somewhat afloat economically. Where has this money come from? In most cases from their savings, second mortgages on their homes, and borrowings from either the Small Business Administration (SBA), their five or six $3,000.00 bank or credit card lines, and from loans from relatives and friends. One need only look at the number of Small Business

Bankruptcies filed in the United States in the years 1990 and 1995 to understand the losses incurred by so many brave souls in so short a period of time. (See Chapter One, "Numbers Can Be Scary")

- AUTHOR'S REVERSE "SPIN" GLOSSARY -

- "WHAT THEY SAY IT MEANS" & "WHAT IT REALLY MEANS."
-

Efficient Allocation of Resources:

What they say it means: The "efficient allocation of resources" is in essence the justification and, allegedly, the result of free market capitalism. The theory embodies the principle that business, unfettered by government interference, will, as a natural consequence of its desire to attain the highest return on investment (profit), efficiently allocate the resources (land labor and capital) of the nation, and ultimately of the world.

What it really means: It's the fairy tales of both historians and economists of the 1800s and early 1900s of a world of seemingly unlimited resources, and the putting to use of those unlimited resources by a few entrepreneurial men who were able to create great industries, railroads, and other great edifices, in spite of themselves, and collectively defined as "capitalism," but which in truth, still denied by many, turned out to be a ruthlessly wasteful system that gobbled-up much of the world's limited resources, while fostering over-population, over-pollution, and overindulgence by a few at the expense of many.

Employee Retirement Income Security Act (ERISA) [See also Pension Benefit Guaranty Corporation (PBGC)]:

What they say it means: A law passed by Congress in 1974, designed to govern the operations of most private pension and benefit plans. The law also eliminated many of the unrealistic vesting requirements that many employers had set with regard to the eligibility of employees becoming vested (i.e. the prior practice of Corporate America shafting the "near retired" out of their retirement benefits) in their various pension plans. The ERISA law also created the Pension Benefit Guaranty Corporation and established legal guidelines for the management of pension funds by both pension managers and private business.

What it really means: The law has proven to be an almost minor insignificant hurdle for the accountants, lawyers, corporate executives and the "M&A Gangs" of Wall Street to overcome. The looting of pension plans during the 1980s bears witness to this. One has only to read the business section of his or her daily newspaper to appreciate the level of pension fund "looting" that occurred in the 1980s: Cannon Mills, Inc. — Raider David H. Murdock — over $36 million looted; Faberge, Inc., McCrory Corp., and Kent Corp. — Raider: Meshulam Ricklis — over $29 million looted; Graniteville Co., Pennsylvania Engineering Corp., National Propane Corp., Birdsboro Corp., Salem Corp., Fishbach Corp., — Raider: Victor Posner — over $56 million looted. Who is unaware of Frank Lorenzo's Eastern Airlines' and the Pan American Airlines' bankruptcies resulting in $700 million and $900 million respectively in pension fund shortfalls that again fell on the back of the Pension Benefit Guaranty Corporation — the federal agency that signs your personal guarantees to these funds and then directly bills you, the U.S. Taxpayer when these funds are "looted".

Employee Stock Ownership Plan (ESOP):

What they say it means: A corporate management sponsored program, given a tax-blessing by the federal government, that encourages employees to purchase stock and participate in the management of the company, and in some cases to even take over the company, in order to rescue the company, or a particular division, or plant that would otherwise be shut-down.

What it really means: After corporate management has "milked" either the company, the division, or the plant down to its last nickel of assets and profitability; or has sufficiently "looted" the employee pension funds as it relates to the division or plant it is selling; or where management has significantly mortgaged or otherwise borrowed against the entity's assets so as to no longer make it viable; it is then that management exercises its final opportunity to realize some additional profit. This is done by convincing the employees that the plant or division or perhaps even the company may have a chance of surviving, if the employees themselves own the company, the division, or the plant directly; and it is under this "fantasy" that it convinces the employee to purchase the entity's skeletal remains, along with usually unknown obligations that seem to always include the entity's super under-funded or "looted" pension plan. On the positive side, there is employee-owned United Airlines and Avis-Rent-A-Car, amongst others that appeared to be success stories, although the jury will remain out on this conclusion for at least another few years.

Glass Ceilings:

What they say it means: A newly coined metaphor used to describe the "invisible barriers" to advancement and promotion resulting from the vestiges of race, sex, and sexual preference discrimination that is believed to secretly still exist in Corporate America.

What it really means: Another political term originated in the basement of the 1992 White House and fed into the pseudo-intellectual element of the lower middle-class as the "buzz" word for the 1990s to keep middle-class Americans divided, as the "top-two-percenters" and America's "representative government" remains unified dividing whatever has not already been "looted" from America or the U.S. Treasury. Now I ask you, do you really believe there are 35 million WASP males meeting in smoke-filled rooms, plotting and conspiring to keep women and America's minorities in general poverty? From what I've seen of these 35 million WASP males, they're all just trying to financially keep their own heads above water, as each of them individually tries to figure out where the other 34,999,999 of their fellow WASPs are meeting to do all of this plotting and conspiring to keep their current and ex-wives from making a few more bucks.

Labor Unions (American):

<u>What they say it means:</u> A group of workers who have organized for the purpose of collective bargaining on behalf of themselves with employers regarding the terms and conditions of their employment. Labor Unions generally deal with employee grievances, labor disputes, wages, rates of pay, hours of employment, conditions of work, and other benefits such as pension, sick time, and vacation time. In the early 1990s certain Unions had even begun to negotiate for child care facilities for their members. For many years in the United States prior to the mid-1930s, Unions were condemned by the courts as being organizations in "restraint-of-trade" and therefore <u>not</u> deserving of legal enforcement for their rights. Today's unions are viewed by a large segment of Americans as nothing more than another segment of "organized crime."

In England, Unions were at one time indictable as criminal conspiracies. After statutes were enacted in England freeing Unions from this criminal liability, they were still condemned by the English Courts as being organizations in "restraint-of-trade" and as in the United States also not deserving legal enforcement of their rights.

In the United States today there are almost 17 million Union members. This represent approximately 16.4% of the American labor force. During the period 1930 to 1960, Labor Unions represented 11.6% of the total nation's labor force to approximately 21.9% in 1960. Thereafter Union membership began its steady decline from approximately 19.8 million in 1960, to the present 17 million members Unions now claim. There are approximately 80 major Unions in the United States of which 68 are affiliated with the AFL-CIO. During the period 1935 through 1947, the primary law governing Unions was the Wagner Act of 1935, also know as the National Labor Relations Act. This Act created the National Labor Relations Board (NLRB) and prohibited anti-labor practices by industry and business management. The Wagner Act was further strengthened in 1937 when the U.S. Supreme Court declared it to be "constitutional." In 1947, Congress passed the Taft-Hartley Act which amended the Wagner Act, and included these more "business favorable" provisions: (1) It outlawed the "closed shop" (i.e. factories closed to all but union members). (2) It created an 8 day cooling off period for strikes threatening the national health, safety or security. (3) It outlawed the use of using Union moneys for national elections. (4) It permitted law suits for breach of contract against Unions. (5) It outlawed Unions from conducting unfair labor practices such as: (a) restraining or coercing employees or employers to discriminate against employees; (b) refusing to bargain; (c) coercing or inducing strikes or boycotts for a specific purpose; (d) the charging of excessive or discriminatory initiation fees; feather bedding; (e) picketing for organizational purposes under certain circumstances; and (f) in the health care industry, picketing or striking on less than 10 days' notice, etc.

Employers, pursuant to this same Act, were specifically forbidden to engage in the following activities: (a) interfering with employees in the exercise of their rights; (b) attempting to infiltrate and dominate labor organizations; (c) directly, or indirectly attempting to encourage or discourage employees union membership through discriminatory terms and conditions of employment, or discriminate against employees for filing labor grievances or testifying in regard to them; (d) refusing to bargain collectively with the representative of the majority of the employees; (e) entering contracts that discriminated against other employers with more favorable union relationships, etc.

What it really means: Labor Unions today cause few if any problems unless it involves a "national strike" or a long-term strike against a powerful American company. And let's all remember, President Reagan's personal, and very effective, strike-busting of the Air Traffic Controllers in 1983. Do you wonder why Unions are so impotent today? Think of the recent (June 1992) "strike" threatened by the Unions that operate America's National Railway System. Another strike of note, was the strike at Caterpillar Inc., again "labor" seemed to collapse with respect to its ability to bring management to any meaningful compromise. National Unions today are so impotent, it is questionable whether they are capable of even influencing the way their members vote in federal, state or local elections. They certainly no longer have the clout with the Democratic Party they did in the mid-1930s and early 1960s — and much of this probably has to do with Corporate America's spending countless millions exposing the corruption of union officials such as Jimmy Hoffa, facilitating strong "negative" public opinion and rigid government enforcement of the Taft-Hartley Act against union activity. And neither should America's stand against Communism (allegedly a "worker based political system") during the past forty-five years be discounted: The "Cold War" was serious business during this period, with countless allegations of "communist infiltration" into union leadership.

And if not viewed as a Communist threat, Labor Unions today are still thought of as being nothing more than a pack of "special interest groups" seeking to get an unfair share of the American "pie," not through hard-work or creativity but through their "collective power of numbers" which, arguably, at one time allowed them to achieve a "fair share" of the American "pie." Unfortunately this "power" was much "abused," as unions and their leaders attempted the "looting" of America through their pre-1947 unfettered "bullying powers" of the "strike." In this writer's opinion, it was this later "abuse" of the unions' "strike power" that played a significant role in allowing the "unchallenged looting" and "destruction" of these same Union's (and America's) Industrial Infrastructure during the 1970s and 1980s by the M&A Gangs of Wall Street. I'm certain many American historians and economists in the future will arrive at this same conclusion.

Pension Benefit Guaranty Corporation (PBGC):

What they say it means: PBGC is a Federal Corporation established by Congress under the ERISA legislation of 1974. This Federal Corporation guarantees basic pension benefits in "covered plans" by administrating terminated plans and placing liens on U.S. Corporation's assets for specific pension liabilities that were not properly funded, if there is anything left after the Corporation has been looted. PBGC Covers all pension plans where benefits are clearly defined, and where there are 25 or more employees.

What it really means: The U.S. Taxpayer is again on-the-hook for those pension retirement benefits due American workers, where neither the Corporation, nor our numerous law enforcement agencies have protected or enforced existing laws requiring the Corporation to properly fund these pension plans; or where they failed to protect the "moneys" in these plans from losses resulting from the M&A Gang lootings, changes in accounting principles by the CPAs, and the redefining by lawyers of existing law with their always questionable "legal opinions." It may also be looked at as a double-dipping into the U.S. Treasury. First, we pay law enforcement and our Legislative Representatives to insure that these lootings do not occur. And secondly, when they do occur in spite of our numerous law enforcement agencies' failed efforts, we then pay for the actual losses. Of final note: PBGC has been bankrupt since 1989. It only remains as a viable entity because of the "full faith & credit" backing of you, the U.S. Taxpayer.

Pension Fund:

What they say it means: Pension Funds are funds set up by corporations, labor unions, government entities, and other organizations to pay pension benefits to retired workers, who have generally complied with the terms of each company's, government's, or labor union's plan. Usually both the union, government or corporation pay in as well as the employee during the course of his or her employment. Absolute ownership of all *employee contributions* are vested as a matter of law when contributed by the employee; labor union, government, and corporate contributions, as the case may be, are vested (meaning they become the property of the worker) based upon vesting schedules as set forth originally in ERISA, and as amended. The moneys held by pension funds are invested primarily in U.S. government and corporate stocks and bonds and are therefore a major factor in the equilibrium of these markets. Earnings on investment portfolios of pension funds are tax-exempt, thus enabling fund managers to focus on income and capital gains without concern for any taxing authorities. Pension Funds make actuarial assumptions about how much money will be required to be paid-out to retired workers and then try to ensure that the earnings of the pension fund portfolios equals, or is greater than the anticipated requirements of future payouts. Pension funds are commonly referred to as one of the many "institutional investors" you hear about on Wall Street, that include such giant industries as America's insurance companies, America's mutual fund companies, and the whole plethora of international institutions who hold money that seeks a home where it can generate new income.

What it really means: Needless to say, an anthology could be written on the abuses that have taken place in pension funds by union leaders, corporate raiders, and U.S. Corporate management. And so long as the U.S. Government and the U.S. Taxpayer insure these pension plans, there is no questions that the beneficiaries of these plans will take little interest in protecting their rights while they are still a part of the American work-force. Only after the "lootings" have taken place, do America's pensioners seem to complain en masse. Then it becomes the U.S. Taxpayer who steps into the shoes to pick-up the "tab" of either the Union, the Corporation, or the former pension plan manager, who had been charged with the fiduciary responsibility of assuring that adequate funds would be available for these retires pension benefits, but who had their children's educations, and their children's children's educations, etc., etc., many of whom were not even born yet, but whose educations had to be funded, even if it were through the looting of your pension plan.

Structural Unemployment:

What they say it means: Structural unemployment has been defined as that "unemployment" which results from "another factor" of production being in short supply; or "unemployment" that results from a worker's inability to relocate; or that "unemployment" caused by the effects of technological advancement that renders certain other out-dated labor skills unusable.

What it really means: A concept created by the "Spin Doctors" to explain why certain unemployment continues within "inner cities" and "ghettos" even when the economy is running at full steam. During Republican Administrations, structural unemployment is said to account for over 30% of all unemployment, while American laziness, due to the Democrat's welfare spending is said to account for another 20% of the Structurally Unemployed.

COMPOSITE DICTIONARY

Anachronism: A chronological misplacement of persons, events, objects, or customs in regard to each other; a person or thing that is chronologically out of place and thus serves no purpose in its present time period. The human appendix is often described as an "anachronism," many believing it once served an important purpose, but for whatever reason, serves no purpose now — thus it is described as an anachronism.

Downsizing: A term currently used to define the effects of the 1990-92 recession and the present and future effects of America's free-trade policies as it relates to the reduction in size of the American Industrial Infrastructure, the number of skilled jobs, and the economy in general. "Political downsizing," is a term the author coined and hopes his fellow citizens will embrace in the near future when it demands a 50% cut in the U.S. Senate, a 66% cut in the U.S. House of Representatives, and a four person reduction in the U.S. Supreme Court, and equivalent reductions across the board for all state legislatures and the top courts of each state.

Initial Public Offering [IPOs]: A corporation's first offering of the company's stock to the public which requires registration initially with the Securities and Exchange Commission (SEC). If such registration is not completed, it is unlawful to "publicly" sell the stock within the United States or its territories.

Unemployment: A condition existing in the economy in which workers are willing and able to work, but cannot find employment for their particular skills or wage requirements.

Under-employment: A condition that exists in the economy when workers are not fully employed based on their education, skills, abilities, and experiences. Examples of under-employment are: An MBA employed full-time flipping hamburgers. A former Executive Vice-President of Marketing of a Fortune 500 Company employed full-time wiping down cars at the local car wash.

4

The American

Business Community

A Lesson to be Learned About Divvying-Up the Pie

Regrettable as it may sound to Americans uninitiated to America's Corporate culture, the vast majority of middle-managers (probably 99.9%) and 100% of the members of top management in America are there because they understand the *pie rules* of Corporate America. The *pie rules* are few, but undeniable as they govern every aspect of Corporate American Culture. If you *don't get it*, you're not now, nor will you ever be an American *team player*, and you will just never *fit*. Now don't confuse these rules with *networking nonsense* you may have wasted months on as you searched for a job after you were laid-off, or just completed re-inventing yourself. Or perhaps you just got out of that new school that re-trained and re-tooled you for the fifth or sixth time to fit into the New World Economic Job Order. The *pie rules* have absolutely nothing to do with any of that sort of thing, but when you complete this chapter, there will not be one of you who won't say: "God, I knew that, I just never put it in those terms!"

So, for those of you who don't know how it really works, or haven't given it as much thought, here are the rules:

PIE RULES

1. The higher up the job, the bigger the piece of *pie* to which you are entitled.

2. You can't see evil; you can't hear evil; and you can't say evil; if you intend to enjoy your own healthy piece of the *pie*.

3. If you are getting your share of the *pie*, don't deny the guy above a larger share of the *pie* than you've got.

4. Always remember, some *pie* is better than no *pie* at all.

5. If you help the "HAZZER" (the Yiddish term for "pig") at the top get an even bigger piece of the *pie*, you might get even luckier than you've been in the past, and have some additional *pie crumbs* drop down to your own plate.

6. No piece of *pie* is too big for the guy you report to, and this is doubly true for anyone above him.

7. Make a mess of the *pie* and you'll be out of the bakery, and the coffee shop too.

The above *pie rules* are innocuously taught to all Americans at a very early age, as demonstrated by an incident that occurred several years ago with a friend's six year old daughter, Nancy.

It all began when my friend's wife heard the quiet crying coming from Nancy's bedroom. My friend's wife being quite *motherly*, went to Nancy's bedroom and knocked on the closed door.

"Nancy," she said, "are you okay?"

Still crying, my friend heard Nancy faintly reply, "Yes."

My friend's wife persisted, "It doesn't sound that way to me. Do you want to talk about what's bothering you?"

Nancy immediately responded, "No," but my friend's wife persisted, "Come on honey, you can tell Mommy what's bothering you."

After several minutes of silence, Nancy finally replied, "I don't want my friends calling me a tattletale!"

"That's right no one should tattle on any one else," my friend's wife reflexively agreed, but then her natural maternal curiosity again kicked-in causing her to prod Nancy further.

"Who was it who called you a tattletale?"

Nancy didn't respond, but my friend's wife, becoming curiously impatient, strongly persisted, "Telling your Mother isn't tattling. That's what Mothers are for."

I heard a faint sigh of relief come from within the room. "Mommy," Nancy said, "this boy at school keeps pulling up my dress and he is always trying to look under it!"

Obviously surprised and somewhat annoyed, my friend's wife responded, "Telling your Mother something like this isn't tattling on anyone. You should be telling Mommy these things." She paused a moment, "Who told you, you weren't supposed to tattle when boys do things to you like this?"

Nancy faintly replied, "It's one of the ten rules my teacher taught us when we started school. She said we were not to tattletale on anyone, because tattletalers always are the one's causing trouble."

So begins the journey for most American children, the journey that leads into American business and American culture, and you ask why there are over 15,000 hidden toxic waste dumps in America, some already dangerously covered-over by fresh new residential home developments? Ask no more. It's just a very acceptable part of American culture.

This point may be further emphasized by honestly answering for yourself the following questions:

1. Have you ever "pined" over the merciless murdering outlaw Jessie James who was shot in the back in cold blood, murdered by the "lousy rotten coward Robert Ford?" Is Jessie James a hero to you?

2. Did you ever applaud when Butch Cassidy and the Sundance Kid met their ends in the movie of the same Name?

3. What of Billy the Kid, Bonnie and Clyde, John Dillinger, and even Al Capone, all of whom are revered by many as heroes of American folklore. Did you ever root for the cops?

4. Twenty years from now, will you also revere Michael Milken, Ivan Boesky, Charles Keating, III as American folklore heroes? The process has already begun.

The Myths of Corporate America and American Government's Involvement:

I. Corporate management from CEO all the way down are truly concerned with corporate earnings, the corporate shareholder, the environment, the well being of lower corporate employees, or the products or services they sell to the public.

II. Creativity is rewarded.

III. Integrity is revered.

IV. The Securities & Exchange Commission (SEC) is an **independent government agency-watchdog** looking-out for the shareholder's interest of publicly traded corporations.

V. The Environmental Protection Agency is an **independent government agency-watchdog** looking out for the best interests of American citizens as it tracks American business and industry polluting the American environment.

VI. The United States Department of Commerce reports accurate statistics as it concerns American industry, investment in the American infrastructure, unemployment data, and other facts to the American public.

The Realities of Corporate America and Government Involvement:

I.   The only thing American Corporate Management is concerned with is maximizing its own wealth and the personal wealth of its top executives, primarily the CEO. How is this **wealth** attainment accomplished? At your expense! Through thousands of ways. For example (and this is just one example): A company may increase the size of its product's outer package and decrease the actual product content (i.e. net weight) in order to justify an increase price to the consumer's eye; the consumer sees a bigger candy bar package, but ends-up getting less product and more paper. The CEO and his cohorts get more bucks at less cost.

You may think this **gimmick** must also benefit the corporate shareholders. Sometimes. Rest assured this "profit" is not for the benefit of the corporation's shareholders. There are other more sophisticated ways to achieve this illusory objective (i.e. press releases, accounting gimmicks, rumors, "blood-baths," out-and-out fabrications, and selling additional common stock to Boobus Americanus). If you review historically the company's stock held by the company's top management you will find that time-and-time again they significantly benefit far more from increases in the price of the stock, than do the outside shareholders. The top members of corporate management are generally out at the stock's high price, and back in when the price is low, and this is especially true as it concerns the exercise of their self-granted alleged "incentive stock options." The term "alleged" is used to emphasize the questionability of the work "incentive": "incentive" menaing to make the company more profitable or "incentive" meaning to make the CEO wealthier.

Much of this aforementioned activity is referred to as legal "Insider Trading," and remains legal so long as it's not based on "limited insider information" (Believe it!) that results in sharp, obvious (and sometimes rather shameless) swings in the company's stock price.

II.   There is no "creativity" in the cadres of America's corporate managers. The "creativity" I refer to in Myth II, is the "creativity" of those "on-the-line" or those in R&D who generally earn between $20,000 and $35,000 a year. "Creativity" in these aforementioned groups is only rewarded if the employee can demonstrate that whatever it was he created previously will be followed up by an even greater second-round of "creativity." His or her reward: a 10% raise, sometimes a small bonus, and he or she gets to keep his or her job another six-months. Otherwise there is "no reward" at all. (You think: Look what's happened to American baseball players, and other professional athletes? They're now getting their share of the "pie." Do I detect you rolling your eyes? Fret not, there's more to come on this later.)

III. There is simply no "integrity" in the majority of American Corporations, or other Businesses whether large of small, public or private. If you've ever worked in this sector you know this to be regrettably true.

IV. The Securities and Exchange Commission [SEC], the FDA, EPA, the U.S. Department of Commerce, and all other governmental agencies in the Executive Branch of U.S. Government (the branch headed by the President) should be viewed as nothing more than "political" information-generators, and when reviewing information released by these federal agencies, one should carefully interpret any data they release as follows:

   a) If its good news, divide it by two.
   b) If its bad news, multiply it by four.

A classic example where the above rule should be applied is the "spin" put on all "information" concerning America's S&L Bailout. One day you read it's going to cost $120 billion, the next thing you hear the industry has become profitable. A day later you read about it again on page 8 of your local newspaper. RTC (or OTS) has again run out of money and needs another $30 billion to close another 191 defunct S&Ls. The bad news always follows the election directly into the Christmas shopping season when most of us are too busy to read it, much less, digest it. This was the case in 1992. God only knows how sour the news will be after the November 1996 Presidential election, and how many more times the name of the federal agency responsible for cleaning up the S&L mess will have its name changed to further confuse the average American who has to pay for all of these "insidious shenanigans" of a government-gone-wild.

- AUTHOR'S REVERSE "SPIN" GLOSSARY -

- "WHAT THEY SAY IT MEANS" & "WHAT IT REALLY MEANS."
-

Corporate Stock:

What they say it means: Corporate stock, also known as Capital Stock represents the <u>equity</u> or <u>ownership</u> interest of those persons who invested in the corporation, as contrary to those investors who acquire corporate bonds (obligations or debt of the corporation). Corporate stock is generally broken down into two categories, one called "preferred" and the other called "common." Preferred stock generally enjoys priority over common stock with respect to distribution of dividends and liquidating distributions in the event of bankruptcy or dissolution of the corporation. Common stockholders, as opposed to preferred stockholders, generally assume greater primary risk of loss if the business does poorly, and generally realize a greater return on their investment if the business is successful. It is generally the common stockholders who elect the Board of Directors that controls the company. (See also Stockholder.) The issuance of common stock has historically been the primary means of raising "capital" (money) for both new and existing corporations, although the 1980s saw this general rule practically nullified (at least on the "money" side) with the "money raising" gimmicks (i.e. Junk Bonds) of the M&A Gangs of Wall Street. All U.S. companies with publicly traded stock must be registered with the SEC.

What it really means: To the common stockholder, it can mean many things; dividends that are taxed as dividend income; appreciation based on the success and growth of the company; a wind-fall profit should the company be "targeted" by an unfriendly predator (i.e. the M&A Gangsters); a frustration when corporate management decides to surreptitiously "loot" the company by taking it private, or just "looting" it directly; and the ultimate realization that those "pretty-pieces-of-paper" that say "Common Shares" have little to do with any real ownership rights of the corporation he or she thought was owned.

Economic Indicators:

What they say it means: These are the key statistics generally compiled and tracked by the U.S. Department of Commerce which show the direction in which the economy is allegedly going. Such indicators include: (1) the unemployment rate, (2) the weekly new jobless claims numbers, (3) the inflation rate, (4) the balance of trade, (5) permits issued for home construction, (6) new housing starts, (7) factory orders, (8) new job creation or loss, (9) factory utilization rate, etc. The U.S. Commerce Department's Bureau of Economic Analysis also created an index of "leading indicators," whose components are adjusted for inflation and which allegedly forecast, six to nine months in advance, the ups and downs of the business cycle. The Composite Index of 12 Leading Indicators are: (1) New orders for consumer goods and materials; (2) The average work week of production workers; (3) The average weekly claims for state unemployment insurance; (4) Vendor performance; (5) Net business formation; (6) Contracts for plants and equipment; (7) New building permits; (8) Inventory changes and adjustments; (9) Sensitive material prices; (10) Stock prices; (11) Money supply (M-2); and (12) Business and consumer borrowing.

What it really means: It's part of the overall "tote board" for the various casinos of Wall Street. To the so-called investors of Wall Street, the "leading indicators" are second in importance to the guessing that goes on concerning The Fed's Discount Rate changes. It is also important to understand that general gambling is also impacted by other factors such as the world's next political or economic crisis, oil spills, the threat of war, monthly independent consumer confidence surveys, and even the "rumors" that precede the U.S. Department of Commerce's announcement of where these 12 leading economic indicators are headed. If the "rumors" are positive (i.e indicators up) the market generally goes down in anticipation of The Fed's raising interest rates to control inflation, and if the economic indicators are down, the market generally goes up as the gamblers expect The Fed to lower interest rates and avoid recession. Given also the manipulation by brokerage houses on Wall Street with their "buy" and "sell" recommendations; the Conference Board's and the University of Michigan's Consumer Confidence Indexes; and the various pronouncements and predications of the so-called Gurus of Wall Street (i.e. the Granvilles, etc.); the moronic utterances of Alan Greenspan, it's no wonder most gamblers find Wall Street to be the most exciting gaming sport in the world.

Economic Theory:

What they say it means: The analysis of recognizable and cohesive groups of quantifiable economic elements (producers, labor, consumers, government, financial institutions, etc.) as they interact largely together to cause either prosperity, poverty, recession, depression or enormous wealth, which economists describe in an esoteric language or abstract principle.

What it really means: A compendium of abstract ideas, relationships, and generally remote and unreliable statistical data used by many government and academic charlatans (who are incapable of being gainfully employed in other productive sectors of the economy) to mislead, misrepresent, and misdirect those who seek solutions to the problems that have confronted human beings since they became addicted to the accumulation of wealth following their being tossed from, what many believe was, the Garden of Eden.

Golden Parachutes:

What they say it means: Those lucrative contracts given to the CEOs (Chief Executive Officers) of America's major corporations and their close executive cohorts, that provide lavish benefits in case their company is taken over or acquired by another one of America's corporations or other organization put together for that purpose. "Golden parachutes" generally include numerous years of generous severance pay, usually in the seven digit range, enormous "quickie" stock options, and fabulous bonuses that are usually paid when a CEO's and his cohorts' employment end.

What it really means: Obviously such benefits would not be offered, nor approved by the owners of the corporation about to be acquired by someone else, as it would only dilute their own possibility of profitability should they sell their stock to the acquiring company. The "golden parachute" is nothing more than the CEO and his Board of Directors handsomely-taking-care-of-themselves and their long-term future needs as a result of their no longer being able to "loot" the corporation "looted" from them. Here again we see the importance of and "efficient allocation of resources" one of the most important underlying principles of American capitalism operating at its very best. Again so much for the "efficient allocation of resources" principle ascribed to by so many of our present-day American capitalistic "Captains of Industry."

Greenmail:

What they say it means: The concept of "greenmail" originated during the M&A Holocaust that began in earnest in the 1970s. Greenmail, like blackmail, was a form of corporate extortion, **not where** the Board of Directors or Corporate Management suffered financially, **but where** the shareholders of the company suffered financially: this being the result of Corporate Management paying a hostile predator a premium to acquire the corporation's stock that had been accumulated by the hostile predator in its efforts to take over the targeted corporation.

What it really meant: Greenmail was the means by which management of the corporation that was threatened with a hostile takeover, sold out its stockholders and corporate treasury in order to preserve their lucrative positions and benefits within the company. One commentator once remarked: "Never have so few, spent so much of someone else's money to preserve so much for themselves." One has to wonder where America would be today if these same Corporate executives would have been as generous and personally motivated when it came to saving the jobs of the blue-collar workers in their own companies? Would the savings of blue-collar American jobs have qualified as an "efficient allocation of resources" in a "free market" capitalistic system? From the empirical evidence of the 1970s and 1980s, obviously not!

Incentive Stock Options (ISOs):

What they say it means: A government-created "entitlement program" for Corporate America's CEOs and lesser stellar senior executives, whereby pursuant to the Economic Recovery Tax Act of 1981 (ERTA) certain qualifying incentive stock options (ISOs) were permitted to be given by corporate management to itself, free and clear of tax on both the day they were granted, and the date they were exercised. These ISOs were only taxed when the CEO or executive finally sold the acquired ISO stock. After much argument, the Congress finally limited the amount of tax-free ISOs to $100,000 per year as part of the Tax Reform Act of 1986.

What it really means: ISOs were just another way for the CEO and senior members of Corporate management to "loot" both the Corporation's Treasury as well as the U.S. Treasury. It baffles the mind why Congress would grant such tax-free benefits to so few unless one considers the nature of this "special interest group": to fully appreciate this, one must consider the $1,000-a-plate fund-raising dinners, the Corporate sponsored PACs (Political Action Committees), and the other more surreptitious fund raising these corporate executive can do given their powerful corporate offices.

Phantom Stock Plans:

What they say it means: A concept of reward for corporate executive management whereby the executive receives a bonus based on the appreciation of the corporation's stock over a fixed period of time. Although actual shares are not involved (hence the term "phantom"), the amount of "phantom" shares involved are generally proportional to the executive's salary level. Should the stock rise to the "phantom stock plan" market appreciation level, within the "plan's" prescribed time, the executive employee is paid the difference in the then appreciated market price and the established lower set "phantom plan" price, multiplied by the number of shares that were assigned to him in the Phantom Stock Plan.

What it really means: Phantom Stock Plans are just another one of the many ways corporate management has devised to "loot" the treasuries of the corporations that employ them. The real power of a Phantom Stock Plan is that it does not involve any form of purchase or sale of security, and therefore, it does not fall under the regulation of any governmental agency (i.e. the SEC).

Stockholder Rights - The Ownership of Corporate America:

What they say it means: In America, stockholder rights are practically non-existent, the concept of "corporate democracy" (i.e. corporate management running the entire show) being paramount.

What it really means: The other commentators have it right for the first time.

COMPOSITE DICTIONARY

Bloodbath (The Corporate): One of the most important tools of Corporate America's CEOs and Board of Directors in the long-term financial management of the corporations they run. It also serves a major need of their out-side independent auditors (their CPAs), in that it reduces their professional malpractice liability, generally for all "prior" years, and saves them from attesting to too-long-a-string of false and misleading financial statements, some already signed-off on in the past year, and others that might have been required to be signed-off in the present, and future years.

How does it work? After numerous years of falsely inflating corporate earnings to cover-up the mismanagement or "looting" of the company, it ultimately comes time to pay some hefty dividends to shareholders. After all, these shareholders have been patient a long time in waiting for the big "dividend check." As corporate management well knows, there were no real profits, and if there were they were either "looted," wasted, or misappropriated.

So now it's time to take the "bloodbath." The strategy is simple. Timing is the most crucial element — the news of the "bloodbath" (the big corporate write-offs for the plundering of the past) are best leaked in the second quarter to the news media and the "Street"; then, the write-offs slam-bang-dunked in the third quarter — a news conference, personal verification by the CEO and the auditors; and then back to work. Time to generate a few paper profits for the fourth quarter (and usually right out of what has been just written-off in the third quarter). That's the game — by the end of the forth quarter corporate management shows Wall Street and the corporation's shareholders that they have again turned around a horrific corporate financial disaster, saving the corporate stockholders millions of dollars. Don't act surprised that even the U.S. Treasury participates in this charade — they're called "tax loss carry-backs," the recovery of all those taxes paid by the corporation on those prior year's inflated or non-existent profits, to be refunded as soon as the appropriate tax returns are filed. Finally, a well orchestrated Shareholders' Meeting in the first quarter of the new year — the CEO taking deserved bows for allegedly saving the company and the shareholder from severe financial losses, and turning the whole financial picture of the corporation around. What better time for the CEO to get his well deserved hefty pay-hike — even a million and a half wouldn't compensate for what he's done for the company this past year — so everyone agrees with the Board of Directors' spontaneous suggestion to make it an even "two" with the promise that additional compensation arrangements will soon follow!

Double Taxation: A term most commonly applied to the taxation of profits earned by corporations, which are then re-taxed again when these same profits are paid to the corporation's shareholders as dividends.

Fortune 500: An annual listing of the 500 largest U.S. Industrial (manufacturing corporations) listed in order by sales and other financial attributes. In addition, Fortune magazine also publishes a list of the Fortune 500 largest U.S. Non-manufacturing Companies referred to as the

<u>Fortune Service 500</u>. For severals years <u>Fortune</u> magazine has also listed the largest international manufacturing, service, and financial organizations around the globe.

Integrity: An "aspiration" professed to be desirable by the vast majority of America's Corporations and citizens. "Corporate Integrity" became a buzz-word during the mid-1970s as a result of the "Watergate Scandal," and the numerous corporate frauds that coincidentally surfaced during this same period. The term itself embodies the elements of honesty, reliability, and fairness.

In reality, the concept of "Corporate Integrity" was nothing more than a clever "marketing gimmick" developed on Madison Avenue to exploit America's consumers — a clever ploy of getting them to believe they could absolutely rely on the product "representations" made by Corporate America. As product-after-product failed to live-up to the "hoopla" and "representations" made by allegedly "integrity oriented" Corporate America, less-and-less heed was given to it by America's consumers, and Corporate America's flirtation with "Corporate Integrity" began to slowly diminish. The whole notion of "Corporate Integrity" virtually disappeared with the emergence of the 1980s.

Laissez-Faire:

What they say it means: Principally an economic doctrine or concept that concludes interference by government in business and economic affairs should be kept at a minimum. <u>The Wealth Of Nations</u>, written by Adam Smith in 1776, described Laissez-Faire economics in terms of the "invisible hand." It was this "invisible hand," according to Adam Smith, that would provide the maximum good for all, if businessman were free to pursue profitable opportunities as they saw them.

What it really means: It does not seem that the "invisible hand" that Adam Smith spoke of was the same "invisible hand" of Alan Greenspan, who has a difficult time keeping his "invisible hand" out of manipulating both the money supply and interest rates in the United States. Neither could Adam Smith have been referring to Ronald Reagan or George Bush, whose "invisible hands" have sent to the Congress the largest spending budgets in the history of the United States over the past twelve years.

Macroeconomics: The study of "aggregates" of incomes, wages, prices, households, firms, and government; as opposed to the single individual analysis of firms or households which is referred to as microeconomics.

Microeconomics: The economic study of "individual" income, wages, prices, households and firms, as opposed to the analysis of "aggregates" which is defined as macroeconomics.

Money Functions: Essentially, there are four generally accepted theories regarding the function of money. (1) A store of value, (2) A medium of exchange, (3) A unit of account, and (4) A standard of deferred payment.

Monopoly: In its most commonly used sense, it refers to the market situation in which one person or a group has such control over the supply of a commodity as to be able to regulate its price. Economists have defined numerous types of monopolies among which are: Buyer's Monopolies: Oligopoly which refers to the condition where more than two, but still only a few "buyers" of a particular commodity exist in the market place; and Monopoly, which refers to the market situation in which there is only "one" buyer for a particular commodity; and Seller's Monopolies: Oligopoly, which refers to that economic condition when there are more than two, but still only a few "sellers" of a particular commodity in the market place.

There exists five sub-subcategories of Oligopoly: Complete Oligopoly, Differentiated Oligopoly, Unperfected Oligopoly, Undifferentiated Oligopoly and partial Oligopolies.

There also exits four lawful monopolies: Natural Monopolies (Public Utilities, such as gas and electric companies); Public Monopolies (the United States Post Office); Legal Monopolies (Copyright, Patent and Trademark created by law); and Fiscal Monopolies (those which are owned and operated only by the government, a rarity in the U.S., the closest of which are the Tennessee Valley Authority (TVA) and NASA).

Monopolistic Competition: The competition that exists among sellers who are individually able to influence the "market" because of the slight differences amongst the products they produce. Prior to Japan's and Germany's entry into the U.S. automobile market, it was generally accepted that General Motors, Ford, and Chrysler were in "Monopolistic Competition" with one another.

Pac-Man Defense Strategy: A defense technique used by the "target company" of an attempted acquisition. The "targeted company" puts the proverbial "screws" to its predator by buying the predators shares of common stock in its own attempt to now acquire the predator. The term Pac-Man comes from the popular video game of the early 1980s, where, when the large yellow character fails to efficiently swallow its opponent, it is itself consumed.

Perks: See "Perquisites" below.

Perquisites (also known as "Perks"): Generally referred to as "perks," these are the fringe benefits generally enjoyed by both U.S. Corporate Executive Management and elected members of both federal and state governments. In business, "perks" generally include amongst other things, company paid automobiles, chauffeur-driven limousines, incentive stock options, phantom stock plans, exorbitant unearned bonuses, Golden Parachutes, special life insurance policies, private corporate jets, and a whole host of other benefits associated with Travel and Expense.

In government, as in business, it is those benefits beyond that of a fair salary and the standard health care plans, etc. enjoyed by the more powerful or senior members of government. It involves such benefits as private housing, house servants, government automobiles for personal use, government reimbursement for personal expenditures, and especially in federal government, the use of government aircraft and government entertainment facilities, special "princely" pension plans, and the best of health care programs, etc.

Depending on the rank of retired government elected official (i.e. Speaker of the House), it includes free offices and government-paid personnel after retirement, for as long as it takes to finish up government business, but generally these former members abuse this perk, using to write their "memoirs" for their personal profit at U.S. Taxpayer expense. Second only to a few of America's top corporate executives, there are no more princely pension plans in America than those provided for the federal government's Executive, Legislative, and Judicial Branches of government. We're talking millions of dollars per elected representative, and contrary to private pension plans, these plans are fully protected against corporate raiders and looters by the "full faith & credit" of the U.S. — you the U.S. Taxpayer.

Poison Pill Defense: The Poison Pill Defense is another strategy employed by the "target company" of an unfriendly acquisition suitor. It is referred to as the Poison Pill Defense because it ultimately results in large financial losses to the stockholders of the "targeted company." The whole essence of the Poison Pill is to make the stock of the "targeted company" more costly to the acquiring company, therefore making the "target company" less attractive. One technique employed is to issue a new series of preferred stock that gives present shareholders the right to have this new preferred stock redeemed at a premium price after the takeover — at a value significantly more than it would have had, had the corporation not been targeted for acquisition. This "defense" is costly to the shareholders of the "targeted company" because: (1) they generally lose the opportunity to sell their shares to the acquirer which is usually at a significant premium above then current worth, and (2) it is the shareholder, not corporate management, who ultimately bears the "cost" of this expensive defense technique, win or lose.

Prime Rate: The interest rate banks charge to their most credit worthy customers; such rate is primarily determined by the Discount Rate as set by The Fed. It should be noted, the bank is not obligated to loan its customers money at its published prime rate; it may both discount this rate for certain customers, and for less preferential customers, charge an interest rate greater than its published prime rate. For these lesser credit worthy customers the bank may charge whatever the customer will pay, so long as the customer is not "consumer" protected under state usury laws.

Privatization: The movement to return to the business and private sectors, functions now performed by government because of the belief that private companies can do the job better, and cheaper.

Shareholder (American Corporations): The mythical owner of one or more shares of stock in a U.S. Corporation entitled basically to four rights of ownership: (1) To, under very unusual circumstances, claim a share of the company's undivided assets in proportion to the numbers of shares he or she holds; (2) To vote his or her shares of stock in the election of Directors and other business conducted at shareholders meetings in proportion to the shares he or she holds; (3) To receive dividends when earned and declared by the Board of Directors; and (4) To exercise his or her preemptive "right" to subscribe to additional stock offerings before they are available to the public, except when such right is overruled by the Articles of Incorporation, or in other special circumstances: (a) such as where the stock is issued to effect a merger, or (b) an issuance of stock is required by corporate management to acquire another company, or (c) the issuance of a combination of debt and equity (executive stock bonus and option plans) instruments are needed by corporate management to allow management to purchase the shareholder's stock and its ownership rights should management wish to own the company.

In most companies the Boards of Directors are controlled by management, eventhough on the surface it appears that they are elected by the shareholders at the shareholders annual meeting. If you own stock in a public corporation, you know first-hand this is true, and if you haven't ever owned stock in a public corporation ask someone you know who has to verify the veracity of this observation. This again is another of the deceptive myths of American capitalism; the "illusory" ownership of America's Corporations by its shareholders.

Whistle-Blower: A term used to define those persons who advises appropriate regulatory or law enforcement authorities of violations of law or criminal acts by their employer, usually for the benefit of the public at large. Although both business and lawmakers generally detest whistle-blowers, the Congress was, due to public outcry and a mauling by the mass media, forced to pass what is known as the Whistle Blower Protection Act of 1989, which affords some protection for whistle-blowers, especially those who seek to protect the federal government against fraud by their employers. Generally speaking, whistle-blowers in American society are not held in high esteem, regardless of their intentions or selfless public service; most Americans generally refer to them collectively as "informants, squealers, rats" or as "narcs," a relatively new term derived from America's illegal drug business, that referencing "undercover" local drug law enforcement officers.

5 | Special Interest Groups

"Sovereigns, Public Servants, Or Just Good Jobs Representing Special Interests"

During the election year of 1992, there were over 20,000 individuals and organizations known as *special interest groups* in Washington, D.C. engaged in "lobbying" activities, at a cost to their supporters of almost $2 billion. An additional $800 million was spent by *special interest groups* on "indirect" or "grass roots" lobbying through newspaper and T.V. advertising, and mass-mailing campaigns, all of this being paid for by U.S. and foreign corporations, as well as foreign governments, and various U.S. trade associations. Also worthy of note, is the growth of these *special interest groups* over the past twenty years. The number of active U.S. Corporation controlled *special interest groups* rose from 100 in 1960, to 500 in 1980, and to almost 1100 in 1995. PACs (Political Action Committees), another form of *special interest group* grew from 608 in 1974, to 1938 in 1979, and to over 4950 in 1995.

Special Interest Groups are subtle, sometimes insidious, and often hard to find, or hard to identify. They are called by different names: lobbyists, PACs, campaign committees, political contributors, professional associations, trade associations, U.S. and foreign corporations acting alone and in concert with others (i.e. a "chemical company" or as a group to include the entire "chemical industry"). *Special interest groups* also include foreign governments (i.e. foreign lobbyists and political consultants representing Arab, Israeli, Chinese, etc. interests), organized ethnic groups, religious groups, racial groups, and subgroups of our own U.S. Senators and U.S. Congressmen (the Black Congressional Caucus, the Jewish Congressional Caucus, etc.).

For election year 1992, it was estimated that the cost to procure (i.e. get elected to) a U.S. Senate seat ran as high as $8 million; and a key House of Representative's seat ran as high as $5 million. All for a job that pays $136,000 a year. Or should we also consider the "perks." As a U.S. Senate you get between $1.0 and $2.2 million to operate your Washington office and district offices back home. If you are a member of the House, you're allocated $500,000 for this same purpose.

Now, we all know that no one sitting in the U.S. House of Representatives or U.S. Senate would be asking this question, but who would be so stupid to put oneself into bankruptcy to be a "public servant"? Yet thousands of Americans are clawing to get themselves into the U.S. Capital "rat's nest" and remain there. Some of our so-called public-service-minded citizens have been clawing to obtain this objective for as many as twenty years, without even a remote chance of success, yet they keep on clawing. Now, would you suck-up to every Lieutenant, Captain, Major, and General in every local Democratic or Republican party cell or ward for a period of twenty years to have the opportunity to bankrupt yourself to become a public servant?

There has to be more to this than meets the eye!

All *you* have to do to figure it out, is to take a close look at the *pie* to be divvied-up and dished-out each year by those 535 public servants who allegedly serve "selflessly" in both the U.S. Senate and House Representatives.

How big is this "pie" you ask?

It's a monster! It's in excess of $1.5 trillion each year, and growing. For those of you who still can't handle this on your computers — just try to imagine 535 piles (one enormous pile for each and every member of the U.S. Senate and House) of single dollars bills. Each member's stack would be 44.15 miles (233,112 feet) high, and each stack would contain 2.8 billion (2,800,000,000) dollar bills. Even Ross Perot would tell you that's one heck of a piece of *pie*!

If you have a depth perception problem with this, you can think of the 1995 "pie" as over three (3) times the cost of running both the United States Government and financing all of World War II, for the period of 1941 through 1945 inclusive. Yes, all of it . . . . all five years — and the cost World War II, if you didn't catch it the first time.

Add to this the unlimited and unchecked borrowing power of the United States Treasury, and one can easily understand why so many of the good citizens of this nation want to be in "public service." Public service that offers the best pension plan not only in the nation, but in the world; the best employment opportunities after you leave "public service," consulting in Washington, (also known as lobbying); working in the boardroom in Corporate America (lobbying from the Boardroom); and with 251 members of the Congress being lawyers, perhaps even entering the practice of law back in your own home state and "lobbying" from your own hometown for one of your local PACs. Let's not forget about the 39,000 patronage jobs that exist in the U.S. Congress, for our elected public servants to give out to friends, family, and those very people who lurk in the smoke-free political party cells in their own congressional districts (better thought of as fiefdoms), who have donated their time and money to see your representative (better thought of as "their" representative) that has been sent to your U.S. Congress.

The Money Interests

In 1988, Political Action Committees (PACs) raised more than $384.6 million and spent $364.2 million. In preparation for the 1990 election, these same PACs raised $372 million, and spent more than $358 million. Worthy of note is that this money doesn't include any of those $1000-a-plate dinners you read about, or those fund raising activities of committees established or administered by candidates, or by the various party committees, or moneys raised by John Q. Public, or matching public funds authorized by U.S. Taxpayers on their personal income tax returns.

It is estimated that as much as $650 million was spent by candidates and their supporters in election year 1992; $700 million is the guesstimate for the 1996 election year. Prior to his withdrawal on July 16, 1992, Ross Perot, the third party Independent, indicated he had personally spent as much as $100 million of his own money on his personal presidential campaign.

The Federal Elections Commission (FEC), is charged with:

1. Administering the public financing of presidential elections;

2. Receiving, reviewing, and maintaining all reports on the campaign finance activities for federal office and the committees that support them; and

3. Monitoring and enforcing compliance with federal election law;

Worthy of note, is that the FEC is the smallest federal agency in federal government, employing less than 250 personnel, it's no wonder that enforcement efforts on part of the FEC are so negotiable with regard to any form of punishment. Now guess who foots the bill for the FEC?

The FEC publicly admits that even those candidates or committees who persist in bending, and outright violating Federal Elections Rules are only slapped with minimal civil penalties. Only on rare occasion does the FEC file civil suits against suspected serious violators of U.S. Election Laws. If the commission should stumble over "knowing and willful" violations of the law, the matter, in the sole discretion of the FEC, may be referred to the U.S. Department of Justice for further investigation and prosecution, and this, as you probably already suspected, is again, at the Justice Department's sole discretion. So you think you smell a "rat."

Your right! Needless to say, this whole process should be an affront to you and every other U.S. Taxpayer and citizen, as we again are required to sit on the sidelines watching the "fox" guard the "chicken coop." The regulatory system governing U.S. federal elections is so obviously ridden with conflict-of-interest, it's disgraceful that the Congress would insult the U.S. Taxpayer by expending any money on the FEC function at all. Remember this when you see your Congressman and Senator after the 1996 elections screaming once more for election reform. Its not election reform that's needed, but real citizen participation in some of the major decisions that these bought-off representatives now make. More about this later when we talk about plebiscite and voter public referendums utilizing what Clinton refers to the *super communications highway*.

The Corporate Employee Political Action Committee

Henry is a part-time Florida State Highway Patrol Trooper working three nights a week, and twelve hours on the weekend. His full-time job is with one of Florida's leading utilities, which requests that each employee in its upper, middle, and lower management groups "voluntarily" contributes to its "corporate employees" Political Action Committee. Does this sound very "voluntary" to you?

Henry, being a part-time Highway Patrol Trooper, also felt there was something wrong with the subtle, but nonetheless coercive tactic, employed by his "major utility" employer in getting him, and other managers to contribute to this PAC. So Henry decided not to contribute at all. Thus began a six year hiatus on Henry's promotion up the corporate ladder, and even the size of his annual raise. Henry may have been principled, but Henry was obviously not in tune with what had become another thread that has been sewn into the comforter known as the American Way. Henry's naiveté regarding the necessity of contributing to his company's PAC even I found initially hard to believe, thinking Henry to be one of the savvy police guys "on-the-beat."

Now, if Henry had contributed to the *corporate employees'* PAC, his annual contributions would have been minuscule compared to the increases he would have received in raises and promotions. Henry, having that rigid personality sometimes found in Highway Patrol Troopers could not rationalize the sale of his soul for neither "family," "comfort," or for what some of you are thinking right now: good old common sense. Henry just wouldn't bend to either this subtle corporate extortion, or the appeal so much a part of the American Way, commonly referred to as "the devil made me do it." Although successful in being independent for six years, Henry finally shook his head and admitted that he had been a bit too rigid in his convictions, and that the "error of his ways" had affected the size of his pocketbook. Yes, Henry had some regrets; the only way Henry's son could attend college was through a supplemental scholarship as opposed to Henry being able to pay his way in full.

On the other side of Henry, in the same utility company, is Jane. Henry is a low level, non-union, middle manager. Jane belongs to the labor union that negotiates the collective bargaining agreements with Henry's utility employer, and she too feels the subtle coercive underpinnings that require her to contribute to her union's PAC. There have been so many cut-backs in employees that Jane wants to contribute double the $100 she gave last year, and was even more happy to do so after hearing George Bush's final endeavor to wrest the remainder of middle-class American jobs for export to Mexico and elsewhere, and Clinton's completion of this Republican initiated sell-out.

As I pondered both Henry's and Jane's stories, one of the better law jokes I've heard over the years came to mind. It dealt with the judge who was paid a bribe of $5,000 by plaintiff's counsel so that he would decide favorably for plaintiff. Two weeks after he had accepted the first $5,000 bribe, defendant's counsel entered his chambers and paid a $10,000 bribe for a decision favorable to the defendant. The judge obviously had just not correctly estimated the true value of this case. Being a fair man, and in order to equitably rectify the matter, the judge, called both lawyers into chambers, where he recited his solution to this dilemma.

"Gentlemen," he began, "several weeks ago I received a $5,000 bribe from plaintiff's counsel. Then two weeks later, I received a $10,000 bribe from defendant's counsel."

All breathing in the room ceased, as the attorneys waited in trepidation for the anticipated judge's wrath and sanctions.

The judge, handing a sealed envelope to defendant's attorney, calmly continued. "Given this circumstance, I am now returning $5,000 to defendant's counsel in order that I might remain impartial in this matter."

As will be repeated several times in this book, it is no secret that U.S. Senators and Congressmen, so desperate to build up their campaign "war chests," now solicit PACs directly for contributions, rather than these PACs having to figure ways to buy their allegiance. This, given the fact that even those novice U.S. Senators and members of the House with the slightest of "common sense" and "intelligence," know there are no free-lunches, nor free handouts in Washington D.C., and that for every request there must be a quid-pro-quo (consideration in return) for those PAC moneys paid. Unfortunately, in every instance, it is the U.S. Taxpayer who ultimately antes-up the "quid pro quo" on the other side of this transaction, usually in proportionate multiples of ten or more dollars in government spending..

Professional PACs

This year, as usual, I received a request to contribute to the American Institute of Certified Public Accountants PAC (the AICPA "Effective Legislation Committee" PAC) along with my annual dues statement. Had I not carefully read the dues statement, I might very well have made an unknowing contribution, since the $10.00 request was already preprinted on the dues statement, requiring only that I sum up my annual dues and PAC contribution to match the amount of my payment check. Now there are 325,000 member CPAs — that's a potential of $3,250,000, and we haven't even gotten to the contributions that the "Big Six CPA Firms" and the lesser firms will make. Different from the coercion felt by Henry and Jane, there was no coercion here at all.

As a matter of fact, the AICPA PAC truly serves the CPA. The "innocuous" flyer that also accompanied the dues statement read as follows:

"The AICPA works hard in Washington to present your views to elected members of congress. Issues of vital importance include legal liability, audit responsibility, individual estimated taxes, fiscal year relief, and investment adviser legislation. To be successful, the profession supports candidates who are willing to consider our views. The Institute's Effective Legislation Committee, a political action committee (PAC), helps us to effectively communicate the profession's message. You can ensure that the profession's voices are heard in the political process by contributing to the AICPA PAC through the voluntary contribution provided on the dues notice. Your participation and involvement is needed and greatly appreciated."

As will be discussed in Chapter Seven, the U.S. Senate might very well have dealt the AICPA's Effective Legislation Committee its perhaps first and most serious blow. New legislation proposed may very well put an end to this somewhat high-flying profession. Of course, this might also be a congressional ploy to increase AICPA PAC contributions next year. (See Chapter Seven or further discussion on this subject.)

Another quasi-PAC (it's not really a PAC, but a genuine anti-PAC, but with the same objective) that annually requests contribution from me, is the Florida Bar's F.L.A.M.E., Inc. This anti-PAC's request is also not coercive in any manner, but should be of general interest to all of you. In 1992, the request was made through a rather economically persuasive letter from then Bar President Alan Dimond. The letter read as follows:

"The lawyers of Florida are under constant attack by *special interest groups*. These groups constantly campaign to divest The Florida Bar of its ability to assist the Supreme Court of Florida in the regulation of attorneys. They continue to influence a negative perception in the public regarding our justice system and the role of lawyers. These groups pressure politicians to change the civil liabilities system by limiting just recovery for victim and by curtailing the citizens' right to a jury trial. Funding decisions for the entire justice system are impacted by a lack of understanding and appreciation of our courts as an independent branch of government. We lawyers of Florida must work together to correct misinformation and faulty beliefs by providing accurate information to the public.

Because the Florida Bar is an integrated Bar, it does not enjoy an unfettered ability to use its funds for such information purposes. For that reason, The Florida Bar established F.L.A.M.E. several years ago. Your voluntary contribution to F.L.A.M.E. enables your Florida Bar leadership to communicate on your behalf with regard to these issues directly and forcibly. We believe that our profession must continue to air direct information campaigns in the mass media to promote a clear understanding of our legal system and of our profession. Your voluntary contribution to F.L.A.M.E. enables your leadership to communicate accurate information and thereby tell "our side" of the story.

We realized that you receive a great many appeals for contributions. Allow me to make this appeal for a voluntary contribution by you of $25 to support F.L.A.M.E. Your contribution will promote the common professional and business interests of the lawyers of Florida and will give your Bar leadership an important tool in our constant battle to maintain the profession we love and our system of justice. We greatly appreciate your contribution and promise that it will be used solely and directly to accomplish these purposes. We thank you for your commitment to the highest ideals of our profession.

Very truly yours,

Alan Dimond, President, 1992-93

The first question I'm sure you are asking is: "What does the acronym F.L.A.M.E. stand for?" The answer: Florida Lawyers Association for the Maintenance of Excellence, Inc.

Important also to recognize is that F.L.A.M.E. is essentially not a PAC, but a non-profit organization where the pooled moneys of Florida attorneys (approximately. 39,000 in total, thus a potential of $975,000 if everyone contributed the minimum and this is, again, without the large contributions from the "large Florida law firms") who are required to be members of The Florida Bar by the State of Florida. F.L.A.M.E. contributions are used to purchase mass media advertising whose objective it is to combat the Insurance Industry PACs, the American Medical Association (AMA) PAC, and other PACs that wish to see "dollar caps" put on civil jury awards. Both the American Bar Association (ABA) and the New York State Bar Association, as do most all other private bar associations, have regular "attack PACs" that directly strike back at the AMA PAC and the Insurance Industry PACs through direct PAC contributions to both federal and state legislators. As you read through this short section if you had a vision or two of the old PACMAN game, you are getting the right vibes.

The Scariest Of All Special Interest Groups

Although PACs have become critically dangerous to American democracy, it will probably be the *Special Interest Creditor Groups* who will finally cause the bankruptcy of the United States and an end to its so-called "democracy." The most dangerous of these *special interest groups* are the foreign creditor nations of the United States; those foreign nations who finance part of America's $5 trillion Nation Debt; and I refer specifically to Japan, Taiwan, Korea, Mexico, Bahrain, Iran, Iraq, Kuwait, Oman, Qatar, Saudi Arabia and the United Arab Emirates. It is these foreign countries that hold both our President and our Congress hostage. So you ask: "How does this work?" Read on.

How shocking it would be for most Americans to know, especially in the context of the "Fast-Track" North American Free Trade Agreement that was initially negotiated by the Bush Administration, that last year Mexico's government and Mexican private investors bought a total of $2.9 billion of U.S. Treasury Notes and Bonds. Do you smell a "rat" somewhere in all of this "Fast-Track" stuff now?

One need not ask, after all the Japanese-bashing of 1991, why the Japanese have become net-sellers in 1992 of U.S. Treasury Instruments, a void that miraculously Taiwan quickly filled, and who are now the biggest foreign net buyers of U.S. Treasury Debt Instruments. Let's not forget who the Taiwanese depend on to defend the Chinese Straights between Red China and Taiwan! Think you might smell a bit of a "rat" here too?

One has to ask why countries such as Great Britain, Spain, and France remain stalwart buyers of U.S. Treasury Debt Instruments when (although blasphemous, if not almost treasonous for any American to say or imply) the U.S. Government teeters on the brink of insolvency, with over $5 trillion in debt and a minimum of at least another $15 trillion in off-balance-sheet obligations.

It would not take the imagination of a Tom Clancy, or perhaps a Stephen King, to structure a scenario setting forth the true meaning of the

G-7. G-7 refers to the seven richest industrial nations of the world, whose finance ministers and financial leaders determine and assure the economic & financial future of their segment of the world's "top-two-percenter's." These seven richest nations are: the U.S., Great Britain, France, Germany, Japan, Italy, and Canada. Its primary mission is global control over the world's money and credit markets. One can only imagine the deals that took, and take place, to assure that the world's greatest debtor nation, the United States, remains "too big to fail." Remember also, the U.S. dollar is the *hoarding currency* of the world's nations and billionaires, and therefore there is no world leader or world billionaire not inextricably entwined with its value, health, and well-being! Until this changes, all Americans (even the middle-class) are safe in our own voracious greed, consumer indifference, and economic wastefulness from out-and-out attack by the rest of the world's financial community, with perhaps the *exception* of some sporadic attacks of profit-taking speculation occurring periodically in the unregulated free-trade international currency exchange markets that trades between $3-5 trillion per day, as discussed later in this book.

AARP
The Biggest Of The Special Interest Groups
&
The Biggest Money Making American Non-Profit Business

It sells Prudential Insurance to its members and earns $100 million a year acting as the middle-man. It has as its members, one-half of the nation's population who are over 50, paying $110 million per year in membership dues; and it owns the largest magazine published in America; Modern Maturity (circulation: 21,430,990), a magazine primarily used to promote its own products and businesses.

AARP's lobbying headquarters in Washington D.C. is referred to as the "Taj Mahal," and is leased for $16.6 million a year and fitted with the most expensive furniture and appointments money can buy; approximately $30 million was spent alone in 1990 to opulesce this palace. The Taj Mahal, houses 1125 AARP employees at a payroll cost of $43.2 million per year.

The U.S. Congress itself scratches AARP's back with almost $100 million in federal grants for programs that have been questioned as being practically non-existent by AARP's own members.

"Why all of these disgusting statistics?", you ask. "You think there wasn't enough to make me sick in the earlier chapters of this book? Sure I remember the 1992 United Way scandals! So why tell me about AARP? I really don't want to hear about it."

Well, don't put the book down just yet. Let's get a better picture of why *special interest groups* like AARP are so dangerous to America and

American "family values." Don't miss Chapter Fifteen, where Social Security is explored as part of the solution to America's problems as contrasted to the AARP solution of America making Social Security a major part of the problem in America.

So, you now want to know: "How does a group like AARP threaten the "family values" of America?"

The Answer: Its "big business," making "big money," under the color of "compassion" for the nation's aging as it divides the nation's youth from its parents and grandparents by continually instilling the fear in the "aging" and "aged" that "entitlement programs" will be eliminated or severely cut-back.

Even as I closed in on 50, I too felt the need to throw in my own $5.00 membership fee to AARP to protect my own personal interest in these "entitlement programs" AARP has us all believing they single-handedly protect from administration and congressional "cuts." The reality is these very fear-merchants take their own large piece of the American "pie" as they profess to do those self-proclaimed good works for us and our allegedly defenseless mothers, fathers, and grandparents, while making millions a year as they line their own pockets derived from dividing America into two camps: The "Gray Panthers," . . . and the under-fifty-age-group who allegedly want to take these benefits away. If you think this analysis is exaggerated, get a membership package from AARP and a couple of past issues of <u>Modern Maturity</u>. Read the propaganda over, then ask your grandparents or parents who it is they trust to keep their "entitlements" flowing?

- The Myths -

I.   There are some *special interest groups* that truly have the interest of the nation's well being as their primary objective.

II.   The U.S. Congress will ultimately restrict or outlaw "lobbyist," "PACs," and other *special interest groups*.

- The Realities -

I.   All *special interest groups*, no matter what their initial motivation, ultimately become "self-interested" in only perpetuating their own existence and the flamboyant life-styles they provide their upper-echelon leaders. This is true even of the most altruistic-sounding of the lot. It's a matter of what we have all come to know as the "American Way" that has everyone ultimately believing they are "underpaid," whether it be for allegedly "charitable work," "good work," or simply "eight-hours of work."

II. The U.S. Congress would outlaw PACs, but only if we provided them with a COLA-oriented $5 million for each election in personal campaign funds to do with what they please. Don't believe this wouldn't change a thing! The present group, and even their successors, would still continue to pretend to "represent" us, as the same large sums of money continued to flow through alternative conduits. That's just the "American Way," and will always remain so, if the present system of "representative government" isn't somewhat revamped and Boobus Americanus refuses to excuse this corrupting conduct. See Chapter Twenty of this book for how you might join in the task of reinventing and revamping our present system of representative government and in "taking back" America politically to your own advantage.

- AUTHOR'S REVERSE "SPIN" GLOSSARY -

- "WHAT THEY SAY IT MEANS" & "WHAT IT REALLY MEANS."

America's Precious Freedoms:

What they say it means: The state of being free; liberty; self-determination; an absence of unlawful restraint; the opposite of slavery. The power derived from acting in the character of a moral personality, according to the dictates of the will, without other checks, hindrance, or prohibition resulting from unjust or unnecessary laws. The prevalence, in the government and the constitution of a country, of such a system of laws and institutions, structured in such a manner so as to secure civil liberty for the individual citizen. Civil liberties are those personal and natural rights guaranteed and protected by the U.S. Constitution. They include: freedom of speech, freedom of the press, freedom of association, amongst others enumerated in the Bill of Rights.

What it really means (1996): The answer here is both postmortem and prospective. Compared to other nations, no one can question the amount of "freedom" enjoyed by Americans especially in the area of constitutionally guaranteed civil liberties and rights. To many of us, presently and prospectively, it seems our "freedoms" are slowly eroding away. Perhaps it was the closing of our frontiers at the beginning of this century? Or perhaps the loss of our national industrial and moral leadership we prided ourselves in over 200 years? Or perhaps it's the loss of "freedom" that one senses as the world becomes a smaller and smaller place. Or the loss of "privacy" that resulted from the computer revolution and its derivative concentration of personal data about each of us? Can one ever feel "free" when his or her most confidential and private information can be accessed by almost anyone? Perhaps the loss of "freedom" we all sense today is a direct result of America's rapidly declining middle-class, the continuing erosion of our former standard-of-living, and the loss of that future promise of prosperity that was believed to be very much a part of our birthright, or so we thought? The most important question of all is: Can we as Americans ever get back the "freedom," or whatever it is that seems to have been gradually, but continuously taken from us during the past thirty years?

Appropriations Committees:

What they say they are: Both the U.S. Senate, and the U.S. House of Representative each have a Committee on Appropriations. Sen. Robert Byrd (D-W. Va.) up until 1994 was the Chairman of the Senate Committee on appropriations, and the House Committee on Appropriations was chaired by Jamie Whitten (D-Miss.), since then the Republicans have held majorities in both the House and Senate. Although every appropriation bill must originate in the House of Representatives, it is both the House and Senate Appropriations Committees who authorize the expenditure of public moneys, stipulating the amount, the manner, and the purpose of these various expenditures.

What these committees really are: The former Chairs of both the Senate and the House Appropriations Committee had between them, 85 years in Congress. Sen. Byrd was elected to the Senate in 1958 and Congressman Whitten was first elected to the House in 1941. With the possible exception of convicted felon, Dan Rostenkowski, the former Chairman of the House Ways and Means Committee, these two previously-named members of Congress were the most powerful and influential members of each body, due to their control over the appropriations process. It is here where all of the "pork" is "pork-barreled," a term you will later become more familiar with.

Entitlement Programs:

What they say they mean: Any government program either federal or state, that pays benefits to those who meet what ever eligibility standards that are established. Such entitlement programs include Social Security, Medicare, Medicaid, and Food Stamps, etc.

What these programs really mean: Entitlement programs are another weapon in the arsenal of the Congress and President to control the largest of all "special interest voting groups," those persons on or close to Social Security and Medicare benefits. These voters represent approximately 25% of all votes in national elections. If continued to go unchecked, it is estimated by the year 2010 Social Security and Medicare benefits paid to the "baby-boomers" of today will account for more than 66% of the U.S. Federal Budget. In fiscal year 1990, Social Security, Medicare, and other retirement outlays represented 31% of all federal spending. In June of 1996, it was announced by the Congressional Office of the Budget that Medicare would be bankrupt in two years or less without some kind of reform. Remember the formula I gave you before with regard to discounting good government news (divide by two) and bad government news (multiply it by four).

Federal Deficit:

What they say it means: The result when the government spends more in a fiscal year than it receives in revenue. To cover the difference the government borrows from the "public" (and foreign governments and anyone else that has money that can't find a home elsewhere) by floating long and short term treasury debt instruments. Federal deficits started to rise in the 1970s, and exploded in the early 1980s. Many economists believe the National Debt (the result of adding on each annual federal deficit onto the aggregate of past federal deficits) is the cause of both high interest rates (this is questionable, given the role of The Fed) and inflation since they compete with private borrowing by businesses and people seeking to purchase amongst other things, new cars, homes, and to pay catastrophic medical bills that have also risen disproportionately to middle-class wages. One has to wonder, if these unnamed economists are aware of the day-to-day operations of The Fed and their power to lower the "interest rates" to historical low levels, while the National Debt is at all time highs with no ceiling in sight, and the debtor (the U.S. Taxpayer) has so little promise of long-term employment to pay-off this obligation?

What it really means: The Federal Deficit in reality is what remains after the President and the Congress of the United States have satisfied the *needs*, that is, *paid-off* <u>both</u> the key *special interest groups* that have financially supported their election (directly bought them) or had the aggregate entitlement recipient or the *special interest voter groups* to elect them.   It is the *special interest voter group's* voting power of Americans over age fifty (historically the largest voting segment of our citizenry), who coincidentally are also the beneficiaries of the largest of the "entitlement program" expenditures. That, in the final analysis, absolutely assures the re-election or appropriate replacement of each member of Congress and the President in their current and subsequent terms. And helpless we are, those of us with parents and/or grandparents to oppose these "entitlements," since this opposition is so contrary to Mother, Apple Pie, and the American Dream, and especially since we are able to keep our nation's creditors paying for it. I estimate that at the rate the annual federal deficit is rising, by 2000 the newest generation (those who today are under 18), will not wish to carry the ball (the burden). Now, don't all of you out there reading this book think this punishment (An $8 Trillion Dollar National Debt by the year 2000) we're hanging on them is a bit unusual for their crimes? (i.e. their own "gimmie-gimmie-gimmie" routines). Keep in mind, the majority of this 100% TV generation believes that "money grows on trees," that Mommy and Daddy have jobs like Bill Cosby and his TV wife, and that vegetable and fruits are grown in the Freezer and Produce Sections of the Supermarket. Does anyone out there really believe this group is going to contribute to Social Security for their own future "entitlements," much less the "ones" being consumed today, or the "ones" we, in the Baby Boom Generation believe we'll be consuming in our "golden years?" It would be miraculous, considering their inadequate education, the "burned-out" resources we're leaving them, and the "moral decadence" and "voracious consumption appetites" we've allowed our marketing MBAs and TV media to brainwash them with since birth?

Federal Farm Credit System:

What they say it means: Congress created the Federal Farm Credit System (FFCS) with its passage of the Farm Credit Act of 1971. The Federal Farm Credit System operates through a network of twelve Farm Credit districts, each having a Federal Land Bank and a Federal Intermediate Credit Bank, and a Bank for Cooperatives to carry out its policies (getting federal money to America's farmers). The FFCS is authorized to sell short-term notes in increments of $50,000 on a discounted basis through a national syndicate of securities dealers, and it is the Federal Farm Credit Bank, who establishes the "interest rates" for these short-term notes. Congress has also seen fit to exempt from federal, state, and local taxation all capital, reserves, surplus and the income derived by FFCS.

What FFCS really means: Here again another powerful "special interest group" has caused another violation of the somewhat hypocritical American "free market" system of capitalism and free competition America supposedly supports. Taking no place on the back-burner, the farmers in this country have long been one of America's most important and powerful *special interest groups*. One need only count the number of farm states and the number of U.S. Senators from those farm states to understand how important *special interest group* farmers truly are; and it's not their "numbers," but the actual size of their land that counts here. As just noted, their power lies in the U.S. Senate. What non-farm state members of the U.S. Senate could afford to alienate so many other U.S. Senators from our farm states by not approving legislation submitted on behalf of the "farmers?" Simply put, it boils down to: "You scratch my back and I'll scratch yours." The American taxpayer picks-up the tab.

Federal Home Loan Bank System (FHLBS):

What they say it means: The FHLBS was created in 1932, after the collapse of the banking system in the United States. The purpose of the FHLBS was to supply credit reserves for Savings & Loans, cooperative banks, and other mortgage lenders in a fashion similar to The Fed's participation with the commercial banking system. The FHLBS comprises twelve regional Federal Home Loan Banks. Money for funds are raised by issuing notes and bonds, and the proceeds are then loaned to Savings & Loans and other mortgage lenders based on the amount of collateral that the institution can provide. The FHLBS also acts as the trustee for all of the stock of the Federal Home Loan Mortgage Corporation, also known as Freddie Mac. Freddie Mac is a publicly charted agency that buys qualifying residential mortgages from lenders, then packages them into "new securities" backed by those pooled mortgages, and further attaches certain federal guarantees as to possible investor losses on those "new securities," and then resells these "new securities" on the open market. Freddie Mac has created a large secondary market for federally insured security-backed mortgages which provides more funds for mortgage lending and allows investors to buy high yield securities backed by federal guarantees. Freddie Mac packages mortgages backed by the Veterans Administration (VA), the Federal Housing Administration (FHA), and also nongovernment insured mortgages. Freddie Mac was established in 1970, and is regulated by the U.S. Department of Housing and Urban Development (HUD).

What FHLSB & Freddie Mac really mean: Here again we see another violation of our American concept of "free market" capitalism. The most significant industry in the U.S., the one most relied upon to lead us out of the majority of our past recessions, the housing industry is just another government subsidized industry, which in 1996 was supported by you and me to the tune of $950 billion in federal government guarantees. Taken together with the nation's mortgage-interest rates that are indirectly controlled by the Fed, one has to wonder where the notions of "free market" and "free competition" exist in this area. Obviously the housing market in the United States is not controlled solely by the "free market" forces of supply and demand. How many of you are aware that back on July 1, 1992, the United States Senate approved legislation aimed at preventing "massive taxpayer bailouts" of the two government-backed enterprises known as Fannie Mae and Freddie Mac through added federal guarantees to investors in these enterprises. Between these two enterprises, the Federal Government (the U.S. Taxpayer) stands behind (guarantees) $900 Billion worth of federally insured home mortgages. The Senate vote was 77 to 19 on July 1, 1992 as the majority of America had just begun their annual vacation season.

Federal Housing Administration (FHA):

What they say it means: The FHA is a federal agency within the U.S. Department of Housing and Urban Development. The agency was created in 1934 to administer housing loans, loan guarantees, and loan insurance programs designed to increase the availability of housing in America.

What it really means: [See Federal Home Loan Bank System above.]

Federal National Mortgage Association (FNMA) or (FANNIE MAE):

What they say it means: A publicly owned (its stock is traded on the New York Stock Exchange), government-sponsored corporation that was charted in 1938 to purchase mortgages from lenders and resell them to investors. Similar to Freddie Mac, Fannie Mae mostly packages mortgages backed by the Federal Housing Administration (See FHA above), but it also deals in (sells) non-government backed mortgages. Keeping in mind the impact of the Fed on interest rates, it is important to know that the price of Fannie Maes "soars" when interest rates fall, and "nose-dives" when interest rates rise, evidencing the absolute dependency of both the "home construction industry" and "residential mortgage business" on interest rates. Fannie Mae also represents the fourth largest financial institution in America, and as such, it shows no "shame" in paying enormous bonuses, benefits and other perquisites to its senior executives. In 1991, its retiring chairman was paid a bonus of $29 million. Keep in mind that this agency: its capital, its reserves, its surplus, its mortgages, and other securities holdings, and all of its income are exempt from all taxation by the United States.

What it really means: If you think the estimated $500 Billion dollar S&L Bailout was expensive just keep your eye on Fannie Mae and its little brother Freddie Mac. Follow the number of "foreclosures" on residential real property around you. Keep your eye also on the "unemployment rate," especially if it should dramatically increase. Recognize that as more-and-more Americans lose their "jobs," and as more-and-more home mortgages are foreclosed, it is inevitable that many of these losses will ultimately flow-back into Fannie Mae and Freddie Mac and ultimately to the U.S. Taxpayer's pocketbook.

Again, as it was with Freddie Mac, Fannie Mae represents just another contradiction of our system of "free market" capitalism. The American Housing Industry is alleged to be the driving force to both take us out of recessions and to keep the overall economy healthy. Approximately 1.1 million new homes are sold annually in the United States, and one can only guess at the amount of economic activity truly generated by the trickle-down effect into the Durable Goods (home appliance) Industry, the Home Furnishings Industry, etc., etc.

Fence Mending:

What they say it means: A term used in political circles referring to the "making of peace" with a former political opponent or opposing political group.

What it really means: "Unless you scratch my back, I won't scratch yours, and thus neither of us will have our backs scratched." This "back scratching" occurs most frequently when one political party is only marginally empowered to thwart the opposition party from taking all the "pie" (the moneys in either the federal, state, or local treasury) for itself.

Freddie Mac [See Federal Home Loan Mortgage Corporation, Ginnie Mae, and Fannie Mae]

The Freedom of Information Act (FOIA):

What they say it means: Legislation enacted by Congress requiring that, with specified exemptions, documents and materials generated or held by Federal Agencies be made available to the public under specific guidelines established for their disclosure. Documents and materials relating to the "national security" are exempt from this legislation.

What it really means: Since passage of the Freedom of Information Act, the Federal Government has probably spent over $100 million to reclassify documents and information as still affecting *national security*. An additional $10 million in black ink magic markers have also been authorized and expended by the U.S. Government in its attempt to thwart the spirit of this law.

Full Faith & Credit:

What they say it means: A phrase employed by politicians when seeking enormous loans or issuing paper money facsimiles. This pledge is used as backing for all U.S. Government Securities and General Obligation Bonds of the United States. This phrase is also used by all state and local governments in the guarantee of their borrowings, and is understood to mean that the full taxing and borrowing power, and other revenues other than taxes, are pledged in payment of "interest" and of "principal" on that debt obligation issued by the applicable government.

What it really means: Your government is again signing your name to IOUs it believes it can enforce you to pay. Implicit in the phrase is that you, your children, your grandchildren, and now your great-grandchildren, have agreed to work and pay for such ridiculous things as:

    1. Last year's Foreign Aid;

2. Your 1980s and 1990s elected representatives' past and present princely salaries, royal pensions, and the other perquisites they provided themselves;

3. The "spoils" those delivered to *special interest groups* that kept them in office over the past thirty years, while they "looted" the nation's, the state's, and local government treasuries.

House Ways and Means Committee:

What they say it means: The Standing Committee of the U.S. House of Representatives responsible for supervising legislation dealing with the nation's financial matters. These "matters" include inquiry, examination, and consideration as to the methods and sources for raising revenue; and to propose and draft legislation (bills) to provide the funds (taxes) need to both run the federal government and provide the moneys necessary for its legislated programs (i.e. defense funding, general welfare funding, Social Security, etc.). Tax legislation, like any other form of legislation (bill), follows the same flow from its inception as an "idea" to its final passage through the legislature (the House and Senate) and either final signing or veto by the President.

What it really means: As important as the House and Senate Appropriations Committees are in "divvying-up" the moneys of the American people in the U.S. Treasury or attained through its immense borrowing power, it is the House Ways and Means Committee in its power to "steal" directly from the American people. The House Ways and Means Committee determines where tax moneys are to come from (i.e. From the wealthy? The middle-class?)

For many years, it was Dan Rostenkowski, Chairman of the House Way & Means Committee and a Democratic member of the House of Representatives for almost 34 years, who virtually decided this on the House side. I point out again that he was a Democrat, and not a Republican. What should be of interest to all U.S. Taxpayers is the "honoraria" that this allegedly Democratic Congressman earned during the period 1980 to 1990 from a various, and sometimes unusual mix of *special interest groups* which included: Total — $1.7 million. These *special interest groups* included Blue Cross-Blue Shield (our leading health care insurer), the Chicago Board of Trade (a major Chicago "casino"), Citicorp (one of America's largest banks that required a lot of help from both Congress and the Fed to survive in 1991), the American Stock Exchange (another "casino," but located in N.Y.), the American Bankers Association (representing all the nation's banks), and the National Automobile Dealers Association. It should be obvious to most, that unless a rather strenuously spun "spin" is put on the endeavors of these "special interests groups," it would be difficult to see how these groups' "interests" were even "coincidentally concurrent" with the "interests" of most ordinary Americans.

Honoraria (Honorarium):

What they say it means: An "honorarium" is a free gift or gratuitous payment, as distinguished from a fee for services or earnings for work performed. It has also been defined as a voluntary reward for which no remuneration could be collected by law. In 1989, the U.S. Congress banned all honoraria, in exchange for one of its "middle-of-the- night" pay raises that brought all House members' salaries to $125,100 per year, with all future raises triggered by a new congressional trick: COLAs! In 1996, Congressional salaries for all members topped $136,000 per year, which I remind you did not include the cost of their benefit programs or other perks previously noted.

What it really means: Prior to honoraria being banned by the Congress it was merely an overt "special interest group" payment to those of our legislators who were members (i.e Chairman) of the more significant and powerful House and Senate committees (as a result of House and Senate Seniority Rules). Now that the Congress has banned honoraria, at least temporarily, we still have the same "cat," but now dressed in a different "uniform": both Representatives and Senators now direct these payments to their personal Congressional foundations or to certain tax exempt related organizations, or committees. U.S. Senator Robert Dole has his Dole Foundation. U.S Senator Garn has his University Foundation. Even the Democratic Senator Patrick Moynihan has a foundation known as Derrymore. The implication here is not fraud, or malfeasance of office; it's merely the circumvention of the spirit of the "rule," for who could deny that the enormous amounts of money generated by present-day honoraria, even though not applied directly to a politician's re-election campaign fund or personal pocketbook, is still not an indirect "power hook" into the overall re-election effort of these incumbents? (See also "Bundling" and "Inner Circle")

National Debt:

What they say it means: The National Debt is the debt owed by the United States to its creditors. This debt is made-up of such debt obligation as Treasury Bills, Treasury Notes, and Treasury Bonds. In 1960, the National Debt totaled $284.1 Billion dollars; in 1970 it had increased to $370.1 Billion; in 1980 it rose to $970 Billion dollars, approximately $100 Billion dollars less than the Trillion Dollar mark. After twelve-years of Republican Administrations, in June of 1992 the National Debt exploded, hitting an all time high of $4 trillion, this representing an increase of over $3.1 trillion, almost three-and-one-half (3 1/2) times what it had been in 1980. To understand the magnitude of this problem, consider it your personal debt. Then presume the bank wishes you to pay a 10% interest rate on this debt. If this were the case, the "interest" alone would be a whopping $400 Billion dollars a year, a sum larger than the "whole" National Debt twenty years earlier in 1970. In 1996, the National Debt topped the $5 trillion mark.

What it really means: Approximately $20,000 per every man, woman, and child in principle alone. If the debt neither decreases, nor increases this would further require every man, woman, and child in the United States to pay his or her first $1,450 of income taxes forever to just cover the "interest" on this debt. The worst is not over. The National Debt does not include such things as the off-balance-sheet $500 Billion S&L Bailout, and the yet low-key present and future bailout of the Commercial Banks. Nor does it include the future funding requirements of the Pension Benefits Guarantee Corporation (PBGC); nor the future funding forecasts of such "entitlement programs" as Social Security, Medicare, or Medicaid. What about Social Security and Medicare, and all of the other federal pension moneys that are vested in our civil servants who include each and every Congressman and Senator, all federal employees, all active and retired military personnel, and all those persons who are expecting to be provided future Social Security and Medicare benefits? Few of you know that Bob Dole and his wife must be on the dole, especially since their combined vested federal pensions are currently in excess of $4 million. Now how does this compare to your Social Security benefits in the future? Many of those economists who are also CPAs, and who understand the term "Off-Balance-Sheet" obligation of the United States, if recorded pursuant to generally accepted accounting principals, would have the National Debt at a staggering $20 trillion. Now who is going to pay for all of this debt? I hope nobody is relying on the so-called X-Generation, those born after 1964.

Representative Government:

What they say it means: A system where the people elect representatives, who in turn, exercise (vote) the will of the people. Representative government, in the context of democracy, presumes that those elected to "represent" will respect that the "sovereign power" belongs to, and shall always remain, the "sole power" of the citizens who have chosen to be governed as such.

What it means in the United States: Representation of those *special interest groups* that either have the "buying power" to effect an election or the reelection of an already elected "representative" at the federal, state, or local level.

Two Party System of Government:

What they say it means: This concept refers to the two dominant political parties in the United States, the Republicans and the Democrats, with no significant third party presence. The "two party system of government," without the presence of a third significant party, in theory assures "majority rule," as opposed to "minority" or "plurality" rule where governments or candidates can be elected by less than 50% of the votes cast. For example, in a three party system, one political party may attain as little as 34% of the vote, while each of the other two parties each attain 33% of the vote, and yet, although clearly in the minority, the 34% party would clearly be elected. The two party system is generally credited with preventing this from occurring.

What it really means: Based upon voter turn-out in both local and general elections, it is very questionable whether any elected official, even with America's "two party-system" truly represents a "plurality" of its people, much less than a majority of its people. In some cities, as few as 16% of the registered voters (those voters who are registered as opposed to voters who are not registered at all) have turned out on a particular election day. Whether it be apathy or just political indifference, there exists something very wrong in an alleged "democracy" where the right-to-vote is not exercised by so many of its citizens. Perhaps the answer lies in one of the basic foundations of American Government as stated by Abraham Lincoln in his Gettysburg Address, when he concluded by defining American Government as, "Government of the people, by the people, for the people . . ." What American, other than those in power, or those comprising the top-two-percenters, and perhaps, the "carrot chasers" in the remaining upper 20% of the economic strata, truly believe that American Government is a government of the people, by the people, and especially, a Government for the people?

Political Action Committees in the "Work Place":

What they say it means: Generally the typical Company sponsored PAC focuses on its cadre of middle managers. Each manager is requested to contribute to the PAC under the concept of: "What is good for the company must be good for the employee." Middle managers generally contribute happily and gratefully, since they feel that they have become a part of the real "political process."

What it really means: If you don't contribute you obviously don't see the value in your present job, or the value in any promotion you may have anticipated. It is the rare instance, that the Company PAC is anything more than employer-based extortion fostered upon those who are either financially reliant on their employment, or wish to continue having expectations of raises and promotions.

Special Interest Groups:

What they say it means: *Special Interest Groups* are those formal and informal groups in society that have a common interest in a particular issue, and who attempt to influence government legislation to benefit that "interest." *Special Interest Groups* include a wide range of so-called "lobbyists"; Political Action Committees (PACs); and numerous other associations, corporations and organizations such as the AARP, NAACP, labor unions, the American Medical Association, the American Bar Association, and even the Klu Klux Klan (KKK), who may or may not have a "shill" or other representative roaming the halls and offices of the Congress, with a checkbook-in-hand.

What they really mean: In American democracy, it is the Special Interest Group that generally finances the election of every "elected official," whether it be federal, state, or local. Members of the U.S. House of Representatives and the U.S. Senate have become so reliant on PAC financing that they actually now directly "beg" contributions from these organizations — this now being widely accepted, and certainly no secret in the Congress. The Federal Election Committee (FEC) at last count indicated that there were 1,795 corporate PACs, 346 labor union and related PACs, 1,062 non-connected PACs, 774 trade associations PACs, 136 "ownerless corporation" PACs (those corporations without stockholders), and 59 cooperative PACs. In fiscal 1989-90, PACs raised more than $372 million and spent $358 million to influence the electoral process. The maximum donation a PAC can make to any political candidate is limited to $5,000. Some commentators have estimated that a $5,000 contribution to a political candidate will return at least $100,000 in legislative benefits — not a bad investment for a 2000% return.

During the 101st Congress, a major effort was made to pass campaign financing reform to control the overwhelming influence of the various *special interest groups*. This effort, as might be expected, failed as have the efforts so far in the subsequently elected Congresses.

Specialist Interest "Voter" Groups:

What they say it means: Special Interest "Voter" Groups are not so much politically empowered by the PACs they form, nor the money they contribute to the election campaigns of candidates; their real power lies in the "voting power" that they possess as a result of the particular "interest" that effects them. Probably the single-most-powerful Special Interest Voter Group in the United States are the voters receiving Social Security and Medicare, or those within reaching distance of these entitlement programs based on their present age. This group represents approximately 30% of all those eligible to vote, and in the 1988 election represented approximately 39% of all votes actually cast. It's no wonder that very few U.S. Senators or Congressmen have the courage to even mouth the words "reform," much less attempt any reform of either Social Security or Medicare.

What it really means: So long as there are "entitlement programs," there will be "Special Interest Voter Groups." It's "American" to believe that your group is entitled to special considerations (i.e. unions versus labor as it concerns strike rights, collective bargaining rights, and wages and benefits), and perhaps these groups will persist and perhaps even grow until the "bubble has finally burst." Here lies the only argument for "representative" democracy as opposed to "pure" democracy; but here again, based on the results of 220 years of this "representative" democracy the nation continually hovers on the brink of financial collapse. - - How come you ask? Simply because these "representatives" will always put their own re-election and the small constituencies that locally vote for them ahead of what may be best for the nation. Not given the solutions in Chapter Twenty, perhaps this is the winning argument for "term limitations," outweighing the opposing arguments of "wisdom & experience gained in office," and "he's done a great job in his last four terms."

COMPOSITE DICTIONARY

Bicameral Legislature: A legislature composed of two separate houses or chambers such as the United States Congress and the forty-nine states excluding Nebraska which has the only "unicameral" legislature.

Captive Candidate: A government official who is presently a candidate for office and who is controlled by certain *Special Interest Groups*.

Electoral College: An institution that comes alive every four-years as part of the Presidential election process in the U.S. The Electoral College was created by the U.S. Constitution and the institution has only been amended once (by the 23rd Amendment to the Constitution where the District of Columbia was given three Electoral votes). Besides the three electoral votes held by the District of Columbia, there also exist 435 other electoral votes which coincidentally equals the total number of U.S. Senators and members of the House of Representatives. Thus with a total of 438 members, it takes 220 electoral votes from the Electoral College to elect the President and Vice President of the United States. Customarily, since neither Senators nor Congressmen are permitted to be electors, the political parties nominate their list of electors at their respective state conventions and in some states these names appear at the top of the ballot, while other states print the names of the candidates for President and Vice President in these slots.

The "electors" of the party receiving the highest number of votes then meet on the first Monday after the second Wednesday in December in their respective state capitals and vote for their party's nominees, although the constitution does not require them to do so. All of the state's electoral votes are then awarded to the winners. Although all Americans know who their President and Vice President are usually the first Wednesday in November (the day after election day), it is not official until all the electors in all states have mailed to the President of the U.S. Senate, a certified and sealed list of the votes of the electors from all their respective states. The President of the Senate then opens these lists in the presence of the members of the Senate and the House of Representatives in a joint session held on January 6, or the next day, if it falls on a Sunday, and the electoral votes of all the states are counted. If no candidate for President has achieved a true majority, the House of Representative chooses a president from among the three highest candidates with all representatives from each state combining to cast one vote for that state. If no Vice Presidential candidate has the needed majority, the Senate chooses from the top two, each Senator voting as an individual. The President and Vice President-elect are not sworn in until January 20, the month in which they are elected by the Electoral College or by the process described above, if no candidate has achieved a majority of the Electoral Votes.

Golden Fleece Award: An award created by Sen. William Proxmire (D-Wis.) who served in the U.S. Senate from 1957 to 1989 notably as chairman of the Senate Banking Committee. Senator Proxmire bestowed his annual award based upon the most wasteful, fraudulent, or useless government project for which the U.S. Congress appropriated money. With the retirement of Sen. Proxmire, came the end of the Golden Fleece Award era, no other Senator in the U.S. Senate has had the courage to continue this "whistle-blowing" truly public service program.

Gramm-Rudman-Hollings Act: Legislation passed in 1985 which mandated that the Federal Deficit be lowered to a certain declining amount each year until a balanced budget was reached. If the ceiling wasn't reached, the law acts to automatically reduce government expenditures in an across-the-board manner to reach that year's required ceiling. When enacted in 1985 the bill called for a balance budget by 1991; the date has now been extended to 1997. Currently there is no expectation by the Congress that the Gramm-Rudman-Hollings Act will ever be truly enforced by themselves or the White House.

Grassroots: The average voter and citizen who has no history of political activism. The term is also somewhat diminished by attributing its meaning to the rank and file of a political party. In most circles the term "grassroots," refers to those persons who are not associated with either the Democratic Party, the Republican Party or any other form of organized political group.

Grid-Lock: A term derived from the traffic patterns in the city of New York. A condition where north and south bound traffic as well as east and west bound traffic were of such magnitude that all traffic stopped in a form of a grid-lock. As it regards the U.S. political and government system, it refers to the stalemate that exists between either the Executive Branch when controlled by one party, where the Congress is controlled by the other, or where each of the two chambers of the Congress are controlled by opposing parties, thus giving further rise to "government's" general inability to get anything done. The author believes the primary reason grid-lock occurs is because of the overloading of the Congress during the past 200 years, with 435 House, and 100 Senate members. (See Downsizings in the Dictionary)

Inner Circle: An "Inner Circle" describes that group of people who have made $1,000 donations to the National Republican Senatorial Committee in exchange for promised personal access to the highest ranking members of the Republican Party.

Lobbyist: Those persons, public relations firms, representatives of *special interest groups*, corporations, etc., engaged in the business of persuading legislatures at both the federal and state levels to pass laws that are favorable, and to defeat those that are unfavorable to either themselves or their clients. The activities of lobbyist are controlled and regulated by statute in most states. At the Federal Government level, lobbying activities are subject to the provisions of the Federal Regulation of Lobbying Act of 1946. This Act requires the registration of lobbyists with the Secretary of the Senate and the Clerk of the House; and their reporting of various contributions, expenditures, and any other considerations for the purpose of attempting to influence the passage of the defeat of any legislation by the Congress of the United States and the criminal penalties involved for violating this statute.

Logrolling: An anti-democratic conspiracy of politicians or political groups helping one another, usually in the context of, "You vote for my bill, and I'll vote for yours."

Power Broker: A political leader who controls a block of votes and can deliver them; someone who employs political power behind the scenes. Any of the ethnic, racial, or religious coalitions of Congressmen or

Senators that have developed within the Congress over the past 200 years. Make no mistake, these congressional coalitions are as wrongfully empowered as any other "special interest group," and certainly are, and have been a much greater threat to the U.S. Treasury than any of even the most moneyed or powerful outside *special interest groups.*

Precinct: The location of the polling place in the lowest level of political subdivision authorized to have voters vote at that site. It is usually a particular location in the neighborhood where voters vote at a single polling place. In urban centers it can be as small as a large apartment building; in the suburbs it might cover two or three square miles. In most states today, the *precinct* is located at the local schools or community centers.

Separation of Powers Doctrine: The Legislative, Executive, and Judicial Branches. The function of the Legislative Branch is to make laws. The Executive Branch is charged with carrying out those laws, and the Judicial Branch is charged with interpreting and adjudicating disputes arising under these laws. Pursuant to the U.S. Constitution and its interpretation over the years by the U.S. Supreme Court, under the Separation of Powers Doctrine, one branch is not permitted to encroach on the power or duties of the other.

Suffrage: The right to vote. Women's Suffrage has nothing to do with the present economic plight of women in the U.S. or the world. It simply refers to their right to vote.

Sunshine Law: A law that requires government meetings to be open to the public.

Teflon Politician: The term was first used to describe President Ronald Reagan, and is now applied to all politicians who are so popular that even merited criticism, seems to harmlessly deflect away from them.

Trade and Professional Associations: All associations are organizations of persons who have joined together for a certain common object, or to promote a "special interest." Business associations include such organizations as the National Associations of Realtors, the National Association of Manufacturers, and the National Retail Merchants Association. Professional associations include the American Medical Association, the American Bar Association, the American Institute of Certified Public Accounts, the American Trial Lawyers Association, and the American Dental Association. Each of the aforementioned business or professional associations have also created political action committees

(PACs) which represent their "special interests" within the U.S. Congress and the Administration.

Ward: A specific division of a city or town created for purposes of either elections, police coverage, or other political and/or economic purposes.

6 | The Legal Profession

The Most Notorious of America's Primary Professions

Contrary to the opinion held by so many Americans, not all lawyers, doctors, dentists, and CPAs are patently evil, or even bad. Many are just insecure or have an insatiable need for recognition, comfort, or a voracious need to succeed; and in some instances, an insatiable need for "pleasure." This is not just an American professional phenomenon, the insatiable need for "pleasure" has become epidemic worldwide; from the "busboy," who is looking to make his first illegal drug deal, right up to the "CEO," who spends most of his time without conscience, dreaming up new and greater compensation plans for himself.

Who of you hasn't seen on a bumper sticker or heard on one of the TV sitcoms, one or more of the following:

1. "You only live once! Make the most of it!"
2. "This ain't no dress rehearsal! Enjoy it while you can!"
3. "I'd rather have been born rich, than beautiful!"
4. Or simply, "Go for it!"

As the vast majority of you know, the quickest assessment of one's success is the "amount" of assets one has accumulated, the "rate" at which these "assets" were accumulated, and the derivative powers and pleasures one enjoys from them.

For the American *professional* especially, this phenomenon is known as achieving the American Dream. And once upon a time, it involved some notions of fair play; as well as a touch of morals, ethics, and at least a *surface facade of obedience to law*. But for a significant number of America's professionals, the need for more security, greater pleasure, or just plain power, has overcome all else. And as their appetites expanded exponentially, the "nuts-to-crack" got bigger-and-bigger; and if you are unfamiliar with what a "nut-to-crack" is, it is simply the hole you've dug for yourself with those business and personal monthly bills you have to pay for all those things you and your family have gotten, all those things you and your family want, and all of those things you and your family must consume every month.

The doctors, dentists, lawyers, and CPAs, and other "bad apples" that I describe in this, and the next two chapters are <u>not</u> your sons or daughters; they're <u>not</u> your mothers or fathers; <u>nor</u> your grandparents; and <u>nor</u> are they your grandchildren. This I promise; just as certain that it's not your individual Congressman, or the two U.S. Senators from your state. It's just the U.S. Congress that I refer to as "bad" and those other doctors, dentists, lawyers, and CPAs that you hear about on T.V., or read about in the morning newspaper.

Now that I have dispelled any notion that this is an attack on your family members, let me also dispel this same notion as to my friends, colleagues, acquaintances and clients — most of whom are lawyers, CPAs, dentists, and doctors. This book is not about any of you, so don't attempt to identify with any of the character traits, individually or collectively, unless of course, the shoe-begins-to-fit!

The second part of this Chapter will primarily deal with the "legal profession," and my perception of it from having been on both the "inside" and "outside" for more years than I care to remember.

Chapter Seven will deal with the CPA profession, the first profession I became a member of after graduating from New York University in 1969. Here again, I will deal with my perception of this so-called profession as I saw "it" develop in the early 1970s, and what I see "it" as today.

Chapter Eight will deal with America's medical professions: Our physicians and dentists. Perhaps those of you who are doctors and dentists, after completing Chapters Six and Seven will be glad that I was never an "inside" member of either of your professions.

Before we get into the "legal profession" there are a few characteristics, alluded to before, of professionals in general that are better summarily treated than repeated over and over for each of the four professions specifically discussed in this book. So in an attempt to minimize time and paper, I offer you the following insights that apply to all of the four professions in general — and some of the causes why they and America are perhaps where they are today.

First, How Many of These Professionals Are There?

Profession	Number
Lawyers	805,000
Doctors	670,000
Dentists	192,000
CPAs	570,000

Total Professionals In the Four Groups   <u>2,237,000</u>

What is awesome about the total number of these four professional groups, is almost everyone of them votes, and 99%, as columnist Mike Royko would note: have "full bellies." Of great importance, is that these four professional groups represent as much as 4.6% of those voting in the 1992 Presidential Election and 5.0% of those voting in the 1994 mid-term elections.

What is a Professional?

The term "professional," up until the early 1900s, contemplated only law, medicine and theology. The term "professional" today is also applied to athletes who've gone from "amateur" status to "paid-performance" status, and is even applied to kids who shine shoes inside shoe repair shops, versus those who still try to hustle on the local street corner. Professional sports personnel are also broken into two groups; mere professionals and super-professionals, there being at least a five million dollar a year income difference separating these two categories.

For the purpose of the "professions" examined in this book it means: (1) someone who has worked to acquire a vocation or occupation; (2) that requires, special advanced training; (3) where the labor or skills involved are predominantly mental or intellectual, rather than physical or manual; and (4) for which either the federal or state government requires examination and educational requirements for licensing.

Why Are Professionals Revered By Society?

In my case, it was probably both my father's ignorance passed on to me, and my own narrow interpretation of what I was taught in school; but it wasn't until 1985 that I completely dismissed the conviction that "professionals" possessed certain higher social or moral qualities and attributes than those of "ordinary mortals," including the ghetto dwellers, the hillbillies, the bubbas, and the other sub-groups comprising *Boobus Americanus.*

Growing-up, I can remember believing **physicians** were situated at the right-hand of God; **lawyers** were all in the mold of Abraham Lincoln; **CPAs** were the protectors of the nation's wealth; and **dentists** the great relievers of pain. And which one of you, who attended Junior High School back in the 1950s wasn't made aware of the Hippocratic Oath, an "oath" most American medical schools today regard as either "antiquated" or too high a standard to have their graduates follow!

In the 1950s there was a special respect afforded all those who had achieved one of the four aforementioned professions and most of us coming of age in this decade wanted to emulate these "professional giants" of our time. It was also those 1950s "professionals" we trusted to be our guardians and protectors in America just as had been the Dr. Salks, Darrows and the Lincolns before them. They were the "educated-class," and the rest of us were essentially their "flocks," who looked to these professionals for leadership, advice, and as our models of integrity. I remind you in the 1950s, America's rock' n roll heroes hadn't yet arrived, and professional athletes (the megabuck heroes of today, who make the words "work" and "play" synonymous) were just happy to avoid general work and the stress of "the 9 to 5 job" as they kept themselves in great physical shape "working" four months a year, and sunning themselves in Florida during the winters.

To be certain, society recognized the value of these 1950s "professionals" with both "respect" and relative "financial reward." They generally had the better homes in the neighborhood, the newest and most expensive cars, the best-dressed children — and as insignificant as it may sound, these professionals both lived in the "neighborhood" and were an integral part of the community.

Sometime near the end of the 1950s, things began to change. First it was the doctors and the lawyers who moved out of their local neighborhoods to where the better folks lived. Then it was the dentists and the CPAs. By the mid-1960s you could not find a single shingle hanging in front of a doctor's, dentist's, or lawyer's house. Their practices changed also. They became impersonal and strangers to their clients who no longer saw them in their churches or the synagogues, but only at the office or medical building located in the center of town or at the mall.

The small black leather medical bag of the 1950s that accompanied doctors on house calls also disappeared along with the house calls themselves. By the mid-1960s most of America's professionals had estranged themselves personally, emotionally, and psychologically from the neighborhoods they served, and with their consciences severed from these same neighborhoods, these professionals were now positioned to charge fees for their services at whatever the market would bear, especially after their former neighbors came to see them as businessmen as opposed to professionals.

For you "outsiders" (non-professionals), I shall now take you through the mind-sets of the vast majority of the four aforementioned American "professionals." I do this so you might understand, not condone, what "drives" or "possesses" many of them. Hopefully you'll even get some initial insight how these "drives" cause some of the problems we are facing in America today. Now just sit back and put yourselves in their shoes: Think of their expectations, their wives' expectations, their children's expectations, and their children's children's expectations.

Walking In The Gucci Moccasins (Shoes) of One of the Typical Members of the Four Professions

So you think you've got it made, not only are you going to be rich, but you're also going to have that much sought after *license-to-steal*. Four years of college, then you went to law school, medical school, dental school, or suffered the rigors of the MBA or the horrific CPA or Bar Exam. Exams, exams, and more exams. Years-and-years of sleepless nights, cramming in the "useful" and the more "useless," and now you're required to have between ten and forty-hours of Continuing Professional Education (CPE) each year to keep your "professional status" in society. Whole industries have arisen, making millions, separating you from your money, in order that you may cram in your annually required CPE hours or in the alternative, if you do not complete these CPE hours you may lose that very *license-to-steal* that has been the object to facilitate your dreams of wealth. And they tell you you're a "success."

Some success! If you're a doctor, the new HMO, PPO, or other corporate-oriented medical insurance managed care corporation are in the process of both robbing your patients and reducing you to perform medical treatments and other procedures for a dollar a visit; if a dentist or a lawyer, the swelling in your ranks of your own kind has shrunk your client base, and if you are not a CPA employed by the megabuck *Big Six* or the group known as the lesser, but still megabuck Twenty Large CPA firms, the flat tax will finally finish you off, and if this doesn't, the plethora of newly licensed CPAs and those being terminated at the aforementioned major firms enter your solo world of practice that has already grown so small and unprofitable that you yourself are looking for second jobs in real estate sales and restaurant management.

After ten years in practice you think: My God, the "nut-to-crack" has grown to $20,000 a month ($240,000.00 a year) and this is "net," without the government getting its share, and you haven't got a "dime" left to put away for your own "golden years," if you're lucky enough to even keep up the pace and live that long.

Each month you have your bookkeeper telling you you've got to up your client or patient "billings," as the bills get bigger and bigger, as more and more of your clients or patients are "stiffing" you. You get the summary of this month's cash-outflows, your monthly "nut-to-crack."

- THE MONTHLY "NUT-TO-CRACK" -

THE VARIOUS "NUTS":	THE MONTHLY COST:
Three automobiles, one for pleasure, one for work, and one in case the other two breakdown: @ avg. lease payment $425.00 per month.	$ 1,275.00

Automobile Insurance: @ auto $250
per month $ 750.00

The Homestead:
    The Mortgage-$3,500 per month: $ 3,500.00
    Real Estate Taxes-$1,000 per month: $ 1,000.00
    Maintenance & Repairs-$500 per month: $ 500.00
    Homeowners Insurance-$200 per month: $ 200.00
    A/C, Heating, Telephone-$400.00 per month: $ 400.00
    Groceries & Sundries-$1,000.00 per month: $ 1,000.00

A Modest Retreat in the Poconos-The Country Home:
    The Mortgage-$1,500 per month: $ 1,500.00
    Real Estate Taxes-$100 per month: $ 100.00
    Maintenance & Repairs-$300 per month: $ 300.00
    Homeowners Insurance-$75.00 per month: $ 75.00

Designer Clothing and Wardrobe:
    For the Spouse-$800 per month: $ 800.00
    For the 1.6 Children-$800 per month: $ 800.00
    For Thyself-$600.00 per month: $ 600.00

Dining out, recreation, and the annual
Vacation $1,500 per month: $ 1,500.00

The small boat, maintenance, insurance,
and slip rental $1,500 per month: $ 1,500.00

Family members conditioned to demand more and more:
    The children: Their own room, their own
    T.V., their own stereo system, their own
    Nintendo set, and two $39 Nintendo game
    cartridges a month, one concert, and four
    movies: avg. cost per child $200.00: $ 320.00

Braces and cosmetic surgery-$300 a month: $ 300.00

The child's personal automobile, preferably
a sports car-$1,000.00 per month (includes
insurance), only for 15 years and older: $ 1,000.00

Private School, $6,000 to $8,000 per year
per child. Avg. monthly cost 1.6 children: $ 930.00

Private summer camp, $5,000 per year
per child. Avg. monthly cost 1.6 children: $ 675.00

Finally College — minimally $500 per month
required savings for the life of each child
and hopefully this won't be wasted while the
child enjoys a four-year vacation. 1.6 children: $ 800.00

Mobile phones for all. $75.00 per family member: $ 270.00

The Monthly Total "Nut-To-Crack":   **$ 20,095.00**

I already sense many of you "professionals," who have "arrived" (i.e. have broken the "glass-ceiling" and are in the upper 2% of the economic strata) are already scratching your heads. You're asking: Hasn't this idiot ever experienced a $50,000 Bar Mitzvah, an $80,000 Wedding, or a $10,000 Vacation?

Doesn't he understand the necessity for a "small plane" in order that I might relax and reduce the "stress" involved with earning sufficient funds to cover my "nut" each month. And what of my "first and second" wife and children: the alimony and child support I have to drop off there? And aren't I too entitled to a $200.00 an hour therapy session at least twice a week that I'm too embarrassed to charge to my medical insurance plan?

To those of you *top-two-percenters* who are thinking this, I can only respond in typical lawyer fashion: The list of "nuts" is not exhaustive, but merely attempts to demonstrate a sample panoramic view of your American Dream come true to the average "American" middle-class and poor who also bought this book.

I'm certain that every sole practitioner who still runs his or her own office and pays his or her own staff, and who lives hand to mouth usually based upon the season is asking: Doesn't this author know anything about my plate? Obviously I do, having been one of you for twenty years and seeing so much of your work. The majority of you have already slipped out of the middle-class and are now inconsequential to those who have done all of that unnecessary financial and tax planning for those who could ill-afford it, or for you dentists who have learned to program the capping of teeth, needed or not, based on the annual earnings of your patients or who have joined in those local dentist referral groups where you seek out patients who have life savings of between $5,000 and $10,000 that can be mutually divided amongst the referral group members since it would look rather suspicious if only one of you boys took the whole thing, patient after patient. I also want every reader of this book to know that there are still numerous professionals who are still honest and who still perform at a level of excellence within reasonable and fair price ranges. Unfortunately, in America's present environment, it becomes impossible for many of these professionals to continue to perform as the professionals of yester-year. I don't apologize in any manner to the majority of wayward professionals that this book is directly addressing.

For those who did achieve the American Dream, it was not without consequence. As the "nut-to-crack" got bigger and bigger, no longer did any of these "successful professionals" have time to do anything but work, plot, conspire, and figure-out new angles to separate their patients, the federal government, and their clients, from their money.

Who of these, allegedly the "brightest and best," have had any time left over to figure out what the local County Commissioners, the State Legislatures, and the State Governors were plotting day-to-day, much less what the U.S. Congress or the President of the United States was up to in their reinvention of Government which enabled them to, and their families, to buoy-up into the top two percenters? There too, as previously noted in Chapter One, a "spending frenzy" was going on. Legislators themselves were achieving the same American Dream. More taxes were required to support their lifestyles. More taxes, and worse, huge borrowings, to be paid by this generation, and future generations of what would probably no longer be American Dreamers, but Third World Country status American citizens.

By the end of 1996, there still seemed no end to how big the "nut-to-crack" could grow. With all of these enormous "nuts" and "visions of wealth," the threat of loss to America's "professionals" also got bigger-and-bigger; lawyers gobbling-up CPAs, doctors and dentists, other lawyers, and everything else that appeared to have a deep pocket. The 1980s America, from the eyes of the American lawyer, both looking inward (where the lawyer himself was the victim) and looking outward (where the lawyer made everyone else the victim), was as follows:

The Divorce:
   Humongous Court Ordered Divisions of the "Nuts."
   Horrific Legal Fees.
   Fear of Millions of Dollars in Spousal Alimony.
   Child Support.
   Rehabilitation Support.

The Million Dollar Malpractice Suit:
   Medical Malpractice.
   Legal Malpractice.
   CPA Malpractice.
   Dental Malpractice.

The Criminal Law Suit:
   Tax Evasion.
   Securities Fraud (10b-5, etc.)
   Fraud Against Insurance Companies.
   Medicare or Medicaid Fraud.
   Client Fraud.
   Business Fraud.

The Ordinary Civil Law Suit (Amongst Numerous Others):

By the Jerk Who Fell Off Your Boat.
By the Person You Sexually Harassed At Work.
By the Family of the Kid Who Drowned in Your Pool.

The Catastrophic Calamities:

Cancellation of Your Major Medical Insurance.
Cancellation of Your Malpractice Insurance.
Termination of Your Tenure by your Firm's Executive Committee.
The Conviction of Your Major Client for Tax Fraud.
Half of Your Partners Leaving the Firm With All of Your Profitable Clients.
Criminal Indictment By The Government For Your Billing Practices.

The list goes on and on. The fears for the future become magnified. The professional cannibals are everywhere. And even your children have begun to ask, "How much money will I get when you die?"

It has even become common, if not vogue, for the children of these "professionals" to ask how much money will be provided for their (the children's) retirement! Just ask any one of the 10,000 Personal Financial Planners in this country. There have even been reported cases of America's teenaged children becoming "insecure" or getting impatient for "the real good life" and murdering their parents in order to ensure continued and undiminished enjoyment of their parents' wealth before and after reaching "maturity."

Who pays for all of the indulgences and extravagances of the "top-two-percenters" of wealthy Americans? To some degree the poor, sometimes with hard earned money, but mostly with less opportunity for themselves to ever get out of their cycle of poverty. When one of these children of the bottom two percent does succeed, he becomes the rule, rather than the exception and every Republican in America tells you: "You see, it doesn't matter that America is divided into such disparate economic classes, the fact is anyone who wants to make it can!"

It's America's middle-class who pays dearest for these extravagances through either higher taxes; mortgaged futures (government) debt burdens; increased medical insurance premiums; increased legal, medical, hospital, and other professional fees; and through the purchase of higher priced consumer products or services where these "extravagances" are ultimately passed onto.

Now that you have an overall perspective of the "driving" forces behind America's "professionals," and who pays for it, you are now ready to focus on the legal profession.

The Legal Profession

Since December 1982, after having completed more than half my law school curriculum, I became firmly convinced that any sort of grouping, social or otherwise, of five or more lawyers was a "conspiracy" against both American "democracy" and the government of the United States. Little that I experienced over the next fourteen years changed my thinking on this issue one iota.

Also, keep in mind as you read this, and the next two chapters that none of the members of these four American professions could "practice" their trade, if they weren't "licensed" by their respective state governments. If you too conclude that one or more of these professions is out of control, you know where the "valve" is to turn off the abuses you conclude are unacceptable. . . .You say your Governor or state government doesn't give a damn! That aspect of the problem is covered in Chapter Twenty of this book.

Entering the Practice of Law

Although I had been admitted to the N.Y.S. Bar, it didn't qualify me to practice in any N.Y.S. federal court. The federal court is a separate admissions process and varies from state to state. In all states though, you must first be admitted to the State Bar before you can be admitted to that state's federal bar. In N.Y.S. there are four federal district court bars, known as SDNY, EDNY, WDNY and NDNY, reflecting the four major compass points.

Having the necessity to file a client's cause of action in a federal court, I asked a long-time attorney I knew if he would sponsor my admission to the SDNY Federal District Court. Incidentally, this attorney has been disbarred and was convicted of a felony two years ago. If anyone was a victim of the exploding "nut to crack," it was certainly this individual who had to subsidize his lifestyle to the tune of $350,000.00 in borrowed trust funds.

Although being admitted to a federal bar is no where near as exciting as being initiated into the Mafia according to The Godfather, I tell you this story because of the implications it has for all Americans. I also point out that I don't know if this goes on anywhere else, or for that matter, if it went on with anyone else even in New York, but on the day I was to be admitted to practice in SDNY, it happened to me and I would find it hard to believe I was the only one ever singled-out for this "message."

The attorney who sponsored me for admission warned me, as we were walking up the federal courthouse steps: "Ron, as long as you never screw another lawyer, you'll always make a good living in this business . . . you just don't screw another attorney, and you'll do okay."

I became somewhat apprehensive when told this, not only because it sounded like what I had heard in the movie The Godfather, but also because my briefcase contained my first federal complaint ever, which coincidentally named a whole slew of attorneys as defendants in a civil securities fraud action. Immediately after being admitted to this bar and before leaving the Courthouse, I advised my attorney sponsor of the contents of my briefcase. He shook his head in dismay, but oddly enough secretly assisted me over the next three years in prosecuting this case. I think this says something about the continuing battle over conscience and American legal culture. You just can't be too overt when you're breaking one of the clandestine rules of the profession.

Before including this short story in this Chapter, I called my lawyer sponsor and asked if he wanted to become "infamous?" I advised him ("lawyer courtesy") that I was going to put this story in the book. Even though he had been disbarred, and had been convicted of a felony, he replied, "Okay," and even said he didn't mind if I used his name. Trust me folks, the vast majority of lawyers, who are not teaching or in other non-lawyer occupations, generally have little if any shame, and in most instances, no consciences. I'm not sure that it isn't the rigors of the law school "experience," or just having to deal with the vast array of mean-spirited, and sometimes sociopathic clients, or clients who themselves have insatiable desires that causes the vast majority of lawyers to become so lacking in compassion and devoid of conscience. Obviously there are also those lawyers and other professionals who are just born without conscience or compassion. I've personally met several of these in the generic form.

Where It All Began In America

As may surprise you, and most of my fellow attorneys who didn't go to Harvard, the Harvard Law School was neither the first law school in America, nor did it even offer the first law course in America, even though the University itself dates back to 1636, and is the oldest in America. The Harvard Law School did not come into existence until 1817, and its business school (The Harvard MBA) not until 1908, two horrendous mistakes, I am convinced, should haunt this otherwise proud University forever more.

It is the college of William & Mary in 1780, supported by then Virginia Governor, Thomas Jefferson, that has the rather questionable distinction of having had the very first "professorship of law" in the United States, graduating such notable lawyers as John Marshall, the first Chief Justice of the U.S. Supreme Court; James Monroe, the fifth U.S. President; and Edmund Randolf, the first U.S. Attorney General.

It wasn't until 1784, that America's first stand-alone "law school" unattached to a major university was founded in Litchfield, Connecticut, graduating the likes of Aaron Burr, and 20 other lawyers each year during its fifty-year tenure.

As you may have already known, through much of the 19th Century most persons who were admitted to the practice of law did not have a formal legal education, but were primarily trained as apprentices under the tutelage of other lawyers. Abraham Lincoln so earned his "license" to practice law in Illinois on September 9, 1863.

As meager as all of these humble beginnings make the legal profession sound, by 1970, there were approximately 350,000 lawyers in the U.S., a number which has more than doubled in the decade of the 1980s, to over 727,000. By 1970 there was one lawyer for every 600 citizens, and in 1996, there is one lawyer for every 327 citizens. If this geometric rate of growth continues, there will be "one lawyer" for "each citizen" by the year 2075. The obvious and simple solution to this problem is to immediately close 60% of the law schools in America.

A comparison of the number of lawyers in other industrial countries also demonstrates the seriousness of this growing "cancer" in America:

The American Lawyer Epidemic In International Perspective

Country	Lawyers	Population	No. of Lawyers per No. of Citizens
United States	805,000	260,000,000	1 to 309
Japan	17,700	122,783,000	1 to 6942
Germany	37,500	65,000,000	1 to 1735
Great Britain	40,800	58,000,000	1 to 1422
France	16,500	57,000,000	1 to 3467

As surprising as these statistics may seem, you will be further shocked to know that if you totaled-up all of the lawyers outside of the United States, there would still be less lawyers outside the U.S. than the menacing number that exists in the U.S. today. Are you still wondering why there is so much mischief going on in America today?

The Size, Wealth, and Power of America's Law Firms

There is an old joke that has been making the circuit of the nation's legal circles. It goes like this:

"A single lawyer in town, and he'll starve to death. A second lawyer comes to town, and they both became millionaires."

The reason lawyers find this joke humorous is because they understand the reality that protracted (long term) litigation requires at least two attorneys and something (anything!) at issue. Who of you readers have not had personally, or know of at least someone else's experience, where the person (client) receives a $10,000.00 bill from a lawyer for a divorce that seemed almost simple when the action was first initiated? Remember, lawyers have big-nuts-to-crack, so when they come across domestic or any other kind of disagreement, to improve their financial productivity (remuneration), they must *expand* the *facts-in-dispute* and *legal issues* by inciting both parties as to what the other party will ultimately seek to "grab."

Once either of the attorneys have convinced either of the parties that World War III has commenced, he or she believes the attorney's fees are merely a means of preserving his or her share of the marital pot. If one of the spouses is ordered by the court to pay the other spouse's legal fees, then serious legal fees can be generated, especially if there is a nice size marital estate (i.e. you and your spose own a house or have other assets in excess of $50, 000). With a nice size marital estate, you will find twenty to a hundred mailings to your new residence advising of motions for any thing your very creative lawyer can imagine, especially if he perceives you are pleased by the pain he is inflicting on the *former love of your life!* Of course ultimately these legal fees usually come out of the general pot, which most of you, *in the heat of the battle*, have forgotten is the "marital estate," which you should think of as being at least half of your own money, and which is now being gobbled-up by both attorneys. Yes, you are both being milked as you both enjoy the misery you are seemingly inflicting on the other, while shooting yourselves simultaneously in your own feet.

Can you imagine how many cases would be resolved if each attorney told his client separately that unless the matter was settled before serious litigation began, that two-thirds (2/3rds) of the "marital estate," or whatever the stake, would be going in his and the opposing attorney's pockets, and the two of you would be dividing **only** one-third (1/3rd) left between your selves? I dare you to apply these fractions to your marital estate if you should ever consider divorcing your spose. I have had great success using this technique and have probably resolved more cases resulting in happy divorced campers than 95% of my contemporaries out there. Of course, regrettably this has not made me a millionaire, as it has made many others. This is probably the reason, among others, why I don't have many friends who are lawyers. After this book is read by those who fit the patterns decribed throughout this book, I don't expect this circumstance to much change, although, I do hold out hope that lawyer Jerry Spence will come to like me.

Some Statistics About Lawyers Out of <u>The National Law Journal</u>

The September 30, 1991 edition of the <u>National Law Journal</u> heralded the first good news concerning the growth of the legal profession in the profession's over 200 year history. The good news, contained as part of "<u>The NLJ 250</u>," more descriptively known as "<u>Annual Survey of the Nation's Largest Law Firms</u>" was that America's law firms (not lawyers) for the first time in history were contracting — 44% of all firms in 1991, decreasing their staffs as a result of the 1990-1992 recession. In 1996, the good news continues, the contraction of the top 250 law firms is going forward. The "bad news" is the "infection" has spread worldwide. The nation's largest 250 firms now have more than 2000 lawyers in 244 branch offices in 48 cities around the world, and before Lenin could be dislodged from his tomb, "thirteen attorneys from six U.S. firms were transferred to Moscow."

To be listed in The <u>NLJ 250</u> in 1991, a law firm had to have at least 129 attorneys — the 1991 cut-off. In 1990, the cut-off was 131. In 1983, when the survey first began, the cut-off was 79.

Worthy of note, in 1972, Baker & McKenzie, headquartered in Chicago, was the largest of the "international" law firms, with a total of 240 lawyers. In 1991, Baker & McKenzie was still the largest "international" law firm, but had grown 658% to 1,580 lawyers, a small army by anyone's assessment.

In 1972, Sherman & Sterling, "New York's" largest firm had 200 lawyers in its ranks. In 1991, this same firm had grown to 617 lawyers, down from its 1990 high of 624 lawyers but still, an increase of over a 300% over its 1972 size.

Also worthy of note, the <u>National Law Journal</u> reported that the *profits-per-partner* in 1990 at Sherman & Sterling (the most profitable of the larger firms) was $860,000 per partner, while the *profits-per-partner* at Baker & McKenzie were a paltry $319,000. Also reported in this edition of the <u>NLJ:</u> Sole practitioners were earning approximately $91,000 in 1990 after expenses, and the average annual starting salary for attorneys just out of law school and going to work in cities with populations in excess of 1 million was $56,200, the top-end of newcomer salaries reaching $82,000. Not bad for no experience. In 1996, it is estimated that over 30,000 lawyers, with ten or more years of experience, will leave the legal profession in pursuit of non-law endeavors and law school applications have been decreasing at a rate of approximately 5% a year since 1992.

ACLU lawyers in 1991 also reported in the <u>NLJ</u>, were starting at $31,000, and the top salary in the organization in 1991 was $98,000. It's no wonder the lawyers in this organization are so "vile," especially knowing that they too read the <u>NLJ</u> and know the salaries of their brothers and sisters at the mega-firms.

As will be noted several times in this book, one of the largest "law firms" in the United States is the U.S. Congress, there being 59 lawyers in the U.S. Senate and 192 lawyers in the House of Representatives, a total of 251 lawyers. If ranked in the 1991, "NLJ 250," this Congressional law firm would have ranked Number 3 in the U.S., and surely number one if all their Congressional staff attorneys were added in.

The Legal Profession: A Menace to America

In this chapter's subsection, I offer to you my comments on excerpts from articles that have appeared in America's leading law periodicals in order that you don't see me as some "lawyer-basher" as many of my colleagues surely will. To appreciate the awesome power of the legal profession and the large firms that dominate it, one need only remember that it was this profession that both facilitated the "lootings" of the S&Ls, and the "lootings" of the American Industrial and Retail Infrastructures, as 251 more of those lawyers condoned it as members of Congress. CPAs alone could have never done it, neither could the Raiders, or the Investment Bankers. Nor could the actual S&L looters have been as effective without the aid of the legal profession. And how many of the insidious "ideas" to expedite and enhance both the S&L and M&A "lootings" do you think originated in the offices of these same law firms? I leave this to your imagination . . as fueled by what you read below.

I first defer to the May 1991, ABA Journal, The Lawyer's Magazine (the monthly publication of the American Bar Association) to an article entitled: The S&L Mess — Savings and Loan Lawyers, written by Steve France, a lawyer and writer from Washington D.C. The first five enlightening paragraphs of Mr. France's article read as follows:

"A scientist seeking to measure the professionalism and ethics of the American bar probably could not improve upon the experiment that legislators, regulators, economists and bankers unintentionally devised in deregulating the savings-and-loan industry in the early 1980s. The policy makers did exactly what was necessary to run a successful experiment. Not only did they immerse thrift-industry lawyers in an environment that invited corner-cutting, obfuscation and outright fraud, they also provided the perfect mechanism to find out in detail what the lawyers then did wrong.

The mechanism is simple: When the government takes over a failed S&L, it assumes the institution's right to sue the lawyers, and the institution's right to all the lawyers' files. In addition, it usually can find several nervous former directors and officers only too willing to point out how the lawyers led them astray.

So, thrift lawyers have experienced a kind of reverse 'Jekyll and Hyde' dilemma — representing clients who first exhibited the predatory instincts of a Mr. Hyde, but who now, in the afterlife of receivership, have turned into Dr. Jekyll-like puritans bent on punishing their former companions in delinquency. Attorneys who were prone to scanting their duties are quite likely both to have sinned and to be caught.

It will be years before the courts and the profession fully evaluate all the data emanating from hundreds of S&L investigations and lawsuits implicating lawyers. However, it is already clear that fallout from the largest financial scandal in American history will give the public an extraordinary chance to see and judge the way corporate lawyers used their license to practice law.

Nor does the controversy find the profession united. While many lawyers fear they are being scapegoated by a lawyer-hating public, it is lawyers who are doing the dirty work of prosecution. Other lawyers are suggesting that the profession fell down in its obligations, and hope prosecutions lead to reform and greater sensitivity to the public interest."

Later in this same article, Mr. France makes note of comments by Federal Judge Stanley Sporkin, who I'd made the acquaintance of when I was unraveling the Cook Industries insurance fraud as a CPA in 1974. It was then that Judge Sporkin was the Chief Enforcement Officer of the SEC; a young and rising star in his own right. From the picture of Judge Sporkin published with the France article, I suspect even Stanley has had enough of the "shenanigans" of his brothers and sisters at the bar. According to Mr. France, Judge Sporkin remarked:

"Where were the attorneys, when these clearly improper transactions were effectuated?"

Mr. France goes on to describe the reaction of certain attorneys defending the role of those lawyers, as it relates to Judge Sporkin's comment above, and perhaps Mr. France's comments here are even more insightful than the first five paragraphs of his article. Keep in mind, the comments below are all from distinguished members of The American "Bar.":

"His [Sporkin's] mere posing of the question has been criticized as a gratuitous bit of rabble-rousing, since it ranged well beyond the issues actually presented in the case. But it also has served as a rallying cry for those intent on not letting lawyers just walk away from a mess they failed to prevent.

"Everybody knows Sporkin wrote about the Keating case not as a U.S. District Judge, but as former chief of enforcement at the Securities and Exchange Commission," says banking litigator Warren Dennis of Proskauer, Rose, Goetz & Mendelsohn, in Washington, D.C.

Keith Fisher, another Washington banking lawyer, with Mintz, Levin, Cohn, Ferris, Glovsky & Popeo, refers to 'Sporkin's Crazy dicta.' He believes the comments have contributed to an atmosphere of hysteria surrounding the S&L mess. As chair of an ABA task force on the Liability of counsel representing depository institutions, Fisher is concerned that people are jumping to conclusions before the courts have had a chance to render judgment.

That concern was heightened last fall when Harris Weinstein, chief counsel of the Office of Thrifts Supervision, declared that lawyers "must take Judge Sporkin's comments to heart." According to Weinstein, a "significant minority" of attorneys failed in their duty "*to provide sound advice and decline to represent clients whose objective [was] evasion rather than ... fulfillment of their fiduciary obligations.*" [Emphasis added]

Now folks, remembering Mr. France's article appeared in May 1991, let's turn (over a year later) to the July 13, 1992, edition of the National Law Journal to find out how "crazy" Judge Sporkin's "dicta" was. The article to which I refer is the same article quoted later in Chapter Nine — American Crime & Law Enforcement, entitled S&L Legal Shake-Up written by Marianne Lavelle. The three excerpts below from Ms. Lavelle's article sum up better than any other source how "crazy" Judge Sporkin, you, or I are when we suspect there's something rotten within "legal-land" and our U.S. government. And perhaps we may even find out where some of those lawyers Judge Sporkin referred to in 1991 are employed now! For sure we know they weren't the attorneys canned from RTC in June of 1991 referenced in excerpt 1 below.

- Excerpt 1 -

WASHINGTON — Major changes in the Resolution Trust Corp.'s legal staff reflect an apparent policy shift by the Bush administration to ease off of aggressive lawsuits to recover millions of dollars from ex-officials of failed savings and loans, according to high-level government lawyers.

Most of these sources labeled as a political move, the removals and resignations in recent weeks of 28 attorneys of the 75-lawyer unit responsible for the lawsuits; one well-placed insider ascribed the shake-up to a long internal battle between two rival legal offices in the RTC. But the sources agree that the RTC now has rid itself of the key lawyers who favored holding liable — under the strict legal theory of negligence — the well-connected, well-to-do people who populated the boards of failed thrifts.

One inside attorney said many colleagues perceived the shakeup as "gross election-year interference by the White House" because so many targets of investigations and lawsuits happened to be prominent individuals with strong Republican ties."

- Excerpt 2 -

"There is no doubt that the roster of defunct savings and loan directors includes high-profile figures in politics and business. Best known is Arizona Gov. Fife Symington, sued by the RTC in December in the $250 million demise of Southwest Savings and Loan, a case that prompted one of the most brutal battles among agency lawyers, sources said.

Tied to thrifts that have yet to be investigated fully are two Bush administration cabinet members. Agriculture Secretary Edward R. Madigan and Veterans Affairs Chief Edward J. Derwinski served in the 1980s as directors of two failed institutions from Illinois — a state that suffered among the greatest thrift losses, but saw few lawsuits for recovery until the recent spate of RTC legal activity.

- Excerpt 3 -

"The recasting of the [RTC] legal division thus prompted Congress immediately to order its watchdog agency, the General Accounting Office, to launch a wide-ranging probe into the treatment of the fired personnel, the policy implications of the move, and even the backgrounds of the lawyers now running the RTC's legal shop.

You had the attorneys in the field doing a heck of a job, filing a bunch of lawsuits under terrible time constraints, because [the RTC was] very slow to staff up in the place," said GAO

Assistant Director Edward Stephenson Jr., who already has spent a year looking at the professional liability program. "They were going out and getting the job done. What was the basis for their removal?"

"Civil War"

Five former or current government lawyers spoke to The National Law Journal on the condition that their names and positions not be used, nor their regions of the country be revealed. All were in a position to know the details of the siege within the agency during the last six weeks. One of them contended that the staff shakeup was a turf dispute gone out of control, while the others are certain that policy and political motives lay at the root of the changes. In any case, their stories squared with one another's and with that told by the GAO's Mr. Stephenson.

So you think you've heard enough — both lawyers and politicians, all getting in there to cover-their-cans, as you sit back and foot the bill for all of their big-time looting of America's S&Ls.

Are you now *angered enough* to demand your state governor and legislature do something about the legal profession and the "bar" in your state? Are you ready to ask your former President, George Bush, and your other political leaders for their "resignations" for their malfeasance of office?

Well, forget it — you won't get one of them to answer, or those who still remain, to leave office voluntarily, and none of them are going to gang-up on any one of their own kind when there's so much "fat" to be "fried" amongst all of them.

I can readily assure you the S&L Lawyer Scandals on both sides of the S&L mess will be the only part of the "iceberg" you'll ever see — as the appellate courts years from now overturn all of the past and future convictions, and new scandals of greater magnitude, displace these former tidbits.

The Ordinary Practice Of Law, and Other Heinous Acts

The 1991 Florida Bar President James Fox Miller, during his tenure as Bar President, wrote a column called the President's Page for each issue of the monthly Florida Bar Journal. I comment here on one of Mr. Miller's articles that appeared in the February 1991 issue, entitled: The Curse of the Legal Profession, because it demonstrates what I believe is the "madness" or perhaps the "sickness" that has completely replaced the "honor" and "integrity" that some of us once believed was the hallmark of the majority in this profession.

Now, what is the "curse" that former Bar President Miller refers to? Believe it or not, it's "hourly billing!" That's right — "hourly billing" — the same hourly billing the members of the legal profession take so much arrogant pleasure in flaunting amongst themselves, and their victims. You've all heard it -- $200 and $300 an hour for the local "boys" and as much as $1,200 an hour for the few top "boys" in New York and Washington, D.C.

So you're now cynically scowling: How about zapping some of this "curse" on me! Right! I mean you could sure make "ends meet" for a month on half of what some of these "boys" are taking down in two or three hours. So what's the "deal?", you ask.

Well, former Florida Bar President Miller is upset because in America's "free market" system, some of his fellow attorneys have had to resort to cheating in their billings to clients to, in their minds, "so they might be paid fairly." Get that one! They agree to work for a set dollar rate per hour and then proceed to rip-off their clients anyway. Mr. Miller seemingly justifies this by stating:

> **"Hourly billing promotes inefficiency, and penalizes productivity. Unfortunately, in some cases it promotes outright dishonesty. Certainly, and I know this happens frequently, lawyers exaggerate the actual time spent on a task so that, in their minds, they are paid fairly."**

Yes, the above is quoted right out of the <u>Florida Bar Journal</u>! I haven't even gotten to the "slick" part. It's called "value billing," and Miller relates a marvelous tale as to how it works. He talks about an "imaginary" broken-down machine that no one could fix, and that almost caused a factory owner to go out of business. Then along comes a fellow with a "nail clipper" who offers to fix the machine. The fellow turns a screw twice, and magic — the machine begins to run! The "bill" — $25,000! That's "value billing." As summarized in so may words by Attorney Miller: It's not the turning twice of the screw — but "knowing which screw to turn." (No pun intended by Attorney Miller I'm sure!)

Now get this "quantum leap" Attorney Miller makes in his argument to replace *hourly billing* with *value-added-billing* — he states: "clients should not care and some don't, how much time is involved. Clients should be interested in the efforts and the results obtained."

I found Miller's choice of reference (a "manufacturing" example) and his choice of words (knowing which screw to turn) to be an outward expression of what I'm certain is the last vestige of his nearly-dead conscience trying to scream out above the "madness" that has over-taken his and the majority of the legal profession's current insatiability for the accumulation of wealth.

Can you imagine, given the brief synopsis I've presented of the legal profession so far in this chapter (and just wait until you get to the bizarre bankruptcy fees and other lawyer/client fee rip-offs later in this chapter), and add to this your own personal experience (everyone's been stung once) with this "professional group," and then imagine giving them the "green-light" to "value-bill" all of America for their good works? Could Mr. Miller believe that you, *Boobus Americanus*, will be suckered into believing that this would make our present lot of attorneys any more honest?

I not only think **not** — but from my personal knowledge of all the "boys and girls" I've met in this profession; I <u>know</u> "**not!**" Unfortunately, I have come to the conclusion the only way to make the boys in this profession honest is to put the fear of "real" prison in their hearts — long prison sentences in places like Rahway, instead of the local Club Feds, where they should be mixed in amongst what they themselves refer to as the ordinary prison population of gangsters, child molesters, murderers and other thieves that pale in their comparison. You want to see how honest this "bunch" can quickly become? Even if they were just put them to the same mercy of the law that the DUI and "street hoodlum,"are subjected, I assure you, you will see 90% of these white-collar, jelly-cans to limit their shameless public and private "lootings."

So you thought you heard the last of the Bar President Miller's article, well you didn't because he makes one other important point that deserves exposure to not just "lawyers," but to every American who is subjected to the legal profession.

Here is where we get into some of the real nitty-gritty. On the third page of Miller's article he mentions that his son will soon be completing law school, and pines over the thought that "some very good and huge [Can everyone of you sense Miller "salivating" as he speaks these words?] Wall Street [law] firm will no doubt hire him at an outrageous starting salary," where Miller painfully relates that a "minimum of 2000 billable hours a year and maybe more will be expected." In this context, Miller goes on to describe the comments of a person who he describes as being the "father of a seventh-year Wall Street firm associate, on the brink of a very financially rewarding partnership." Miller relates that this father told him that "his child billed 3100 hours last year," to which Miller replied, "being the diplomat" that he is: "You are nuts, your kid is even nuttier, and/or this firm's clients are getting ripped-off."

In light of the Bar President Miller's comments, I relate my indirect encounter with a medium-sized law firm in southeast Florida, which was primarily dedicated to medical malpractice defense. I had the great misfortune to see some of their "secret" detailed billings to the medical malpractice insurance companies they represented: paralegals and secretaries being billed as attorneys, the top-billing partner in the firm with over 3426 billed hours in the first "ten months" of their fiscal year, and the other partners averaging over 2649 a piece for the same ten-month time frame. These boys know who they are, and if they can't figure it out, their top-billing associate (non-partner lawyer) in this 1991 "ten month" period had billed just over 3068 billable hours, and all other associates with the firm for the full ten-months averaging just over 2389 billable hours.

Even the worst of the "naughty boys" in the New York law firms don't reach these "peaks," although I've been privy to some "billing mania" stories (they're also part of public record). Now remember, these are not the Dole/Gingrich "tort lawyers" that the 1994 Contract with America is all about. These are the good Republicans who are not taking advantage of those large punitive jury awards and ludicrous personal injury awards. These are just a bunch of hard working lawyers, whose computers have been programmed to automatically bill in multiples of 1000. Some of the "wildest" of this recent "billing mania," I set forth below:

1. The Eastern Airline Bankruptcy (January 1989 - November 1991) - Lawyers, accountants (CPAs), and advisors billed $95 million. Weil, Gotshal & Manges, the primary law firm on the case ran up a tab of $21.7 million.

2. The Drexel Burnham Bankruptcy (February 1980 - November 1991) - The Kings of "M&A" and the "junk bond" heroes of the 1980s (Milken and the gang) finally put their own firm in bankruptcy — a result of everyone suing them for their wrongdoings of the 1980s. Well these alleged investment bankers had the vultures picking on their bones (or more correctly, the bones of their creditors and defrauded clients). Again Weil, Gotshal & Manges had $15.4 million; but this was a small fraction of the total fee, and the second biggest of all lawyer bankruptcy fees: $109 million.

3. The Carter Hawley Hale (CHH) Bankruptcy (January 1991 - January 1992) - The most honest American businessman I've ever met was Philip Hawley, who, when I had first met in 1981, had then been recently named Chairman, CEO, and President of this major retail chain, the "Hawley" name being his own. In 1991 CHH filed Chapter 11 bankruptcy, and from both the legal periodicals and the "scandal sheets," I understand that CHH has

had close to $16.8 million separated from its coffers by the lawyers who assisted them in their bankruptcy filing. Perhaps this story is the most painful to me because of the decency of the company's namesake, Phil Hawley, but I assure you the list goes on and on. Decent lives disrupted, companies destroyed, all by the M&A scourge that struck America in the early 1970s and lasted through the decade of the 1980s, a scourge whose devastation will be with us for years, and perhaps decades to come.

4. The most notorious horror story coming from the bankruptcy courts, and the "grand daddy" of them all: Federated Department Stores (January 1990 - February 1992) - $120 million in bankruptcy lawyer fees. And the all time fourth-place finisher on the bankruptcy lawyer fee "horror list" is Revco D.S. Inc. (June 1988 - February 1992) at a mere $90 million in bankruptcy lawyer fees.

5. The notorious West Palm Beach Court battle between Dr. Zbigniew Scheller, and his attorney Jack Scarola over the $8 million in legal fees and $80,000 in court cost Scarola demanded from Dr. Scheller's $19.2 million settlement with AMI, the giant health-care corporation accused of attempting to sabotage Dr. Scheller's pathology practice. Who would ever think the attorneys or doctors in Florida were operating in these "eight-digit" figures?

Now, what do you think of the above examples of "legal fees" charged by American lawyers, other than Gingrich's "tort reform" lawyers? Does it motivate you to put aside the necessary cash to get your "kid" into this lucrative profession? If you answered this question "yes," you've probably been hopelessly "Reaganized" by the 1980s decade. If you answered "no," I think you can conclude there might still be some hope for America, once referred to by Abraham Lincoln as the "hope for the world." And, again I remind you that all of these legal fees will ultimately be paid for out of your pockets in the form of increased consumer product costs, larger legal fees, increased insurance premiums, increased taxes, and a long list of other indirect conduits that are just too long to list here.

The Threat To American Democracy
The So-Called Lawyer "Sleaze Factor"

It's collusive, corrupt, clever, and its consequences, as you now know are paid-for by you. You've heard it called the "sleaze factor" before, mainly because so many of them appear to have such evil beady-eyes, drawn-gray faces, and are always wearing those expensive slick-looking, French-cut, body-fitting suits, and lizard shoes. And for a long-time you've suspected there's more to this "sleaze stuff" than what's on the surface, but it's tough to get a handle on it with all their smooth-talk and confusing rhetoric. You're still not sure if they're there to protect you, or if they're there to gobble you up and everything else in their path like the locust swarms you see in those 1930 depression movies.

To assist you once and for all in getting your "rope" around this dilemma, I offer the three examples below to demonstrate how criminality, or what should be criminal, is converted to money that is taken right out of your pocket!

Example One — Product Liability

You cheer as you read about the multi-million dollar judgment in the "this" or "that" *product liability* suit. You are told the "manufacturer" has been punished! The message is clear to them, and all the others who would dare to release a faulty product into the market place — yet no corporate CEO has gone to jail, no corporate CEO has paid a "penny" out of his personal pocket, and no one, especially the corporate CEO has lost his job.

Now, who do you think has been punished? Ninety-nine percent of the time — you! The American Consumer! The cost of the lawyers, the damage award, and the CEO's bonus for concluding the litigation are all passed along to you, sometimes in pennies, and sometimes in dollars, but all in down-the-road product prices, or increased insurance premiums. Rest assured it's you who pays and it's the lawyers who are always fabulously enriched, not the victims.

That's the American legal profession's gimmick: keep it in the civil court where large "monetary" settlements are available so the lawyer can share in what is called the "pain and suffering" aspect of the damage award. That's why this aspect of the damage awards are always so large.

Ask yourself: "Do you know anyone involved in a product liability suit who has made out better "financially" than the plaintiff's lawyers?"

This is a hundred-times more true when the lawyers and the court divide up any "damages award" that results from a "class action" products liability suit, or for that matter, any "class action" suit. I was once a class action plaintiff in one of these suits against a New York bank known as Goldome. Goldome, through a deceitful prospectus convinced me to invest $20,000.00 of my previously FDIC insured IRA account in Goldome stock, which was an initial public offering on their part. Obviously, I felt secure in this transaction because I was certain both the CPAs, the lawyers, the SEC, and the bank regulators were all overseeing this public offering. Seven months later Goldome went into bankruptcy, its corporate officers having become very rich and denying any wrong doing. Four years later, $4 million was paid to the class action attorneys. I received $132.00 as recovery for my lost $20,000.00. Nobody went to jail. I wasn't the only attorney or CPA who was stung by Goldome or induced by their misrepresentations or my own greed in believing that the stock would rise 100% over the course of the next year. Greed, and the promise of vast returns are the best bait to catch even the biggest, most skeptical, and best educated fish in the ocean.

Example Two — The Game Of Malpractice Monopoly

Here again you cheer the multi-million dollar awards. The "professional malefactor" is punished! Yeah! Right? Let me assure you, there is rarely, if ever, a multi-million dollar award paid out of a "professional's pocketbook." They're always paid out of his malpractice insurance carrier's pocketbook. And who do you think pays for this? Don't for one minute believe that every "nickel" in increased insurance premiums for malpractice insurance isn't passed onto you!

You ask: "How come the professional malefactor doesn't have his foot-put-into-the-fire?" Frankly, I only wish I had a nickel for every professional in this country, who faced with a malpractice suit didn't become almost instantaneously judgment-proof (i.e. his or her assets under the guidance of his or her attorney are legally transferred to a third-party long before a "judgment" ever comes down). If the professional malefactor has no malpractice insurance or homeowners insurance you won't even be able to find an attorney to sue him or her unless you have $25,000.00 or more to plop down to cover the hourly billing rate of the attorney you seek out to represent you. Lawyers just don't work on contingent fees, in general, unless it is a personal injury case with permanent injury resulting in a loss to you of over $50,000.00. That is the cut off point for the medium size malpractice firm where a contingency fee arrangement is requested. Of course you still might find a sole practitioner of superior competency who might be able to negotiate a settlement without litigation who will accept your case on a contingency fee arrangement, but this species is becoming more and more rare, and this again is contingent upon that sole practitioner knowing that there are assets to negotiate for. The lesson to be learned here is to be certain your professional has or is required to carry malpractice insurance before you give him any sort of informed consent or sign a retainer agreement. Don't be embarrassed to check with the state and local regulators to see if he has had any complaints or malpractice suits filed against him in the past. Follow these suggestions and you will limit at least some of your losses.

Example Three — The Criminal Defense Bar

Let me begin this section with a letter written by a prominent criminal defense attorney to his fifteen year old female client who was charged with a general intent crime, that of leaving the scene of an accident involving a death which under the laws of the state we were in was a second degree felony carrying a five-year maximum prison term. None of the warnings or threats or fee factors (i.e. being earned when paid) included in the below letter was ever discussed with the client or her mother who paid the legal fees to defend her. The letter was received by the young girl after the first $10,000.00 installment of legal fees had been paid and cleared the defense attorney's bank account. The names, dates and law firm involved have been changed in order to avoid a law suit being brought against myself by the attorney who wrote this letter and who obviously would seek to have compensation for the enjoyment or disgust that it brings so many of you now reading it. I must tell you that I discussed this letter with the attorney because its initial reading had shocked me. The attorney told me that this letter was developed over his 30 years of practice. He was elated when I told him it was the most gruesome letter I had ever read from an attorney to a client. The letter, with all names changed to protect the innocent, is as follows:

JOHN DOE, P.A.
Attorney At Law
PALM BEACH, FLORIDA

February 28, 1995

Jane Smith
Palm Beach, Florida

Re: State v. Jane Smith

Dear Jane:

Enclosed please find a copy of the Praecipe for Appearance, Waiver of Arraignment and Not Guilty Plea that has been filed on *your behalf. This is to confirm that you have paid $10,000.00 toward a $15,000.00 fee for our representation of you on your Leaving the Scene of Accident Involving Death and other related charges. It is our agreement that the balance of $5,000.00 is due by March 27, 1995. We have agreed that the fees are non-refundable and are deemed earned when paid. Since we agreed that the fees can be paid in installments, the installments are due on the date agreed to, not two days later, not two weeks later, not two months later. When we accepted your case, we agreed to do so based on the amount and manner of payment agreed to. We do not have the time to call you up and remind you that you forgot to pay as agreed. Please realize that the fee quoted does not include any fees that rarely, but under some circumstances, may be required if an appeal to a higher court is necessary, either by the State or by the Defense, or if a re-trial of your case is required after a mistrial. The only other expense for your defense will be for any costs that are incurred such as for a court reporter, subpoenas, etc. for which you will be billed and any such bills will have to be paid promptly upon billing. Costs are moneys that we have paid on your behalf. When you get a cost bill, it is due immediately, not a month later. The cost bill is not an informational summary for your review. It is a bill that has to be paid. Failure to pay fees and costs as required will result in a motion to withdraw as counsel being filed. However, the costs in your case may be paid by Palm Beach County if the motion to have you declared indigent for costs is granted by the Judge.*

If you have not done so already, please furnish me with the complete names and addresses of any witnesses who are to testify for you.

I have noticed as my practice of law has progressed over the past 20 years that clients whine and complain far more than they ever did before. There are far too many people who are angry at the fact that they have been arrested (which they may or may not have a right to be) and they direct that anger at the lawyer, his associates and his office staff. It is not our fault that you are in trouble. It is not our fault that you have had to pay a lawyer. It is not our fault that society, or the prosecutor, or a jury, views either the crime that you are charged with or the conduct that you are charged with as evil and something that is deserving of punishment. Clients also can be angry at the other driver in an accident or the police officer or someone such as a spouse who caused them to be arrested. It is our job to use our best efforts to get you out of that trouble. However, any anger, whining or abuse at my staff, my associate lawyers or myself will not be tolerated. I am sure that you will not conduct yourself in this fashion, but I have seen it far too often in the recent past and I am too far along in my career and too busy a lawyer to either need to or want to put up with any such type conduct on any client's behalf. Any such conduct will result in this office moving to withdraw as the lawyer. If we cannot get along with a client, we don't want them.

Another disturbing trend that I have noticed increase over the years is that some clients retain a lawyer and then attempt to tell him how to do his job as well as ignore his advice that is based on his full investigation of the case and his expertise and experience. If you want to do either of those things, then you do not want to be represented by this office. You certainly have the right to ultimately make the decision regarding whether or not you accept the best plea offer available from the State or go to trial. However, if you want to approach our handling of the case with you giving us instructions on what motions to file and what questions to ask, then you should handle the case yourself and not be represented by this office or any lawyer. We will always get you the best plea offer available from the State. We will make our recommendation as to whether or not you should take it or go to trial. You obviously should consider that recommendation seriously and probably follow it. I do not have the patience for clients who want to whine and philosophize regarding that the State shouldn't do this or the State shouldn't do that, or the Judge won't do that or the Judge won't do this. You will need to swallow a large dose of reality and not be in denial about the seriousness of the charges, the facts or otherwise. We will do our best as your representative to get you out of the problem that you find yourself in, but remember we are on your side and we are not the enemy and, as indicated otherwise in this letter, we did not create your problem.

Please allow my support staff to help you. I am in the office a very small percentage of time because most of my days are spent trying cases at the Courthouse. Therefore, if you call with a question or if you need assistance and you insist on speaking with me personally, then our ability to assist you will be delayed. I am not an office lawyer who sits behind the desk with his feet on the desk waiting for something to do. If you call and I am not available, I, of course, would try to return your call when I return to the office late after a trial. However, if I am unsuccessful in reaching you, then our ability to help you is delayed. Therefore, when you call, please ask the Receptionist to give you to one of my Legal Assistants, Susan or Rita, who will attempt to help you. If *they cannot be of assistance and cannot answer your questions, then one of my Assistant Lawyers, Sherry Alias, or Candice Alias will attempt to help you. If they cannot be of assistance, they will bring your question to my attention, they will obtain the answer and they will return your call. You have every right to have all of your questions answered, but please work with the staff that you help pay for and that I need to be of assistance to you because of the many hours I spend at the Courthouse.*

Also, you will be required to rely on my judgment in deciding how your case is handled and which one of my staff will handle what part of your case. Every case has many parts, such as in the case of a D.U.I. with the Department of Motor Vehicles administrative hearing, or in any case a pre-trial Motion to Suppress, Motion to Dismiss, depositions and trial. There will be times that many of these matters will be handled by Sherry Alias or Candice Alias because many of these matters are them gathering information, such as the Department of Motor Vehicles hearing or depositions, so that we can have that information available at the time of your trial. Many of the pre-trial hearings, such as a Motion to Suppress, may be handled by Sherry Alias or Candice Alias from time to time, in that many of these pre-trial hearings are our efforts to have evidence excluded from your trial.

You must rely on my judgment as to whether I or one of my assistant lawyers will handle these matters and I do not wish to hear any complaining from you if some of these matters, which other lawyers would not even think of, are handled by one of my assistants. In other words, some of these matters raised by the pre-trial motions would not even be pursued by less diligent and thorough lawyers, and as a result, if I schedule those matters and have one of my assistant lawyers take care of them, I want you to cooperate with them. They would not be working for me if they were not skillful and prepared for these matters.

IF YOU RECEIVE A COURT DATE FROM US THAT INDICATES THAT YOU MUST ATTEND PLEASE WRITE IT ON YOUR CALENDAR AND MAKE ARRANGEMENTS TO BE PRESENT. IF WE TELL YOU MUST ATTEND WE ARE NOT KIDDING AND YOUR FAILURE TO APPEAR WHEN YOU MUST BE IN COURT COULD RESULT IN A WARRANT BEING ISSUED FOR YOUR ARREST. ALSO, THERE ARE MANY DIFFERENT TYPES OF COURT DATES WITHIN EACH CASE SO IF ONE DATE GETS CONTINUED DO NOT ASSUME THAT TAKES OFF ALL OTHER DATES WITH IT. IN OTHER WORDS, TREAT EACH DATE WHERE YOU ARE INFORMED

THAT YOU MUST ATTEND INDEPENDENTLY. MERELY BY WAY OF EXAMPLE, LET US SAY THAT YOUR CASE IS SET FOR TRIAL ON JULY 7TH AND WE UNCOVER GROUNDS FOR A MOTION TO SUPPRESS AND OBTAIN A DATE ON THAT FOR JULY 30TH AND TELL YOU THAT YOU MUST ATTEND THAT DATE, IF YOU LATER HEAR THAT THE JULY 7TH DATE IS CONTINUED DON'T ASSUME THAT THAT CANCELS THE JULY 30TH DATE AS WELL. AGAIN, TREAT EACH DATE WHERE YOU WERE TOLD YOU MUST ATTEND INDEPENDENTLY AND IF YOU WERE TOLD THAT ONE DATE IS CONTINUED DO NOT ASSUME THAT ANY OTHER DATE IS CONTINUED WITHOUT CHECKING WITH US. A SIMPLE PHONE CALL IF YOU ARE IN DOUBT CAN CLEAR UP ANY UNCERTAINTY IN ADVANCE. IF YOU ARE REQUIRED TO BE PRESENT EITHER BECAUSE THE JUDGE WOULD REQUIRE YOUR PRESENCE OR WE MIGHT NEED YOU TO TESTIFY AT A PARTICULAR HEARING, IT IS TOO LATE TO FIX THE PROBLEM IF YOU FAIL TO APPEAR BECAUSE YOU DID NOT FOLLOW INSTRUCTIONS.

Again, the bottom line of all of this discussion about the staff is that you allow us to help you in spite of the chaotic nature of the practice of law. Remember, judges can schedule trials on one-hour call notice, meaning at any time that I am working on something on your case or others, I can be called to trial by a judge who is otherwise ready for me on another matter. That obviously creates chaos and, therefore, I need my staff to help you even more than if these matters were scheduled by the Courts in a more predictable fashion.

In addition, whenever you are required to be in court, please be at least 15 minutes early. That does not mean that we will arrive that early, but what we do not need is to be running around in circles looking for you or calling you to make sure you are on your way. You may wait outside the courtroom until just before your scheduled appearance and by the time of your scheduled appearance, please be sitting in the back of the courtroom. However, you may not see us 15 minutes ahead of time or even at the scheduled time of your hearing because at any one time, especially at early morning hearings, there are 20 or more judges scheduling hearings for the lawyers at the exact same time and at branch courthouses. Thus, if you do not see us at the precise time of your hearing, there is no need to panic and call the office. It is merely because another judge has possession of us and will not release us until that other judge is finished. If your name is called and you do not see us, merely stand up, raise your hand and indicate that you are the person whose name was called and that *your lawyer is in another courtroom and is on the way. Even if judges grumble and growl, they still have to accept the fact that the Court system functions in a fashion where different judges require the lawyers' attendance at the exact same times. This is just to prepare you not to be in a panic if you do not see us at the exact scheduled time of your hearing. It is only because a different or higher or more powerful judge has us and will not release us.*

In spite of the large fees you have paid us, a lawyer's job is to represent a client's interest and present the case in a light most favorable to the client and no matter what the experience of the attorney and what the attorney's fees are, an attorney can never be looked to as a guarantor of a particular result. A judge or jury ultimately decides your fate, and the lawyer no more controls the outcome than you do. If you view a lawyer as a guarantor of a particular result, you are approaching the problems facing you with the wrong attitude and that attitude should be adjusted accordingly. Remember, we have not and cannot promise you any particular result. We can and do promise you our best efforts in representing you.

I will keep you posted as things develop.

Very truly yours,

John Doe, Esquire"

Now that you've completed the letter it is important that you have an understanding of what I believe is a typical example of the American criminal justice system. The first thing you must understand is that each courtroom is a "division" which generally has assigned to it the same judge, the same two or three state prosecutors, the same clerk and bailiff(s), and, believe it or not, the same two or three public defenders. This is the system for the indigent and don't think they are getting off cheap. They pay generally for all of the costs of prosecution, the statutory fines, and compensation to their victims, as usually provided by statute. Now in some cases it doesn't matter if you're innocent or guilty because the plea bargain for most non-violent second and third degree first time felonies will guarantee probation and no jail time. The thought of this being so enticing even to an innocent person versus the threat of going to jail that the plea bargain invariably elected with little thought given to the consequence of what might happen should there ever be a mistaken, or even a justifiable second arrest.

The criminal defense attorney who practices outside of the system I've outlined above is viewed as an outsider. He is not in the courtroom every day during recesses schmoozing with the clerks, the bailiffs, the prosecutors, or the judge. This group views him, the criminal defense attorney, as a sleaze bag, and in most cases they are correct despite what you hear Jerry Spence saying on CNBC Talk Television. Now in the case of the attorney who wrote the letter set forth above, there are two things that he well understood after having received his $10,000.00 retainer and having it cleared through his bank. He knew that his new client had nowhere to complain having been given the shafting revelation that $10,000.00 just made him another client and not this attorney's life work. After all, who could this client complain to? $10,000.00 already down the tube, you certainly don't expect him to search out another unknown lawyer and start the process all over again. Secondly, the criminal defense attorney also knew that if he withdrew his client might find himself with bail revoked and back in the can before new counsel could be found. Thirdly, this criminal defense attorney having, locked in the first $10,000.00 in fees, knew that any other attorney in town would be suspect of a client and his motives for wanting to escape his original criminal attorney's grasp, creating a fear in any new possible successor criminal defense attorney that he would not get paid.

Lastly, the fifteen-year old client has been given the cold realization that if she doesn't behave and conform to all of the new rules and regulations laid down, she may very well find herself doing the full five years for this general intent crime because she has alienated her only hope, the very criminal defense attorney she hired by the very whining or complaining he warned her of in the letter. Perhaps you would like to show your family, friends, and especially the children you know at least this small part of this book so that they might be forewarned about the system and the *fun* that having a couple of extra beers with their friends at the local lounge might cause them, or the nightmare of the criminal justice system they will be subjected to if they simply make a mistake in judgment, and run from the scene of an accident where there has been an injury, property damage, or a death.

Let's look at the other side of the coin from the Republican perspective. For almost twenty-years now you've "wised-up" to the sheer stupidity of protecting the constitutional rights of those who would "murder" you in your sleep or "mug" you on the street, but yet there's been "no" real swing in the pendulum back the other way so that you can again sleep with your doors unlocked, and not fear being mowed-down in a drive-by shooting. Yet you pay your taxes and keep almost 20 million of your fellow citizens employed in government.

Now, I myself have wondered about this phenomenon, and discuss this problem at great length in Chapter Nine of this book where I've come to one absolute conclusion: crime is America's most unregulated big business. If you're a member of the "criminal bar" you sure don't want the pendulum to swing back to the days before the "Warren Court" (1953-1969).

It is here in both the U.S. Supreme Court decisions and our own culture where the fallacy lies. The concept has been "brainwashed" into us since birth: Better a hundred guilty men go free, than one innocent man be wrongfully be convicted. This has been buttressed over the years by such T.V. shows as <u>Perry Mason</u>, <u>Matlock</u>, and <u>L.A. Law</u>.

Who would be surprised to hear that the system has worked far better than expected. There are probably 99,000, yes 99,000, free guilty men out there for every wrongfully convicted innocent man convicted of a crime in America. I have some first-hand knowledge of this, having personally investigated fourteen cases of allegedly "wrongfully convicted" innocent men (all were guilty except one — and he was erroneously found guilty of one crime, but was actually guilty of a greater crime, where the evidence was insufficient to prove his guilt, than the crime he was serving time for. I clearly remember the State Attorney, who had known of all of the circumstances of both crimes. When he had prosecuted the case two years before, he knew that this individual was innocent of the crime he was ultimately convicted of, but his words to me were clear: "You're right, he's innocent of what he's in the can for, but let's just say it's the right time, wrong crime!"). When I discussed this matter with the individual in question he admitted to me that he was trafficking in kilos of cocaine, but he would not rat-out his supplier even then, after the State had agreed to release him into a witness protection program. He would rather spend the next twelve years in jail for armed rape and kidnaping, than lose his criminal connections that would be waiting for him ten years down the road.

"So," you ask, "if this is true why hasn't the pendulum' swung back?"

First, because the same constitutional protections that exist for "street thugs" also exist for America's "white-collar" thieves in "business" and "government," and none of these "boys" are ever going to support the pendulum swinging back to slap them in their heads. Secondly, it's the megabucks. Criminal defense has come of age. Even the 100 year-old "white-shoe" firms are establishing criminal defense sections, in many instances to protect themselves, but also to partake in the lucrative defense fees paid by organized crime, drug kingpins, corrupt government officials, and some of America's *top-two-percenters* who even with today's nominal tax rates still occupy themselves with tax evasion. Yes, believe it or not, even a member of the *top-two-percenters* is occasionally charged and convicted of tax evasion. This generally occurs when her accountants and lawyers "dime" him or her "out" because he or she hasn't paid their fees for having set up the tax conspiracy that resulted in evasion, or he or she hasn't taken care of their employees by sharing some of the fraudulent tax benefits, and the employees, en masse, *dime out* the *top-two-percenter* because they haven't been sufficiently compensated. For those of you who co not know, the term *dime-out*, is a term from the 1930s when public telephones only cost a dime for a call. Since the call could not be traced, the squealer could anonymously rat-out his or her intended quarry, without any fear of retribution.

A View From The Top

Second only in depth to U.S. Supreme Court Chief Justice Rehnquist's speech dedicating the Indiana University Law School on September 12, 1986 (included in the Appendices section), is an excerpt from the keynote speech given by a Harvard University undergraduate alumni during Harvard's 350th commencement exercise. Unfortunately I was unable to locate the precise text, and the University itself was unable to point me in any direction, but in either event, the recorded tapes went something like this:

Ladies and Gentlemen: I thank you all for being here with us today to celebrate the 350th Commencement Exercise at Harvard, a school rich in tradition and history in its 350 years.

On this note, I wish to point out to you that America itself is only about to celebrate its 200 years of existence. But in America's short 200 year history, I'm certain you'll agree that America has contributed more to Harvard, than Harvard has to America in its 350 years.

In this regard, and in order that Harvard might give something back to America for all it has received, I suggest this day, we permanently close the Harvard Law School.

Now I ask all of you readers to turn to the aforementioned Appendix section to read the transcript of Chief Justice Rehnquist's September 12, 1986 speech dedicating the Law School at Indiana University.

* * * * * *

Now that you've read the Chief Justice's remarks, I'm certain you'll now concur that America's "legal profession" represents as much a threat to American democracy as does the $5 trillion National Debt, all of the "special interests groups" combined, and the continuing demise of American morality.

As difficult as it is for me to say, I have concluded that today's American legal professionals are the "facilitators" of America's decline.

They are the professionals who blessed and condoned the destruction of America in the 1980s, and who by their very numbers will continue to be American democracy's foremost nemesis into the 21st Century. Who of you reading this book is not in awe of the top 250 mega-law firms, who are of such immeasurable power and influence, that they appear almost as "small sub governments" within American Government?

Mega Law Firms that exist in America today with more lawyers in full combat "paper" regalia and "word processing power" than all of the U.S. Attorneys' offices and 50 states' prosecutors' offices combined. Ask anyone of your sons, daughters, or friends in the practice of law they have ever been "papered into a corner" by one of the top 250 law firms in the United States? These top 250 law firms *do it* to the smaller firms, *do it* to all federal government law enforcement agencies, and *do it* to whole state governments. Sometimes even the threat of a lawsuit by one of these 250 member mega law firms is enough to cause a state legislature or county commission to trash a statute or ordinance that would be beneficial to Americans as a whole. These same mega-firms also revise the Internal Revenue Code and its accompanying regulations almost every day of the week to the benefit of their top two percent class clients.

When one profession can tie-up so many hands of government, especially the judiciary and the executive branches, we as ordinary citizens obviously have less protection, either explicit or implicit, of our state and federal constitutions. The "Separation of Powers Doctrine" itself becomes meaningless when there exists a more influential and powerful "fourth estate," and this fact is evidenced inadvertently now and then in just about every published law journal in America.

The chosen profession of so many past great Americans and defenders of America's liberty and *democracy*: Adams, Jefferson, Madison, Monroe, Lincoln, both Roosevelts, and Truman. What would these past Americans think today, of their "chosen profession," the "majority" of whom have become nothing more than "hired guns" of the new American "aristocracy," the "facilitators" of America's "looters," and, in some cases, the "looters" themselves: a massive pack of thieves disguised in the robes of a once proud and honorable profession, the majority of whose members once aspired to much higher ideals, and certainly worthier principles.

The Myths Of The Legal Profession

I. Most lawyer's are exceptionally intelligent, and specially knowledge-able as it relates to the law.

II. It's not my son or daughter who has given a black-eye to the legal profession, it's the "big firms" controlled by Wall Street and Washington, D.C.

III. You can trust the legal profession to police itself, and to aspire to the ideals set forth in the ABA Code of Ethics already adopted by 39 states since its introduction in 1983.

IV. American capitalism, competition, and free enterprise will as a natural force, cause the number of U.S. attorneys to diminish.

The Realities Of The Legal Profession

I. As disturbing to you as it may sound, on average, CPAs have higher IQs than lawyers, and three years less education. In the majority of cases except for their area of specialization (i.e. divorce, corporate law, workers compensation law, etc.), most lawyers have about the same level of expertise outside of their area of practice as a well-read layman.

II. In geometry there exists an axiom: The whole is equal to the sum of its parts. There is no credible reason to believe this doesn't also apply to America's law firms and the U.S. Congress.

III. The only way the legal profession can be policed is by making lawyers subject to the same criminal laws that are applied to everyone else, and to perhaps punish their wrongdoing with tougher sentencing since their crimes are more often than not compounded by a betrayal of a public or personal trust.

IV. Remember the joke about only one lawyer in town? The only way to put an end to the legal menace that now threatens the foundation of American democracy is to immediately close half of America's law schools and limit, statutorily, the size of law firms to no more than five members. Short of this, the playing field will never be level for the ordinary American citizen, situated either in America's middle-class or in another one of the sub-species of *Boobus Americanus.*

- AUTHOR'S REVERSE "SPIN" GLOSSARY -

- "WHAT THEY SAY IT MEANS" & "WHAT IT REALLY MEANS." -

Legal Profession - Code of Ethics:

What they say it means: The American Bar Associations (ABA) is the largest national lawyer organization in the United States. Almost half of Americas 750,000 lawyers are members of the American Bar Association. The ABA Model Code of Professional Responsibility has been adopted by the majority of states (39 in total since 1983) as the official standard of conduct for lawyers. This 1983 code, designed by the ABA over several years, is called the ABA Model Rules of Professional Conduct. This document was to replace the ABA Code of Professional Responsibility and to become a new model for individual states to follow, in the hope that there might emerge a new meaningful national standard. In addition to the ABA's Model Code, each state now requires the passing of a formal bar examination, and sets its own ethical standards with respect to admitting and retaining lawyers to, and as members of its state Bar. It is not uncommon for states to do extensive background checks, reference checks, and state public records checks for those persons seeking admission to its Bar. In addition each state has an association of lawyers, and many states have an integrated Bar system (i.e every lawyer who is admitted in the state to practice law must also be a member of the state bar association, if the state subscribes to an integrated bar system). In most states, it is the Bar that is responsible for disciplining those attorneys who step outside of the rules of conduct, unless such conduct extends beyond violation of ethics and enters the sphere of criminality. Lawyers, as all other professions, are also subject to civil suit for malpractice. Generally speaking, the code of ethics adopted by most states include both ethical rules and aspirational goals. Most codes of conduct or ethical rules have specific examples to give guidance to lawyers to assure that they do not wander to far from the norm of what is expected from those in the profession.

What it really means: Not a week goes by when an article does not appear in the national or local law journals or the daily newspapers concerning the lack of ethics and criminality of one lawyer or firm of lawyers. Everything you see, read, experience, or hear about lawyers in the various law journals, the daily press, in novels, or in the movies seems to contradict what you might expect would be in a "professional code of ethics." One certainly has to wonder if the present aspirational state statutes, without the force of "criminal penalties," or the voluminous codes of ethics will ever be taken seriously by, not only lawyers, but by all of America's professions that are so loosely regulated? With the economic attitudes as demonstrated by federal, state and local government spending, regulation of all professionals can only become more lax resulting in enormous costs both in money and morality to American society.

COMPOSITE DICTIONARY

Ethics: Generally a compendium of moral and professional opinions, rules, and/or guidelines that may be either in a written format or "generally understood." In business it generally refers to work performed in an honest and diligent way. It is generally accepted in all cultures, that the morality displayed by members of a "profession" is important for continued public confidence in their work. One would be remiss, not to find a formal written professional code of ethics in any one of America's leading professions (i.e. the legal profession, the CPA profession, the dental profession, the medical profession, etc.).

7 | **The CPA Profession**

What It Is Today & How It Became That Way

America's CPA profession's roots began in Scotland in the mid-1850s where the independent accountant first came into being as the arbiter of money matters between disputing parties. In the early-1880s, England followed and was the first country to first recognized independent accountants needed some form of government regulation.

The first state legislature in the U.S. to recognize the Scotch and English equivalent of the **Charted Accountant**, the **Certified Public Accountant**, was New York State, and first college-degreed CPA in America was graduated from New York University in 1896. In 1899, Pennsylvania became the second state to regulate public accounting. By 1923, a mere 24 years later, every state and the District of Columbia had state statutes controlling the issuance of CPA certificates and the practice of "public accounting."

At the turn of the 20th Century there were fewer than 300 CPAs in the U.S., a number that grew to 75,000 by 1970; 140,000 by 1980; and to 480,000 today.

It was until the late 1960s, that the "green-eye-shade" image of the CPA began its metamorphosis to become the high-flying, go-go profession it is today. As late as the early 1970s, the CPA profession, at least on the surface, still retained some modicum of conservatism and attempted to maintain an "image," although quickly in the process of eroding, of integrity, honesty, and complete adherence to a formal code of ethics.

The first step of the CPA's movement into the "go-go" era can be traced back to 1966. Between 1966 and 1968, just two years, **Big Eight CPA Firm** starting annual salaries for new college graduates jumped from $5,800 to $12,500 per year. By the late 1970s, top accounting undergraduates were commanding $28,000 starting salary a year, and those with MBAs were receiving as much as $35,000 a year. Although these numbers may sound small compared to the starting salaries of their professional companions in law, it's quite a different matter at the "partner" level. CPA partner salaries are on a par with their companion law partners. One such partner at a *Big Six CPA Firm* confessed in 1989 to earning over $1,000,000 in total compensation and profits.

Similar to the explosion in size that the legal profession experienced in this same period, by 1983 *not one* of the then *Big Eight CPA Firms* (now the *Big Six*) had fewer than eighty U.S. offices. Touche Ross had the least with eighty offices, and Ernst Whinny the most with 118 U.S. offices. In 1983 Peat, Marwick & Mitchell boasted 1280 partners and almost 10,000 staff auditors; while Arthur Anderson, a little short on the partner side, wit a mere 1075, was boasting an army of over 12,000 staff auditors.

With revenues in 1983 running as high as $909 million for Arthur Anderson, $810 million for the then Peat, Marwick & Mitchell Company, and $380 million at Touche Ross, these firms were able to afford between three and five floors of prime office space in the highest priced rental districts in New York, Chicago, San Francisco, and elsewhere. Anyone who has ever visited the offices of the "Big Eight" can attest to the palatial fiefdoms these powerful CPA firms created for themselves. Partners with corner offices overlooking the whole of Manhattan and elsewhere mimicked scenes right out of the movie "Wall Street."

Even the AICPA, the professional association of the majority of CPAs, and most definitely a wholly-owned subsidiary of all of the *Big Eight* (now the *Big Six*), by 1982 had taken two floors in the McGraw-Hill Building (Rockefeller Center), one of the highest priced buildings in the nation.

By the end of 1960, every state had its own State Society of CPAs and by any standard, these societies became as influential and powerful as any PAC in promoting their self-interests in both state legislatures and with state governors.

By the late 1950s, almost all of the Big Eight CPA Firms had expanded their operations beyond the traditional auditing services to include:

1. Tax Consulting,
2. Management Advisory Services, and
3. Actuarial Services.

By the mid-1970s, most of these Big Eight Firms had:

1. Merger and Acquisition Specialist Groups,
2. Tax Shelter Specialist Groups, and
3. Industry Management Advisory Specialist Groups.

Throughout the 1970s and 1980s, the Big Eight Firms had played an extensive game of "Pac-Man," eating up many of the smaller firms, buying them out or merging them into themselves. By 1989 the Big Eight itself witnessed two major mergers. Four of its firms became two: Touche Ross & Co. merged with Deloitte, Haskins & Sells, to become Deloitte, Touche; and Ernst & Whinny merged with Arthur Young to become Ernst & Young. Although more mergers were rumored at the end of the 1980s, merger fever amongst the remaining Big Six abruptly came to a halt, probably because these firms neither had pension funds, subsidiary companies, or stockholders to loot to support the early retirement of those forced out as a result of the downsizing that is always the natural consequence of a merger.

Only Team Players Allowed!

Before I explain what the term *team player* means in the context of the *Big Eight or Six CPA Firm*, I must first describe the way both CPAs and lawyers in the large firms rise to the top. It's a process of elimination; there being less and less floor-space, desk space, and supervisory positions as you rise to the next level in these pyramid-like structures. Promotions usually occur annually, and the general rule is "up or out." In the typical Big Six CPA Firm there are six levels: (1) Partner, (2) Manager, (3) Supervisor, (4) Senior, (5) Staff Auditor, and (6) First-Year Auditor.

This is similar to the first-year, second-year, third-year, fourth-year, fifth-year, sixth-year associate, then "partner" in the typical major law firm.

Both CPA firms and Law firms use this "up or out" promotion process to: (1) weed out the unambitious, (2) weed out the incompetent, and (3) most importantly, to weed out the misanthropes, the potential whistle blowers, and those who are not *team players*. This process is very similar in concept to the *pie rules* of American business described in Chapter Four, but the "elimination process" in law and certified public accounting is much more fast-paced and assertively more decisive.

It was decided in the latter half of 1974, after I had been promoted to Supervisor in "record time," and after having had worked in stretches of 70 hours a week, three and four months at a time in such faraway places as Memphis, Tennessee, Houston, Texas, and Columbus, Ohio, that I was **not** a *team player.*

The news hadn't come as a shock, since I had recognized after my first year in public accounting that I could never *tunnel-vision* my thinking enough to allow *the audit results to be obscured by size of the client's fee.* This is the way it was, and I just couldn't change. I had seen a lot of my fellow contemporaries get thrown out in the same manner, and quite frankly, I was becoming more concerned with going to jail as a result of some of the questionable audit decisions than being unemployed, or being blackballed. We Americans sometimes equate this phenomenon to the cliche: *No guts, no glory!*

Even the Vesco fraud was an up-hill battle with the partner-in-charge of the engagement; this even after one of the firm's top managers agreed with me that all the Vesco operations were "fraudulent." The partner-in-charge became so annoyed at the two of us, he advised us we would soon be looking at more than the loss of a $3 million fee, whatever that was supposed to mean. That was the name of the game, not only at the firm I worked for, but for all the firms I had friends at who exchanged similar, but obviously less exciting stories with me.

My later experience as an internal auditor, manager of internal audit, and director of internal audit at three Fortune 500 Companies was no better in ethical quality, than the experience I had had in public accounting. Here I learned from the inside how the independent auditors were fooled on the outside. As many of you may, or may *not* know, 1977-1980 was the era of FCPA (the Foreign Corrupt Practices Act-1987), a federal law which, among other things, was enacted to control the illegal payments being made by the once American Multinational Corporations, to low-level foreign government officials in order to procure a greater share of the foreign market place for the MNC's products sold in these foreign countries and to speed the clearance of the MNC's raw materials and finished goods through customs.

Because of the penalties attached to this law (massive fines and jail time), the CEOs of these MNCs, along with their cadre of corporate officers and board of directors were all trying to insulate and separate themselves as far as they could from these illegal payments, and in some cases million dollar bribes, and therefore needed somebody to be the "ax-man" to chop-off the head of the local manager or CEO of the local subsidiary in these South American countries in such a manner that would leave no trail of evidence implicating any of the MNC's corporate officers or members of the Board of Directors. *(Author's comment:* FCPA was not the panacea for de-corrupting low-level local foreign government officials, but rather a clever ploy of the *world's top-two-percenters* to take somewhat surreptitious measures to get these local officials off-the-dole so that these moneys could then be re-distributed to the local country's government *top-two-percenters*. Think of it as the $6 per hour security guard at the retail store where you might be employed requiring a tip from the driver of every truck delivering goods to the store, if that driver wants to get to the shipping dock to unload. Now think about it, wouldn't this required tip be better paid directly to the CEO of the store, after all, isn't the security guard only worth $6 an hour while the CEO is worth a million or more a year? What would the security guard do with all that extra money anyway, except corrupt himself with more sex, drugs, cheap beer? Lastly, with regard to the foreign bribes, who do you think would give you greater influence in the long run, the low level customs agent or members of the cabinet of the foreign country's President?)

But under either circumstance, new, fresh, and highly qualified internal audit "type" CPAs with absolutely "clean hands" were necessary in the U.S. to come on board at these MNCs to clean-up these low level illegal payments and bribes, which by 1977, had grown to large sums based on the amount of free trade going on. These internally employed CPAs with clean-hands were also needed to erase any trail of evidence that would lead to the MNC Management or Board Room, and thus possibly an investigation by the U.S. Justice Department or SEC, which could be avoided if the MNC's independent outside auditors (CPA Firm) said as part of their "opinion" in the following year's annual report that the illegal payments had been cleaned-up.

Needless to say, under this new 1977 FCPA law, the CPA profession knew what the CPA stood for, and most CPAs had guessed what the "F" stood for, since the criminal penalties of the law also extended to them as the independent auditors of these MNCs. But in reality it was all a lot of Spin Doctoring! In retrospect, and in light of the 1990s Salinas $300 Million Telephone Scandal in Mexico, those of you CPAs who still pride yourself on a job-well done at the end of the 1970s, chalk another one up to your just being duped, or perhaps the *top-two-percenters* even then, having found a way to keep you guys happy and preoccupied while they were preparing for the unfettered coronation of Ronald Reagan in 1980!

But nonetheless, in 1977, *non-team players* were now in the *in-group, and* I was immediately embraced because of my reputation as the quintessential *non-team player* and until the rise of Ronald Reagan, we naive *non-team players, whistle blowers* and other *watch dogs* thought we were having a field day in at least wiping out some of the then American Multinational Corporation's obvious foreign corruption. Since the beginning of the Reagan Presidency, and through today, except for the local-level customs agent being paid, everything is back to where it was prior to the enactment of the 1977 FCPA law, this new law being rarely enforced, or if enforced, only to get rid of the local foreign manager or local subsidiary president. I need only point out again the $300 million scandal that just came to the forefront of <u>60 Minutes</u> describing the millions paid to former Mexico's President Salinas's brother to assure that certain American telephone companies could get a foot hold in the Mexican telephone market in this new era of NAFTA, as Mexican government operated companies were privatized, and capitalism was spread from the U.S. down to Mexico. Interestingly enough, since this spread of capitalism to Mexico, this Third World Country now boasts being the fourth largest home of billionaire citizens, oddly enough, only the United States, Germany, and Japan, in that order, being ahead of this Third World Country in this *billionaire club* distinction. Obviously nothing has changed based on NAFTA, FCPA, or any of the other myriad of laws, and probably from the Mexican citizens point of view, things have gotten a lot worse. Remember folks, it was your government's $50 billion loan in the latter part of 1994 that kept the Mexican economic and financial structure from collapsing. Now, I hope none of you reading this book expect that money to be repaid, from other than your own U.S. hard earned tax dollars.

Since the inauguration of President Reagan, almost every **whistle blower, honest regulator, honest CPA, honest lawyer** (of which there are very few as previously noted), and almost every **honest board of director** has virtually been gagged or deep-sixed, unless he or she was desirous of changing to share some of the crumbs, or in some cases, simply survive. Unfortunately, many of these honest folks were never properly socialized, possibly because of their family's lack of business and political savvy, their fathers being just one of the millions of ordinary Americans whose belief, and correctly so, that America is still the best place in the world regardless of the corruption, the greed, and the looting that is believed to be so necessary a part of America's mutation of Capitalism.

Then, of course, I may have just been exposed to some of the worst of America's professionals and some of the worst of American corporations. Unfortunately, I really haven't found but a few good men; and a very few good CPAs; and only two truly honest practicing lawyers. I can also state, without reservation, that of the hundred or so doctors and dentists that I have met in both of my professional practices, and also those doctors and dentists that I myself have also been a victim (i.e. of their malpractice) and having personally witnessed so many of their conspiracies, schemes, and other sundry devices to defraud their patients, and state and local government, I can summarily state that it is my opinion that they are no better than the CPAs or lawyers that have also crossed over my professional career. Even this long in the system, I still have not given up on America, and never will. The solutions to America's awesome problems are certainly out there and we Americans have always come through when times got tough. We can change our destiny, if we realize that this time, the enemy we face is not from Europe or Asia, but this time the enemy we face is from within: our bought-off representative government; our corrupt virtually closed two-party political system; our corrupt professions; our highly over-paid **don't make waves** news media stars; and most important, you, yourselves, in the ever-shrinking middle-class, driven by your own personal greed and illusive dream of wealth that results in your choice to do nothing in the hope of some day having something, and perhaps even fulfilling your illusive dream of yourself joining the ranks of the **top-two-percenters**.

NO SPIN GLOSSARY OR COMPOSITE DICTIONARY EXISTS FOR THIS CHAPTER

8 | The Medical Professions

Some Statistics and Other Facts About U.S. Doctors & Other Health Care Providers

The below chart compares the number of doctors in Canada (our socialized medicine neighbors to the north) Germany, and Japan (our allegedly two greatest competitors in the world economy), and three of the other most prominent industrialized nations of the world.

SELECTED INTERNATIONAL PHYSICIAN ALLOCATION
(1988 DATA)

Country	No. of Doctors	Doctor per 100,000 People
Germany	177,001	1 per 351
Great Britain	92,172	1 per 611
Japan	201,658	1 per 609
France	138,825	1 per 403
Canada	55,275	1 per 464
USA	612,000	1 per 408

Being that the United States is first in the actual number of physicians, and third in physicians per capita of the six listed nations, you would expect that doctors would be somewhat less costly or at least relatively competitively priced in relation to those of our global competitors. To the contrary, American physicians are the most expensive in the world, and the highest paid; and this is not a result of America's physicians being any more efficient, or working longer hours than their contemporaries in Japan, Germany or elsewhere. In 1996, it is estimated America will spend in aggregate $800 billion on health care, and these same costs are projected to increase at three times the rate of inflation, or 10% a year whichever is greater (i.e. or whatever you the U.S. citizen will allow the market to bear).

If you don't know already, I'm sure you're curious as to why this phenomena exists.

First, it's due to the very "structure" of America's Health Care and the fabulous "cookie jar" billing gimmicks they make available to America's doctors through government-paid Medicare, Medicaid and the Medical Insurance Industry's chaotic billing systems and procedures. Doctors are not paid by the hour, but by the procedure. Now does this tell you why your doctor has five to ten little examining rooms into which he pops in and out every three or four minutes? When he saw you, in your little cubicle, did you know that he had performed half a dozen procedures on you that he charged to your medical plan, or to Medicare or Medicaid? Did you even care, so long as you weren't footing the bill? Did you also know that all of the little things his assistant did before he even entered your cubicle was charged as a procedure to your health care carrier? Lastly if you looked at your bill would you know whether your doctor or his assistant did any of the procedures that he billed to your medical insurer? From the eleven medical practices I've audited over the past twenty years, I have been appalled by the outrageously expensive procedures willingly paid for by Medicare, Medicaid, and the health insurance industry, that are very rarely ever audited by an independent third party or the payer agency. If lawyers and CPAs were allowed to "structure" their work and, especially their billings, and get paid similar to the doctors, (not that they haven't their own billing schemes as noted in previous chapters), the U.S. Treasury would have gone bust ten years ago, this is one of the primary reasons the U.S. Treasury is about to go "bust." The only reason the medical insurance companies have not gone "bust" is because they can simply increase their premiums to you.

Look at the cost of your medical insurance coverage today. If you're the typical American, your premiums have probably risen 10 times their 1970 level; and why? First because your health insurance company said they'd drop you, if you didn't ante-up; and, second because you were scared-to-death of having your medical coverage being interrupted in any manner with the "no pre-existing condition" coverage exclusion, if you were forced to change carriers. So in the grip-of-this-fear, the doctors, hospitals, and the pass-along-the-costs health-care-insurers have one heck of a monopoly — and we now have close to 37,000,000 Americans unable to afford health care insurance at all.

If there weren't Health Care Insurance Carriers in the United States and each individual had to pay for his or her medical treatment directly, with the doctor's hand directly extended into each of his patient's pocketbook, instead of it being deep in the impersonal "cookie jar" of the nation's health-care-insurers, and the U.S. Treasury the cost of health care in the U.S. would be between 30% and 40% less than what it is today.

The second reason the American physician is the most expensive in the world is simply a matter of the members of this profession looking at it as a business rather than a profession. What American have you met in the last 40-years, willing to go to sweat-out four years of college, three years of medical school, and two years of internships to improve your living, and not his own? Look over those Medical Economics article titles later in this chapter. Do you think you're looking at profession where the majority of its practitioners are with any "calling," other than "cash?"

The third reason America's physicians are the most expensive in the world is the infectious insecurity and greed that has been inflicted on them by both the legal and CPA professions. First these lawyers and CPAs came as counselors and accountants, then as financial planners, and then as the physician's "profit oriented" practice managers. To cover the fees of their CPAs and lawyer handlers alone, the physicians of America were forced to increase their "billings" by at least 15%, and this doesn't cover the losses many of these physicians suffered (not undeserved) in lawyer and CPA created "tax scams" and other questionable ventures and investments. Not to say that a lot of these CPAs and lawyers didn't make millions for their physician clients, but in those instances where this did happen, I can assure you the only adage that applied to these investment millions being made was: "More is always better!"

The fourth reason, as you all hear about day in and day out from Citizen Robert Dole, are the tort lawyers who solely focus on medical malpractice and the large jury awards that seem to always run into the tens of millions of dollars. These large malpractice awards have also resulted in some very fine doctors paying as much as $100,000. a year in medical malpractice insurance premiums. The doctor without medical malpractice insurance, for whatever reason, is still forced to pay the piper, his lawyer, to make certain that his asset are judgment proof.

The Business Of Medicine

Have you ever heard of the magazine called: <u>Medical Economics</u>? If you're a doctor, you have; and you probably get all twenty-four issues of this 200 page, high-gloss magazine "for free." If you're one of those medical doctors getting <u>Medical Economics</u> "for free," you certainly don't put this publication out in your waiting room for your patients to read. If you did, I probably could have eliminated more than 50% of this chapter — your patients would have already known about half of what they are about to read here.

If you're not a medical doctor, I'm certain you're now really curious about this publication <u>Medical Economics</u> and what it's all about?

Well, first it's one of the main sources for many doctors to update their knowledge of the latest drugs offered by America's and Europe's Pharmaceutical Industries — one drug being advertised over four, five, six, and sometimes even as many as eight full pages of full-color advertisements describing the drug and its pharmacology — and sometimes in contrast, in one of those less expense half-page advertisements, just a short explanation of what the drug does and how to prescribe it. If you think the automobile, or the designer clothes industries can put on superb ads, just breeze through the ads of the pharmaceutical companies who pay for this "free-bee" publication and you'll know where the real creative talent lies in America's advertising industry.

It was but three months after I had received my first issue of <u>Medical Economics</u> in 1987, that I bought my first copy of <u>Physician's Desk Reference</u> (<u>PDR</u>) so that I myself might feel more secure about the dozens of prescription drugs our family doctor was prescribing for us, realizing that if he was relying on the super-hype in <u>Medical Economics</u>, that I should at least offer my immediate family a minuscule chance at surviving this pharmacological "information over-load" that I was convinced no human being could deal with, not even a trained doctor.

Now, I'm sure you're all saying: "So what. A doctor has to get his information some how, and so what if it comes from <u>Medical Economics</u> — Would it be better if he didn't have the information at all?"

I don't disagree with this argument, but <u>Medical Economics</u> is not called "<u>Medical Economics</u>," because it's just an "advance sheet" for new drugs (<u>PDR</u> is also published by the same publisher of <u>Medical Economics</u>). <u>Medical Economics</u> is the educational equivalent of a Harvard MBA and JD wrapped-up in one, and offers some of the most comprehensive information concerning:

- Domestic & Foreign Investment Strategies.
- Retirement Planning.
- Real Estate Investment Strategies.
- Medical Practice Marketing.
- Vacation Planning.
- Malpractice Avoidance Techniques.
- Anti-Trust Avoidance Techniques.
- Tax Avoidance Techniques.
- How Others Got Caught In Medicare and Medicaid Frauds.
- How To Make Kick-Backs and Bribes (Referral Fees) Legal.

Below are some of the telltale articles that have appeared in <u>Medical Economics</u> in 1988 and 1989:

Loss Avoidance Articles

- The Dumbest Thing A Malpractice Defendant Can Do. (June 19, 1989)
- How Much Do You Risk When You Review a Colleague's Case? (September 4, 1989)
- Did This Doctor's Penalty Fit The Crime? (August 7, 1989)

- Never Think You've Got A Lock On A Malpractice Victory. (July 3, 1989)
- A Lawyer Put Your Malpractice Defense to The Test. (May 15, 1989)
- Don't Get Cute With Your Ex-Wife's Money. (October 17, 1988)
- A Tactic That's Heading Off Malpractice Suits. (October 17, 1988)
- My Most Unforgettable Lawyer Suit. (October 17, 1988)
- My Countersuit Victory Sent A Message. (June 19, 1989)
- The Kinds Of Patients Your Colleagues Are Turning Away. (February 6, 1989)
- If You Should Lose A Peer Review Suit ... (December 5, 1988)
- This Might Be Your Best Weapon Against Malpractice. (November 7, 1988)
- Don't Make These Informed-Consent Mistakes. (August 15, 1988)
- If You Forgive Copayments, The Carrier May Not Forgive You. (May 1, 1989)
- How I Killed My "Can't Lose Practice." (April 17, 1989)
- Will Congress Put Canadian-Style Curbs On Medicare Fees? (April 4, 1988)
- Why Did It Take So Long To Nail This Crooked Doctor? (March 20, 1989)
- To the Medicops [Uncle Sam's Gumshoes], There are No Honest Mistakes. (July 4, 1988)
- How Lawyers Stack Juries Against Doctors. (December 5, 1988)
- When Do Hospital Perks Become Indictable Bribes? (May 1, 1989)
- Will This Antitrust Victory Back Fire On Doctors? (August 15, 1988)
- One More Way To Get Sued For Malpractice. (June 19, 1989)

Wealth Enhancement Articles

- Bleeding Hearts Are Making Hard Cash On Wall Street. (July 17, 1989)
- Are You Ready When Europe Unites? (July 7, 1989)
- Garbage Can Turn To Gold In Your Portfolio. (June 19, 1989)
- Can You Clean Up By Playing With Vultures? (June 5, 1989)
- Why Investors Are Suddenly Flocking To Raw Land? (June 5, 1989)
- High-Tech Stocks May Take Off. (June 5, 1989)
- How Much Junk Is In Your Bond Fund Holdings? (April 3, 1989)
- How To Focus On A Snappy Investment. (March 20, 1989)
- The Smartest Way To Jump Into The Bond Market. (December 19, 1988)
- I'm Fattening My Pension Fund With Second Mortgages. (September 5, 1988)
- Tax-Shelter Losses Can Still Pay Off. (March 6, 1988)
- More Trouble Ahead — Congress Has "Fixed" the Tax Law. (January 2, 1989)

The Rebellion Articles

- To Many Of Us Are Just Plan Greedy. (February 6, 1989)
- Why Was The Love Surgeon Allowed To Keep Cutting? (July 17, 1989)

If you are one of those fortunate enough to have both private medical and dental health-care-coverage (or old enough to be on

Medicare or poor enough to be on Medicaid), do you ever examine your carrier's or the government's statements of amounts paid on your behalf once you've gotten passed your deductible? Did you know that your health insurance carrier and the government thinks you're out there checking these "charges" to assure that your health care professionals are not:

- Double billing your health care insurer or the government,
- Billing for health care services not provided, and
- Billing your health care insurer for services you were told you were required to pay for directly.

How often has your doctor or dentist told you "not to worry about the deductible" — that he or she would "take care of it?"

As long as you paid "nothing" — and got one of those <u>zero-balance</u> due billing statements from your carrier or Medicare — why should you give "one hoot" how much your health-care-provider "bilked" your health-care-insurer or the government. After all, you may have saved a $600 deductible, and perhaps even the 20% copayment you were required to pay directly, but all you can think is that this is just a part of the American Way: "Better in my pocket, than the next guys!" — Now whose pocket do you think this money ultimately comes out of? It may take time for the circle to be complete, but ultimately it comes out of your pocket and those of us who also pay our taxes.

Now I know in America's busy health-care offices, neither doctors nor dentists have the time, nor the inclination to review the "billings" to your health-care-insurer or the government — or the dozens of other patient's bills that go out daily. That's the receptionist's job!

I ask: "Would you really be surprised to find out that those receptionist's mistakes always benefit the doctor's "pocketbook," and rarely ever your insurance carrier's or the government's pocketbook?" One medical claims audit expert advised me: "Billing mistakes are so rampant, we couldn't keep up with them if we wanted to — in fact, it's cheaper to pay these erroneous claims than to even attempt to track them down or correct them."

Although this next comment may seem in contradiction to the aforementioned medical claims audit expert's comment that "it's cheaper to pay these claims," it's estimated these several million per year in medical claims "mistakes" cost the health-care-insurers and the government between $20 billion and $50 billion a year.

The second of the major scams rampant in both the medical and dental professions are the "referral clubs!" If a member of either of these professions involved in this "scam" smell either "money, or the hoard in your savings account," or the "right health-care-insurance-coverage," you'll be immediately put into what I like to refer to it as the "referral loop" — that's your body being shifted around to one or more members of the referral club, first for "consult tion," then for "treatment," and so on, and so on, until every member in the club has had his fill of billing.

A dentist client of mine in West Palm Beach told me to test the "referral club" mechanism out amongst a group of dentists he knew had formed such a "club." Sure enough, in the course of two weeks my savings had been reduced $275.00 for professional consultations, and I was looking at estimates totaling $26,000.00 for all the "dental work" they said was required. This was after I had spent $30,000.00 to have the whole mess repaired six months before.

Now you say, "I thought kickbacks were illegal?" Well they are in some cases, but rarely enforced — and even more difficult to prove. Remember also, none of these "boys" are "ratting" one another out — the one's on the outside of the "club" may know of it, may not like it, but also haven't got the where-with-all to prove it. Because of the number of conspiracies that I've become privy to over the past twenty years within the four "professions" I've become somewhat immune to it. I have also become convinced these four "professions" are quite pleased to see America's law enforcement efforts focused primarily on the alleged war on "illegal drugs" and its related violent crime. You don't have to be a brain surgeon to connect this allegation to the corruption in the health-care professions, nor the rampant lawlessness previously related to the legal or CPA professions, nor the rampant corruption in government and even law enforcement itself.

I'm certain I need not admonish you how much worse this condition will become as the American "pie" continues to get smaller-and-smaller, especially if some serious corrective measures are not employed to thwart this decline in the professional morality amongst all of our professions.

Now its your turn to act as the empiricist, and through your own observation of the evidence in your own city, town, or state, attest to whether or not the U.S. Health Care System and its health care providers are or aren't giving you the "fair-shake" you deserve as both a citizen and a taxpayer. You don't think you've got the right to ask? . . . Well then, let me ask you: "Who do these professionals rely on to provide them with this free and unfettered economic environment (America) to function in, if not you? As most of you know, when it comes down to the actual fire-fight, the majority of America's professionals are the furthest from the combat front lines, either in school ducking the "draft," or too old to serve after having graduated.

No question here, if you're in the "top-two-percenters," the last paragraph is of no consequence to you, but if you are situated anywhere below — beware: One catastrophic illness in your family, should your health care insurer ever drop you, could cost you in excess of $1,000,000 — and that should be "material" to the vast majority of you young lawyers and CPAs who are also reading this book.

The Malpractice Business-Another Cost Factor
It's More than Just Doctors

A short story: As fate would have it, you just mangled yourself and your automobile up after guzzling down "one-too-many beers," and found yourself in the crowded emergency room under the care of the nastiest intern at General Hospital. You immediately started dreaming of that big Mercedes Benz, a house with an Olympic size pool, and never working again for the rest of your life. The only thing standing between you and your dream, you're certain, is the "right" attorney.

As soon as you regain consciousness following two hours of surgery, you begin your search amongst friends, and maybe even have your wife shoot over to the county library to scour over last year's microfiched-newspapers to see who hit the "tort lottery" (got the big jury award) in your jurisdiction for getting smashed-up in their automobile.

The following week you find yourself sitting in a very plush attorney's office, engrossed in dialogue:

Attorney: "If you <u>don't</u> have these symptoms we'll never be able to sustain the "proofs" necessary to show there was medical malpractice . . . If you <u>don't</u> have <u>all</u> of these symptoms, you're not going to recover anything for the serious "permanent" injuries you sustained . . . . . We'll have enough trouble proving these injuries in any event because there's <u>no</u>, . . . I repeat, <u>no</u> absolute test to say whether they exist or not!"

The attorney hands you the list of symptoms, all true, tried, and well tested, and all very subjective. You carefully study the list. After a few minutes of careful examination, you look up at your new attorney and reply: "You mean if I don't have <u>all</u> of these symptoms, I don't have a case?"

Attorney: "That's right! That's the symptoms you have to be suffering from. . ... all of them. . . . if you expect to recover damages for your injuries."

You then ask: "And if I do have all of these symptoms?"

Attorney: "You've got a shot at getting not only damages for your injuries, but possibly major punitive damages (the jackpot) too!"

This short dialogue that I have set forth above, according to plaintiff's bar medical malpractice lawyers <u>never</u> occurs. If you've been to see a personal injury lawyer, or a medical malpractice specialist, I am certain you understand how cryptically you've been instructed in the symptoms of your "permanent" injury.

Of the twenty-three cases I've been privy to (referral and walk-in clients seeking recommendations for a medical malpractice lawyer), seven I am certain were absolute frauds. One of these seven "con-artists" advised me that if we "sued for a million dollars we could split a quick $20,000 settlement check — advising me his best friend had just pulled-it-off two weeks before.

On the other side-of-the-coin, remember the story of my Podiatrist client —he admitted to me confidentially that he had used a "radical medical procedure" that he admitted to me should have only been used as a "last resort," and as a result of his aggressive stupidity, he literally crippled a young woman for the rest of her life. Remember how the law firm the young woman had selected was criminally indicted for insurance fraud a week before her case came to trial, the doctor's malpractice insurer was able to settle a genuine million dollar suit for an unconscionable $6,000. Let me further assure you, the judge overseeing the settlement negotiations didn't blink-an-eye at this injustice.

One last point I wish to make concerning medical malpractice. If you suffer less than $25,000, and in some parts of the country less than $50,000 in damages as a result of medical malpractice, there is <u>no</u> remedy for you — there's just no cost-benefit justification for the medical malpractice attorney to take your case, unless of course you can come up with a $25,000 retainer and are willing to cover the attorney's fees out of your own pocket.

The message here is straight-forward. There has got to be a better way to handle both Doctor fraud, greed, and medical malpractice cases so that neither the doctor, nor the patient, nor the American consumer is egregiously wronged. Lawyers will tell you it is only the "jury system" that can work fairly under these circumstances, and with this conclusion, I very much agree — providing there were no lawyers, judges, or certain technical rules of procedure and evidence involved. No need for my bothers and sisters at the bar to write or call, I am well aware of all the arguments requiring the need for certain court procedures and the exclusion of certain evidence — as much as I am aware of how lucrative medical malpractice is to both plaintiff's bar, and defendant's bar as well.

Nevertheless, it seems logical to me that an elected five-person panel made up of two doctors and three ordinary citizens serving maximum paid terms of two years, with no "manipulation" or "filtering" of evidence as occurs in the present legal process, could better decide these medical malpractice matters than the "justice system" we rely on today. Certainly if the nation adopts a National Health Insurance System, this sort of, or similar, panel system would almost be required.

CONCLUSION

Now, I know this book so far has been nothing more than a castigation of much of America, its business culture, its professions, and certainly its values. To those of you who comprise the decent doctors and other professionals of America, I apologize for making everyone of you seem bad or evil, or even suspect. My references are not to you, but to the ever growing number of "bad apples" in what most Americans believed was once its foremost four professions. Those of you professionals, who are genuinely insulted or truly innocent of all the allegations I've made, what about your "omissions," - - your looking-the-other-way and doing nothing, as if none of this were going on - - it is these very "omissions" and looking the other way that facilitates much of the theft by others in our respective professions.

The Myths Of The Medical Professions

I.   Dentistry or Medicine is a "calling" for most, not for financial gains, but for the spiritual and emotional rewards it provides.

II. Spiraling health care costs can be contained by existing proposals set forth in the Republican insurance health care reform.

III. A National Health Care Plan will add hundreds of billions of dollars to America's present health care costs and will cause a rationing of America's health care services.

The Realities Of The Health Care Professions

I.   Perhaps one doctor in 100 today enters the Medical profession for spiritual or emotional rewards, and less than 1 in 10,000 enter the dental profession for this same purpose.

II. Myth II above is probably one of the "biggest" Republican Party myths in America today. By throwing more "loose money" into the "cookie jar" of the present cesspool of health care providers, America will not only make them more voracious, but wealthier than ever before. Needless to say, this is also consistent with all of the economic programs the Republican Party has on its agenda to allegedly grow America's economy.

III. If a National Health Care Plan (1) replaces all of the present hundreds of "payers" in the health-care-insurance industry with one federal "payer," with only one ledger per doctor while simultaneously implementing strict federal fraud penalties for any and all billing abuses (such previously noted abuses blamed on the receptionist's mistakes), and (2) has as its primary objective for increasing the number of physicians by seeking them out amongst America's poor and minorities, to be trained at the expense of the government, can there be any doubt that health care costs would be held, at a minimum, constant, and even reduced in the long term. Just closing the current Medicare/Medicaid "cookie jar" would save between $20 and $50 billion, and no one argues that $120 billion could be saved if there was a uniform "one payer system," with a "singular claim form," and a single ledger for each doctor. The single ledger concept per doctor would in and of itself highlight the abuses of many of our physicians and the large medical facilities that they have established in order to bilk Medicare, etc.

The only downside, I see of a National Health Care Program is for the ***top-two-percenters*** who would <u>not</u> have the same level of care they now enjoy, and which <u>only</u> they can now afford under America's present health care system. There is also the "imagined fear" of the middle-class that "this same level of care" will not be available to them should they ever achieve ***top-two-percenter*** status.

9 | American Crime and
Law Enforcement

She closes every show with the reassuring line:

"Remember, we're in touch, so you be in touch."

You've watched her show with her side-kick Hugh Downs for almost ten years, so as a matter of almost habit, every Thursday night, you turn it on. It's July 23, 1992. You push your pillow comfortably under your head, and get ready for an hour of critical social analysis by America's foremost woman "in touch." You begin to hear Barbara Walters talking about Japan, and you immediately think, tonight's show is going to be just a little more Japan "bashing."

"Imagine," she says, "being arrested, then put in isolation, denied bail or even the right to make a phone call, and brutally forced to confess to a crime?"

You rub your eyes to improve the clarity of your vision. You feel dyslexic, as all of Walter's words seem to flow in complete contradiction to ABC reporter Lynn Sherr's video panning the safe and clean "streets" in the inner cities of Japan, the nation with the lowest crime rate of all industrial nations.

Walters is heard again, but now in her sinister "usually overworked" inquiring tone: "But tonight, Lynn Sherr brings us the most shocking and revealing evidence ever about how far the government of Japan goes in order to maintain its safe streets."

The show now shifts again to Lynn Sherr's video report. Sherr voice is heard as the video goes forward: "This is, after all, Japan, one of the most envied of modern societies, a country where visitors and residents feel safe. Street crime is practically unheard of hear, thanks partly to the police, who are very visible. By making themselves so available to the community, they're considered friendly, local heroes, but this comforting routine masks a very disturbing reality."

Lynn Sherr's words: "masks a very disturbing reality" stabs at your curiosity. You sharpen your ears as she continues.

"The system the Japanese trust to protect them actually robs them of their basic human rights!"

For the next twenty-minutes Walters and Sherr condemn the lack of Japan's "constitutional rights" for both Japanese and foreign citizens accused and found guilty of
crimes. Both women go on the condemn the entire Japanese government and the Japanese prison system — prison cells without televisions, stereo sets, bathing facilities, and only three-feet by five-feet in dimension. Prisoners having to sit or kneel all day, not even being allowed to stand or lean against the prison cell's walls.

You keep waiting for the "punch line," as Lynn Sherr, along with some relatives of an American and other foreigners arrested, continue to lambaste the Japanese police, as the peaceful scenes of Japanese streets and communities continue to flash across the 20/20 screen. You finally conclude these "idiots" are very serious, all the while you're thinking in the back of your mind: "What the hell, have the two of them gone completely "bananas?" Condemning law and order and on T.V.?" In fact, you've so fully enjoyed the few minutes of peacefulness, law, and order you've seen flashing across the 20/20 screen (the clean streets and civilized people, etc.) you begin to think even deeper, "Hey, maybe they're accepting immigration from the U.S.?" You scratch your head, as you continue to think: "Hey, ... it's at least worth inquiring into."

It isn't until the last segment of this night's 20/20 show that you wonder whether Walters has completely lost "it," or perhaps never had "it." This thought occurs to you as she moderates the third 20-minute segment of tonight's 20/20 show. You're back in America!

This segment begins with pictures of several American armed bank-robbers pointing and shooting their guns indiscriminately over the counter at tellers, who appear, and later confirm, they are near scared-to-death to return to work.

"With bank robberies continuing at an all-time high, we thought you might want to see again these extremely interesting and unusual cops and robbers," are the words used by the "women-in-touch" to describe the 2,000 bank robberies a year in the Los Angeles area — robberies that are becoming more and more violent.

One of the caught bank robbers, who is now suing the FBI is interviewed. He'd been nicknamed by the FBI as the "Clearasil" bandit because of his bad complexion — he says to John Stossel: "I've been greeted as "Hey, Clearasil" by officers and inmates. It's hurt my feelings, it's caused me emotional distress." On this, the "woman-in-touch" does not comment, but in closing she ruefully concludes shaking her head as she looks over to John Stossel. "John, this report makes a difference? Are there fewer robberies now?"

To which Stossel replies, in obvious disbelief to the "woman-in-touch's" question: "I don't think the robbers watch or- . . "

Walters breaks in: "They didn't wise up"?

To which Stossel replies: "Well, if they watched, they're still so stupid, they still don't realize that 85% get caught, because the robberies are up. It was about 40 a week last year. Now it's 50 a week."

Walters replies, "Gee, that's a big number."

"And they're more violent," Stossel interjects, "more takeovers. They're not just robbing banks, but the customers, too."

Showing her first sign of somewhat "becoming-in-touch" after Stossel comments that it's "one more reason to hate going to the bank", Walters, appearing somewhat distraught concludes, "Oh, John. I won't even comment."

You now wonder whether she has any respect for either your "intelligence" or your "span-of-attention," or, perhaps, your ability to control your hand-held-channel-changer? Or perhaps Walters truly believes, after this third-segment of 20/20 that she and her cohorts have convinced the Japanese to adopt the American system of "law enforcement" and "justice." Can't you just see the Japanese now turning their whole society over to similar "lawless elements" that now dominate America, especially after seeing and hearing the "one-in-touch's" idiotic commentary on the third segment of 20/20? I, for one, as an American, apologize for the intellectual insult cast at the Japanese by Walters in the "Japan's Iron Hand" 20/20 piece, and admonish them to chalk up Ms. Walter's stupidity, for what it is — sheer stupidity.

For both the Americans and Japanese who might be reading this book, I think it important for you to know what the "woman-in-touch" has failed to tell you about America and Japan in the context of the "law enforcement" and "justice" systems:

1. Japan has 556 police officers for every 100,000 Japanese citizen. Japanese citizens gladly pay for this serious police service and protection. The U.S. has only 459 police officers for every 100,000 citizens — and it certainly seems evident, few Americans are happy with the quality of service, or happy about paying for it.

2. There is no widespread use of illegal drugs and its related violent crime in Japan. In Japan, only 29 pounds of cocaine a year is confiscated and there are 2 related drug crimes per 100,000 people; whereas the U.S. has approximately 280,000 pounds of cocaine confiscated every year with 238 drug related crimes per 100,000 people — the U.S. having 8.3% of all arrest related to drugs, while the Japanese have only .3% of all of its arrest related to drugs.

3. What should be of even more importance to the "one-in-touch," the U.S. has 4.4 prison inmates per 1,000 people, while the Japanese have .4 (less than a half-of-a-person) person per 1,000 people of population serving as prison inmates.

Putting The "One In Touch" In Touch With Crime & Reality

The United States Justice Department reported in the 1991 Edition of Statistical Abstract of the United States that in its most current year of complete statistics (1989) there were in excess 14,250,000 "serious crimes" committed in the United States. The number of "arrests" made during this same year, for these same "serious crimes," amounted to less than 2,400,000; an arrest rate of less than 17%. Remarkably, 83% of serious crimes in America went unanswered and without apprehension of the perpetrator.

Convictions rates result in a much even lower percentage "punishment" to "crime", and even then, actual sentencing of convicted felons is rarely for the statutory period prescribed for the offense, but usually for a lesser crime, putting the convicted felon back onto public streets in a mere fraction of the time prescribed by law.

Also worthy of note, the aforementioned 14,250,000 "serious crimes" do not include the 20,000 S&L lootings, the securities frauds of the Wall Street "crowd" and M&A Gangs, government corruption, defense contractor government fraud, forgery, counterfeiting, general fraud, sex offenses other than forcible rape, drug possession and abuse, stolen property, disorderly conduct, unlawful carrying of weapons, prostitution and gambling, amongst numerous other lesser crimes.

If the above 1989 U.S. Justice Department statistics aren't awesome and scary enough for the "woman-in-touch," in April of 1992 the FBI reported that it was their guestimate that the total number of "serious crimes" that occurred in the U.S. (reported and unreported) had reached the astronomical number of 37,000,000 in 1991. One can only imagine how many unreported crimes occurred between 1992 and 1995 since the FBI stopped guestimating unreported crimes in 1992.

Some More News For The "Woman-In-Touch"
The State Of The U.S. Criminal Justice System

1. Loss of Public Confidence In State and Local Police Protection Throughout The United States.
   (a) Rodney King Incident - Los Angeles 1991-1992.
   (b) Robert Jewett Incident - West Palm Beach 1991- 1992.
   (c) Jeffrey Daumer Incident - Milwaukee 1991-1992.

2. Today's Public Perception of State and Local Police.
   (a) Improperly Trained and Overworked.
   (b) Corruption Plagued, Generally from Drug Money.
   (c) Crime Prevention Efforts Negligible or Impossible Due to Alleged Disproportional Use of Police Resources in America's Inner Cities.

(d) No Longer Dedicated to The Fundamental Protection of Private Citizens.

(e) Crime Investigation Beyond "Informant" Level Connections Negligible.

(f) Based on Risks, etc., Police Officers are Underpaid, and are Generally at Odds with Their Own Constituents.

(g) Police Brutality Itself has Become a Serious Citizen Concern.

3. Emergence of "new" types and levels of American, not Japanese, criminality:

(a) Home Invasions and Home Driveway Armed Robberies.

(b) Carjackings, and Related Vehicular Violence.

(c) Rise in In-Home Murders By Outside Assailants.

(d) Drive-By Shootings.

(e) Open and Notorious Use of Crack Houses and Street Sale of Drugs.

(f) Major Rise in the Number of U.S. Mass Murderers.

(g) Major Rise in the Number of U.S. Serial Murderers.

(h) Increase in Violence Associated with Stalking Crimes.

(i) Major Rise in Violent Crimes amongst Adolescents and Preadolescents.

(j) Major Rise in The Number of Crimes and the Number of Weapons Carried in Schools.

(k) Dramatic Rise in Organized Youth Gangs (ages 10-30) and Their Serious Violence.

(GO DIRECTLY TO NEXT PAGE)

Whose Out There Protecting You?
State & Local Police Data (1989)

1. Number of State & Local Police Agencies: 15,118

2. Number of Sworn Officers:

(a) Local Police	376,023
(b) Sheriffs & Deputies	128,728
(c) State Police	50,613
Total	555,364

How Safe Are You?
Reported Crimes Versus Arrests (1989)

Crime	No. of Crimes	No. of Arrests	Arrest %
Forcible Rape*	94,500	31,000	32%
Robbery	578,000	134,000	23%
Burglary	3,218,000	357,000	11%
Larceny	7,706,000	1,254,000	16%
Aggravated Assaults*	952,000	355,000	37%
Auto Theft	1,565,000	183,000	12%
Murder	21,500	18,000	83%
Totals	**14,135,000**	**2,332,000**	**16%**

* Unreported crimes in these categories are estimated to be five and three times more than those actually reported, respectively.

The Private Sector - The U.S. Security Industry

In addition to the various levels of U.S. state, and local government law enforcement, there exists the U.S. Security Industry, the private sector's "personal protectors" and "law enforcers," which compared to its equivalent in Japan is like comparing the "elephant" to the "flea" on the elephant's "you-know-what."

For those of you who don't know, the U.S. Security Industry includes all Private Security Guard Services Companies (i.e. Pinkerton, Wells Fargo, Burns, K-9 Patrol, Advance, Globe, etc.), Armored Car Companies (Brinks, Wells Fargo, etc.), Burglar Alarm Companies, Crime Consulting Companies, Private Investigators, and Protective Device Manufacturers. In 1991, this U.S. industry grossed $11 Billion and employed 1.3 million Americans.

That comes to 515 additional Americans employed per 100,000 trying to keep other Americans from stealing one thing or another. Again, keep in mind that America has 429 sworn federal, state, and local law enforcement officers per 100,000, bringing the total public and private law enforcement force to 944 per 100,000.

There are also well over 20,000,000 burglar alarms (approximately 2 out 9 of every household's in America has one type or another) installed in the U.S. today, costing those Americans who can afford them between $200 and $5,000 for installation, and monthly charges, depending on the monitoring services requested, of between $20 to $500 per month.

It is estimated that in 1992, the cost of this additional security protection will cost the American Consumer almost $12 Billion, and that consumer is you, me, and all of our friends, neighbors and fellow citizens living in the "one-in-touch's" and George Bush's crime-ridden America. Although it may seem un-American, for some reason, researching this chapter, I seem to have developed a greater respect for the Japanese systems of "law enforcement" and "justice" in spite of what the "one-in-touch" has decried it to be.

Where Were Presidents George, Bill, and "The G-Men?" (Is It "Dirty Harry" or "Barney Pfeif?")

You can skim the Glossary in this Chapter for some real insight, but for beginners you might want to read one of the final updates on Mr. Bush's getting all of those S&L looters punished for costing all of us $500 Billion. The up-to-date to which I refer appeared in an article written by Marianne Lavelle for the July 13, 1992 <u>National Law Journal</u> — top left hand corner, front page news. The first three paragraphs of the article are quoted below:

> **WASHINGTON** — Major changes in the Resolution Trust Corp.'s legal staff reflect an apparent policy shift by the Bush administration to ease off of aggressive lawsuits to recover millions of dollars from ex-officials of failed savings and loans, according to high-level government lawyers.
>
> Most of these sources labeled as a political move, the removals and resignations in recent weeks of 28 attorneys of the 75-lawyer unit responsible for the lawsuits; one well-placed insider ascribed the shake-up to a long internal battle between two rival legal offices in the RTC. The sources agree that the RTC now has rid itself of the key lawyers who favored holding liable — under the strict legal theory of negligence — the well-connected, well-to-do people who populated the boards of failed thrifts.

One inside attorney said many colleagues perceived the shakeup as "gross election-year interference by the White House" because so many targets of investigations and lawsuits happened to be prominent individuals with strong Republican ties.

RTC officials flatly deny that either politics of policy changes were behind the personnel decisions. Dismissals of lawyers working on professional liability cases stemmed simply from efforts to streamline agency management, they said, and the number of lawyers in the unit will remain virtually unchanged at 71. "Pursuit of wrongdoers in the savings and loan crisis has been, and continues to be, one of the top priorities for the RTC and its Legal Division, said RTC chief Albert V. Casey in a June 16 statement in response to initial Senate Banking Committee questions about the restructuring.

Now if this is the way "Dirty Harry" gets after the S&L Looters, how much law enforcement do you think you're going to see when it comes to, "or-it- came-to" prosecuting:

1. The United Technologies Corporation (Pratt & Whitney) Defense Contractor bribery-fraud and influence peddling operation dubbed "Operation III Wind," which allegedly bilked our Navy and Marine Corp. out of $250,000,000? No question it'll be a settlement without prosecution if one of Mr. Bush's "two-percenters" is involved. Nothing at all about this should appear unusual to you. Obviously, if George won't tax them, what make you think he'll prosecute them for stealing whatever is left?

2. General Electric Co. and its $69 million fraud against the government in the sale of military jet engines to Israel? Rest assured, no one's going to the "can" on this one, except maybe the "whistle blower" who spilled his guts — there has got to be something, somewhere in his last three year's tax returns that the IRS can dig up!

3. The now defunct Western Savings & Loan Association and the failed $39 million Dicor Loan (total cost of the Western Savings & Loan Association collapse to U.S. Taxpayers $1.7 Billion), where the "fox" watching whatever was left of the "chicken coop" was found out to be none other than RTC's present General Counsel Gerald L. Jacobs found also to be linked previously to Western and Dicor.

First, you've got to ask yourself, how Attorney Jacobs got the General Counsel job at RTC in the first place? Secondly, do you think there will ever be sufficient evidence found now to ever prosecute him, if he did commit any criminal acts?

4. The class-action price-fixing *civil law suit* brought against American Airlines, Delta Airlines, United Airlines, U.S. Air, et al., *by 50 U.S. citizens*, and *not* the U.S. Justice Department, and which was settled in June 1992, after much public outcry, for $44 million in cash and $368.5 million in vouchers. Noteworthy is that Northwest Airlines and TWA had previously settled out of this civil class-action suit for $37.5 million. Pan Am and Continental, both in bankruptcy, but also named in this suit have not settled as of the writing of this book.

You ask: "Where was the U.S. Justice Department?" — Still investigating the allegations; that where! .. You can bet the "mortgage," there won't be any federal "criminal prosecutions" in this case either.

5. You may still have some faint recollection of the infant formula price-fixing case involving:

    - Mead Johnson, a subsidiary of Bristol-Meyers-Squibb.
    - American Home Products Corporation.
    - Abbot Laboratories.

You also may recall the months of settlement negotiations by the F.T.C., and how in July 1992, Mead Johnson settled for $38.76 million. I know lawyers are expensive, but does anyone out there believe that this $38.76 million was paid to avoid the cost of litigation.

You ask: "Where was the criminal division of the U.S. Justice Department?" — Again, don't hold your breath waiting for the criminal division of the U.S. Justice Department to get involved — no one goes to jail in America for anti-trust or grand larceny, especially if they are well connected in Corporate America.

6. The ultimate embarrassment. The Securities and Exchange Commission (SEC) and the U.S. Justice Department and their "settlements" with some members of the M&A Gangs of America, who wantonly "looted" American Industry.

The recovery and criminal penalties — mere fractions of the M&A Gang's ill-gotten-gains given back as their "armies-of-lawyers" paid with the "looted moneys" tied-up the "big-bad-prosecutor-wolves" at both the SEC and the U.S. Justice Department in allegedly "complex negotiations"

— i.e. Michael Milken's $800 million settlement for almost $4 Billion looted — plus four years of soft-time at the "Club Fed" tennis courts — now for that kind of money and minimum prison time, who do you know in America isn't already waiting on line to get in on the next round of "lootings?"

Now that you're really ticked-off, think about this: How many of us, including you, don't root for the romantically inspired "bad guys" in the movies? The Butch Cassidy's and the Sundance Kids, the Bonnies and Clydes, the John Dillengers, and the Al Capones?

How many of us don't fret over a man being hanged or electrocuted, no matter how heinous his crime? Who in America would deny that there exists a special reverence for the multi-million dollar embezzler, the clever jewel thief, or even the S&L "looter?" It's almost as if we admire the courage or "guts" we attribute to these people who went out and made "it" anyway they could.

A young CPA who worked for me during my "Big 8" days summed it up best, after a long discourse on the subject: "So who cares; you gotta live . . . Don't ya?" I've also heard the argument on numerous occasion that this is the very essence of American Capitalism, that it's greed and stealing that makes it all work. Over the years, more than one high-ranking assistant U.S. Attorney (division chief or higher) has advised me that none of us would be employed, honest or not, if it wasn't for the "daring" of others to steal, loot, and pillage — like the hurricane Andrew of August 24, 1992, $30 Billion in property damages, if you want to look at it that way; . . . or was it really $30 Billion in new construction and business opportunity in southeast Florida, putting thousands of people to work for the next two years. It's all has to do with "money" and "profit" — and what else they argue, is American capitalism all about? Insurance fraud resulting from Hurricane Andrew in January 1996 was estimated to have cost the Insurance Industry between $5-6 Billion. Today, insurance costs across all of Florida have more than quadrupled, if you can find someone to insure you at all.

U.S. Business or Corporate Crime

It is estimated that business or corporate crime (internal fraud, bribery, embezzlement, kickbacks, and business property theft) soared to $114 Billion in 1991; and it is expected to rise to over $200 Billion by the year 2000.

So you ask: What is American Business going to do about it? In light of the last paragraph of the last section above, you further ask: Should anything be done about it at all?

As long as this glorification and romancing of past and present American outlaws continues, anyone with a clever personality, good-looks, or great daring, will never be brought to appropriate justice in the United States.

the solutions to our cultural criminal behavior does not lie in the creation of new criminal statutes, but in the enforcement of the criminal statutes that exist without exceptions applying, or special treatment given to white-collar criminals, corrupt government officials, or others who believe themselves to be above the law because of their station in life or profession. Obviously, this preferential favoritism that now exists for certain of our citizens will continue so long as U.S. Attorneys remain political appointees, and as long as state and local prosecutors and the top law enforcement officers at the local level are products of political parties, and as long as judges predominately come from the ranks of lawyers vis-a-vis the same two political parties from which they all come. If we continue to romanticize crime and build hero-folklore around all of our more infamous criminals, neither we, nor they will view their lowest conduct as an excusable part of the *American Way* of life. Chapters 18, 19, and 20 confront the changes necessary to eliminate most of the above criticisms, but even when these American attitudes, and the way American prosecutors and judges are selected for office is changed, there will still be America's illegal drug problem, pornography, organized crime, youth gangs, and there will always be domestic violence. We will never completely eliminate crime or criminal behavior, until you begin to understand the underlying causes of the American criminal behavior, and are willing to participate in the solutions set forth in Chapters 18, 19, and 20 of this book.. These solutions should go a long way in reducing this criminal behavior.

To do nothing will result in ultimate American anarchy where we will surely end up as a nation where every American man, woman, and child individually or in gangs will be fending for themselves against everyone else. The seeds for this eventuality have already been sewn.

The answer is somewhat complex, but very American. First you have to identify the perpetrators. According to the U.S. Sentencing Commission 51.6% of all corporate looting occurs by the owners themselves; another 16.1% is attributable to top executives; middle managers account for 7%; lower level employees account for 1.1% and 25.1% simply disappears, with no known or identifiable perpetrator.

There's always the question of funding a program to catch criminal wrong-doing within the corporation, when it may be the CEO or the business owners who are conducting the criminal wrong doing?

Many public corporations have beefed-up their internal audit departments, but, as is well known to those who have worked in American business or industry, it is very difficult to find highly qualified personnel for this function; after all, how can you attract highly qualified personnel to run an internal-audit-function when there is generally no career path to which it leads? It should be obvious to anyone, whether or not he or she has participated in business, that an internal auditor cannot rectify Corporate Crime where 67.7% of the people he reports to are the owners and top executives of the corporation are doing the stealing. Thus it may be concluded that the internal "policing" function of the internal auditor is only effective, at maximum, to perhaps prevent between 8.8% and 33.3% of existing corporate crime.

What if a million dollar corporate crime is discovered? Now we get to corporate America's aversion to the "airing-of-the-dirty-laundry-syndrome." I know of not one American Corporation that would embarrass itself by revealing it had been the victim of any major corporate crime, and thus most of these crimes go unpunished. As a general rule, the perpetrator of corporate crime has the "mind-set" that in Corporate America, crime-does-pay.

I am personally aware of one corporate CEO who stole over $5,000,000 and was never prosecuted criminally. When asked to make restitution, he refused, saying he'd rather "go public" — the matter was quietly dropped.

Now what of the corporate crimes that are not of the "incestuous" nature as described previously, but "external" in nature? Such as defense contractor fraud, and criminal violation of the antitrust laws?

What is the Federal Government Doing About It?

Well, first of all, the United Stated Sentencing Board created by the U.S. Congress in 1984, instituted on November 1, 1991, stiffer fines for corporate misconduct — now you know who ultimately pay these fines — either the consumer (you) who gets it passed along in the product's "price," or the Corporate shareholder whose profit share is reduced as a result of the "fine." Even the federal and state governments share a little of the cost of the "fine" in a "trickle down" sort of way, vis-a-vis the tax system: The lower the corporation's profits, the less paid in corporate income taxes. What of our present cadre of G-men, the so-called Elliott Nesses? This aspect America's "law enforcement" efforts is set forth in the Author's Glossary at the end of this chapter.

What Can You Do About It?

Nothing. Unless you want to be known as a "Rat," "Squealer," or "Whistle-blower," and have severe limitations put on whatever advancement potential you might have had in the corporation, or elsewhere. (Read Chapter Four again, if you seem to be missing the gist of this conclusion.)

A Final Note To The "One-In-Touch"

Based on all of the data presented in this chapter on American criminality, and the last 20 minutes of your own program, perhaps you ought to re-examine your criticism of the Japanese "law enforcement" and "justice" systems, or perhaps you should really get "in-touch" and spend a few weeks in one of America's "inner cities" or one of America's middle-class suburbs and then be required to do a twenty minute comparative piece on the American prison system and the constitutional rights of the American criminal in light of her despair over the police system in Japan.

- AUTHOR'S REVERSE "SPIN" GLOSSARY -

- "WHAT THEY SAY IT MEANS" & "WHAT IT REALLY MEANS" -

Antitrust Laws:

What they say these laws mean: Federal laws that regulate trade in order to maintain competition and prevent monopolies. The Clayton Antitrust Act of 1914 and the Robinson-Patman Act of 1936 made illegal various forms of price discrimination. No longer could companies charge different prices to different buyers (dealers), such as offering different advertising and promotional allowances, unless offered to all buyers on equal terms. Also made unlawful was "collaboration" for the purpose of restraining trade by and between two or more business enterprises that operated in the same market.

The Clayton Act further prohibited "tying" (the sale of one product on the condition that the purchaser also buy another product, or agree "not" to buy the other product from anyone else); prohibited "exclusive dealing" agreements (generally agreements to deal exclusively with one seller or buyer); prohibited "total requirement agreements" (an agreement whereby the seller of raw materials or other goods is required to sell all of these raw materials or goods to meet the "future requirements" of the buyer at a fixed price, regardless of future price increases, solely because of the buyer's superior bargaining position in the market); prohibited "corporate mergers" that tended to substantially lessen competition; and prohibited "interlocking directorates" (prohibited members of the Board of Directors of one corporation or bank, to also serve on their competitor's Board of Directors). Antitrust Laws carry both severe civil and criminal penalties and are generally prosecuted, although rarely, by the U.S. Justice Department. In most cases it is damaged plaintiffs who seek redress in civil antitrust actions.

What these laws really mean: There have been so few cases prosecuted under the Antitrust laws by the U.S. Justice Department, one has to wonder if Congress repealed this legislation along with one of their midnight pay raises to repeal these laws. Can there be any question George Bush or his successor, Bill Clinton would have signed such legislation? Needless to say, with the "horse-long-gone-from-the-barn," the U.S. Attorney General, now, is looking to use these same antitrust laws to thwart the nasty trading practices of one of our so-called "trading partners."

Federal Aviation Administration (FAA):

What they say it means: An agency that is apart of the Department of Transportation, the FAA being charged with regulating air commerce to foster aviation safety; promoting civil aviation and a national system of airports; achieving efficient use of navigable airspace; and developing and operating a common system of air traffic control and air navigation for both civilian and military aircraft.

What it really means: One need only look at the current state of the American Airlines Industry to understand the effectiveness of the Federal Aviation Administration. Since 1985, three major American Airlines have gone out of business and three other remain on the brink. All this, while failing also in its primary role or maintaining air safety standards for the vast majority of American air carriers.

Federal Communications Commission:

What they say it means: Created in 1934 by the Communications Act, its mission is to regulate interstate and foreign communications that are done via wire, radio, television, telephone, telegraph, and cable television operations as well as two-way-radios and radio-hand-operators. The FCC is also responsible for all U.S. Satellite Communications.

What it really means: One need only look at the quality of network broadcasting, the quality of cablevision broadcasting, and the state of radio broadcasting in the United States to evaluate the effectiveness of the FCC. It is extremely difficult to understand how after twelve years of Republican Administration with direct Administrative control over the FCC along with the Republican Party's philosophy of "family and moral values," when both our televisions and radios airwaves are so clogged up with so much pornography and hourly attacks on both family and moral values. One has to question whether this is not just another example of the Republican laissez-faire principle of "no" government regulation, "free market," "money-making-at-any-price" business enterprise.

Independent Counsel:

What they say it means: Pursuant to Public Law 100-199, also known as The Independent Counsel Reauthorization Act of 1987, the Attorney General of the United States is authorized to request the appointment of an "Independent Counsel" whenever the Attorney General receives information sufficient to constitute grounds to investigate whether any person of significant power in the Executive Branch of Government (generally top-level White House Staff, Cabinet members and Federal Agency Heads as set forth in Title 5 U.S. Code, Sections 5312 and 5313) may have violated any Federal criminal law other than a violation classified as a class B or C misdemeanor or infraction. Two note worthy examples where Independent Counsel were appointed: The "Iran-Contra Scandal," and "The HUD-Samuel R. Pierce Jr. Scandal."

The request and appointment of Independent Counsel is neither a "free," nor "nonpolitical" decision of the U.S. Attorney General; the essences of the legislation putting the U.S. Attorney General into the position where he becomes a "criminal violator" should he not appoint the Independent Counsel to investigate the alleged criminal violations of federal law that usually comes to his attention from the Congress. The Independent Counsel Law is structured in this manner (the U.S. Attorney General charged with the preliminary investigation) to avoid the appearance of a breakdown in the "Separation of Powers Doctrine," and for lengthy Executive Branch constitutional challenges. The Independent Counsel Reauthorization Act of 1987 is codified in Title 28, Sections 591 through 599 of the U.S. Code.

What it really means: As eluded to above, it is the "well warranted" distrust of the Democratic Congress for the Republican controlled Executive Branch of Government, between 1988-1992, and vise-versa between 1992-1996 and "actually" an extension of the "Separations of Powers Doctrine" whereby, indirectly, the Congress breaks its way into the Administration's "chicken coop" vis-a-vis the U.S. Attorney General's forced appointment of Independent Counsel (i.e. the Administration is otherwise charged with investigating and bringing itself to justice for its own wrong doings — the most classic of " the-fox-guarding-the-chicken-coup" situations). For whatever argument, after the abuses of power by Presidents Nixon, Reagan, Bush, and certainly Clinton, it would appear that the Independent Counsel Law should probably remain intact for as long as there is an American Government.

Insider Trading—Rule 10b-5:

What they say it means: Under rule 10b-5 of the Securities Exchange Act of 1934, persons, generally directors, officers, and key employees, and their relatives and others in positions to capitalize on "insider information" (non-public information that would effect the share price of the stock, if known to the public) are prohibited from trading on this information.

What it really means: As much a integral part of American Capitalism and the business of Wall Street, as oxygen is necessary for human life. About 99.99% of "insider trading" abuse occurs, not in the primary market (IPO market) where investment is made in PP&E, but in the secondary markets, where the high-rolling takes place, and where fortunes can be exchanged around the world in seconds. Given human nature, and the daily abuses of those operating with "insider information," it's surprising the federal government wastes U.S. Taxpayer money on trying to enforce the 10b-5 rule, especially when handicapping stocks on just the rumor of such information could very well become the hottest handicapping item on the Wall Street's gamblers' "tote board," if the rule itself were rescinded.

National Security:

What they say it means: What they see it means is covered in Title 50, U.S. Code, Sections 401 through 432, entitled "War and National Defense." Section 401 specifically states that it is the intent of the Congress to provide a comprehensive program for future security of the United States; to provide for the establishment of integrated policies and procedures for all the departments, agencies, and functions of the Government related to National Security; to provide a Department of Defense, including the three military Departments of the Army, the Navy (including Naval Aviation and the United States Marine Corps.) and the Air Force under the direction, authority, and control of the Secretary of Defense; to provide that each military Department shall be separately organized under its own control of the Secretary of Defense; to provide for the unified direction under civilian control of the Secretary of Defense but not to merge these Departments or Services; to provide for the establishment of a unified or specified combatant command, and a clear and direct line of command to such commands; to eliminate unnecessary duplication in the Department of Defense, and particularly in the field of research and engineering by vesting its overall direction of control in the Secretary of Defense; to provide more effective, efficient, and economical administration in a Department of Defense; to provide for the unified strategic direction of combatant forces, for their operation on the unified command, and for their integration into an efficient team of land, naval, and air forces but to establish a single Chief of Staff over the armed forces nor an overall armed forces general staff.

Now that you have an idea of what the Congress has sought to include under the umbrella of National Security, we can now turn to the White House's "National Security" umbrella coverage. And here there exists the "President's Intelligences Oversight Board," created by Presidential Executive Order No. 12334, dated December 4, 1981, and later amended by Executive Order No. 12701 on February 14, 1990.

The President's Intelligence Oversight Board is comprised of three members, who are unpaid and serve at the pleasure of the President. The President also has the sole power to appoint the three members of this board from among allegedly trustworthy and distinguished citizens outside of the Government, who are qualified on the basis of achievement, experience, and independence. The Board has the authority to use such full time staff and consultants as authorized by the President, so that it may fulfill its duty to inform the President (yes, the President not the Congress or anyone else) of all intelligence activities that any member of the Board believes to be in violation of the Constitution or laws of the United States, Executives orders, or Presidential directives. And if this independent Board finds the White House or any of its staff personnel violating the "law" under the guise of National Security, the Board in its discretion is to forward to the "Attorney General" (not an Independent Counsel) its reports concerning these intelligence activities that the Board believes may be unlawful, so that the U.S. Attorney General, who coincidentally reports also to the President, might review the Board's concern regarding the "unlawfulness" of intelligence activities.

As loaded with conflict-of-interest, and as "intellectually retarded" as the last paragraph might sound, Section 5 of this Executive Order 12334 contains probably the most nonsensical aspect of this Order. It states: "Each member of the Board, each member of the Board's staff, and each of the Board's consultants shall execute an agreement **never** to reveal any classified information obtained by virtue of his or her service with the Board except to the President or to such persons as the President may designate (i.e. squealers get ten-years in the "Can" for going "public").

Lastly we have Executive Order No. 12356, Section 1.6, subsection (a), which states: In no case shall information be classified in order to conceal violation of law, inefficiency, or administrative error; to prevent embarrassment to a person, organization, or agency; to restrain competition; or to prevent or delay the release of information that does not require protection in the interest of National Security.

What it really means: A term flippantly used by our elected and appointed officials of the federal government, when it is in their best interest, not to reveal government information that might be harmful to themselves. It rarely has anything to do with the "National Security" or welfare of the United States. The privilege of National Security has been invoked by such Presidents as Richard Nixon, Ronald Reagan, and George Bush in various scandals such as Water Gate, Irangate, and the shooting down of an Iranian Airliner by the USS Vincennes over the Persian Gulf that killed 290 civilians on July 3, 1988. The National Security "ploy" was also used extensively during the Persian Gulf War, and as a matter of common knowledge, it is still unknown how effective our trillion dollar weapons systems performed, how much aid and assistance the U.S. Government gave Iraq just prior to the commencement of Desert Shield and Desert Storm, and the real cost of American lives due to "friendly fire."

With respect to above Executive Order No. 12356, Section 1.6 (a): How much more confidence might we Americans have if the Section were reworded as follows: Any information, classified or to be classified, which may include, or appears to include or conceal any violations of law, inefficiency, or administrative error; or prevents embarrassment to a person, organization, or agency; or restrains competition; or prevents the delay of release of information that does not require protection in the interest of National Security shall be immediately communicated to the **U.S. Senate's Select Committee on Intelligence** and the **U.S. House of Representative's Permanent Select Committee on Intelligence**.

Perhaps this is what our "founding fathers" might have had in mind when they incorporated the "Separation of Powers Doctrine" into the Constitution they drafted in 1787?

Saturday Night Special:

What they say it means: In some areas of America it refers to a cheap thirty-eight caliber hand gun used to stickup the local convenience store. In the context used here, it refers to the sudden attempt of one company to take over another through a public tender offer, utilizing a rash of surprise maneuvers that were generally announced at 8 A.M. on the Saturday morning of a three day weekend. This martial art form of the M&A Gang was so distasteful even to the Congress, that in 1968 it saw fit to pass the Williams Act which placed severe restriction on tender offers and required disclosure of direct or indirect acquisition of 5% percent or more of any class of stock ownership in any publicly traded American company.

What it really meant: Up until at least 1968, American history will show the "M&A Gang" hadn't taken care of enough members of Congress to callous their sensitivities as to the "lootings" of American Industries that were then beginning, and quickly multiplying like cancer.

Securities & Exchange Commission [SEC]:

What they say it means: Created by the Securities Exchange Act of 1934, the Securities and Exchange Commission is charged with administering, enforcing, and promulgating the rules and regulations permitted by the Securities Act of 1933. The SEC is made up of five commissioners appointed by the President on a rotating basis, each for five-year terms. No more than three commissioners may be from the same political party, this allegedly to assure the "independence" of the SEC from political pressure (Are you now ready to puke?).

As the chief law enforcement agency and regulator over the securities industry, the SEC is charged with: (1) promoting full public disclosure and protection of the investment public against malpractice in the securities market; (2) preventing fraud or misrepresentation in the issue of securities offered in interstate commerce or through the mail; (3) regulating all operations of the National Securities Exchanges and Associations, which include investment companies, investment counselors, and advisors, over-the-counter brokers and dealers, and virtually all other persons and firms operating in the investment or securities industry; (4) approving the rules promulgated by the Municipal Securities Rulemaking Board, a self regulatory organization responsible for regulating the municipals securities industry; and (5) pursuant to the Securities Act amendments in 1975, establishing a National Market System and a nationwide system for clearance and settlement of transactions of all securities exchanges.

What it really means: This is America's most expensive training ground for the most ambitious of America's Lawyers and CPAs, who swing into of the SEC generally for periods of between one and five years, and then who return to their CPA or Law Firms to command princely salaries far in excess of their peers, who were less astute in maximizing their career potential. The SEC is to Lawyers and CPAs who enter the securities industry, as the U.S. Attorney's office is to those entering into the Law Firms specializing in such areas as antitrust, white-collar criminal defense, illegal-drug criminal defense, etc.

And, as long as we're on the subject of career potential, it is no less prospectively lucrative to the law school graduate who takes his first job as a "clerk" to either a federal district court judge, an appellate court judge, or if great fortunes are to be had, to a U.S. Supreme Court Justice. Here again, for an initial sacrifice of some up-front-money, one can command lucrative salaries from law firms joined later, because of the connections established in these initial lower-paid positions.

To further demonstrate the incestuous relationships that exists, one need only recall SEC Commissioner John S.R. Shad, who prior to serving as SEC commissioner was the Chairmen of the major securities firm E.F. Hutton. It was during Shad's tenure as chairman of Hutton that the check-kiting scandal occurred. Scandal or not, in 1982, Shad was appointed SEC Commissioner by President Ronald Reagan. One need not be a "Sherlock Holmes" to figure how this obvious conflict-of-interest played itself out in the actual prosecution of E.F. Hutton, with John S.R. Shad at the helm of the SEC during the period this case was prosecuted.

Finally, contrary to must wishful thinking by "investors," the SEC does not read, nor analyze any registration statements, whether it be an Initial Public Offering (IPO), or Shelf-Registration, or any other filing unless there is some form of public outcry. In fiscal 1992, approximately $150 million of U.S. Taxpayer money was spent to operate the SEC.

Selective Prosecution (U.S. Dept. of Justice):

<u>What they say it means:</u> Also referred to as "prosecutorial discretion" this term refers to the wide range of alternatives available to the U.S. Attorney in both criminal and civil cases. It includes such matters as the decision not to prosecute, to prosecute, the particular charges to be prosecuted; or the realm of government civil litigation, the discretion as to which claims are to be prosecuted; plea bargaining and subsequent prison term reduction deal-making; and recommendations for sentencing in criminal actions. U.S. Attorneys and the Department of Justice, justifies "selective prosecution" on the grounds that the "biggest spending" government in the history lacks sufficient resources to prosecute certain kinds of cases, and other cases are merely just not cost/benefit justified. Get that, you get murdered or swindled and it may not be cost beneficial to prosecute the case!

<u>What it really means:</u> During Republican Administrations, the majority of Republicans don't get prosecuted. During Democratic Administrations, the majority of Democrats don't get prosecuted. Any individual or corporation represented by anyone of the top 250 law firms in the United States has a "much lesser" chance of getting prosecuted than someone who cannot afford representation at all. It should also be noted that it is traditional for most U.S. Attorneys, or Assistant U.S. Attorneys, to rotates either in from one of these 250 major firms or upon leaving the U.S. Attorney's Office, returns to one of these major firms at a substantially larger salary than he had prior to his "public service" in the U.S. Attorney's Office.

U.S. Attorneys - The U.S. Justice Department:

<u>What they say it means:</u> Each U.S. Attorney in the United States is appointed for a four-year term by the President of the United States with the advise and consent of the U.S. Senate. Each appointed U.S. Attorney must reside in the district from which he or she is appointed, except those appointed in the District of Columbia and the Southern District of New York so long as they reside within twenty miles of these two federal judicial districts. (Very few Republicans reside within the "inner cities" of Washington D.C. or New York City. For that matter, neither do many Democrats.) On expiration of his or her term, the U.S. Attorney continues to perform the duties of his or her office until a successor is appointed and qualifies; and each is subject to removal from office by the President of the United States. Assistant U.S. Attorneys are appointed by the Attorney General of the United States and are subject to removal by the U.S. Attorney General during their tenure. Pursuant to Title 28 U.S.C. Section 547 the duties of the U.S. Attorney within his district is to prosecute all offenses against the United States, prosecute or defend, for the Government, all civil actions, suits or proceeding in which the United States is concerned unless satisfied on investigation that justice does not require the proceedings; appear on behalf of the U.S. to defend all civil

actions, suits or proceedings pending in his district against the United States; and make such reports as the U.S. Attorney General may direct. Pursuant to Title 28 U.S.C. Section 546 the Attorney General may appoint a U.S. Attorney for the district in which the office of the U.S. Attorney is vacant, except where the President has appointed the same individual but where the U.S. Senate has refused to give advise and consent (i.e. "approval"). Prior to 1986, vacancies which occurred in the office of U.S. Attorney were filled by the district court for that district. Now the district court may only appoint a U.S. Attorney until the vacancy is filled, which is now clearly in the sole purview of the Attorney General of the United States.

What it really means: One must first ask: Where candidates for the office of U.S. Attorney come from? Who measures their qualification to serve in this office? Who recommends them for appointment? The answers to these questions might be enlightening to many. U.S. Attorneys generally come from large law firms and are generally (in 99% of the cases) an active member in the political party of the then serving President. It is generally the local Bar or Bar Association that evaluates the qualifications of the candidates to perform the function of U.S. Attorney. It is usually the U.S. Senator of the state who recommends appointment of U.S. Attorneys in his state, and if the Senator happens to be of the same political party as the President, the appointment is literally assured and only the advise and consent of the U.S. Senate remains an obstacle thereafter. The office of U.S. Attorney has always been a "special patronage plum," in that it permits the office holder to serve government in a very influential position for generally a four-year term, and then returns him to a very lucrative position in the law firm generally from which he came. (See Selective Prosecution.) Now how well does all of this work for all of us Americans working 9 to 9? One need only ask: Where were all of our U.S. Attorneys during and after the "looting" of America's S&Ls? Where were they during the destruction of America's Industrial Infrastructure as looters violated U.S. Securities laws, and Antitrust laws? And what were they doing to prevent the laundering of Billions of Dollars of drug related money as revealed by the BCCI-First American Bankshares-Clark Clifford Scandal? So much for political patronage and merit selection by America's bar associations!

COMPOSITE DICTIONARY

Anarchy: The absence of government. A state of society where there is no law or supreme power; lawlessness and political disorder; destruction of, and confusion in government. At its best, it pertains to a society made orderly by "good manners" rather than law, in which each person produces according to his powers and receives according to his needs; and at its worst, a terroristic resistance of all present government and social order.

Federal Trade Commission (FTC): The FTC was created in 1915, pursuant to the Federal Trade Commission Act of 1914. Its purpose is to protect America's free system of enterprise and competition in the interest of a strong economy. The FTC is directly responsible for promoting "free" and "fair competition" in interstate commerce in the interest of the public through prevention of price-fixing agreements, boycotts, combinations in restraint of trade, unfair methods of competition, and unfair and deceptive acts and practices. The Federal Trade Commission has five commissioners, who each serve a seven-year term. Not more than three members may be selected from the "same" political party. Not only empowered to investigate interstate commerce, the FTC is also empowered to investigate certain aspects of foreign commerce (i.e. foreign goods falsely labeled as made in America) as well as to take legal action to enforce the laws that fall under its jurisdiction. The FTC also has jurisdiction over the advertising industry, and one of its prime functions is to prevent fraudulent and deceptive advertising, as well as advertising that creates or results in unfair trade practices.

Food and Drug Administration (FDA): The FDA, is an agency of the U.S. Department of Health and Human Services, responsible for setting safety and quality standards for food, drugs, cosmetics, and other household substances sold as consumer products. The FDA is also charged with conducting research, inspection and licensing of drugs for manufacture and distribution, and all food content labeling. The FDA is also in charge of administering the requirements set forth in the Food, Drug, and Cosmetic Act of 1938, which prohibits the transportation and interstate commerce of adulterated or misbranded foods, drugs or cosmetics.

Interstate Commerce Commission [ICC]: The Interstate Commerce Commission was created by Congress pursuant to the Interstate Commerce Act of 1887. The ICC regulates railroads, trucking companies, bus lines, freight forwarders, water carriers, oil pipelines, and transportation brokers. The ICC is charged with the responsibility of assuring that the carriers it regulates provide the public with rates and services that are fair and reasonable. The ICC does not regulate the airline, air-freight, or air-passenger business in the United States. The ICC is also responsible for: prohibiting unjust price discrimination, rebates, draw-backs, preferences, pooling of freights, etc., and requiring schedules of rates to be published.

Maloney Act [Section 15A of the Security & Exchange Act of 1934]: Legislation passed by Congress in 1938 to amend the Securities and

Exchanges Act of 1934 by adding Section 15A, which extended the regulation of the Securities and Exchange Commission (SEC) to the Over-The-Counter market (OTC) through a requirement that National Securities Firms doing business in this market register with the SEC. This group of firms is also known as the National Associations of Securities Dealers (NASD).

Sandbagging: A term used to describe the efforts of government officials, or those testifying under oath to avoid telling the truth; or to avoid describing their roles or efforts in an illegal activity or its continued "cover-up;" or to avoid exposing themselves to the wrath of the public for their questionable and sometimes illegal acts.

Sandbagging, when under penalty of perjury, involves the use of such techniques as: "I don't remember!"; utilization of the Separation of Powers Doctrine by the Executive Branch of Government when subpoenaed by Congress to offer testimony on certain government actions; and out-and-out fabrication of events, facts and records to cover-up what has actually occurred.

10

The Government's Role in Greed, Wealth, and Capitalism

It was in the latter part of 1985, and all of America's **top-two-percenters** were going wild. Word had it that personal fortunes were being doubled and tripled and that anyone finding himself asleep for even the shortest period of time, might find himself back in the **middle-class.** It was during this time that one of my millionaire clients called upon me in order that he might not miss the last train out of town. This client is now dead, so I don't think it matters much that I tell his story. Even if he were alive, I don't think he would mind the whole world knowing, as shameless as he was, of how absolutely certain he was that he was the "greediest man in the whole world."

It was one of those drizzly days in New Purchase, New York, when I arrived at his home. The overcast and bleakness created by the low-hanging afternoon clouds seemed to make the rows of five-acre estates with their brick and slate-roofed mansions more imposing than usual.

As I pulled into the long driveway that led to George's house, I still didn't have a clue as to what was on his agenda nor the reason for his sense of secrecy and urgency. I could only hope he hadn't gone completely overboard and done something as ridiculous as murder. The relationship between George and his wife Anita was always on the brink of very serious violence.

I was relieved when Anita opened the door and directed me into the study; a room that was more of a boardroom than what you would expect of a home study. George was sitting with his back toward me in front of the large desk, which was nothing more than a large conference room table, in the seat that he always referred to as the **power seat**, the seat directly in the center of the table that commanded a view of the entire room. It was also the seat that gave George the closest proximity to the person he had invited to his lair for a quick swindle or other nefarious deed.

"It's not so much any more **how full my plate is**," George began, "**it's now a matter of high my plate is filled**. We're living in a new era and I'm not going to be left behind!"

George and Anita, in 1985, already had a net worth in excess of $100 million, and that was on a balance sheet that excluded their three fully paid homes, two yachts, and eight or nine antique and other sundry automobiles, a count even they were never sure of.

George continued, "I'm putting you in charge. Find out who's making the `big money' and let's get in with them as fast as we can."

By the first quarter of 1989, the now dead George had more than tripled his 1985 $100 million net worth to over $340 million, and if he hadn't gotten himself killed falling off a horse while endeavoring to be a star polo player at 46, he might very well have quadrupled his wealth again by 1996. George was in the export-import business: "exporting" his financial wealth into plants he owned in some of the biggest slum centers of Mexico, and "importing" the goods those plants manufactured back into the U.S.

George was said by many to have been a **visionary**. A **Great Architect** of the **new American Capitalism** formulated in the late 1970s. That's what they said in his eulogy. A truly great American. A man, whose basic understanding of "free-markets," "free-trade," and a "global economy" and "the efficient allocation of resources" made him hundreds of millions of dollars. What wasn't said about George was the special "mastery" he had at the "efficient allocation of all those resources" into his own pocketbook.

To some of you fans of the TV show, <u>The Rich & Famous</u>, you're probably asking: "So what's wrong with making a couple of hundred million bucks? It's the **American Way**! **Isn't that what America is all about?"**

To others of you who were in the Reagan, Bush, or Clinton Administrations and/or in America's economic **top-two-percenters,** this is a wonderful example of American Capitalism working at its best.

For those of you who haven't "made it," or who can't get beyond your own amoral "envy," George was probably best described to me in a comment by his wife two days after his funeral when I showed up with his Last Will & Testament. I, of course, was still attempting to demonstrate my condolences to her when she remarked: "What the hell are you looking so sad about? He was nothing but a loathsome shallow human being, who just never got enough. So don't give me any of the sympathy crap . . . besides it's all mine now, and I've also got my own lawyer."

Now, let's put George and all of the rest of us in economic perspective. A quick trip though some theories of government and economics may very well help some of you make millions. For those of you with no millions, and just "envy,"— a better understanding of your present plight and where you might very well be ten years down the road.

If you have neither "millions" nor suffer from "envy," and really don't care about the growing "economic chasm" in America and the rest of the world, you may just want to go on to the last two chapters of this book to at least get the "solutions" that first lured you to this book. I urge the rest of you to read on so that you might better understand the reasons why America has gotten to where it has.

THE FRAGILITY OF WEALTH

First, it's important that we all get a better handle on the term "wealth." Something beyond the concept of simply "lots of cash," "megabucks," or such comforting proverbial notions of the envious, such as: "You can't take it with you!", or "Easy come, Easy go!", etc.

So what is "wealth"? My twenty years as a CPA has taught me that "wealth" is the "measure" or "value" others place on what you possess and vice-versa, or what you can provide in goods and services, conditioned upon:

1. The actual or perceived scarcity of an asset in context of "aggregate demand" by others for that same asset.

2. Underlying the said "aggregate demand" for this asset, whether it be goods or services, is the aggregate base of consumers or collectors who are desirous of it, willing and able-to-afford-it, or bid-it-up. If there is absolutely no desire or demand for the possession, good, or service, it has "no" value whatsoever. Thus, what is "wealth" today, could very well be "worthless" tomorrow, if no one wants the asset at all.

3. All possessions, services, and goods, including money (wealth) may, at times, be of little or no value in certain circumstances. For example:

    (a)   There exists no desire, or willingness, or ability to exchange money or other goods or services for the possession, service, or good.

    (b)   The government, where the asset owner and asset reside, is no longer able to enforce the laws that protect the rights of ownership of the asset or other personal or real property, or public property, thus subjecting it to be stolen, robbed, looted, or pillaged by the hordes of have-nots and wannabees.

    (c)   The majority of people, who include amongst others, the American consumer, the American taxpayer, and the American blue-collar and white-collar working classes become so disenfranchised (the significant loss of confidence in the government, the society, their employment, and themselves) that they refuse to produce "necessities" (i.e. bread, electricity, etc.), except in return for prepayments of large blocks of currency or other wealth-related assets. Once confidence is lost in the "currency" commodity itself, those tangible assets once thought to be of great value, now fetch a fraction of their former worth. One need only study the history of post-World War I Germany, the Great Depression of 1929-1938, or even the collapse of the American Real Estate Market of 1989-1992, to gain further insight into this asset-value-depletion phenomenon. Stay tuned! By 2000, there is more apt to unravel in the American economy, especially since the nation's fragile economic structure currently hangs squarely on the shoulders of "Wall Street" and its ability to hold on to at least a 4000 Dow Jones Industrial Average. The "Dow" is in the 5000-6000 trading range as this book is being written.

Now, if "wealth" can be so fragile, especially when concentrated in the hands of so few as to deprive the majority of its desire to preserve its value, why would so many be obsessed, or perhaps possessed by the sole ambition to possess most, if not all of the world's wealth? The answer: It's simply "human nature" for most, "insecurity" for a lot of others, and "easy pickings" for the rest.

How do such individuals accumulate such large fortunes in a nation supposedly founded upon the primary democratic principle of "government of the people, by the people, and for the people?"   The answer: The willful failure of present day American "representative government" to regulate, *in any manner*, the present <u>inefficient</u> allocation of the nation's resources, or to control the continuous lawless looting of America's assets and resources.

We have at last revealed the ***American fantasy***, that the unlimited accumulation of wealth and power by the "individual" is the very proof that our ***so-called*** American Democracy is working.

In this present environment, the two words "government regulation," have been so successfully maligned by the Reagan, Bush, and Clinton Administrations (i.e. there fifteen minute second sound bites on the subject) that it has become a part of our dysfunctional American Culture to believe any form of "government regulation" is paramount to restoring the evils of Communism, not just in the former USSR, but right here in America.

Contrary to America's present cultural assessment of "government regulation" being "evil," it was precisely the <u>absence</u> of this so-called "evil" that will cost every American man, woman, and child not less, and probably a great deal more than $20.00 a month every month for the next 30 years: The estimated cost is $500 billion to the U.S. Taxpayer for the

S&L Lootings subsequent to government <u>deregulation</u> of America's S&Ls as imposed by the Congress in 1982 at the insistence of President Reagan: understandably America's rich man's hero and unexplainably, also America's poor man's hero.

One need only ask: Is there any discernible difference between "freedom" being snuffed-out by the forces of "mighty weapons" versus the forces of "economic greed" which are deeply camouflaged by the colors of "red, white, and blue" and the absurdity that the unfettered accumulation of wealth by the "few" to the detriment of the nation is a part of America's constitutional protections bequeathed by our nation's founding fathers.

It appears almost axiomatic that there exists a necessity for some "government regulation" by a government premised on the principles of "government of the people, by the people, and for the people." However, it is *not* logical to rely on those whose only aspiration is to amass wealth to both regulate and govern; as demonstrated by the aristocracies of Europe at the turn of the millennium and through the early part of the twentieth century.

The empirical evidence is clear. The unfettered accumulation of wealth by the "few" *does not* result in even the slightest "trickle-down" of wealth to those in the lower economic classes.

The inertia the last three Administrations in this area *is not* based on "national security," nor "national welfare," nor any of America's democratic ideals or principles. This inertia is based on the Republican Party's own unique Darwinian concept of American democracy and economics, later adopted by Bill Clinton to ward off the 1994 Republican threat of dethroning him in 1996. This subject will be more fully discussed from different perspectives in Chapters Ten, Eleven, and Thirteen.

WHAT IS ECONOMICS?

We talk about it every day. We know it has to do with jobs, inflation, and whether or not our standard-of-living will improve or decline. Since as early as 1972, the majority of Americans have voiced their concern by making every presidential candidate since Richard Nixon make economics the focal point of their election campaign.

To these ends, it is important that every American understand the "five" most important questions economic theory addresses. It is with this understanding that the primary objectives and workings of any economic system (capitalism, communism, etc.) can be gained by the individual citizen. The five basic questions are:

1. What goods and services are to be produced in terms of quality, quantity, and nature to satisfy the needs and desires of the nation's citizens?

2. How are these goods and services going to be produced, delivered, and made available to the consumer?

3. How will both national and world resources be allocated, used, and replenished?

4. For all of those goods and services that are produced, how will they be allocated amongst the nation's consumers?

5. How will changing circumstances and conditions that effect the efficient allocation of the nation's resources be dealt with? Some of the present-day circumstances and conditions that must be forthrightly dealt with are:

    (a)   World Overpopulation.
    (b)   The Depletion of the Nation's and World's Natural
    resources.
    (c)   Global Warming.
    (d)   The Deterioration of Law & Order.
    (e)   The Use of Illegal Drugs.
    (f) Racial & Ethnic Violence.
    (g)   The Decline in National and World Morality.
    (h)   The Decline of the American Family Structure.

Most important, but not listed above, is the decline of American nationalism and patriotism in every economic class, racial group, ethnic group, and religious group.

Complicating the five questions set forth above are American greed; the decline in the American standard of living; profit motives and incentives; limited resources; natural disasters; the current chaos in America's social and economic class system; racial, cultural and ethnic differences; and America's competition for world resources, the control of which is now concentrated in America's and the world's ***top-two-percenters.***

Further complicating all of the above is the supply-side of the marketplace where suppliers may "purely" compete, "monopolistically" compete, compete in a "structured oligopoly." The forces on the demand-side of the marketplace also compete, consumers competing only against the forces of scarcity, contrived scarcity, and the most powerful of psychologically influencing forces of advertising or marketing. (see the Author's Spin Glossary and Definitions Section at the end of this Chapter for specific definitions of the previous terms.)

As both simple and or complicated as all of this seems to be, it has but one singular objective: "The efficient allocation of resources," which is synonymous with the "supply-side of the equation." The supply-side resources have always been:

1. Land
2. Labor
3. Investment Capital
4. Raw Materials

The "efficient allocation" refers simply to who, given the four above resources can produce the "finished product" at the lowest cost and thus, in theory, sell it for the lowest price. I use the term "theory," because in theory this works, but in reality as soon as market share is concentrated in the hands of a few, prices become set at whatever the market will bear; there being no competition in the marketplace when the market is controlled by a few. This is also known, in economic parlance, as "monopoly."

Notwithstanding The Propaganda Of The Bush & Reagan Years, What Should Be The Economic Objectives & Obligations Of American Government?

The same economic objectives of government are taught in every entry-level high school economics course, and repeated in every entry-level college economics course given in America. I myself went back to some of the textbooks I used over twenty years ago to see if much had changed.

It was all the same. Somewhat boring, somewhat complex, and a lot of progressively more difficult statistics and graphs as I proceeded to turn each page. Then I came across some penciled-in lecture notes at the top of one page which read:

"Economics is only as complex as the society itself makes it. No matter how complex it's made out to be, economics will never be more than the fruitless study of the interaction of irrational men, their money, their government, their wealth, their poverty, their power, and their institutions, in the context of trying to explain and predict quantitatively, their insatiable need for greater-and-greater consumption. Nevertheless, the study of "economics" alone serves the indispensable function of occasionally identifying, sometimes excusing, and always quantifying the natural resources, and the social, moral, and consumption objectives of each and every nation-state — nothing more, and nothing less."

Oddly enough, not only did the lecturer's notes above still seem to have the same relevance today as it did twenty years ago, but the economic objectives of government in general had also not changed.

Now, it's time for you to measure these six basic economic objectives of government against those "obligations" and promises owed you, and made by the Reagan, Bush, and Clinton Administrations and the U.S. Congress. As you may have noted, I do not restrict my standards to "aspirations" as implied by the term "objectives," but use the word "obligations" to engender the notion that in America, it's government that serves the people, and not vice-versa.

Does the present Administration and Congress:

1. Provide an adequate system of defense to assure the security and safety of it citizens?

2. Assure the efficient and free continued flow of resources to maintain and improve its citizens' standard-of-living?

3. Regulate economic growth to assure adequate employment opportunities for its citizens?

4. Within it domestic borders, provide an adequate and efficient system of law enforcement, social order, and justice to protect its citizens from violent crime, white-collar crime, and organized crime (i.e. illegal drug importation, trafficking, and production), etc?

5. Provide to its citizens an adequate system of education and job training to assure that each citizen may achieve his or her required educational level, or the level of technical skills to further himself or herself, and thus the nation as a whole?

6. Provide a sound social and economic environment that assures price stability, free-competition, true entrepreneurial growth, free entry (admission) for all of its citizens into both government and business sectors based solely on the factors of ability, hard-work, creativity, experience, education, and specific learned and licensed skills?

With the possible exception of the first objective above, were you able to reconcile any of the other five objectives to the objectives or accomplishments of the past three Administrations? I certainly could not!

If you choose to argue that objectives 2 through 6 are not the obligations of government due the people, then for what purpose does such a government serve, or exist, given the argument by this government itself that its foundation relies on the concept "of the people, by the people, and for the people?" Perhaps the question that should be asked is: Has our two-party system so divided us as a "people" that our present form of government is no longer appropriate, if America is to survive the twenty-first century, a century that will certainly be one of very limited resources? It is this question that will inevitably have to be addressed if America finds no other solution to avoid its present divisive and destructive course.

Some of our major policy makers and leading academicians have suggested that the only way the decline in America's standard of living can be reversed, is to divide the country into five or six smaller nation-states, so that they might be more manageable, especially as the population continues to explode. I reject that solution for two basic reasons: First, it would reduce America as a world force to something comparable to the nation-states that formerly comprised Yugoslavia. Second, the chaos that would result from the division itself, given the greed and current ownership of land in America, would be even greater than the chaos that followed after the 1948 breakup of India and Pakistan and the 1989 breakup of the Soviet Union, combined.

A SECOND LOOK AT MY CLIENT, DEAD GEORGE.

Now that you possibly have some additional scary concepts and other tools to add to your own, you can now begin to work in this general framework to understand what dead George was all about. You should also now be able to better deal with the complexity and simplicity of both economics and government, as it effects you and America. We can now go back and take a closer look at George.

First, we should now understand that George was (he has been dead seven years) the quintessential laissez-faire capitalist on the far right side of the economic spectrum. Not only did George detest all governmental regulation, he also detested the notion of paying one cent in taxes to support "government regulation," except as it related to national defense (the military), national security (the military), or the "state's" police power (the state's para-military).

Especially abhorrent to George were taxes used to fund securities regulation, bank regulation, the FDA, the FCC, and those welfare and retirement "entitlement programs" which George certainly didn't need for himself or his family. George never failed in his belief that his tax contributions should be earmarked only for a strong national defense system, and his state taxes should be strictly earmarked for strong local law enforcement.

Even George, before his early death at age 46, recognized that there had been a *quid pro quo*. George had given up some things: the comfort of believing he didn't have to lock his door at night was gone by 1960; the early evening picnics he had enjoyed with his family in New York's Central

Park ceased in 1965; his joy of late evening walks to window-shop the stores up and down Fifth Avenue came to an end in 1982, the street cluttered with too many muggers and too many homeless begging vagrants to allow George to feel secure; and by 1985, he had become a slave to his insurance company, paying over $120,000 a year in annual insurance premiums to protect his personal fleet of automobiles, his two boats, and the three homes he hardly had time to enjoy.

AMERICAN DREAMS AND FANTASIES

It seems all Americans want to be millionaires, and some find nothing less than entry into the ranks of billionaires as minimally acceptable. We all know that this is an impossible dream for but a few of America's 266 million citizens, but we all cling to the belief that each of us has that "one" chance. Now the bad news, the odds of becoming a billionaire, are approximately twenty times the odds of hitting the state lottery. The odds of becoming a millionaire are about the same as hitting the lottery. The odds of being born into a family of millionaires by far the best shot, is slightly less than 1 in 125. For those of you still clawing to get up that ladder, the "stats" suggest your best hope is reincarnation.

What if you did have the wonderful good fortune to "make it" and you got to live like George in a place where you could practically enjoy every penny of it, America, the home of the stretch limo, the 20 bedroom home, the Olympic size swimming pool, and the wonderful cadre of cultured people. Those are the other *top-two-percenters* that you could mingle with at the finest hotels, country clubs, and elite private schools from kindergarten to Harvard, and with whom you could share the sheer joy of having as many as 260 million other Americans "sucking-up" to you! Wow! Now pretend you've made it, and you're now there. You're now a part of the elite.

Now think about this, and I'm not asking you to answer out loud. Now that you've made it, would you want *everyone* else to be able to enjoy your private club?

Well, for most of us that would defeat the very purpose of getting there in the first place. So we play out our fantasies, always keeping alive our hopes of someday "making it" ourselves. We buy lottery tickets in record numbers for record jackpots and praise those others who've "made it," lawfully, unlawfully or luckily, in the hope there's still a place up there for us. In the case of the Milkens, Boeskys, and Keatings our initial reaction was, "live and let live," as we all secretly aspired to have the same good fortune and status as they achieved. Unfortunately, thousands of Americans, even knowing of the crimes committed by Milken, Boesky, and Keating, still see these three individuals as three of the America's quintessential success stories.

On The Subject Of Greed & Capitalism

Some people, like my deceased client George, are just born greedy. Others learn it quickly as they assimilate into the most current version of the American Dream. "More is always better. Having most is best!" You certainly can never have enough if you intend to provide for your children's children and their children's children, ad nauseam.

Greed should never be confused with ambition, nor saving, nor the reasonable accumulation of wealth, nor the fruits of legitimate capital investment. Neither should it be dismissed as a virtue just because it allows the "likes" of a Michael Milken to contribute tens of millions of dollars to charities of his own choice from the money misappropriated from others.

Nor should greed ever be perceived as the common-denominator "virtue" of American Capitalism; nor should it be accepted as necessary or be described as the driving force of American Capitalism. Nor should greed ever be likened to the "invisible hand" behind the "efficient allocation of resources" as espoused by many of the so-called gurus of modern American Capitalism.

Greed and capitalism can be kept as mutually exclusive as oil and water, or as explosively mixed as tossing a lit match into a can of gasoline. The agent for the former is "government regulation," and the catalyst for the latter is simply "deregulation." It was not capitalism that brought America from the end of World War II to where it is today, but rather the unregulated greed that was allowed to infect America in the early and mid-1970s and which was allowed to run rampant through the 1980s that brought on this once-unimaginable decline.

It was when greed was elevated to this false virtue of being the driving force behind American capitalism that the seeds of Reaganomics were sown. It was those same seeds that grew into our dilapidated industrial infrastructures, our drug and crime ridden cities and suburbs, our grid-locked corrupt government, and most importantly, the loss by the majority of Americans of their hopes and dreams.

The fact is there is no better economic system than that of capitalism, and certainly no other economic system that can better put America back on its feet. I do not refer here to the mutation of the American capitalism experienced in the 1980s, but the American capitalism set forth in Chapter Nineteen of this book. This is American capitalism that is truly "of the people, by the people, and for the people" and which, for the benefit of all Americans, is "regulated" by an American "government" that is also truly "of the people, by the people, and for the people," an American government described in Chapter Twenty of this book.

- AUTHOR'S REVERSE "SPIN" GLOSSARY -

- "WHAT THEY SAY IT MEANS" & "WHAT IT REALLY MEAN" -

Cost-Push Inflation

What they say it means: A rise in "prices" caused by the competition amongst different groups or whole sectors of the economy attempting to increase their relative share of the national income — such as when labor unions strike for higher wages, thus resulting in their employers passing along these increases in product price increases to consumers; or where corporate management decides to triple their salaries and pass these added costs again to consumers. The cycle doesn't end here since the consumer who has had to pay more must demand more in terms of his own income requirements; and so the "cycle" goes.

What it really means: To some: American capitalism working at its very best. To others: American capitalism working at its worst.

Deflation:

What they say it means: A period of time when the purchasing power of the dollar is rising where both prices and wages are in a period of decline. However, when prices are rising, but their underlying costs are rising faster (profits are decreasing), the term "relative deflation" is said to be occurring.

What it really means: A recession is in progress, or a depression is on the horizon.

Demand-Pull Inflation:

What they say it means: A rise in the price level that is occasioned by too much money chasing too few goods. If these price increases occur at the time when some of the resources of the economy are idle (during recessions or depressions) it is called "reflation."

What it really means: Historically, in America, demand-pull inflation is generally a consequence of both American and foreign manufacturers controlling the "supply-of-goods" in violation of antitrust laws. It is effected mostly by utilizing such techniques as stock control, threatened cancellation of shipments, substantial advertising expenditures creating excessive artificial demand, and direct impact "over-sell" marketing, generally to those consumer groups least able to deal with the concept of money, the "infant" and "adolescent" consumer markets of the United States.

Disinflation:

What they say it means: A deliberate decrease in the general price level by governmental action generally as a result of the effects of long-term inflationary trends.

What it really means: Something so contrary to American capitalism and its profit-motive that such governmental action is propagandized by Corporate America as either latent Communism or treason.

Franchising:

What they say it means: In the private sector of the U.S. economy, this term refers to the granting of a contractual "license" to generally use the name, or sell the products or services of a manufacturer or franchisor (those firms such as McDonald's, Burger King, Dunkin' Donuts, that are in the "franchising" business) to generally a "retailing-entrepreneurial-motivated investor" with upwards of $500,000.00 net worth to use the franchisor's name and or products on terms and conditions mutually agreed upon. In the Sports Industry, it is a grant by a professional sports associations such as the National Football League (NFL), the National Basketball Association (NBA), etc.) to field a sports team (sports franchise) in a given geographic location under the auspices of the "league" that issues it. The business of "franchising" has its foundation in Patent Law, Copyright Law, Trademark Law, federal and state trade-name law, state trade secret laws, and general contract law.

What "franchising" really means: One need only ask what it would cost to start a new sports team or sports league, or start a new hamburger, or other fast food business to compete with those already franchised in the United States. As many of you will or have found out, "franchising" has had a chilling effect on the concept of "free competition," contrary to the "free market" capitalism our government professes. Anyone who wishes to compete in any one of the mature franchise industries, requires enormous amounts of capital, the purchasing power to achieve the volume discounts enjoyed by the major "franchisors" currently, and be able to expend significant resources to achieve market share. As the franchising industry has matured, so have the profit opportunities for those seeking to be franchised (franchisees). Here again, pseudo-American capitalism has created another form of quasi-monopoly, if not a true monopoly in the absolute sense of economic theory, again contradicting the very premise of capitalism's economic foundation; free and open markets and the unfettered freedom to compete. I point to so many of these contradictions of "American capitalism" throughout this book, not because I condemn them, but because I believe that the contradictions are inevitable and necessary, and more importantly, of great "precedence" value to the economic solutions put forth in Chapter Nineteen. It is essentially my first defense against America's *top-two-percenters* saying that the concepts in this book are an attempt to dismantle an American capitalism that in reality doesn't exist for most Americans who are not already in the top-two-percent.

Gentrification:

What they say it means: A term used to define the economic process of rehabilitation and revitalization of an older neighborhood by those of greater wealth, who expend large sums of money to improve the property that its last owner was financially incapable of doing. Gentrification occurs as many homes are sold by lower income people to those wealthier persons, and the wave generally continues through entire neighborhoods.

What it really means: Money not only buys convenience, but more wealth. In America, it wasn't long before the quickly rising suburban upper middle-class discovered that it was spending more time traveling between their homes in the suburbs and their place of employment in the financial centers of the city, than they were spending at work. In order to minimize the commutation time between home and work, the process of "gentrification" was begun. In most instances, enormous profits were realized by those persons with sufficient wealth, who had the foresight to purchase certain dilapidated properties within certain slum areas in the "inner city." As whole neighborhoods turned over, the former residents realized that the purchase price received for their former property was far below the current value of the rehabilitated price, even when the cost of rehabilitation was added on. In some instances, properties that had been sold for $20,000, and rehabilitated for a cost of an additional $200,000, were resold within one year of the rehabilitation for as much as $2 and $3 million. It has been asserted by many of those lower income persons displaced from their neighborhoods, that the gentrification was nothing more than a conspiracy of the middle and upper classes to deprive them of the unknown profits that existed in their former homes. Close, but no cigar! What they still haven't figured out, is that it was a "conspiracy," not by the ordinary upper-middle-class, but by the "banking-upper-middle-class" who were well versed in the use of "other people's money" (OPM), and who financed many of these "deals" with the same bank's money they worked for.

Greed:

What they say it means: As viewed from the top, a rather reprehensible insatiable desire for wealth, power, and comfort for those have-nots in America's middle and the poor-classes. As viewed, looking from the bottom: "Sonovabitches can't get enough! I just know I'll get there someday myself, *whether by hook or by crook.*"

What it really means: The most important singular driving force in America, effecting every aspect of American life from business ethics to family relationships. Over 80% of all Americans believe "greed" is synonymous with the "American Way," and one of the most important qualities necessary if one is going to succeed.

Inflation:

What they say it means: The rise in the price of both goods and services that results in lost purchasing power of one's money. Spiraling inflation is said to occur when prices for those same goods and services occur at an increasing rate as opposed to a constant rate, thus causing the money or currency effected to even more rapidly lose its value.

What it really means: It's the "F" word of capitalism. "Fear." First the middle-class is frightened-to-death that it might lose the purchasing power of both its already illusory pension fund savings, as well as the wages it anticipates in the future; secondly the "aged" have the fear-of-death put to them in that their life's savings will deteriorate so rapidly that they will no longer be able to eat, much less survive; and finally the real "fear," the fear that is felt by America's *top-two-percenters*. It is the mortifying "fear" that their vast fortunes, accumulated through exhaustive hours of plotting, conspiring, stealing, and efficient exploiting of the capitalistic system, will be drastically reduced, or possibly lost completely, as did happen in pre-WW II Germany. Several of today's underground economists believe that a strong dose of inflation might be the only way to make the National Debt manageable; the theory being to pay off a $5 trillion debt with dollars, perhaps worth one-tenth of their present value.

Intellectual Property Rights and Law:

What they say it means: The body of law which includes Patent Law, Copyright Law, and Trademark Law. Patent Law grants to an individual or corporations exclusive rights to make and sell a new invention during a specified period of time; it constitutes a legitimate monopoly. Persons who violate or infringe on another's patent without legal permission may be found guilty of patent infringement, for which both significant damages and equitable relief (i.e. court imposed injunctions) may be granted. Patents generally are for a period of 17 years and are presently codified in Title 35 of the U.S. Code.

Copyright protects the works of artists and authors, giving them the exclusive right to publish their works or to determine who may publish them; copyright is exclusively a matter of federal law and exists for a limited period of time, presently 28 years, with a renewal available for an additional 28 years. Copyright is presently codified in Title 17 of the U.S. Code. Trademark protects the trademark owner of any mark, word, letter, number, design, picture or combination thereof in any form or arrangement which is: (a) adopted and used by a person to denominate goods which he marks; (b) is affixed to his goods; and (c) is not a common or generic name for the goods or a picture of them, or a geographical, personal, or corporate, or other associated name, or design descriptive of the goods or their qualities, ingredients, properties, or functions; and (d) the use of which is prohibited neither by legislative enactment, nor in otherwise defined public policy. Trademark protection infringement is afforded by common law actions of "unfair competition" once the trademark has been sufficiently identified with the goods, by various state statutes, and federal law as codified in Title 15 of the U.S. Code.

What it really means: Although well intentioned by the original drafters of this legislation, these laws have resulted in the greatest exploitation of America by corporations and the legal profession, and an even greater exploitation: that of the "M&A Gangs" and the "looters" of the S&Ls. For example: one singular record release, that reaches "number one" on the charts in American popular music is worth approximately $15 million today. You can rest assured that it is not the "artist" who is receiving the bulk of these monies. On the consumer side, this exploitation is directed at those below the age of eighteen (indirectly, an exploitation of the pocketbooks of the parents of this group). And if you already haven't caught on, it is not necessarily the artist or writers who make the vast sums of money from copyright protection, although no one should be thinking "benefit dinners" for these multi-millionaires. It is just that the vast bulk of the "bucks" are made by the producers, the corporations who own the recording labels, the distributors who bring the records to market, and the retail sellers who deliver these products at the retail level. Important here is to also recognize we again have another example of Government's need to limit the "free market" aspect of capitalism, or perhaps this is just another element of today's American capitalism that allows those "top-two-percenters" to control and manipulate it? I shall not discuss the downside of "patents" (think "patented drugs"), nor "trademarks" (think "hamburgers"), but here also you have numerous examples of significant, and I'm certain unintended legislative consequences.

Maslow's Hierarchy of Needs:

What they say it means: Maslow, one of America's leading sociologists in the 20th Century defined five human motivational needs by order of their importance in the overall scheme of emotional development. These five "needs" in descending order of achievability are: (1) physiological (the body must be fed, (2) safety — the body needs a fort, (3) social — the body needs friends, (4) esteem — the body has to like itself, and (5) self-actualization — the body finds "peace of mind." According to Maslow, once each "need" is satisfied, the next "need" as set forth in the above hierarchy then emerges as the next motivator. Once "self-actualization" is achieved, according to Maslow, "man" has reach fulfillment as regards his inner peace.

What it really means: Obviously Maslow either preferred the abstract, or was unaware of America's and the world's "self-actualizing" capitalists;

for sure he couldn't have possibly read the July 13, 1992 edition of <u>Forbes Magazine</u>, that listed the world's 401 billionaires, 101 of whom are Americans. And, perhaps it would have been too offensive for Maslow to have just boiled it down to the acquisition of different levels of "money?" Do I hear some of you yelling "foul" out there? Calm down, I was just testing your emotions not espousing a new school of sociology.

Price-Wage Controls:

<u>What they say it means:</u> Government employed controls over both prices and wages which are generally implemented during server periods of inflation. Oddly enough, it was a Republican Administration under President Richard Nixon that ordered the only price-wage controls (commonly referred to as wage-price controls) in recent American history. This occurred on August 25, 1971, when Nixon ordered sweeping economic changes in an effort to curb inflation and strengthen the dollar. Oddly enough, it was organized labor (unions) that were most adamant about not cooperating with these controls. It was also during this same period that Nixon decreed the U.S. would no longer convert U.S. Dollars into gold, and thus the era of American money backed by U.S. gold reserves ended. As Nixon had noted in 1971 regarding this decision, "The chips had just run out."

It should be noted, that many European countries that experimented in the past with permanent price-wage controls concluded that they really "don't work" — this based on the fact that their citizens always developed methods of getting around these controls, making them both ineffective and even more inequitable than the usual inequities resulting from "free market" capitalism.

<u>What it really means:</u> Since both U.S. Organized Labor and Corporate America will always seek unrestrained wage and price increases to inequitably increase their "piece of the American pie," inflation's worst enemy, price-wage´ controls, cannot be employed regardless of the suffering by those members of the middle-class or the "poor," who are neither associated with Organized Labor, nor directly benefited by the profits of Corporate America. The "top-two-percenters" have always been in favor of "wage controls," regardless of any "free market" hoopla, but see "price controls as the death-knell of American capitalism.

Stagflation:

<u>What they say it means:</u> The condition where the economic condition of the country is plagued by a combination of slow economic growth, high employment, and rising prices. "Stag" prefix referencing "stagnation" referring to the slow economic growth and high employment, and the "Flation" suffix derived from "inflation," or rising prices. In periods of stagflation, characteristically, fiscal and monetary policies intended to

stimulate and economy generally tend to only heighten the inflationary effects.

What it really means: A condition that has generally been absent from the American economic condition since 1973-1974, when OPEC imposed four bold increases in oil prices challenging all previous economic theories, but which could return so long as the United States remains dependent upon foreign oil or any other commodity or good it must import to survive.

Structural Inflation:

What they say it means: Probably the most insidious form of inflation that exists, in that it exists as a matter of law, either through statute or contract, and automatically triggers certain price or wage increases based upon price rises in one or more inflation tracking indices (i.e. Consumer Price Index). Examples of structural inflation are the COLAs (cost-of-living-adjustments) legislated into such "entitlement programs" as Social Security, Congressional salaries, and wage increases predicated upon contractual agreements between labor and management where wages are increased based upon the CPI.

What it really means: Once the United States falls into a general pattern of inflation, the factors of "structural inflation" as set forth above tends to cause the "spiral inflation effect," where one price increase, in turn causes another, which in turn, then again causes another. Such inflationary conditions may require government intervention with such tools as price-wage controls, etc., especially if these structural inflationary elements are not legislated out of existing law, and legislatively outlawed in the private sector. As stated previously, government has other, more equitable means, of controlling inflation in its initial stages than by attempting to correct its effects by continually shooting itself in the foot.

Upward Mobility:

What they say it means: Upward Mobility is the axiomatic result of the forces of American capitalism when left undisturbed by government. As it pertains to the individual, it only requires tireless work, entrepreneurship, and an unfettered desire to succeed. The acquisition of an MBA, JD, MD, DDS or other advanced degree or professional certificate (i.e. CPA) can only accelerate the process of "Upward Mobility."

What it really means: An occurrence as natural as river flowing down a stream, prior to 1900 given America's (1) natural resources, (2) unlimited land, and (3) geographic location, setting it three-thousand miles away from Europe and almost seven-thousand miles away from Asia. Although unnoticed by most Americans, all of the three aforementioned factors quietly disappeared sometime long before the beginning of the

1950s. The Upward Mobility of the 1980s was not a result of America's unlimited resources, unlimited land, or America's proximity to Europe or Asia, but rather a function of America's unlimited ability to borrow Trillions of Dollars both domestically and internationally, while completely unconcerned and unfettered by any thought of ever having to pay any back.

Yuppie:

What they say it means: A young and upwardly mobile MBA, lawyer, investment banker, or "dealmaker" who usually works (plays) in and about Wall Street earning between $100,000 and $5,000,000 a year, and resides in a $500,000 plus condominium on the upper east side of Manhattan.

What it really means: Another one of America's long list of inferior "products!" — Designed in the early 1970s, requiring too much energy to run it, being too large and grotesque to be exported, and no longer deemed to be "fashionable" by the present crop of "wannabees" who today are having trouble getting placed in "stockrooms," much less "boardrooms."

COMPOSITE DICTIONARY

Dumpie: A word coined in the early 1990s to describe the new plight of the 1980s "yuppie" — now a "dumpie" or "downwardly mobile professional."

11 | American Government -

Representative Betrayal

How A Bill Becomes A Law?

Step One. First there is the perceived need for a new law (legislation) that is first born out of some idea or necessity to regulate or deregulate the social order, commerce, or the present governmental process. Simply said: Someone, or some group wants to change the way someone else, business, industry, the clergy, or government has been or not been doing business.

Step Two. Either a Senator or Representative introduces this "idea" or "need" by drafting a bill and sending it to the clerk of the House who assigns it a number and title. This procedure is termed the "first reading." The clerk then refers the bill to the appropriate Senate or House committee.

Step Three. If the committee (a small minority of our elected powerful representatives) opposes the bill, they immediately table or kill it; the perceived *need* or *idea* is dead. If the bill is not opposed, the committee holds hearings to listen to opinions and facts offered by members and other interested people; usually other *representatives* of the *special interest groups* who, 90% of the time, are the originators of the *idea* or *need* behind the bill in the first place. After these hearings, the committee then debates the bill and usually offers amendments. A vote is taken and, if favorable, the bill is sent back to the clerk of the House.

Step Four. The clerk reads the bill to the House. This is termed the "second reading." Members may then debate the bill and suggest amendments to satisfy other demand of *special interest groups* who have found out about the bill and caucused with their personally bought- off congressman.

Step Five. The "third reading" is simply by "title" and the bill is put to a voice, or "roll-call" vote of the House of Representatives. For the bill to remain alive it must pass by a majority of the House, if not, it will be "killed" on the floor.

Step Six. The House passed bill then goes to the Senate for a vote, and here it may also be defeated, or passed, with or without amendments to satisfy more *special interest groups* demands. If defeated, the bill dies. If passed with amendments, a joint Congressional committee works out the differences and arrives at a compromise to make all the *special interest groups* happy.

Step Seven. After its final passage by both the House and Senate, the bill is "enrolled" and sent to the President. If he signs the bill it then becomes law. However, he may also veto the bill by refusing to sign it, and send it back to Congress with his reasons for the veto.

Step Eight. If the bill has been vetoed, the President's objections are then read in the Senate and debated, and a role-call vote is taken. If the bill receives less than two-thirds (66%) vote, it's defeated (66 of 100 Senators, are needed to override the President's veto in the Senate.). If the bill receives at least two-thirds, it is sent to the House. If the House also passes it by at least two-thirds, (It takes 272 of 435 Representatives of the House to override the President's veto.) the President's veto is overridden and the bill becomes a law. If both chambers don't override the President's veto the bill is killed. It should also be noted that if the bill had originated in the House it would have been first read and debated and voted upon, then sent to the Senate.

Step Nine. If the President wishes to neither sign nor to veto the bill he may retain it for 10 days — not including Sunday — after which it automatically becomes a law even without his signature. However, if Congress has adjourned within those 10 days, the bill is automatically killed; this indirect rejection is termed a "pocket veto."

The above set of Nine Steps demonstrates how a bill becomes a law, but does not really show the true genesis of legislation, nor does it show how "bills" are ultimately funded or paid for. Legislation is born in many ways. Organized groups and individual citizens barrage the Congress with petitions and suggestions for new laws every day. Every department of government submits so-called "executive communications" to the Congress calling for legislative action. In many cases a bill which a government department may want to see legislated into law will almost be in its complete form when delivered to the Congress. Again, the only way a bill can be introduced officially is by a Senator or Representative as set forth in Step Two.

By present practice of Congress, the first "two readings" (see steps two through four above) are accomplished simply by introducing, printing, and distributing the proposed legislation to the body's members. The bill is then catalogued, recorded onto the computer, and referred to the appropriate Standing Committee or Committees of the House or Senate. It is usual practice for the full committee that gets the proposed legislation to immediately refer it to one of its Standing Sub-committees that holds hearings, studies the legislation, and then reports back to the whole committee.

The final and most important process is called the "mark-up." This is when the committee goes over the proposed legislation ad infinitum, word-for-word, and section-by-section to ensure that the legislation conforms to the purpose and intent of the controlling Standing Committee or Committees of the House and/or Senate. The "marked-up" bill is then returned to the Senate or House and placed on the legislative calendar for floor action which sometimes appears to the uninitiated as inaction. Each bill that reaches this stage is also accompanied by a statement from the Rules Committee, known as the "rule" which sets forth the length and form of House debate; and what type of amendments, if any, will be considered appropriate and acceptable for debate. One must never underestimate the power of the "Rules Committee" if he or she is to ever have a full grasp of government grid-lock.

Resolutions as well as bills, are processed similarly in both the House and the Senate. Each chamber can end up with different versions of the same bill, and each chamber can amend the other's bill. Differences are generally resolved by the appointed representatives of both chambers meeting in conference. The result of their efforts is a "Conference Report" which is sent back to both chambers for final approval on the floor. If both chambers adopt the Conference Report the legislative process is complete and the bill is "enrolled" (See Step Seven above.), which means that it is published in final form by the Government Printing Office and signed by both the Speaker of the House and the President Pro Tempore of the Senate (The Vice-President of the United States acting in his constitutional role as President of the Senate) or by the then presiding officer of the Senate. Once this is done the bill is then dispatched by messenger to the White House for consideration by the President (See Steps Seven through Nine above.).

If the bill does become law (i.e. it has survived the initial phase of the Nine-Step grid-lock process set forth above), this new law then enters the "budget" and "appropriations" grid-lock. This is the planning and funding phase where the U.S. Taxpayers' monies are allocated so that this new law, and all other laws requiring expenditure of government monies, may be lawfully financed.

The Federal Budget process created by Congress in 1974 established an elaborate series of procedures for arriving at each year's new federal spending plan. Although the process seems childishly simple on paper (Remember the influence of just one segment of the *special interest groups*? That one segment of 4172 PACs must all be satisfied.), it has proven to be all but unworkable, or so complains the President and many members of the Congress. First, there is the deadline of September 30th. Since the Federal Government operates on a fiscal year (October 1st through September 30), the Federal Budget must be passed by the Congress and signed by the President no later than midnight of September 30th of each year, or government shuts down.

Now, consider all of the *special interest groups* and the *pork* needed for all of the *special pork barrels* of our elected representatives, and let's not forget the pork needed to satiate those *special interest voter groups,* such as the Gray Panthers. Try to imagine these formidable pressures upon the 435 members of the House and the 100 members of the U.S. Senate. The deadline for the looting, pork barreling, and other sundry and miscellaneous "divvies-up" of the U.S. Treasury and its "power-to-borrow" must be in place by the final deadline date set by budget time table, September 25th of each year.

One can only imagine, how in the short period of nine months, 535 members in the House and Senate can come to "back-room" agreements to accommodate all of the thousands of *special interest and lobbying groups* to whom they are obligated. At this juncture, these members of the House and Senate are either *re-financed* and *re-elected* or put back into the *real world*. Most times this results in an even more lucrative life style than they've enjoyed as a so-called public servant — joining the ranks of the"top paid" corps of Washington Consultants and Lobbying Specialists.

The last hurdle in the "appropriation process" is the President of the United States. He signs all appropriation bills. After all, it was his original Budget that was sent to the Congress 15 days after the Congress had convened the previous January. This is not to imply that the President's Office of Management and Budget Director has not been involved in every phase of the Congress's eight month partisan bickering process. The overall objective of all this bickering, as you have already gathered, is essentially one of each political party and their *special interest groups* ultimately having a complete victory that can only be achieved when one or the other gets complete control of both chambers of Congress as well as the Presidency so that the U.S. Treasury, the biggest *"pie"* of all, need not be shared at all.

Returning to "process," it is ultimately the President who must sign the Budget Reconciliation (the final resolution of all "special interest group" differences) in order that the Budget may become law effective October 1st, the first day of the Government's fiscal year. If the President doesn't sign the Budget Reconciliation, neither the budget nor the appropriations become law and government must cease to operate.

Every President (Carter for altruistic reasons, Reagan and Bush for political power, Clinton for switching power) who has operated under the present U.S. Budget System has been publicly hostile to the reality that he was ultimately faced with the choice of either approving, or disapproving the entire Federal Budget. If he disagreed with the allocation and the appropriations passed by the Congress for a specific department or program (the other party's "special interest group" got more of the "quid pro quo," his only option was to veto the entire Budget and then watch government cease operating. One commentator's Note: "Several Americans have suggested that this would be a noble experiment on the part of the President, giving us all an opportunity to see if the Federal Government and its operations are all that necessary."

Thus there has been a call by the last three Presidents for the "line-item veto" — a veto power that would allow the veto of specific "appropriations," while allowing approval of the overall Federal Budget. As should be obvious to most, this would not square well with the eight months of bickering that went on amongst the 100 Senators in the U.S. Senate or the 435 members of the U.S. House of Representatives. Imagine the horrifying nightmares each of them must have! The possibility of the President undoing all of his or her, and sometimes their, "good works" with a single line-item veto could be the determining factor whether he or she would be re-elected. This very powerful "line-item veto" might very well be the forbearer of the very power our already less-than-trustworthy President might need to finally end America's Two-Party System of Government. Can there be any doubt who will then control all of the cash flows out to the *special interest groups* and its derivative power?

Now, for those of you who don't remember George Bush, he was the staunchest supporter of the line-item-veto, a "power" he told us he require if he was ever going to get control over that wildly free-spending Democratic Congress of the 1990-1992. Oddly enough, this same George Bush, the last Republican President, submitted to the Congress a record-spending 1993 Federal Budget of $1.515 Trillion, this compared to his first Federal Budget request in 1989, for the period October 1, 1989 through September 30, 1990 which approximated $1.252 Trillion. Worthy of note, Mr. Bush's Budget in 1989 was submitted when the country was not being ravaged by a two year recession and while there was still some hope left in the country that there might yet be a future for America. Mr. Bush's 1989 Budget resulted in a deficit of $220.4 Billion, capped by the government's failure or inability to raise more than $1.031 Trillion in federal taxes for the 1989 Fiscal Year.

Now folks, given all of this can there be *any reasonable explanation* for Republican President George Bush's 1993 record-spending Federal

Budget? Perhaps, George believed America was populated by 260 million people suffering from dyslexia. How does our last Republican President's 1993 Federal Budget square with his twelve years of political rhetoric that demanded the balancing of the federal budget, a reduction in taxes for the middle-class, a reduction the annual federal deficit, and a capital gains tax for the rich? Obviously it is the U.S. Taxpayer who is in need of the line-item-veto, and not George or Bill, or any of the other politicians who have or will occupy the White House regardless of party affiliation. And George Bush till this day believes that he lost the 1992 election to Clinton because Perot split the vote. Perhaps, George, it was the double-talk of **what you said**, and then **what you did,** and the fact that we former Republicans did just **get it,** just before you could get yourself **re-elected!**

WHAT A MEMBER OF THE U.S. SENATE AND HOUSE OF REPRESENTATIVES COST AMERICANS ANNUALLY

As a CPA, I feel obliged to tell you that the "costs" set forth below do not include for our Senators or House members the most princely of retirement benefits, the numerous, but invisible **perks** (perquisites) of high office (everybody's taking care of you — luncheons, use of private corporate jets, the right financial deals for families and close friends, patronage, etc.), nor do I quantify such benefits as Representative Harry Smith (D-FL) was able to acquire nefariously as a result of the power of his high office, which unfortunately for Harry, hit the front page of every Florida newspaper in May of 1992 and ultimately causing his demise.

As of July 1, 1996, each member of the House and Senate is paid a base salary of $136,000.00 annually. In addition, each Congressmen and Senator is appropriated funds to run his Washington office and district offices within his state. Congressmen are allowed a total of $500,000.00 annually to operate their offices in Washington and their home districts. In addition to this $500,000.00, each Congressman in 1996, was allowed an annual "franking" allowance (free U.S. postage), so that he or she might correspond with his constituents and others. No question, it's going to be a tough election year for some. Most Congressmen maintain staffs of between 5 and 12 people, depending on their seniority in the House of Representatives and the geographic size of their Congressional District.

U.S. Senators are also paid $136,000 annually, but they are appropriated much larger sums of money to run their offices, both in Washington and in his or her home states. The amount of money each Senator is provided depends upon the size of their state. The Senators from the largest populated state, California, receive approximately $2.2 million each and employ between 55 and 65 people each, whereas the Senators from the fourth largest state, Florida, receive $1.7 million and employ between 45 and 55 staff people each in both Washington and their home state. Because U.S. Senators serve larger constituencies than do House members, they are allowed substantially larger "franking" allowances determined by the number of citizens residing in their state. Now if each Congressman is allowed $330,000 in "franking" for his or her 500,000 constituents, I leave it to your imagination how much your two Senators receive, especially those representing such states as California and New York with almost 30 million constituents each.

Many of you are now scratching your heads and asking: "How did congressional salaries jump from $125,100 to $136,000? Wasn't that $125,100 everyone was up in arms about during that sneaky 1991 after midnight pay-hike they passed for themselves and the judiciary?" The answer is quite simple. To avoid the unpleasantry and shamelessness of ever again having to debate amongst themselves or before the U.S. Taxpayer future increases in their salaries, the members of both the U.S. House of Representatives and U.S. Senate when voting their pay raises in 1991 almost unanimously included in this bill a COLA (Cost-of-Living-Adjustments) provision, that now automatically raises their pay based upon increases in the cost-of-living index. You guessed it! No automatic decreases in congressional salaries were legislated for decreases in the cost-of-living-index, or for malfeasance of office, absenteeism, tardiness, or incompetence. These boys and girls in the congress are now fully recession and depression proof, and will never feel the pain of their fellow citizens if a recession or depression ever comes about again? Now aren't we all supposed to be in the same boat? Or has this *cola pay raise deal* have that ring to it of a lot of rats leaving a sinking ship even before the seas begin to become rough?

If you wish to find out which of your *dedicated public service-oriented* Congressmen or Senators have refused to accept their last few cola raises, or wish to know precisely how much money he or she has appropriated from the U.S. Treasury to operate his or her "public relations business" (Washington and local district offices) that you are paying for, you may call them directly. Each has a public listing with your local telephone information.

BECOMING A U.S. SENATOR OR CONGRESSMEN

No doubt that you are wondering how you too might get into one of these lucrative positions in the Federal Government. Let me warn you, it's not simply getting your name on the ballot like Ross Perot on election day and persuading 50% or more of the people in your congressional district or state to vote for you. In some cases it maybe as simple as all this, but this is not the general rule. Although described by many as part of the democratic political process, it's probably one of the sleaziest of employment endeavors in America.

If you are outside of the system (defined as not being one of America's ***top-two-percenters***) and you are neither related to nor connected with any high-ranked government elected or appointed government officials, you have to start by first selecting, then joining one of the two major political parties. The next step is to register to vote in the primaries of that "party," officially making your existence known to the political party of your choice and your local elections board.

You are now ready for your first local party political meeting. Now, unless you are one of those already anointed either by appropriate birth or wealth to accelerate you through the ranks of "party loyalists" to the first available ballot slot, it will be three or four years of intensive party work and demonstration of party loyalty, as well as, party "cleansing" (a term used to define the "indoctrination process" conducted by both parties whereby the party assures that the cell member is generally pure of any " party offending" ideology) before you will be given your first opportunity to be elected to a low level job in your own local district. You generally get about $25,000 a year as your "first plum." Don't be disheartened by this mere pittance of a salary. This is your first test of "party loyalty," not compensation for your ultimate "level of incompetence."

During this entire internship period you will be required to be actively involved in the process of electing and supporting other members of your local and national party. You will participate in local, state, and national party conventions if you are aggressive enough, and you will literally pay your "dues" by both making financial contributions to the party and raising funds for the party on your own time and at your own expense.

Unless you are one of the aforementioned "anointed group" (i.e. your father is a former Governor, etc.), you will not have the opportunity to run for a seat in the House of Representatives unless you have at least 10 years of successful party affiliation. You certainly won't be permitted to even dream of a U.S. Senate seat until you have at least attained election first to the U.S. House of Representatives or have held numerous elected, and most importantly, ascending local, then state elected offices.

So, you think you can still do it? You're still saying to yourself, "Not a bad career path when you think of its ultimate rewards!" After seeing some of the speeches given during the last National Party Conventions and either reading or hearing about the lackluster track records of those who hold the majority of high political offices, you're ready to make the plunge. Career Politics here you come! And why not? You've just lost your job, you are in dire need of money, and you need something more to do than pretending to be starting a new business at home for the sake of the neighbors.

Wait a minute, you haven't considered some of the hidden barriers. Although not a prerequisite to running for public office it would appear that you would have a greater chance if you were already a lawyer. Of the 100 members of the senate, 59 are lawyers. Of the 435 members of the House, 192 are lawyers. Not only that, you find that in every one of those small smoke-free rooms where the local political party cells meet, 25% of the chairs are taken by practicing members of the Bar. Your odds of getting one of the real "plums" has just plummeted to perhaps 1 in 10,000, that is if you have no J.D., no wealth, and your father isn't in politics.

If you're like the majority of Americans, you will find the new friends and company you will have to keep within these local political party cells are generally different than the group you thought you saw on T.V. participating at either party's National Convention. Attending those "big bashes" are the best of the lot, all dressed up to give the appearance of being ordinary middle-class Americans. When back home, they turn into a rather sleazy bunch that you wouldn't ever have to your home for dinner, much less drive 20 miles to meet with once a month.

So, if you're like the average John Doe, you're out of politics in three months or less, only to pine time-and-time again every four years afterwards, as you tune-in to the pomp-and-glitter of either the GOP or Democratic National Conventions: "Oh how it might have been. So close, yet so far away."

SO FOR YOUR WHOLE LIFE YOU'VE BEEN APOLITICAL

This doesn't imply that you didn't do your civic duty and go out to vote. Nor does it imply that you didn't pay your taxes and didn't occasionally write your Congressmen or Senator about a matter that you took issue with.

The inference here is merely that you were unaware that 17,588,000 of your fellow Americans (approximately 10% of the total American work force) work in federal, state, and local government jobs which generally pay substantially more than flipping burgers at McDonald's, or delivering pizzas for Domino's.

Re-reflecting on the political process described immediately above and giving full consideration to your current job security, do you still have reservations about not making a commitment of time and money to your local and national political party? Do you think most of these jobs require civil service examination or special training? Not the better paying ones; not the ones requiring political or local cell appointment.. So get back in there and get your share of the *pie* — you owe it to yourself, your community, and your country, and most importantly, you owe it to your pocketbook.

PATRONAGE: THE BASIS OF CONTINUED LOYALTY

How many times have you wondered how that fellow you read about in this morning's newspaper got his job as the local U.S. Attorney or as the Federal District Court Judge in your district? You don't recall having voted for either of them and you're not even sure when they took office. Your only real thought and hope is that you never have to meet with either of them, whether socially, or on business.

How these U.S. Attorneys and Federal Judges get their jobs (appointments) is the patronage junction where your elected representative and your local lawyers converge (both the State Bar Associations and National Bar Associations are involved in these matters) . Although I've described the "appointment process" for U.S. Attorneys at great length in the Glossary Section, the only real difference in the process is there is more and more scrutiny by each party's bosses and regulars as one goes up the ladder from Federal District Judge, to U.S. Appellate Court Judge, and to U.S. Supreme Court Justice, and this does not mean to imply that it is a promotion process requiring that one hold one level of judgeship before he or she can go to the next level. Remember the ridiculous suggestion about *parking* defeated New York Governor Mario Como.. on the U.S. Supreme Court? Wouldn't you have liked to been *the fly on the wall* when after this trial balloon was launched by the Clinton administration when the awesome 800 lb. Gorilla, U.S. Senator Alfonse D'Amato got on the hotline with Clinton to go over this one! Only the fly knows the expletives used, the threats made, and the possible trade-offs made on this no-brainer! Nonetheless, almost all of these political judicial appointee hacks originate directly or indirectly from the smoke-free local political cells. They're all political appointees, appointed by the President of the United States with the advice and consent of the U.S. Senate.

It is noteworthy, that all Federal District Court Judges and all the higher ranking Federal Judges of above them have *life tenure* appointments. Although sometimes the job might be a little dangerous — you might have to sit as the trial judge in a "Gotti" type case — it's a wonderful job with a starting salary of around $105,000 a year, with the best of retirement and family health care benefits, along with some of the most wonderful *perks* imaginable. The only way you can lose your job is if the U.S. Senate brings an impeachment proceeding against you and then chooses to find you guilty — and that's about as likely as the "Second Coming" occurring at either of the Democrat's or Republican's National Convention.

You're all now wondering: How do these judicial appointments square against the *Separation of Powers Doctrine*, the *principle doctrine* put into place by America's founding fathers to protect its citizens from the abuses that happen when two or three of the branches of government are no longer in check of one another! The answer is, it simply doesn't..

Because of the lack of life tenure appointment, in the appointment process of U.S. Attorneys, certainly the *Separation of Powers Doctrine* simply doesn't have application. In the case of the Federal Judiciary (federal judgeships), most political scientists and constitutional scholars argue that the appointment of federal judges for *life tenure* assures independence from future political manipulation. Regrettably, this argument bears little if any truth in the majority instances, the future demonstration of gratitude by judges being more the surreptitious rule, than the exception. Remember many of these *life-tenured* jurists have cousins, friends, girlfriends, etc. who also wait in the wings for these and other prestigious, and often less prestigious *federal appointments* — and as adamantly as these "jurists" will deny their loyalties, all Americans today are now sufficiently experienced in the *American Way* to no longer be fooled by the false dignity portrayed by many who wear these "black robes" of justice.

Why does the *Separations of Powers Doctrine* fail as it pertains to the appointment of U.S. Attorneys? Simply because U.S. Attorneys are appointed for six-year terms, thus minimizing even the appearance of "political independence. Acknowledging this lack of independence is the need for the appointment of the special prosecutors in both Iran-Conta and Whitewatergate.   This subject was also examined under the entry "Independent Counsel" in the Spin Glossary Section of Chapter Nine.

Perhaps there should be no political process more offensive to Americans than this process by which Federal Judges and U.S. Attorneys are selected by the political party in power. One can only guess the cost to U.S. Taxpayers, as the party in power scours 365 days a year to locate "politically correct" judges with their same political philosophy, while the majority of Americans believe there is some sort of independent merit review process is being performed by one of the local or national Bar Associations, or some genuine character assessment is made from the FBI background investigation. How many brothers or sisters of mine at the Bar, or perhaps now ex-brothers and sisters, haven't heard at least one story of a major law firm partner being moved out of the firm and into a Federal District Court Judgeship to make room for the a more aggressive junior partner? Or a five-year associate being rotated into the U.S. Attorneys office or U.S. Justice Department for *the three-year grooming process*, and other nefarious purposes?

If you still believe that the American Federal Judicial System is truly free of politics, as demonstrated by their symbolic black robes, take a look under those robes and I'm sure you'll find a lot of blue pin-striped suits, especially if they were appointed in the last 16 years. Lastly, think about all of the antitrust cases, securities cases, and defense-contractor- fraud cases that are tried by those same U.S. Attorneys and Federal District Court Judges that were appointed by the last two Republican Administrations? Reflect on whether you've really seen an exercise in Justice, or an exercise in Politics?

Not covered in this book is the process by which state and local judges attain their positions. Most of you probably haven't read recent law journal articles supporting the elimination of elected judges and replacing this process with an alleged merit system similar to the Federal System. The argument is always for *merit selection*, but one has to wonder how much trust citizens can put in a *merit system* run primarily by lawyers that commences in the smoke-free political party back-room cells that the two political parties would have us falsely believe are the "grassroots" of American democratic government?

I suggest you carefully read both the Glossary and Definition Sections below to fill in some of the blanks you may still have in this vert complicated area of democratic government. Hopefully at the end of this endeavor, you'll have a better feel for processes that diminish it for you and every other American not on the inside of the system.

- AUTHOR'S REVERSE "SPIN" GLOSSARY -

- "WHAT THEY SAY IT MEANS" & "WHAT IT REALLY MEANS" -

Housing and Urban Development (HUD):
What they say it means: HUD was created as a cabinet-level executive department on September 9, 1965 as part of President Lyndon B. Johnson's Great Society Program. This new cabinet-level executive department absorbed all of the activities of the former Housing and Home Finance Agency and brought to a single focus the Federal programs relating to housing and urban problems. HUD's mission was to reverse the factors that made the U.S. cities a dangerous place for the people who lived in them and for outsiders (remember, this was 1965). HUD's function was to coordinate 115 federal housing and urban development programs within a single department. HUD administers, through various internal departments, public housing, urban renewal, college housing, housing for the elderly and the handicapped, central city open space, demonstration housing, rehabilitation of existing housing, community planning and new communities, community renewal demonstration cities, temporary housing, rent subsidies, urban mass transportation, and public facilities such as water and sewage, airports, municipal buildings, and

street improvements. There are approximately 13,218 employees on the payroll of HUD almost all of whom are located in the Washington D.C. area, with a total payroll cost approximately totaling $32.6 million. HUD's piece of the Federal Budget in 1995 approximated $27 billion.

What it really means: A Cabinet-level U.S. Government Agency, notably headed up during the Bush Administration by the former "Buffalo Bills quarterback," New York Congressman, and supply-side economic proponent, Jack Kemp. (Mr. Kemp was and still a proponent of Enterprise Zones for renewing America's inner-cities' infrastructures, and for his frequent clashing with the Administration he served.). How many of you can forget the $1 billion loss HUD suffered under the leadership of Samuel R. Pierce Jr., President Reagan's cabinet appointee as Secretary of HUD for eight years. When Mr. Pierce appeared before a Congressional panel investigating this eight-year HUD scandal, he refused to answer questions invoking his Fifth Amendment protection against self-incrimination. Fortunately for Pierce at about this same time the $500 Billion S&L scandal was knocking everything else from the "front pages" of newspapers, and off the Six O'clock News. Since the initial news of this scandal, who has ever heard anything regarding a criminal prosecution of Secretary Pierce? How many of us will ever forget the CBS 60-Minutes piece on U.S. Senator Alfonse D'Amato (R-N.Y.) and his directing funds from HUD to pet projects (projects "run" and "controlled" by those who generally contributed to his campaign to have him elected). Interestingly enough, Senator D'Amato serves on both the Senate Appropriations Committee as well as on the Senate Committee on Banking, Housing and Urban Affairs, as well as its subcommittee on Housing and Urban Affairs.

Office of Management and Budget (OMB):

What they say it means: An agency, presently headed by Leon Panetta of the Clinton Administration, and formerly by Richard Darman as its Director under the Bush Administration. The OMB is structured within the Office of the President, and responsible for: (1) the preparation and presentation of the President's budget to the Congress; (2) developing fiscal program with the Counsel of Economic Advisers and the Treasury Department; (3) the financial and budgetary review of the cost associated with implementation and execution of administrative policies and the performance of government agencies; and (4) advising the President on all legislative matters that involve funding.

What it really means: From the number of TV. appearances made by Leon Panetta during the Clinton Administration and Richard Darman during the Bush Administration, OMB appears to be more a part of each Party's propaganda machine, and based on the size of the seven budgets to date developed by this "office," Americans have to wonder if there is much, if any, difference between either the Republican or Democratic Parties, although under Panetta deficit growth was slowed and so during Clinton's watch the national debt has only risen 25% to $5 trillion as of June 30,1996. Well, stop grimacing, it could have gone easily to $6 trillion or more if George Bush had been elected based on the previous twelve years of Republican Administration in the White House.

Taxing Jurisdiction:

What they say it means: Any government or quasi-government agency, organization, or corporation given the authority to assess, determine, regulate, raise, execute, exact, or collect a portion of your income, savings, assets, or other saved or accumulated property or wealth under the color of law. These taxing jurisdictions are created by the federal government, the state governments, county governments, and municipal governments. Examples of "taxing jurisdictions" are: the Department of Motor Vehicles; the local Fish and Game Department; the tax authority issuing "tax stamps" required on the deed of your home so you might transfer it; the excise taxes paid on your phone bill, on your gasoline and on your beer, etc. Recently I was advised by one of the leading Tax Abolitionists in Palm Beach County, Florida that there are 126 different taxing jurisdictions and or authorities in this one Florida county conspiring daily to separate every man, woman, and child from his or her income and wealth.

What it really means: Tax jurisdictions or "authorities" are those "special interests groups" that have at one time, or another, convinced the people, or the powers that reigned in government at the time they were created, that either the country, the state, the city, or town couldn't survive without the particular tax that was then deemed necessary. A classic example of this is the toll road that supports the pay-down of the various government-issued bonds that paid for its initial construction. Long after the road has been paid for, the tolls remain. The continuing taxes (tolls) generated are used to keep the tax collectors, in many cases, still employed. Many of these taxing jurisdictions or authorities have become "habit" or "tradition," as well as, "job security" for those assessing and collecting the tax. It was the concept of "zero-based budgeting" that greatly threatened many of these taxing jurisdictions. However, with business-as-usual, the *special interest groups* buried this concept along with every other government reform ever proposed that would threaten many of the needless tax collector's ever increasing piece of America's shrinking *pie*. It is also these *special interest groups* that make the argument that these taxes (i.e. subsidies, surtaxes, duties, tolls, and synonym taxes, such as excise, indirect, direct, sales, luxury, etc.) are not taxes at all but direct charges for specific government services provided. Now you, as a U.S. Taxpayer, try to keep a score sheet on, say, those 126 different county and local-levied taxes. Need any more be said!

Tax Fairness:

What they say it means: A concept that generally arises as part of the democratic political agenda generally nine to twelve months before any federal, state, or local election. The concept generally says that the "rich" will have to pay a greater share of the tax burden of the government in order to create "fairness" to those over-burdened Taxpayers in the middle-class.

What it really means: Something the Democrats generally aspire to do in theory, but never really achieve. Something the Republicans never aspire to do at all, but unconditionally and unashamedly make worse.

COMPOSITE DICTIONARY

Aristocracy: A government that is ruled by a "class of men and or women," who are believed (by themselves at least) to be superior. A form of government that is governed by a minority consisting of those believed to be best qualified; a rich or privileged class of people; nobles, people of wealth and station, dignitaries, and those believed to be of superior breeding.

Authoritarianism: A form of government where the governed blindly submit to authority. A system of government relating to, or favoring a concentration of power in one leader or small elite group, not constitutionally responsible to the people.

Big Brother: The concept of government collecting information on every aspect of the individual's private business and private life for the ultimate purpose of regulation and control.

Bipartisan: The rare event when both Democrats and Republicans work together for the passage of a law to resolve a problem; that event when the members of both political parties work together for the passage of a piece of legislation, or to resolve an issue, or crisis that effects the American people.

Boondoggle: Government legislation that creates expensive and wasteful projects benefitting particular individuals or groups. This term was originally used to describe the "jobs programs" created by the Congress during the 1929-1938 Depression.

Bureaucracy: The Government. The term is also applied to the various government agencies and permanent career employees protected by civil service laws and who stay regardless of how often the Administration is changed. Considered by many Americans to be America's political infrastructure, the term is also used synonymously with the expression "red tape."

Civil Liberties: Those personal and natural rights guaranteed and protected by the Constitution. Civil liberties are those restraints on certain government actions necessary to protect certain freedoms and natural rights of the individual.

Communism: A system of government and social organization in which goods are held in common as a opposed to the system of private property. Communism is a form of government in which the state controls (1) the means of production, (2) the distribution what's produced, and (3) the consumption of all products industrial or agricultural produced in, and by the state.

Demagogue: A political office holder, candidate, or any speaker, who appeals to greed, hatred, fear, or to various other negative emotions or ideologies to create a personal following for himself or his cause.

Dictatorship: A system of government where one individual is placed in, or ascends to, or usurps supreme authority over those governed and rules autocratically and authoritatively, generally governing oppressively.

Fascism: A system of government, political movement, or regime that exalts nationalism and race superiority, and stands for a centralized autocratic government headed by a dictatorial leader who generally imposes severe social order through regimentation and forcible suppression of all opposition.

Federalism: A system of government where power is divided constitutionally between a central government and local governments, the local governments maintaining control over local affairs and the central government being accorded sufficient authority to deal with national needs and affairs. The classic example of Federalism exists here in the United States, where fifty state governments support and interact with one central Federal Government.

Gerrymandering: The drawing of boundaries for legislative districts, especially congressional districts of the U.S. House of Representatives, in such a way as to help the party that controls the state legislature, consolidate areas where they are assured of having members of their own party elected to either the Congressional seats of those new congressional districts or the local state official elected from new state districts.

GOP: The Republican Party (Grand Old Party).

Libertarian: One who advocates an absolute minimum of governmental interference or involvement in the lives of the nation's citizens.

Mudslinging: A term used by politicians to minimize the impact of their opponent's "negative" campaigning or the press's derogatory charges against them or someone in their party, and often used as a "cover" for a party's own mudslinging.

Monarchy: A system of government in which the supreme power is vested in a single person. If the power is deemed to be absolute, the Monarch is deemed to be "despotic." The Queen of England is deemed to be a Constitutional monarch. This is based on the notion that she reigns subject to the supreme power to govern being vested in the constitution and laws as created by elected representatives of the people.

National Socialism [Nazism]: A political party that controlled Germany from 1933 to 1945 under Adolf Hitler. The National Socialist Party employed a fascist form of government during its period of power in Germany (see also Fascism).

Nepotism: The handing out of patronage by public officials in appointing others to positions by reason of blood or marital relationship. In corporations or business, the term is used to refer to family members being employed by the same corporation or business.

Oligarchy: A form of government where power to govern remains in the hands of a few persons as opposed to one person. The power is generally retained through the exercise of authoritarian or totalitarian principles.

Parliamentary Form of Government: A form of government practiced in such countries as Great Britain, Ireland, and Israel, where the power lies in the legislature which chooses one of its members to be prime minister and the de facto head-of-state. It is generally the majority party with its majority votes that selects the prime minister, but in the case where three or more parties participate in this form of political government, and where a majority is not achieved, a "coalition" of two or more parties may be formed to elect a prime minister, or where this fails, new elections of every member of the legislature may be required. Technically, the prime minister and his colleagues exercise legal authority at the discretion of the Monarch, In fact, the prime minister and his government must retain confidence of the House of Commons and must resign when that confidence is lost. If a party with an overall majority in the House of Commons has a recognized leader, then the Monarch must appoint that person as prime minister.

Under the parliamentary system, the prime minister is only indirectly accountable to the voters since he or she is elected by the members of parliament, not directly by the people. In the parliamentary system of government, the voting solidarity is generally maintained by a sophisticated organizational network. In England, under each party leader there is a "chief whip," who is responsible for, along with several junior whips who assist him, in maintaining party unity. It should also be noted that in Great Britain, the House of Lords, is not the equivalent of the U.S. Senate; it is not elected and has little influence in the legislative process.

Partisan: In American politics, it refers to the circumstance where an elected official votes along with, or makes decisions according to party lines. (See Bipartisan.)

Patronage: An exchange of government favors (such as the granting of special contracts, appointment to political jobs, and special treatment) for political support.

Platform: Positions taken on major issues by a politician running for office or by a political party. Each position taken in the platform is considered a "plank."

Plutocracy: A form of government where power is controlled by a select group with wealth or power, who generally govern oppressively. Where all civil liberties, if any, are granted by the group with power, as opposed to being guaranteed by a constitution approved by the people.

Pork-Barrel: A term that describes the favoritism given in government appropriations, usually for public works projects which are often of dubious merit and that are designed to bring economic vantage to one legislative district and are allocated as a favor to that district's legislator.

Republican Form of Government: A form of government in which the administration of affairs is open to all of the citizens. A government of the people; or a government of representatives, chosen by the people. Do you believe the U.S. government still adheres to a Republican Form of Government? Or do you agree with most Americans that certain things have subtly changed over the past thirty years?

Socialism: An economic system in which government owns or controls many major industries and businesses, but may allow markets to set prices in many certain areas. Socialism is sometimes thought of as a middle ground between capitalism and communism. Socialism when employed in a capitalist government generally includes such entitlement programs as welfare, Social Security, Medicare, and Medicaid.

Totalitarianism: A system of government under the centralized control of an autocratic leader or hierarchy. A political regime based on subordination of the individual to the state and strict control of all aspects of life, productive capacity, and civil liberties, where such strict control is exercised through coercive measures such as censorship, terrorism, and restriction of all civil liberties.

12 | The United States Supreme Court

Final justice in the United States resides in the U.S. Supreme Court. It is here where statutes and other laws, both federal and state, are ultimately found to be constitutional or unconstitutional. It is here where power and authority disputes, and other constitutional disagreements between the executive branch and legislative branch of the Federal Government are ultimately resolved. It is also the third branch of Government in which is reposed the power granted by the Constitution to oversee each and every interpretation of the very document, the U.S. Constitution, that is responsible for its own creation. Lawyers, CPAs, politicians, federal agencies, state governments, stock brokers, bankers, corporations, charities, educational institutions from the public school to the University, and every other organization, association, and individual have felt the impact of the U.S. Supreme Court in one way or another over the last 200 years.

As a result of the power granted to this Supreme Court, consisting of now nine men and women, by the U.S. Constitution, this body has also been responsible for (directly and indirectly) the moral decadence which this nation now finds itself immersed. Little if any moral leadership ever occurs in this body. One needs only to remember the meaning of "political free speech" of the nineteenth century and compare it to the current "free speech" doctrines that this Court has unlawfully expanded to include in its purview, i.e. commercial "free speech" (pornography) and common "free speech" (vulgarity). Think also about prayer in school, and this Court's interpretation of the U.S. Constitution's separation of church and state doctrine. Eighty percent of Americans approve of some form of school prayer. But this body of **nine** men and women, relying on unusual abstract logic that should have remained in their law school closets, continue to deny the will of the American people; while "In God We Trust" remains on every denomination of U.S. currency and coin. For those of you who don't know, every session of each new Congress and new U.S. Supreme Court term are commenced with an invocation of prayer.

I point out to you that the nine life-tenured justices who sit on this renowned Court were all lawyers at one time. All of these nine justices were at one time or another political hacks in either the Democratic or Republican party prior to his or her being appointed either directly to this Court, a Court below this Court, or other federal or state jobs by the then political leader or party boss of their political persuasion. It would take a trip into *Alice In Wonderland* to ascribe any more, or any less, to these nine individual Justices, especially when the media has dissected for each and every one of you, the political ideologies and loyalties of each of these Justices before their appointment and approval by the U.S. Senate.

The last five Justices appointed to the U.S. Supreme Court have had no less than sixty hours of televised media analysis and scrutiny; including, the televised hearings of the U.S. Senate Judicial Committee as to their judicial ideology, as well as their academic, philosophical, spiritual, and moral ideological qualifications to serve. One has to wonder if this is not a function of "exclusion" rather than a function of "inclusion." In either event, once approved by the U.S. Senate and appointed, each of these new Justices ascend to the most powerful tenured position in Government.

We all remember the Clarence Thomas-Anita Hill hearings in 1991. This scandalous affair again brought the U.S. Supreme Court and the U.S. Senate Judiciary Committee to the attention of the vast majority of Americans. It wasn't Clarence Thomas's political ideology, his politics, his moral persuasion, or his being given one-ninth "constitutional power" that the Court possesses or his ability to abuse its power, once confirmed. It was the sexual harassment aspect of Prof. Hill's allegations against him that invited and stirred the interest of Boobus Americanus.

Contrary to the alleged majority of Americans and lawyers who supposedly sided with Thomas, my personal poll of lawyers I know came down on Prof. Hill's side. Although I did not do an extensive survey, I also found that the majority of non-lawyers I spoke with who sided with Thomas, did so primarily on the basis of Prof. Hill waiting so long to make her charges "public." After all, it was argued, she certainly could have made the allegations when Thomas was appointed to the U.S. Court of Appeals just a few years before.

Finally, others who sided with Thomas have argued it wasn't a matter of "rape," just "sexual harassment." Just a little "boy-girl" talk, which, had it occurred anywhere but in the context of the "office" hierarchy, it would have been viewed as mere flirtatious advertising of one's rather unique qualities for romantic advantage.

The "fundamental reason" I believe Anita Hill stepped forward in 1991 was because she was a product of the American legal education system, where a lawyer's reverence for the U.S. Supreme Court becomes so paramount, it can only be explained a *spiritual*. As believers of many faiths have sacrificed their lives for their faith, so was Prof. Hill compelled to do the same for her "profession." For this was "no" ordinary political court appointment. This was a "political appointment" that might very well change the whole moral and social fabric of the nation; a "political appointment" that could very well impact the scope of American democracy for three or four decades to come. Prof. Hill well understood that this "one" political appointment reflected as much as 20, or more, of the President's *hand-from-the-grave* veto power — a "veto power" that is even more powerful than the president's, reaching into the fifty-states and U.S. territories. This is a *life tenured* "power" to strike down or uphold the "laws" legislated by both the federal and state governments . . . an absolute "power of veto" that, if put in the wrong hands, could itself quash American "democracy."

The Composition Of Court Today

You probably already know it has one Chief Justice, currently William Rehnquist (appointed 1971-RMN, indicating the year and initials of the President who made the appointment), and eight Associate Justices that include: one Afro-American, Clarence Thomas (appointed 1991-GHWB); and two women, Sandra Day O'Connor (appointed 1981-RR) and Ruth Bader Ginsburg (appointed 1992-BC). The six other Associate Justices are John Paul Stevens III (appointed 1975-GF), Antonin Scalia (appointed 1986-RR), Anthony M. Kennedy (appointed 1988-RR), and David H. Souter (appointed 1990-GHWB), Stephen G. Breyer (appointed 1993-BC). RMN are Richard Milhous Nixon's initials, and GF are Gerald Ford's for those of you too young to remember.

SOME MEMORABLE COURT OPINIONS

You are certainly also familiar with <u>Roe vs. Wade</u> (1973) which made abortion legal in the United States; <u>Miranda vs. Arizona</u> (1966) which created those "Miranda Rights" you've seen read to every criminal being arrested on T.V. since 1966; and <u>Brown vs. The Board of Education</u> (1953) tried by the late then NAACP attorney and later Supreme Justice Thurgood Marshall (appointed to the U.S.S.C. in 1967 by Lyndon Johnson, and retired in 1991). It was <u>Brown vs. The Board of Education</u> (1953) that resulted in today's school busing the racial integration of all American public schools.

Lastly, although you probably don't remember <u>Engel vs. Vitale</u> (1962), you do remember that it was the U.S. Supreme Court that banned all official prayer (after almost 190 years of its cultural existence in the United States) in all public schools.

How The Court Works

The court has "exclusive" and "original jurisdiction" (meaning that acts as a court of "first resort") in controversies involving foreign ministers and cases between "states" as "parties." The Court's most important authority is the "review" (judicial review) of certain lower federal and state court decisions arising under the "Constitution" or "federal law" and in a variety of specialized matters (i.e. admiralty, bankruptcy, patent, copyright, postal service and Internal Revenue Service). The Court reviews "final decisions" from the highest courts of each state, where "Constitutional" issue are involved, as the Court of last resort.

In certain special cases, appeals may be taken directly from a federal district court. Cases heard by the Court of Claims are also reviewable by the U.S. Supreme Court if the Court of Claims "certifies" that there exists a question-of-law in the instant case being heard by them. Cases in both the Court of Claims, and the Courts of Customs and Patent Appeals may be reviewed on a writ of certiorari, by direct appeal, or by certification.

The "writ of certiorari" is the term most of us are familiar with when it comes to appeals sent to the U.S. Supreme Court. However, the "writ" is not a "matter-of-right." Whether or not to hear an "appeal" under a Petition of Certiorari is within the absolute discretion of the Court. The Court will grant the petition of certiorari only when there is a special and important reason for reviewing the lower court's decision.

Review by "appeal," to the U.S. Supreme Court, as opposed to "certiorari," is a matter-of-right and is restricted to cases involving a party relying on a State Statute held by a U.S. Court of Appeals to be invalid as repugnant to the Constitution, treaties, or laws of the United States. This right of "appeal" is always restricted to the "federal questions" of law presented, and not a review or re-argument of the "facts" presented at trial.

Now that you have an idea of how the court works, it's time to ask a very important question. Do you want nine "political appointees" of the President (with the advice and consent of the U.S. Senate) dictating the social and moral fabric of America, especially in such areas as:

1. Schools Prayer
2. Abortion, and
3. Pornography,

or should the vote of the majority of the people rule on these and other similar issues? This argument has been heated for years and focuses directly on the concept of "judicial review" discussed below.

The History of Judicial Review

Although "judicial review" is not explicitly set forth in the Constitution, seventeen of the leading members of the Constitutional Convention in 1789, openly stated their views. Contrary to what you might have thought, these seventeen "founding fathers" firmly believed that federal courts "should have" the right to determine the validity of the act of Congress (Judicial Review).

In 1803, then Chief Justice of the U.S. Supreme Court John Marshall in the historic case of <u>Marbury vs. Madison</u> (1803) asserted that the power of "judicial review" was within <u>the province</u>, and <u>the duty</u> of the judiciary to determine whether a "law" is constitutional or unconstitutional. Marshall stated:

> "It is emphatically the province and duty of the judicial department to say what the law is. Those who apply the rule to particular cases, must of necessity expound and interpret that rule. If two laws conflict with each other, the court must decide on the operation of each.

> So if a law being in opposition to the Constitution; if both the law and the Constitution apply to a particular case, so that the court must either decide that the case conformably to the law, disregarding the Constitution; or conformably to the Constitution, disregarding the law; the court must determine which of these conflicting rules governs the case. This is the very essence of judicial duty.

> If, then, the courts are to regard the Constitution and the Constitution as superior to any ordinary Act of the legislature, the Constitution, and not such ordinary Act, must govern the case to which they both apply."

Certainly no scholar, or ordinary lawyer such as myself, would question the validity or the necessity of "judicial review." But many Americas today believe the old argument that "judicial review" of "legislation" designed to enhance a nation's morals and values **should not be within the ultimate purview** of an appointed political elite who, under Article III, Section 1, serve for life, and where impeachment is rare and requires an enormously high burden of proof. Given their **life tenures,** U.S. Supreme Court Justices are not accountable to the electorate (the people) and thus have enormous power to nullify the will of the majority as expressed in legislation, or to change American culture as they so deem fit. Even Justice Frankfurter described "judicial review" as, "A limitation on popular government" and "inherently oligarchic."

On the other hand, no citizen should ever be foolish enough to surrender the needed political protections provided by "judicial review." Striking the balance *requires* that citizens (*you*) participate actively and consistently in the political process, as later described in Chapter Twenty. It is this participation, and not "judicial review," that will save and maintain America's democracy, and for the first time, provide a role for Americans in their own self-government.

In further argument for the need to curtail "judicial review" in specific areas, one need only look at the list of Supreme Court Justices and their political ideologies. It's commonly understood Presidents seek to appoint justices who will serve for two or three decades, forcing on future generations their views which may have already been proven unrealistic, or not in conformity with the needs of the times.

The following schedule summarizes the age and basic political ideology of today's Court.

Justice	Pres. Age	Date Appt.	Age Appt.	Appt. By	Party Affiliation
W. Rehnquist (C.J.)	74	1971	47	Nixon	Republican
J. Stevens	76	1975	55	Ford	Republican
S. O'Connor	65	1981	62	Reagan	Republican
A. Scalia	61	1986	50	Reagan	Republican
A. Kennedy	61	1988	52	Reagan	Republican
D. Souter	59	1990	51	Bush	Republican
C. Thomas	49	1991	44	Bush	Republican
R. Ginsburg	46	1992	47	Clinton	Democrat
S. Breyer	45	1993	48	Clinton	Democrat

*(C.J.) Current Chief Justice

Remember what was said at the beginning of this Chapter about the shocking and disgraceful Clarence Thomas-Anita Hill Senate Judicial hearings of 1991. Are there any of you readers who aren't convinced that the U.S. Supreme Court appointment process is *not* simply an application of the *Separation of Powers Doctrine*, but also another means of America's two party system to usurp from Americans the last vestiges of what *democracy* is erroneously believed to be by Boobus Americanus? It should be obvious to everyone that the U.S. Supreme Court is "loaded" with each party's "political" and "ideological" hacks, as much as it also allegedly protects all of our constitutional rights, as the nine of them so determine.

Now, ask yourself again: "Do you want the "nine men or women" selected by George Bush, Bill Clinton, and approved by the likes of Spector, Hatch, and Simpson either deciding the "law" or creating "law" on every American issue of "culture," life-style," and "moral value" in America?

If you wish to limit this authority, the "tools" are already in place. Perhaps it's time we again added a new amendment to our Constitution to limit "judicial review" to the preservation of our Constitutional Rights and not the elimination of those "rights" (i.e. the right of Americans to have public airways free of pornographic filth, etc.) that are essential to the preservation of our moral values and our unique American culture and civilization.

- AUTHOR'S REVERSE "SPIN" GLOSSARY -

- "WHAT THEY SAY IT MEANS" & "WHAT IT REALLY MEANS" -

Separation of Church & State Doctrine:

What they say it means: This doctrine is embodied in the words of the first amendment to the U.S. Constitution where it states: "Congress shall make no law respecting an establishment of religion, or prohibiting the free exercise thereof; . . ." The doctrine is also referred to as the "Establishment Clause." Only since the later part of the 20th Century has the U.S. Supreme Court applied its interpretation of the "establishment clause" to bible reading, public school financial aid, release time, school prayers, and Sunday-closing laws. Today, almost every federal district court, appellate court, and the U.S. Supreme Court has at least one or more "establishment clause cases pending before it. A recent federal district court case involved the "Boy Scouts of America's" refusal to admit young men who will not take the eighty-year-old oath confirming their belief in, and duty to God.

What it really means: Almost without limitation, all cases reaching the U.S. Supreme Court have come down "contrary" to those favoring the expression of religion in any form in the United States. The most notorious of these cases was the ban on school prayer: the Court held that since public schools are paid for by government, that prayer within them is, in effect, an offense against the "Establishment Clause," which I again repeat here: "Congress shall make no law respecting an establishment of religion, or prohibiting the free exercise thereof; . . ." It would seem that the Court has completely overlooked the last six words: "or prohibiting the free exercise thereof; . . .." The question here is simply whether or not the "Establishment Clause" was really intended by our "founding fathers" (the drafters of the U.S. Constitution) to protect those who don't wish to hear any reference to God, versus protecting the "rights" of those who do?

It is the belief of many, including myself, that the first amendment "Establishment Clause" does not protect those who might be offended by those who believe in God and are willing to express it openly, but only protects against the state creating a prototype of the Church of England, the "state religion" of England when the U.S. Constitution and its Bill of Rights were drawn. The "primary" argument voiced by Constitutional scholars concerning the "establishment clause": It's "offensive" for some to hear that others believe in, and wish to give reference, to God! However, the U.S. Supreme Court does not protect those citizens who are offended by the foulest language, even when printed boldly on a tee shirt and paraded in the U.S. Supreme Courthouse. Nor does this Court protect the rights of those who sit in front of their televisions, in the privacy of their homes, and are offended every night by some of the sleaziest pornography broadcasted on both cable and network television. To this, those same Constitutional scholars say: Turn your TV to a different station! Now how come they don't tell those offended by the thought of God in a classroom, to leave the room for a moment or two? It would seem, that in a true democracy, it should be the majority of the people who should prevail on these issues, as opposed to the nine political appointees of the U.S. Supreme Court. It is for this reason I believe that such issues should be put forth to the American people in the context of either broad national, or state-confined referendums.

Taking many of these personal and moral value "issues" out of this Third Branch of American Government, and empowering the people to directly decide these "issues" by national or state referendum would eliminate a great deal of unnecessary government "grid-lock." It would enfranchise citizens with the power to decide their own moral values and standards in the most direct and meaningful manner possible, and probably reduce the cost of government and election rhetoric by 25%.

COMPOSITE DICTIONARY

Judicial Activism: Periods of time, and situations whereby judges make new public policy through their broad decision-making powers, especially as it relates to their power of Judicial Review.

Judicial Review: The review by a court of law of some act or failure to act, by a government official or agency, or by some other legally appointed person or organized body. In a constitutional law context, "judicial review" expresses the concept first articulated in <u>Marbury V. Madison,</u> (1803) that it is "the province and duty of the judicial department to say what the law is." Under this doctrine the U.S. Supreme Court and the highest courts of every state have assumed the power and responsibility to decide the constitutionality of the acts of the legislative and executive branches of their respective jurisdictions.

13

The Free Trade

Myth

Webster's dictionary defines *nation* as: (1): nationality; (2): politically organized nationality; (a) a community of people composed of one or more nationalities and possessing a more or less defined territory and government; (b) a territorial division containing a body of people of one or more nationalities, and usually characterized by a relatively large size and independent status.

Webster further defines *nationalism* as a sense of national consciousness exalting one's nation above all others and placing primary emphasis on promotion of its culture and interests as opposed to those of other nations or supranational groups. A *nationalist* is defined as: an advocate or believer in nationalism, or believing in strong national independence or strong national government. Anthropologists have expanded the definition of *nation* as a large number of people, who view themselves as a *community,* who place *loyalty* to the *community* above those *loyalties conflicting* with that of the *community.* It is the concept of *non-conflicting loyalties*, and sense of *community* within a *nation,* which ultimately constitutes its power, prestige, independence, self-defense, survival, and, what is more important, its prosperity. A *nation*, where a small percentage of the populace have conflicting *loyalties* detrimental to most of its populace. And where those *conflicting loyalties* result in detriment to the majority of the populace, for that majority of that *nation's* populace, these *conflicting loyalties* of the minority ultimately end the need for the *nation* itself to exist for the majority.

Such a state of *conflict of loyalty* is evident in America today, as well as in America's recent past. This has been overtly demonstrated, especially by those who have occupied the office of the President of the United States, the highest elected representative office of this nation.

This *conflict of interest* is, and has been, rampant in the U.S. Congress since as early as our nation was formed, but never has its intensity been so overt, blatant, and bipartisan, as in the past sixteen years. Mr. Clinton's (and his predecessors) Messrs. Reagan's and Bush's concept of *international free trade* is the absolute manifestation of this *conflict of loyalty* to which I refer — a *conflict* rooted in *international economic class*, *wealth*, and *greed* — a *conflict* that may very well someday explode between America's middle-class and America's *top-two-percenters*. The Clinton, Reagan, and Bush Administrations, and their respective U.S. Congress, especially since the early 1980s, has followed this same *international free trade policy* to which I refer. This is an *international free trade policy* that is in *conflict* with, and *intentionally destructive* of, the very *short-lived fifty-year standard-of-living* of America's quickly disappearing *middle-class* — a *middle-class* that first emerged as such, after the end of W.W.II.

Before you read any further, let me suggest that you re-read Chapter One-<u>Numbers Can Be Scary</u>, the subsection entitled, <u>The U.S. Trade Deficit (1960-1995)</u>. The six stars below will get you back where you left-off after re-reading the above subsection.

***** *

Our aforementioned representative leaders' illusive theory of *international free trade* has its roots and alleged redemption in *Adam Smith's* 1776 classic treatise on microeconomic theory entitled the <u>Wealth of Nations</u>. Based on the economic circumstances of the 18th Century, Smith concluded the following:

1. International "free trade" must be of mutual benefit to both parties to the transaction, and

2. International "free trade's" mutual benefits are derived from the ones trading partner's unique "specializations" and "efficiencies" to more "cheaply" produce certain goods than it can itself.

You ask: *"So what can possibly be wrong with free-trade?"* *"After all,"* . . . *you reason, "according to Adam Smith it allows us to buy goods more cheaply from all over the world, and it allows American industry and agriculture to export their competitive goods into expanding markets. True, or not?"*

This was true in 1991, for <u>perhaps</u> $487.1 Billion in U.S. imports and <u>perhaps</u> $421.7 Billion in U.S. exports. I use the qualification "perhaps," because I'm not remotely convinced, even if *international free trade* could be put on a so-called *level playing field*, that *international free trade* could ever "benefit" America's *middle-class*, as theorized by *Adam Smith*. Remember please, that *Adam Smith* was of the Scottish Aristocracy, published his treatise in 1776, and died in 1790, long before the emergence of America's *middle-class* or, for that matter, before the emergence of any middle-class! In this light, we shall examine one of Smith's leading American proponent's, former President Bush, the greatest of the *international free traders.* (Pardon me if I misheard the word. Maybe they were saying *traitors* instead of *traders* and thus, all of this book would be about nothing). It was from Adam Smith that George came up with the export-job formula for Boobus Americanus. This is the formula that says that for every billion dollars in American exports, 20,000 American jobs are created.

Before we go any further in our analysis of the ramifications of *international free trade* on our fellow American nationals, I want you all to remember Ronnie and Nancy Reagan's trip to Japan in 1988. This is the trip where this great American President, who had trouble remembering his name at the Iran-Contra hearings, received a shameless **$3 million** honorarium from the Japanese for a thirty-minute speech and his $10 billion sell-out of America's *middle-class*. As a result, you must be aware of how American goods have been allowed to freely flow into Japan over the past fifty years? You've almost got to wonder who won WWII when you think of the economic trade trouncing the Japanese have given us each and every year since their *unconditional surrender* in 1945. Perhaps the next surrender by a former American foe might require a *conditional surrender* the next time around, allowing us to at least keep our dignity. Lastly, before we go any further, I ask all of you to remember the *last hurrah* trip you paid for, the one that George and Barbara took in December 1992. The purpose was to visit those Saudis and Kuwaitees after George's alleged victory over Saddam Hussein in Desert (or was it Dessert) Storm, and after George, himself, was defeated, and tossed out of office by the American people? What do you think that bulging attache case, George was so firmly gripping, was so loaded with when he came off U.S. One from his last trip as a lame-duck President? I first ask, would the Bush "export formula" of creating 20,000 jobs also apply if this same "billion dollars" of exportable goods were instead imported goods purchased by Americans? Does an equivalent "billion dollars" in imports also result in 20,000 lost American jobs? If the answer to both questions is yes, *then America in 1991 had 8,434,000 jobs resulting from its export trade, and lost 9,742,000 resulting from its import trade — a net loss of 1,308,000 jobs.* Ordinary common sense tells me this certainly could not be the "mutual benefit" Adam Smith had in mind in his 1776 treatise. Now, what if we factored into the Bush equation the difference in the wage rate, for example, between the U.S. and Mexico! You don't have to be an Einstein to figure that a "billion dollars" in exports from Mexico at their labor rate has to be creating at least ten times the number of jobs that the same "one billion" in exports create in the U.S.; that is the difference in wage rate, alone, between the two nations. That would mean that 200,000 jobs could be created in Mexico making American products in Mexico instead of Americans making American products in America, for each "billion dollars" in Mexican exports of Mexican-made American products to *anywhere*! With all of today's emphasis on technology, efficiency, and productivity, how many jobs do you think are really needed worldwide? Can Americans **exchange jobs at the rate of 10 for 1** and expect to have sufficient jobs for Americans, much less, sufficient jobs for all of our illegal immigrants? Now, do any of you reading this book really believe that there is an emerging middle-class in Mexico or anywhere else that American middle-class jobs were exported to? Or, perhaps you are thinking there is just a lot of *skimming* going on among America's *top-two-percenters*; *skimming-off* the difference between what they were paying you and what they are paying your replacements overseas?

Possibly with Reagan it was just a little greed. But who of you believe that those two Yale graduates, George Bush and Bill Clinton, didn't fully understand the *international free trade benefits* **Adam Smith** had was alluded? That such *international free trade benefits* were economic benefits that were only to flow to each nation's *top-two-percenters?* After all, the entire blueprint for this theory of international trade was all put into his book called *The Wealth of Nations.* Let's remember, back in Adam Smith's days he was selling books to the aristocracy, not folks like you who have been disenfranchised from America's middle-class that was unknown to Adam Smith. I am relatively certain that Smith would have **never** expanded his discourse on the "nation's benefits" from *international free trade* had he ever envisioned today's "anti-national" *international free traders*, made up of America's former MNCs, and the former MNCs of some of America's allies. Had he ever envisioned today's world of commerce, his book would **not** have been entitled *The Wealth of Nations*, but rather, *The Wealth of CEOs of The MNCs*.

In summary, it doesn't seem probable that **Adam Smith** ever contemplated the following anti-national organizations, their unlimited power, their ungovernability, or their control of world commerce:

1. The MNCs — The Multinational Companies;

2. The International Banking Community;

3. The International Currency Markets;

4. The International (global) Financial Markets; and

5. The ease by which the two most critical elements of today's capitalism: *money* and *technology*, as opposed to Smith's agricultural and manufactured *goods,* could be exported to

other nation's to profit from significantly lower wage rates, less costly worker benefits, and escape from the laws and regulations deemed desirable by one democracy, to the detriment of another nation's environment, workers, etc.

So you ask: "But isn't that what *international free trade* is all about? . . . Even if it involves *the free trade* of the critical elements and components of *capitalism?* Isn't this just an extension of the ability to have individuals go into the market place and freely negotiate price without any government interference, i.e. tariffs, duties, unreasonable customs inspections, government subsidies for national industries, etc., etc.?"

The answer should be a simple, yes! But here it's two-fold. First, we have to remember we're dealing with MNCs who recognize no governments, whose profit maximization formulae require avoidance of laws (i.e. tax, environmental, worker protection, antitrust, etc.) that effect their profits. Those countries that are the least burdened with such laws is where the MNC, today's *legal international outlaw,* manufactures its products. MNC host "nations" are virtually run by that nation's own group of *top-two-percenters*, who protect the MNC at the expense of their workers and environment. The *carrot* for these low paid foreign workers, who now work for what were formerly American MNCs, is the dream of emulating America's *middle-class* who, unbeknownst to them, are now in the process of becoming extinct. When you think these MNC *international free traders,* think of them as being the equivalent to the *international pirates* of the early 1800s. It took the then nation-states of Adam Smith's time to eradicate the pirates, so the very nation-states themselves would not be subjugated to, and overrun by this international group of cut-throats, who were without allegiance to any nation.

Secondly, to respond to the above question, we have to be able to see through Mr. Bush's concept of the "level playing field" (it was on George's *watch* that this term came into vogue with serious application by America's *top-two-percenters*) and how it operates on the world's playing field. Much of this failure probably has to do with America's lack of ethnic and racial homogeneity. In Japan, you have a homogeneous Japanese population. In Germany, there still remains a very homogeneous population, as in most of Europe, with the exception of a large group of controlled foreign workers who are rarely permitted citizenship. Now do you really believe these homogeneous nations will sacrifice one well-paying job so that you might keep your standard-of-living?

To say there is no impact on the degree nationalism within a nation resulting from the close ties of religion, ethnisticity, and common culture is to deny white is white and black is black. Here America loses. The level of American nationalism today has fairly much gone the way of mother, apple pie, the Brooklyn Dodgers, and more recently, the Cleveland

Browns. We are not a homogenous group; but rather a pressure cooker of racism, ethnocentrism, and already large and growing population of imprisoned criminals. We are a society conquered by illegal drugs, pornography, and corruption in both government and business. Perhaps this was the subliminal reason Ronnie, George, and Bill *willingly sacrificed, with Bill continuing to sacrifice*, without remorse, America's *middle-class* to advance the international *aristocracy* of their *new world order*. This is not to say this *world aristocracy* itself has yet succeeded and that the American *middle-class* is dead and buried, but one need not look too far down the yellow brick road to see where America's *middle-class's* cemetery has been platted in the mind's of America's *top-two-percenters*.

For those of you still hanging on to your fragile middle-class status, you have already dismissed this diatribe. For years you've heard these economic conspiracy theories. You've attributed them to misanthropes, malcontents, or what we in America call "losers." Well for the twenty-years preceding July 1991, as a devout registered Republican, I would have been the first to condemn what I've written here. I myself would have labeled my own words "treasonous," as I suspect many of you have already done. That's also one of your rights, but it won't save your job in the next downsizing. Most important for you to remember as you remain wrapped up in those very two magic American words *free trade* is, it's *your standard-of-living* which will soon be slipping through your very own fingers if you're not one of America's *top-two-percenters*.

Whether you care to accept my conclusions or not, George Bush himself told you the same thing I've related here in his 1992 acceptance speech at the Republican National Convention. As usual, you were just too bored, or patriotic to decipher the *meaning* when you heard these words:

"In the last ten years," Mr. Bush said commandingly during his speech, **"the rest of the world has become more like America . . . Now it's time for America to become like the rest of the world!"**

Do you remember the emphasis and severity he placed on those twenty-eight words? And what do you think Mr. Bush was alluding to, *if it wasn't your standard-of-living?*

Having been an avid watcher of CNN World News for many years, I for one want no part of Mr. Bush's 1992 ambitions or visions for America. From what I've seen of (1) Mr. Bush's "New World Order," (2) Mr. Bush's "Global Economy," and (3) Mr. Bush's "Free Trade," I can't comprehend any *middle-class* American dealing himelf or herself in on any of these "losers" either. Regrettably, Bill Clinton has completely filled the shoes of George Bush since 1992 and has completely adopted Bush's concepts of the new world order, the global economy, and complete unfettered free-trade.

So what has your President and the U.S. Congress got in store for your future? That goes hand-in-hand of what they really think of you? . . . And, since I don't have to listen to your naive replies if you're a **top-two-percenter**, a U.S. Congressmen; or your adamant denials and "spins" if you are or were a part of the Clinton, Reagan, or Bush Administrations, I'll lay it all out, just the way I heard it from one of the **top-two-percenters** in December 1991.

Your government and America's "*top-two-percenters*" believe:

1. You've gotten both "fat" and "lazy" over the past thirty years as you've spent the majority of your time indulging in spectator sports, while stuffing your face with hotdogs and beer, etc., or doing and self-indulging in other American "leisure activities" (i.e. T.V. watching, sexual promiscuity, self-admiration, etc., etc.). You're overpaid, overfed, under-worked, and have too many fringe benefits that you haven't earned and don't deserve. And most important you can be replaced for between $.60 and $1.80 an hour by a Mexican laborer who'll work harder and without benefits, will complain less, and most importantly, steal less.

2. Although, in your heart-of-hearts you won't believe it, the American government you think represents you, *even though you **don't** bother to vote*, is more concerned with the pocketbooks of itself, its families, and the **top-two-percenters** than it is with yours. As a result, you are now on the "fast-track" into "free-trade" as well as on the "fast-track," into the Third World's lower economic class as the "new world order" and "international aristocracy" emerges. Frankly, can you blame them? Don't you watch the reflections of yourself on "Cops," "Top Cops," "America's Ten Most Wanted," or "Married With Children," etc., seven nights a week?

Adding insult to injury, the new "free-world-traders" who bargain and barter for the goods you need from others, and bargain and barter away your goods (if you can still make anything worthwhile), will take an additional 10% fat off for themselves (export-import commissions) which you'll pay for, and it's all done in the name of "free-trade." Now do you think the three Bush Boys, George, Jeb, and Neil now poised in Texas (as Governor), Florida (as a wannabee Governor), and California (probably still trying to perfect S&L looting), respectively, are there because of their close family ties? Or perhaps you think it's just coincidence that they all happen to be resident at the "three free trade gateways" in and out of Mexico? And just how am I so knowledgeable of all this? Because I negotiated a lot of international trade deals when I represented one of America's most prominent International Manufacturer's Reps in the electronics industry.

Lastly, don't think there isn't precedence for all of this movement, through the 1800s to 1929, the ***top-two-percenters*** brought the immigrants to America to slave in their "sweatshops." Today they've discovered it's a lot cheaper to take the "sweatshops" and "pollution" to the immigrants in their own lands where freedom and liberty are scarce, and oppression a way of life.

Well folks, if you don't see any merit in these arguments, I suggest you put this book down and read no further. Enjoy the $30.00 seat at the ball game and the $4.00 hotdogs and $3.50 beers. Soon you'll be paying that much to watch it on cable-T.V., telecast from Mexico.

In closing this Chapter, let me say that even one year ago, I would have thrown out this book myself having read these "wild allegations" that many will say are right out of "paranoia-ville." But careful examination of the past twenty years and my personal involvement on the "level-playing-field" as a lawyer, MBA, and CPA has drawn me to these and only these conclusions. Frankly, I don't want to believe them or hear them myself.

- AUTHOR'S REVERSE "SPIN" GLOSSARY -

- "WHAT THEY SAY IT MEANS" & "WHAT IT REALLY MEANS" -

Balance of Payments:

<u>What they say it means:</u> The system the United States uses to record all of the economic transactions, which its businesses, banks, and citizens conduct with the rest of the world during a one year period. The Balance of Payments is divided into three accounts: the Current Account, the Capital Account, and the Official Reserves Account. Although any one of the three aforementioned accounts can show a surplus or deficit, there can be no surplus or deficit on the overall Balance of Payments because both the "buys" and the "sells" etc., as in "double entry bookkeeping" are recorded on this score sheet.

<u>What it really means:</u> It's the one-year score sheet that defines how much money we owe our trading partners for that year, how much money we invested in our trading partners that year, how much money our banks still have in reserve for that year, how much we receive in return with respect to our investments, how much money is owed us by our trading partners, how much money our trading partners invested in the United States, and how much money our trading partners' central banks are owed by the United States as a whole.

Balance of Trade:

What they say it means: The difference between what the United States imports and exports in merchandise and other goods over a period of time, generally reported monthly, quarterly, and annually. A surplus exists when imports are greater than exports, and a deficit exists when exports exceed imports in that period.

What it really means: It's the monthly score sheet issued by the U.S. Commerce Department concerning the endless voracious appetite of the American Consumer for our foreign trading partner's goods, and a combination of our foreign trading partners' mediocre desire and sometimes, contempt for U.S.-produced goods, as well as, their extraordinary aptitude to keep their own economies manufacturing oriented through such tactics as "dumping," "price fixing," and "government subsidies to industry," something America itself had a virtual lock on until about 1962.

Fair Trade & Fair Trade Acts:

What they say it means: The term "fair trade" in retailing refers to an agreement between a manufacturer and retailer whereby the manufacturer's product is sold at or above an agreed upon price (also known as resale price maintenance), and in many states these agreement were enforceable by state law. In 1975, the Congress passed the Consumer Goods Pricing Act which made unlawful the use of resale price maintenance laws in interstate commerce. On the surface, this law has worked to seemingly eliminate "fair trade" or resale price maintenance arrangements. The Fair Trade Acts (those state laws that protected manufacturers from price-cutting competition by permitting them to establish these minimum retail prices for their goods) were further effectively eliminated in 1975 when Congress repealed all federal laws upholding resale price maintenance agreements.

What it really means: First, can anyone figure out how any form of "price fixing" can be categorized under the words "Fair Trade?" Even after all of our Congress's good efforts back in 1975, haven't you ever wondered why you couldn't purchase a particular "toy" at a cheaper price in any store in your geographic area, even though you know the "toy" has been shipped via interstate commerce from Japan or another State? From personal experience, I assure you a retailer would be cut out completely from all the goods ordered from a particular manufacturer, if he chose to make that manufacture's product that week's "loss leader" (the "sale" item) to draw customers to his retail store. This, is of course, in direct violation of federal law. How many cases have you read about in the past 30 years where the Federal Trade Commission has vigorously investigated or the U.S. Department of Justice has prosecuted violators of the Consumers Goods Pricing Act of 1975?

Free Markets:

What they say it means: An economic phenomenon where price is determined by free, unregulated interchange of supply and demand. A free market economy is the opposite of a controlled market, where supply and demand and price are artificially set.

What it really means: A delirious hoped-for aspiration of the economic "top-two-percenters" that will probably work as well as did the "failed systems" of "totalitarian communism," "Nazism," and the "anarchy" of the post-French Revolution. It's also a bill-of-goods (bunk) our ***special interest group-controlled government*** sells around the world, hoping that competitor nations will also believe this myth. As stated previously, the three "Bush Boys," George Jr. , and Neil of Silverado S&L and Apex Oil Drilling infamy, and Jeb, weren't fooled as they had laid-in-wait in California, Texas, and Florida, being immediately available to pounce on, and exploit these three "free trade-free market" gateway points of wealth, clairvoyantly knowing the Clinton gang would pass their Dad's "Fast Track" NAFTA free-trade strategy in North America, in spite of Clinton's pre-election rhetoric. There was just too much money in it for everyone of America's ***top-two-percenters*** for anyone to say no!

Free Global Economic Markets:

What they say it means: An international global trading market for the exchange of all countries' goods services and other sundry items (intangibles such as stocks, bonds, options, etc.) where the transfer and freedom of movement of all such goods, services, and intangibles are free from all trade barriers, trade tariffs, trade discrimination, or other, open or surreptitious, direct or indirect trade impediments (including those subtle barriers resulting from ethnic, racial, or religious prejudices), and free of such practices as "dumping," government price support, and any other form of government regulation or control, etc. This results in the global situation where the only determinative of **price** is the free, unregulated interchange of supply and demand for labor, capital, raw materials, technology, etc.

What it really means: One need not be an expert on international trade, politics, or economics to understand that there has **got** to be more to this myth than first meets the eye. All one has to do is turn on the six o'clock news to know we are dealing with "impossibility." Even the average child of eight or nine has a better understanding of human nature than the proponents of this total global "free trade-free market" concept. Unfortunately, governments tend to cheat (take a close look at ourselves, Watergate, Iran-Contra, etc.). Sub-governmental units within governments also cheat. Need I remind you of the frauds that surfaced at HUD and within the Department of Defense, etc? Businessmen generally cheat as a matter of habit, and the overwhelming majority of individuals will always cheat, especially when it comes to making money. Even more unfortunate for those proponents of the "global free trade-free market" myth: All the world's people were not created equal, and neither were they given equal access to the same resources. Saudi Arabia and Kuwait have the largest oil reserves; South Africa the largest diamond mines; Canada and the United States the largest lumber reserves; and China the most industrious people willing to work the longest hours for the least pay, possibly with the exception of India. Now which of these groups are throwing their "national wealth" into the "pot" for the benefit of all? Who will be the first to believe he or she is not being somehow exploited by the other? And who will regulate this "mess" to assure everyone is playing on a "level playing field" when even the likes of a Saddam Hussein, having had his "can" kicked so soundly in 1990, still shakes "it" in George's face practically every other week on the evening news? Further, I ask those proponents of "global free trade-free markets": Show me which of our seven super Industrialized Nations (the G-7) has been able to regulate its own internal financial affairs in this or any other century so I might be somewhat assured that there is the **potential** for regulating this future global "mess" Ronnie, George, and Bill envision. Show me **one**, and I shall be glad to join with Ronnie, George, and Bill in their run-away efforts to subvert the spirit of America and its wealth.

Free Trade:

What they say it means: The government policy of having no quantity, quality, price, etc., controls over imports or exports; thus letting the law of "competitive cost" operate freely. The policy of "free trade" presumes also that "government" will neither subsidize nor offer direct or indirect tax subsides or support in any other way to the "businesses" or "industries" within its borders. Under a "free trade" policy, government also neither insures goods, provides financing, nor subsidizes shipping and freight of its country's products.

What it really means: For America's "top-two-percenters" it means further substantial investment opportunities and profit returns for investment in, and exploitation of the Third World's sub-poverty-level-wage-rate labor forces. For middle-class Americans it means a severe loss of jobs and a significantly lowered standard-of-living. For America's poorest-class, it means the complete loss of any hope or dream of ever attaining American middle-class status.

Trade-Balance of:

What they say it means: Commonly referred to as the "Balance of Trade," it is the difference between the total exports of U.S. goods and services and the total imports of foreign goods and services into the United States in a given month, quarter, or year, and is the most important of the five (5) categories that make up the nation's Balance of Payments. These five categories are: (1) exports of goods, services and income to foreign countries, (2) income receipts on a nation's assets that are invested abroad, (3) imports of goods, services and income from its foreign trading partners, (4) income payments on its foreign trading partners assets that are invested in its borders, (5) unilateral transfers (i.e. those included in the U.S. Balance of Payments include U.S. government grants made abroad, U.S. government pensions and other transfers made to Americans and foreigners living abroad, and private remittances and other transfers to foreign countries by private individuals).

Getting back to our focus on the U.S. Balance of Trade, when exports exceed imports, the Balance of Trade is said to have a surplus or be "positive." When total imports of goods and services from foreign countries exceeds the total exports of goods and services by the United States to foreign countries a "negative" balance or "trade deficit" is said to exist. For the trade-year 1996, as just reported by the U.S. Commerce Department on August 5, 1996, the United States is expected to have a **negative record trade deficit** or imbalance of $200 billion! This will be almost double any previous annual trade deficit in American history.

<u>**What it really means:**</u> The Balance of Trade not only reflects the wealth and borrowing power of a nation, but also the perception of foreigners and Americans in general on the quality and price of each others goods and services available for export. A Trade Deficit also indicates a nation's voracious appetite for consumption, or lack thereof. Even when the entire value of our oil imports are excluded from total foreign imports, the United States shows, as does the rest of the world, a significant preference for Japanese and German goods and merchandise. Obvious from the list of American exports, very few categories of American products, with the exception of agriculture products, farm equipment, defense equipment, and technology, are deemed desirable by our foreign trading partners. Now, given this information, what American products can you think of that our trading partners would want to buy which would help America get back to at least an even balance of trade?

Trade Barriers:

<u>**What they say they mean:**</u> Any type of governmental activity or restriction which renders the import or export of some goods into or out of a country difficult or impossible. Some examples of "trade barriers" are: (1) tariffs, duties, specific product regulation and inspection routines, and (2) government and private-sector-supported "negative imaging" of products from other countries. Trade barriers also include the anti-competitive tools of direct or indirect government subsidizing of industries to create an environment of unfair pricing and "dumping," amongst other numerous surreptitious government and private sector practices.

<u>**What they really mean:**</u> The U.S. had better start learning to play the game of international trade as it is played by its trading partners. This essentially means that government, business, labor, and the American

consumer must all work together under one National Economic Plan that assures both American economic growth in American Manufacturing and a rebuilding of America's Manufacturing and Industrial sectors.

Trading Partners:

What they say it means: Those nations that trade with the United States such as Germany, Japan, Great Britain, Canada, Taiwan, etc. The term "partner" connotes the notion that these trading partners have joined the United States in some form of generally beneficial agreement whereby each one profits equitably, as opposed to any one nation benefiting to the detriment of the other.

What it really means: The term "trading partner" is generally confined to the economic and government community of the United States; elsewhere in the world it translates to "foreign trading competitor." Even with the advent of the free-trade-zones being created in Europe (EEC), in South America, and in North America, it is unlikely that the United States will benefit economically from any of these endeavors. This conclusion is based on the notion that the Western European free-trade-zone and the South American free-trade-zone have been specifically set up to benefit their respective regions, not to benefit their trading competitors of three-thousand or ten-thousand miles away. If this conclusion were inaccurate, the United States, Japan, and Taiwan would not be excluded, nor limited in participation, in these trade pacts.

Trade Representative (U.S.):

What they say it means: The U.S. Trade Representative is a principal adviser of the President of the United States and the principal negotiator for all U.S. Trade Treaties. The U.S. Trade Representative also acts as chief enforcer of the terms, conditions, and covenants of all existing U.S. Trade Treaties. Although armed with numerous trade sanctions that may be imposed against both foreign governments and industries within foreign countries that violate U.S. Trade Treaties, rarely are these sanctions ever imposed and when they are they're rarely ever enforced.

What it really means: Historically the position of U.S. Trade Representative, and those persons employed on his or her staff, provides advancement of personal ambitions and careers. Most persons, after completing their "public service" in this generally anti-American agency, continue their careers in selling out America usually in the representation of foreign governments in Washington D.C., or become trade consultants (lobbyists for foreign governments) earning princely fees and or salaries while lobbying against U.S. trade interests.

Free and Open Markets:

What they say it means: Markets that exist in a capitalist economy in which price is determined by the free, unregulated interchange of supply and demand; as opposed to a "controlled market" where both supply and demand, and thus price are artificially determined.

What it really means: In the final analysis there is no economic, political, or social system that has been able to sustain a "free and open market" system of business enterprise. The reasons for this, although obvious, are often muted by academicians, government, and the business community in favor of the world's and America's *top-two-percenters*. But it simply a matter of choice: choosing to protect a nation's overall **standard-of-living,** or sacrificing it through a **conduit of free-trade** for the benefit of the nation's *top-two-percenters'* long-term profitability, and ever growing enormous fortunes. To the lower-class and middle-class, this simply interprets to: "The rich get richer, and the poor get poorer."

COMPOSITE DICTIONARY

Export-Import Bank [Eximbank]: A bank created by Congress in 1934 to encourage trade (mostly U.S. agricultural exports) between the United States and foreign countries. The Eximbank, although an independent entity in theory, borrows money from the U.S. Treasury to: (1) finance both exports and imports; (2) grant direct credits to non-U.S. borrowers; (3) provide insurance against commercial and political risk, and (4) provide export guarantees and discount loans to both Americans and foreigners involved in trade with the United States citizens. Here again is another example of the contradiction of the free market principle many of us believe such a vital element of American capitalism and it "efficient allocation of resources." Without the billions of dollars of U.S. Treasury financing of Eximbank, many a farm in the U.S. could not have effectively competed with their foreign competitors, even if it meant starvation for certain areas of the world. And we're not even talking about the billions spent in direct U.S. government farm subsidies over the past forty-years. How can we still think agricultural exports are one of our "strong suits" in the international trade game?" I think we got to guess again! Our strongest suit today is simply the export of all American manufacturing jobs, American capital, and little else; and when all these assets are all gone, and America's top-two-percenters internationalized like the former American MNCs, the United States will then be positioned to legitimately file for Chapter 7 Bankruptcy and also wipe out all of its own debts!

Durable Goods: Those goods that can be used over and over again and are contrary to the notion of nondurable goods which do not last a long time and which are quickly consumed, therefore requiring continual replacement by consumers. Fuel for automobiles, food products, and office supplies are examples of nondurable goods, whereas televisions, home appliances, and home furnishings are examples of durable goods.

EEC: See European Economic Community below.

European Economic Community (EEC): The EEC currently consist of Great Britain, Ireland, Denmark, Greece, Spain, Portugal, Belgium, France, Italy, Luxembourg, Holland, and Germany. The EEC is an economic alliance that was initially formed in 1957 to foster trade and cooperation among its members by gradually abolishing trade barriers and import duties amongst themselves, and standardizing import duties with non-EEC countries. The most current objective of the ECC today is to replace all of its member countries' currencies with a singular currency so as to further facilitate trade amongst its members. Also worthy of note, is the EEC's limitation on the import of Japanese automobiles by member nations within their trading block, and other trade restrictions placed on other non-EEC nations — so much for Messrs. Reagan's, Bush's, and Clinton's "free trade" world.

G-7: See "Group of 7" below.

Group of 7 (G-7): The Group of 7 includes Canada, the United States, Great Britain, Japan, Germany, France, and Italy. Known also as the G-7, these countries periodically hold meetings among their finance ministers and foreign ministers in an effort to coordinate international political policy, as well as, economic policy. The heads-of-state of the G-7 also meet periodically at summit meetings in an effort to develop global policies affecting their own group and the rest of the world, as well as, to iron out any matters that were not resolved at lower level staff meetings.

International Monetary Fund (IMF): An international lending organization that helps developing nations pay their debts and also focuses on lowering trade barriers and stabilizing currencies. The IMF usually imposes tough guidelines for lowering inflation, cutting imports, and raising exports when dealing with Third World Nations. Founded in 1945, the IMF is headquartered in Washington D.C. and is an agency of the United Nations. I know, you thought the U.N. and the world's financial center were both in New York. So now you're asking: What the heck is the IMF doing down in Washington, D.C.? The answer is simple, just think of where the U.S. Treasury, and your tax dollars are located.

14 | American Financial Institutions

As a result of the blurred lines that now distinguish the relationships between the various agencies of federal government and America's Financial Institutions, all of America's Financial Institutions that are alleged to be "private" or those that are acknowledged to be government and quasi-government have been included in this chapter, with their detailed descriptions presented in the Glossary and Dictionary sections of this Chapter.

By the end of this chapter, it is hoped you will have a basic understanding of the wide variety of America's Financial Institutions and how they interact with government, domestic and international commerce, and how they affect you. Also, it is hoped you will be able to dispel any notion you might have had previously that there exists one iota of truth in the Bush or Reagan Administrations' rhetoric between 1980-1992 that they were opposed to "big government" or "big government's" involvement in business. The only opposition by Mssrs. Bush and Reagan to "big government" was "big government's" involvement in the taxation of America's "top-two-percenters" and "big government's" involvement in maintaining the status quo of America's poor classes and the demise of its middle-classes. Perhaps at the end of this book you may come to these same conclusions.

In order to sharpen your understanding of the "ins" and "outs" of America's Financial Institutions, there are four concepts explained below in the four subsections of this chapter that will help you get a handle on all of the "money flows" you've been mystified about all these years.

Money Must Find a Home

This concept is fairly easy to understand. Individuals, organizations, associations, charities, banks, insurance companies, pension funds, and just about every other kind of entity you might be able to think of, at one time or another has excess "money," defined more specifically, as "money" earning little or no interest or other income. If this excess "money" is not earmarked for immediate expenditure, it has to find a "home." A "home" where it can earn the highest "interest" or "dividends," or perhaps even other "equity" that might be available in the market place.

In the U.S., a nation of 266 million people, and over two million businesses and organizations, there are easily well over 100 million individuals and entities seeking to place their excess "money" in the most favorable (highest return) "homes" available.

For example, take the one-in-a-thousand retired American, who has saved $100,000 over his life time, and who maintains his retirement lifestyle by supplementing his Social Security and private pension fund benefits with the "interest income" earned on his $100,000. What happens after he has become accustomed to earning 15% per year ($15,000 per year as he did in the late 1970s and early 1980s) in a federally insured jumbo CD, but because of a major decline in interest rates, he can now only earn a mere 3% return on his $100,000 cash savings? The previously comfortable "home" is no longer comfortable, or available for the income he now has available. Making matters worse, his county just increased his real estate taxes by 12% to a total of $1760.00 per.

This was precisely the economic circumstances that Wall Street, and especially the mutual fund operators, were waiting for, they themselves knowing that this "money" must find a more comfortable "home" that will provide its *owner* with a better return. So immediately following any long decline in interest rates, America is bombarded with thirty-second commercials from the boys on Wall Street announcing yields of three to four times the 3% now offered by American banking institutions, that is, if those Americans are willing to take-on some additional "risk," and invest in a ***non-federally-insured investment***. Especially attractive to these former federally-insured investors are "mutual funds," which almost sound as if they are banks themselves.

After long assurances by the mutual fund operator, the retiree's $100,000 is invested in a "stock fund." As the Dow Jones rises every day reaching new highs, the investor is pleased seeing both dividends and appreciation in his new mutual fund shares. Everything goes along fine for several months and then in one day, the stock market crashes. The Dow Jones drops 500 points. The next month's dividend checks are cut by one-third, and one-fifth of the investor's investment is gone. The mutual fund operator tells him to hang-in, assuring him that this 500 point drop is only a technical adjustment that will soon reverse. (**Author's note:** This 500 point drop would be almost impossible today with all of the trading limitations and brakes implemented by the various stock exchanges after the crash of October 19, 1987. These very brakes and trading limitations have probably been the most important factor in the rise of all of the U.S.

stock markets, since these braking mechanisms reduce the downside risk at least on a daily basis and also give the markets a great deal more price stability. However, a drop of 500 points **could** easily happen over a three or four day period.)

And so you ask: "So why did the damn fool run to the stock market?"

The answer is quite simple. Our hypothetical American retiree had two less palatable choices: (1) he could have sold his small condominium in a deteriorating real estate market, or (2) he could have reduced his food consumption.

He could not have given up his car because he had no other means of getting to the supermarket to purchase food, and he certainly never thought of spending some of his remaining $80,000 principal to support his present needs, for the fear he might live well beyond the years that the current morbidity tables call for. Thus, our once-secure American retiree either gets a job bagging groceries at the super-market, commences looking in the want-ads for another job, or calls AARP for possible job referrals.

If you understand this micro-analysis, you will understand why falling interest rates have an enormous impact on stock prices, for it is not only the retired individual who moves his "money," but also the major financial institutions such as life insurance companies, banks, and pension funds, etc. who also move their money in this manner, away from low income yielding debt and other interest-bearing instruments, or other interest-bearing *financial products* (i.e. corporate bonds, CDS, Munis, etc.). Perhaps you now have figured out why Americans have been saving less in savings banks over the past thirty years! With U.S. stock markets offering historical returns twice that of saving institutions over the past thirty years, is there any wonder that Americans are only too happy to leave their savings at a hot Wall Street brokerage house or in a hot super-growth mutual fund?

There are also other reasons why investors are tempted to jump into the stock market and assume same risks. Historically, equities have far out-paced bonds, CDS, and other fixed-rate debt instruments with their rate of returns. This is evidenced on the Dow Jones Industrial Average chart on the net page.

The question is whether this trend of the Dow Jones Industrials or the trend of the stock market as a whole will continue in the same direction as it has over the last fifty-six years? Lord Maynard Keynes, the great economist of the first-half of the Twentieth Century theorized that there was no such thing as the *long-run* or the *long-term*, *only* the *short-term*, when looking at savings, investments, or even assets. In the *long-run*, he said, we're all dead. This is probably the soundest advice anyone can give you, and this has been the advice of realistic financial advisor gurus for as long as I can remember. However the old chestnut of Wall Street goes like this: *Don't worry about the ups and downs of the market that take place day-to-day, in the long-run your investment and its returns will be there.*

DOW JONES INDUSTRIAL AVERAGE 1940-1996					
	1940-1987			1988-1996	
YEAR	LOW	HIGH	YEAR	LOW	HIGH
1940	147.42	172.51	1988	1879.14	2183.50
1945	168.46	201.06	1989	2144.64	2791.41
1950	201.62	250.24	1990	2365.75	2999.75
1955	381.43	402.48	1991	2470.30	3168.83
1960	326.54	426.24	1992	3136.58	3413.21
1965	840.59	969.26	1993	3241.95	3794.33
1970	631.16	842.00	1994	3593.35	3978.36
1975	632.04	881.81	1995	3832.08	5199.01
1980	759.13	1000.17	1996	5006.09	5801.01*
1985	1184.96	1553.10			
1987	1738.74	2722.44		* THROUGH JULY 30, 1996	

I'm not so sure about all of this continued long-term astronomical growth going on forever, especially with the Dow Jones Industrials (commonly referred to as the "market") hovering just below 6000, and every broker on Wall Street looking for this average to bust through the unbelievable 6000 point barrier.

As you will note from the above historical chart of the Dow Jones Industrial Average, the market in 1991 was well below 3000. Do you believe that the thirty industrial companies included in this Dow Jones Average are worth *twice* what they were in 1991? I don't think so. But I also didn't think that these thirty industrial stocks were worth *twice* what they were worth in 1987, a mere 2722, and yet they are about to break the 6000 barrier. Obviously, valuing the "market" was never my *forte*.

Some of my theories for the monstrous growth in the Dow and all other stocks since 1987 are as follows:

1. There had to be a major expansion in wealth to cover all of America's domestic and international IOUs, debts, and other sundry obligations which neither the U.S. Treasury, nor the U.S. Mint, nor the U.S. Banks, nor the U.S. Credit Card Companies could keep up with. These folks were still under the limiting restraints of law, conscience, and some minimal sanity. Therefore,

the task fell upon the boys of Wall Street and the numerous printing firms that could print millions of stock certificates on short notice, over night. The uncanny coincidental timing and convergence of computer technology and the Telecommunications Superhighway occurring in 1987 was also a key ingredient to creating a *Dow 6000*. This allowed unlimited daily trading of stocks, even by pre-programmed computers themselves, and precise, instantaneous record keeping, that permitted the back offices of Wall Street to manage this new avalanche of money, of trading, and of new complex equities; such as derivatives, which ultimately bankrupted some local government entities like Orange County, California in 1994.

2. The small investor was lured back into the market vis-à-vis the new trading limits put in place after the October 19, 1987 crash. The most important trading limit was that after a fifty point drop in the Dow, for any reason, all trading is halted so that the herd mentality that used to exist prior to 1987 would have the opportunity to realize they were shooting themselves in the foot if they continued to sell out their positions, especially if they were the last to get in on that day's sell-off.

3. The advent of the enormous appeal and marketing acumen of Mutual Fund Industry and its portfolio diversity, as well as, its ability to analyze its own growth within the parameters of its own statistical criteria, caused enormous amounts of individual stockholder moneys to flow through them as a conduit into the stock market and numerous other investments. One day, out of curiosity, I added up all of the shares of one particular company held by four of these mutual funds, and found that their holdings were 150% times the number of shares that the company itself said it had outstanding. Notwithstanding my possible errors in addition, a full understanding of the bookkeeping methods employed by these four mutual funds, or the company's stock ledger bookkeeping, I refuse to lose faith in any one of these mutual funds, until the day I see them refuse to cash in any of their outstanding fund shares. With the Dow approaching 6000, nothing is something, just as well as something is nothing.

4. The *multiplier effect* that applies to the expansion of money in the banking industry, also applies to the brokerage industry i.e. deposits of money by depositors to their banks, and the lending thereafter by the bank having only a fractional reserve requirement, is equivalent to the stockholder depositing his or her money with the brokerage house with a 50% margin requirement,

but in the case of the brokerage house, there is also that wonderful creation of wealth by the artificial inflation of stock prices, which if unnoticed, undetected, or intentionally ignored will have the affect of making the *multiplier effect* appear arithmetic in relation to the exponential growth possibilities realizable in the stock markets of Wall Street and the rest of the world. How else in the world could our insurance companies have paid for all of the disasters that occurred since 1990, i.e. Hurricane Andrew, The Hundred Year Flood, etc., if there weren't these wonderfully inflated Wall Street dollars around. So you see, the boys of Wall Street aren't all bad, and their greed is not all one-sided. There are some very positive side-effects to their madness. When the ultimate crash comes, as it always does on average once every fifty years, 80% of the boys of Wall Street will be on the sidelines (the remaining 20% usually get caught as *bulls* or *pigs*), as all of that imaginary wealth that you and they thought you and they had earned without either of you working for it, disappears with the same mystery attached to it, as was, when this wealth was created. That's both the end result and a major distinction between American Capitalism and Pure Capitalism.

Why Bad News Is Good News On Wall Street!

You probably don't know much about the *inner-workings* of Wall Street, but you know that whenever there is *bad* economic news the market seems to go up; and when there is *good* economic news the market seems to drop.

You wonder why this phenomenon occurs, since one would expect that most of the investors on Wall Street would be thinking that good economic news could only result in higher corporate profits, and thus higher stock prices. What you *don't know*, and all sophisticated Wall Streeters *do know*, is that in many instances, corporate profits are massaged, and sometimes even manufactured, for the very purpose of manipulating the company's stock price. Therefore sophisticated Wall Streeters prefer to gamble more on whether or not the stock market will rise as a result of an increase or decrease in the interest rate, the employment rate, or any one of the thirteen *leading, concurrent, or lagging* economic indicators manipulated and published by the somewhat more disinterested Federal Reserve Board (The Fed). Even the boys of Wall Street like to play on a somewhat level playing field without the potholes created by those greedy CEOs manipulating earnings so they might exercise their stock options in order to triple their personal earnings. The "Money Must Find A Home" section above may have given you some insight into part of the phenomenon of money growth - growth without sunlight, water, or fertilizer, but perhaps *fed* with some variations of *Miracle-Gro* and certainly a lot of *manure!*

With the information set forth below, your overall picture of the Fed's role in the U.S. economy, as well as, the world's economy will even be clearer. One other major *kicker* that you should also have in your new arsenal of knowledge is how Wall Streeters, their commercial banks, and the other of America's *top-two-percenters*, with their enormous wealth and borrowing power of today, have even greater control than Fed Chairman Alan Greenspan, to expand, contract, or destroy both the nation's and world's money supplies, as well as their economic infrastructures. Here I make reference to America's *top-two-percenters'* control and trading in the completely unregulated international currency market, where international currency traders hold their knives to the throats of everyone of the world's central bankers each day. These currency traders are the world's most ferocious speculators, who trade in as much as $5 trillion a day, yes a day. This dollar amount equals America's $5 trillion National Debt, and is two to three times the dollar volume traded on all U.S. stock markets.

An example of what I've just described took place in 1994 when the Mexican peso went into a free-fall in its value against most of the other world's currencies. Seeking to stabilize the Mexican peso, the central banks of certain nations purchased (supported) the peso at market price. As the peso continued to fall, these banks continued to purchase (support) pesos at dropping market prices. Finally, it was realized that the intervention of these purchases was insufficient to stop the dumping of pesos by the international currency traders onto the market. The pesos that had been purchased by these different central banks or governments now had a value equivalent to the low market value that the unregulated International Currency Exchange traders forced the currency to drop to. A similar scenario, or attacks on world currencies and central reserve banks (including America's Federal Reserve Bank) have been quite common over the past twenty years.

Some of these attacks by the international currency traders have been so severe that the central governments of some counties were almost brought down. So you ask: What is the consequence of this international currency trading to me? The answer is that the gold and foreign reserves in your central bank have been looted by this International Gang of Currency Traders. The treasury of your country has lost the amount of money that was lost when your central bank sold its reserves of gold, foreign currencies, and its own currency, for those dropping pesos that it now owns. Who do you think these losses in the value of these newly held pesos are going to be passed onto? It's you, if your country was one of the trading partners of Mexico and had to support the peso, and it was your central bank who purchased the pesos at the time it required international support. None of these attacks are a secret to the world financial community. They are all anticipated and pre-orchestrated by the world's current traders in open conspiracy to loot a nation of its reserves whenever the need or whim arises. Even Alan Greenspan sits back in awe of these pit-bull terriers of the world's financial community.

Let's return to the relatively small world of Chairman Greenspan, the Federal Reserve Bank, and The Fed's power over the money supply and the nation's interests rates, including the rate paid on U.S. government debt obligations, the prime rate charged by banks, and the interest rates you pay for your home mortgage in our so-called free market system.

When the bad economic news, say **higher unemployment** , hits the proverbial "fan" our elected officials, both the Administration and the U.S. Congress, flock to Federal Reserve Board to demand *stimulation* of the economy. "The Fed" then lowers interest rates causing money to seek new "homes," and may also increase the money supply (by buying government debt and putting more "dollars" out into country's money supply, a function known as *open market operations*) which also expands the money-supply. This in turn, causes the commercial banking system to have more money to lend Americans resulting in a general expansion of business, requiring additional employment of Americans, and thus, expansion of the economy. Unfortunately, with theses lower interest rates, certain savers, unlike our previous retiree, who invested in a hot mutual fund, are now required to seek a more rewarding "home" for their money. The cycle of the previously described retiree starts all over, only with a new retiree in search of his or her higher yielding mutual fund.

In this period of higher unemployment, The Fed may also lower the commercial banks' "cash reserve requirements," which again effectively creates more "money" in theory. Increasing the money available to the nation's borrowers, allows banks to make more loans (with lower reserve requirements, banks can loan out proportionately greater sums of money with less deposits or less cash reserves). Again, all of this newly created money must find a "home." Thus, with all this new "money" seeking "homes," the feeding frenzy on Wall Street also begins again: the "money" itself outstrips the supply of stocks. This demand for stock not only drives-up stock market prices, but also allows the Wall Street "pros" to make enormous profits as they reposition their own portfolios for the next major swing. For the top Wall Street pros, it doesn't matter whether the market moves up or down, so long as it keeps trading and they hedge their bets correctly by selling **long** or **short,** as their portfolio position requires.

You now have a brief outline of the market philosophy of "don't fight interest rate trends" that has made some "market gurus" very wealthy selling this very same advice. It is important for you to have an even greater understanding how the price of a stock is determined, and how fortunes are made, not only stock markets, but elsewhere. If you quickly read through the Spin Glossary and Composite Dictionary sections of this Chapter prior to going on to the next subsection, you will not only have a better feel for how all of this occurs, but you may well learn the meaning of a few of the terms that appear later in this chapter. Remember, a little bit of knowledge can be very dangerous. So be warned, if you haven't been doing the trading or investing described above and you don't have enormous cash reserves: beware you are swimming in a fish tank full of piranhas and you're the only fresh meat in the water. Be sure to read the section below for additional protection of your assets if you intend to take the dive in the tank.

The Make Believe Story Of One Stock's Price Rise

It is in this subsection that you will learn why America's stock exchanges can create overnight personal and national wealth. You will also understand why Americans tend to invest more in Wall Street than in America itself. Before we begin, I ask that you review two definitions in the Definition Section below: The "Primary Market" and the "Secondary Market."

Now that you are aware of what "primary" and "secondary markets" mean, we can now go on with our hypothetical creation of wealth vis-à-vis the stock exchanges of America.

That Late Afternoon Broker's Phone Call

Late one afternoon, you get a call from the aggressive young fellow at the brokerage house down the block from where you work. He's been pestering you during the past three months to put some money into stocks. His voice, in an almost inaudible whisper, tells you he has a hot stock "tip."

A particular company, XYZ Corp., is going public and will be offering its shares at $10 a piece commencing on Friday. The young stock broker implores you to invest, but again you decline. Several months go by. You've heard nothing from the young stock broker and nothing about XYZ Corp. Your phone rings and it's the same stock broker you haven't heard from in several months, and again he has some "important news." His muted voice advises you that XYZ Corp. is on the verge of discovering a cure for AIDS. He further advises that the news is not yet out on the Street. He can still get a hold of 1000 shares for you at the $12 price.

Unable to control your excitement, you immediately jump on this "hot" information and purchase the 1000 shares. Over the next five weeks the rumors spread all over Wall Street. The price of the stock jumps to $100 per share. Your $12,000 investment is now worth $100,000, a tidy $88,000 profit. This is only part of the story. The sold-out initial public offering of 1,000,000 shares has created an aggregate

$90 million in profits and new national wealth. All of this "new wealth"is based on "anticipation," the "anticipation" that XYZ Corp. will soon have the cure for AIDS.

What does this mean to the nation? The ABC Pension Fund, the portfolio value has risen $9 million because the pension plan manager had the "smarts" to purchase 100,000 shares during the initial public offering. MNO Banking Corporation, who had the greatest foresight of all, purchased half of the initial public offering and has profited by $45 million.

For several months thereafter, the stock trades in a range between $100 and $130 per share as some portfolio managers realign their portfolios. Then one day you hear all trading in XYZ Corp. is halted by the "exchange." There's a news release. The FDA will not approve the cure for AIDS that XYZ Corp. has been developing because it has discovered that it not only kills the AIDS virus but also kills the patient.

That night you pick up the evening newspaper with the closing stock prices. You quietly read the bad news. XYZ Corp. stock has fallen to $.50 a share. No longer are you worth between $100,000 and $130,000. You are worth $500.00. No longer do you have thousands of dollars in profit, but a loss of $9500.

So goes Wall Street sometimes, and so go expectations. As you can see by this example, money (wealth) can be created merely from expectation. It wasn't due to earnings that every share of stock rose penny by penny all the up until each share of XYZ Corporation was worth $130.00. It may have been only ten or twelve bids in this instance, with no more than a couple of hundred shares traded, to cause the entire initial public offering of 1 million shares to rise to between that $100 and $130 trading range. Surprising as it may sound, it might've only taken one trade to bring the XYZ Corp. stock down to $.50 a share. That's another of the possible consequences of the market.

And then the usual anecdotes: You hear your friends commiserating to you after you tell them of your losses, "It is better to have loved and lost than to have never loved at all!" You yourself will always relish in the notion that you did "make-it" big one time to the tune of over $100,000. Ultimately only cost you $9,500; not that expensive for the experience you had.

This subsection is not meant to be a criticism of Wall Street in its entirety, but rather an example of how Wall Street can create fortunes and money overnight. Anyone with any sophistication at all in the financial markets recognizes the need to have a "secondary market" where stock may be traded when individuals or organizations require liquidity.

The criticism of Wall Street arises when the short-term "profits" in these short-term "secondary markets" appears to eclipse the long-term "profits" attainable in the long-term "primary market" (the market where moneys are invested in actual property plant and equipment).

This phenomenon is analogous to the "inverted yield curve." Short-term debt instruments fetching higher interest rates (higher yields) than equivalent long-term debt instruments because their long-term nature should be considered riskier (i.e. a debtor has a greater chance of going bankrupt in the long-term, rather than the short-term with respect to not paying his debt). Not just I, but many others attribute the state of America's industrial infrastructure to this "inverted yield" investment phenomenon that has developed on Wall Street and its "global" equivalents over the past forty-five years. Clearly, the result is an America with half of its once-great industrial infrastructure, now primarily dependent on an overpriced stock market that will inevitably "crash" as the underlying "industrial infrastructure" beneath it is further allowed to deteriorate.

How Your Wealth is Taken Without Taxation

If you have carefully read the first three subsections of this chapter, you can probably guess what this final section is all about. It's about your money finding a new "home" and getting kidnaped ("cash-napped") while in that new "home." This is precisely what happens when "The Fed" drops interest rates.

Remember the $12,000 in "interest income" our hypothetical retiree lost in the first subsection of this chapter. Here a quasi-government agency's actions virtually "took" $12,000 in income from this hypothetical retiree. When you are required to pay 12% as opposed to 7% on your home mortgage, or 14% versus 9% on your car loan due to "The Fed's" setting "interest rates" for these and practically all other loans in America, is this not a *controlled taking* of your wealth? It is not a direct tax by any federal, state, or local government, but it is an indirect tax nonetheless simply because it results in an artificial redistribution of wealth not determined solely by the "free forces" of the marketplace. It doesn't matter that it's not called a "tax," it's still a "government taking" that results in an artificial redistribution of its citizens' wealth. Look in the Dictionary section in Chapters Eleven and Twenty under "Tax" to see the different names given to camouflage such "taking."

Conclusion

On October 19th, 1987, the Dow Jones Industrial Average plummeted 22.6%, the highest percentage decline in seventy-three years. The volume that day was 604,330,000 shares traded, still almost twice the all-time record for one day of trading on the New York Stock Exchange.

There were many causes for this "crash." Some say it was anxiety about U.S. International Trade Deficits. Some blamed the Federal Budget Deficit. Others blamed then U.S. Treasury Secretary James Baker, who the week before had subtly hinted at a willingness to let the U.S. Dollar continue its previous days' free-fall. Still others blamed the "crash" on Wall Street's new "programmed trading" in which computers automatically "buy" or "sell" large volumes of stock, given certain circumstances.

Oddly enough, prior to, and immediately following the 1987 "crash," the U.S. economy showed steady growth. By mid-spring of 1988, just six months after the worst "crash" in seventy-three years, it seemed as though the "crash" had never occurred. Except for the loss of fifteen thousand Wall Street jobs (some refer to this as a "technical correction") and the temporary abandonment of the Street by the small investor, there were no other noticeable effects.

Five years after the crash of October 19, 1987, the Dow Jones Industrial Average reached new peaks closing well over 500 points above its 1987 "crash" level. All this while: (1) the American economy was said to be in its worst long-term "slump" since the "Great Depression," (2) unemployment was at its highest level since 1984, (3) the "dollar" reached its historic low (September 4, 1992), and (4) the National Debt increased by more than $1.6 trillion over its 1987 level of $3.4 trillion to $5 trillion. The U.S. Trade Deficit in August, 1992 was the worst reported in the previous two-years and has remained at these levels up until today. In 1996, the Dow Jones Industrial Average trades between 5000-5800, and is poised to go over 6000 in the very near term. How and why has this all occurred, you ask?

"Is there any reason for concern"? you also worriedly ask. The answer is clear: Not any more or less than there was a month ago, a year ago, or ten years ago. With investments in "real estate" in their current unfavorable tax climate, America's middle-class in serious trouble, and the National Debt at $5 trillion there should be plenty of reason for concern. There's none in the Administration or the U.S. Congress. I suggest you wait like everyone else for the "madness" to unwind. In our present environment, to do anything more might get you committed. Should a "crash" take place between now and before you complete this book, immediately go to Chapters Nineteen and Twenty. Read them both thoroughly, and then set your mind to taking part in what may very well be a very meaningful recovery.

Lastly, for those of you who wish to delve further into a more expansive study of America's Financial Institutions the two books listed below are must reading:

1. Inside Job: The Looting of America's Savings and Loans: By Stephen Pizzo, Mary Fricker, & Paul Muolo, Published by HarperPerennial, a division of HarperCollins Publishers.

2. <u>The World's Money</u>: By Michael Moffitt, Published by Simon & Schuster.

A FINAL WORD ABOUT THE STOCK MARKET

In May of 1990, I advised several of my *top-two-percenter* clients to put all of their money into the stock market and to convert all other investments such as their gold ingots and silver bars, gold coin collections, stamp collections, art collections, antique automobile collections, and real estate investments to cash, and put it all the proceeds into the stock market. I then made the statement that I would see the Dow Jones Industrial Average over 6000 before I would ever see gold above $400 an ounce for any sustained period. The Dow hasn't yet gone over 6000 and neither has gold sustained a price over $400, except for one day in 1995. Although the 6000-point goal of the Dow has not been reached yet, I still remain confident, even with the bad news of July 5, 1996 (the drop of 114.88 in the Dow), that the Dow will go over 6000 points before the price of gold stays over $400 per ounce for more than one day.

One of my clients insisted upon knowing why I was so adamant about disrupting his investment advisor's diversified investment program. It was an irrational answer, but I simply responded: "Gold is too scarce, and too dangerous to hold. None of your other investments such as your antique cars, the coins, etc. can grow unless the demand for these trinkets also grows, an unlikely event, given the severe decline in the upward mobility of America's *middle-class* who, as novices, usually create the demand for these sort of occasionally appreciating assets."

Underlying my investment theory were all of the headlines in the 1980s describing the downsizing of Corporate America and the number of Boobus Americanus *falling out of the middle-class* at an exponentially quicker rate, versus those Boobus Americanus in America's *middle-class* that were buoying up into America's *top-two-percenters*. But of greater importance to my theory was the humongous amount of money that had been virtually growing like alfalfa since the crash of October 19, 1987. I was certain the boys on Wall Street were somehow responsible for the creation of all this new wealth.

Combined with the knowledge that America had nothing else left to manufacture, I had in the middle of the night of the day before, concluded that the only place where scarcity would be of no limitation, and safety paramount because of the trading limitations now in place to avoid the downside risks of the pre-1987 market, was the equity markets of the United States. I likened it to the U.S. Mint printing money. What difference between that and the local printer printing stock certificates and all sorts of other financial instruments than the U.S. Mint printing money, except a little less regulation. Certainly this idea didn't contradict my belief that wealth was nothing more than what you and everyone else thought it to be, and demanded. Application of the banking multiplier effect was applied, and I concluded that the only investment game in town was Wall Street.

Many of you may find this contradictory to everything else in this book but I think its important that each and every one of you know that the victim of every natural disaster in the United States between 1990 and 1996, including Hurricane Andrew and the Hundred Year Flood, amongst others, can thank the boys of Wall Street for the insurance proceeds they received for their losses. The boys of Wall Street provided all of the make believe money for all of the payments made by the insurance industry to these victims. Insurance companies, as many of you may know, keep vast parts of their portfolios full of those same equities that I advised my clients to acquire, as opposed to all of those other non-performing assets I recommended my *top-two-percenter* clients divest himself of back in 1990. Conclusion: Although American Capitalism always seem generally evil to most except the *top-two-percenters*, sometimes it isn't all that bad.

Occasionally, another's greed inadvertently has benefit to some third party non-participants as in the case of all the victims of America's natural disasters occuring in the 1990s. Don't depend on this same phenomenon being repeated when the next round of natural disasters occur. *Top-two-percenters* once burned, are *twice* learned.

- AUTHOR'S REVERSE "SPIN" GLOSSARY -

- "WHAT THEY SAY IT MEANS" & "WHAT IT REALLY MEANS" -

Bank Insurance Fund (BIF) [See FSLIC]:

What they say it means: A new fund mandated by FIRREA after the dismantling of FSLIC to insure "bank depositor's" money deposited in America's S&Ls.

What it really means: A "new fund" to be "looted" by the next generation of: Our elected politicians children and friends, certain "special interest groups," and the crop of "looters" and thieves that will inherit America.

Commercial Banks:

What they say it means: In America's banking structure, the commercial bank as opposed to the "savings and loan" banks, are the most unrestricted type of bank concerning the latitude of services it can provide its customers and the types of loans it can make to its customers. FDIC insures commercial bank depositors against $100,000.00 of losses in deposits made in accounts of these banks.

What it really means: To truly understand the role of the commercial bank in the world and American economies, one must understand its most important officer: the bank's loan officer. It's his job is to get every available depositor "penny" out into the world borrowing community, and in most cases this is irrelevant to the financial risks involved, the "character" of those borrowing the money, or the nature or purpose of the loan. Assisting the loan officer is a relatively whole new industry in the United States, the Loan Broker, whose multi-purpose job it is: (1) to locate borrowers (those in need of money for whatever reason), or (2) create borrowers i.e. convincing those who don't need liquidity to take on additional or new debt based upon the Loan Broker's portfolio of financial schemes and "investment opportunities," or (3) identify "roll-over-borrowers" who generally might benefit (again based upon the Loan Broker's portfolio of financial schemes and "investment opportunities") from larger loans than they already have, Even though the larger loans require a higher rate of interest and additional up-front points. Bank loan officers are promoted and generally remunerated based upon their volume of lending. One only needs to look into the real estate portfolios, the Third World Debt portfolios, and the corporate debt portfolios to appreciate the indifference most of these loan officers have respecting the Commercial Bank's federally insured Moines. For those of you interested in an in-depth analysis of the commercial banking industry and its economic ramifications, <u>The World's Money</u> by Michael Moffitt, published by Simon and Schuster in 1983, is absolutely "must" reading. On further reflection, I heighten my recommendation to say Moffitt's book should be required reading for every American citizen.

Commodities Futures Trading Commission [CFTC]:

What they say it means: The CFTC was created in 1974 by the U.S. Congress, succeeding the regulatory agency that had previously been authorized by Commodities Exchange Act of 1936. The CFTC has jurisdiction over: (1) all commodities traded in all organized commodities markets; (2) policing matters of information and disclosure, registration of firms and individuals, and bad trading practices; and (3) the protection of customer funds, record keeping, and the maintenance of orderly futures and options markets. The CFTC is to the Commodities Exchanges and commodities, what the SEC is to the Securities Exchanges and stock and bonds.

What the CFTC really means: It is the second largest U.S. Taxpayer paid-for gambling regulatory agency (i.e. similar to state racing commissions and casino regulators) that gives false assurance to the small high-flying American middle-class gambler (sometimes erroneously referred to as "investors") that the gambling operations conducted at the Commodities Exchanges are never "rigged."

Commercial Paper:

What they say it means: Commercial Paper are the short-term debt obligations issued by banks, corporations, and other borrowers to investors, who have millions-of-dollars sitting around in "idle cash" in need of finding a home. Commercial Paper may have maturities ranging from as little as two days, to as much as two hundred and seventy days, and is usually discounted, although some of this paper is interest-bearing. In 1970 there was approximately $33.4 billion of Commercial Paper outstanding in the United States. By 1980, these unsecured promissory notes had almost quadrupled to $124.4 billion, and by 1990, another quadrupling occurred to approximately $535 billion.

What all this Commercial Paper really means: There's a lot of money around looking for a "home," but certainly not finding "it" in any PP&E investment, or job creation in the United States. Compare this amount of money to Bill Clinton's $200 billion program, suggested during his 1992 campaign, to revitalize America out of its 1992 recession.

Corporate Bonds:

What they say it means: These are debt instruments issued by Corporate America as distinguished from U.S. Treasury Bonds which are issued by the federal government, and Municipal Bonds which are issued by state and local governments and agencies. Corporate Bonds generally have a par or face value of $1,000 and are usually of a fixed maturity and interest. Bonds holders earn "interest income" as opposed to "dividend income." Corporate Bonds are traded on the major Security Exchanges at prices reflecting current interest rates: for example, if a bond with a $1,000 value (face value) carries a fixed interest rate of 4% and the current rate of interest in the market place is 12%, the bond will sell at a discounted price where the new investor purchasing the bond will receive an effective current yield of 12%. As a rule, when interest rates fall below the fixed interest rate set forth on the face of the bond, the bond price rises; and when interests fall below the fixed interest rate set forth on the bond, the bond price falls. Corporate Bond prices are also effected by such things as overall market liquidity, the rating given to them by rating services such as Standard & Poor's, Moody's, etc.; the anticipation of interest rate movements by the Federal Reserve Bank; and "news" concerning the economy — good news, oddly enough, generally drives bond prices down (i.e. the fear of a prosperous economy always raises inflation fears, and thus the fear of rising interest rates, thus for good reason (lower bond prices) causing money to move from this market to the stock market (called a sell-off).

Unless there is a "conversion privilege," corporate bonds remain the obligation of corporation until their redemption date. Lastly, it should be noted that most corporate bonds today include a "call" feature, allowing the corporation to effectively recall the bond from the investor at any time, especially when interest rates drop below the face interest rate of the bond, thus allowing the corporation to refinance this bond debt at a lower cost of interest after the bond has been issued.

What it really means: One scenario, proposed by one economist, who is not a member of the "inner circle," is that a corporate bond (including corporate junk bonds) are one of the primary "vehicles" that corporate management has for stealing the company from its stockholders. The scheme generally works along these lines: (1) The corporation issues $50 million in corporate bonds pursuant to a prospectus which indicates it wishes to build a new manufacturing plant. (2) The corporate bonds are sold and the $50 million is maintained in the Corporate Treasury, until such time as corporate management decides that the manufacturing plant has become unfeasible (really known from day one). (3) The idle $50 million is then used to purchase the company's stock that is offered on the various Securities Exchanges. (4) This procedure is repeated over-and-over again for four or five more years (know as corporate long range strategic planning) until a majority of the corporation's stock has been retired into the Corporate Treasury. (5) Corporate management has during this same "strategic planning period," issued to itself numerous Incentives Stock Options and general stock bonuses which complement their own purchases of stock over the same three or four years so that ultimately corporate management owns a large percentage of the stock that remains outstanding. (6) Management of the corporation then determines that it is in the best interest of the corporation to repurchase all of its outstanding stock and then makes the appropriate tender offer at a price where the remaining stockholders, especially those in management, are substantially rewarded. (7) Once all of the stock has been retired, all ownership is effectively transferred to the company's management. (See also Junk Bonds.)

Corporate Stock:

What they say it means: Corporate stock, also known as Capital Stock represents the equity or ownership interest of those persons who invested in the corporation, as contrary to those investors who acquire corporate bonds (obligations or debt of the corporation). Corporate stock is generally broken down into two categories, one called "preferred" and the other called "common." Preferred stock generally enjoys priority over common stock with respect to distribution of dividends and liquidating distributions in the event of bankruptcy or dissolution of the corporation. Common stockholders, as opposed to preferred stockholders, generally assume greater primary risk of loss if the business does poorly, and generally realize a greater return on their investment if the business is successful. It is generally the common stockholders who elect the Board of Directors that controls the company. (See also Stockholder.) The issuance of common stock has historically been the primary means of raising "capital" (money) for both new and existing corporations, although the 1980s saw this general rule practically nullified (at least on the "money" side) with the "money raising" gimmicks (i.e. Junk Bonds) of the M&A Gangs of Wall Street. All U.S. companies with publicly traded stock must be registered with the SEC.

What it really means: To the common stockholder, it can mean many things; dividends that are taxed as dividend income; appreciation based on the success and growth of the company; a wind-fall profit should the company be "targeted" by an unfriendly predator (i.e. the M&A Gangsters); a frustration when corporate management decides to surreptitiously "loot" the company by taking it private, or just "looting" it directly; and the ultimate realization that those "pretty-pieces-of-paper" that say "Common Shares" have little to do with any real ownership rights of the corporation he or she thought they owned.

Discount Rate [see also Federal Reserve Bank, Moral Suasion, Open Market Operations, Reserve Requirements.]

What they say it means: The interest rate charged by the Federal Reserve (The Fed) for collateralized loans by member banks using government securities or other government prescribed eligible collateral. The Discount Rate also sets a floor on interest rates from which banks determine their prime rate, the rate they generally charge their best customers.

What it really means: The Discount Rate is the first contradiction of the concept of American "free market" capitalism. Obviously it is not the supply or demand of lenders that determines the "interest rate" (the cost-of-money), but the Federal Reserve Board, a quasi-governmental institution parallel to our foreign trading partners' Central Banks. To understand the awesome power of being able to control the nation's cost-of-money ("interests rates") through the Discount Rate (there are other tools also in "the Fed's" arsenal), one need only focus on home mortgage rates especially those variable rate mortgages; savings bank interest rates; certificate of deposit interest rates; and the integral role the "Discount Rate" plays in financing our own National Debt. Some underground economic theorists contend the United States Government would literally have gone out of business, if it had truly let the "free market" determine the interest rate at which the National Debt had to be financed. Given the notion of a "free market," it is certainly questionable how many of America's creditors would finance our very dubious $4 Trillion National Debt.

Federal Deposit Insurance Corporation [FDIC]

What they say it means: FDIC is a federal agency established in 1933 to guarantee funds on deposit in member banks and performs other functions such as making loans to its member banks or buying assets from member banks to facilitate mergers or prevent failures. Currently FDIC insures deposits in member banks of up to $100,000 per depositor. Initially FDIC only insured deposits at commercial banks, but with the great S&L debacle of the 1980s, and the bankrupting of the Federal Savings & Loan Insurance Incorporation, today all Savings & Loans as well as saving bank deposits of up to $100,000 are insured under FDIC.

What it really means: FDIC, in its purest form, is probably one of the most important federal agencies in America today. It insures the savings of individuals in aggregates of up to $100,000, thus assuring those people who are able to save in these large sums, that their money will be protected by the "full faith and credit" of the United States. This allows for our banking system to attract deposits, which in turn become their reserves, which, then in turn become the money available for lending and investment in the United States. Unfortunately, after the "late" FSLIC, and perhaps Ginnie Mae and Freddie Mac, the FDIC will probably become, if it has not already, the most abused federal agency in the history of the United States. Why is that you might ask? Simply because FDIC insurance allows banks to attract enormous amount of depositors with almost unlimited money. This is accomplished through loopholes that the banks themselves create. For example, if you open up a first account in your own name, you're insured for up to $100,000. You then opened up a second account in your name, but "in trust" for your child; you're insured for a second $100,000. You may then open another account in your own name but this time "in trust" for your mother, and similarly then one "in trust" for your father, and your uncle and just about any other member of your family. Each one of these accounts are insured for a maximum of $100,000. Most of you are already scratching your heads asking? "So what's wrong with insuring one's money in this manner?" The answer is not simply. For it is not the saver who is the culprit here, but the banker. As some of you are already aware, this was one of the reasons for the Great S&L failure of the 1980s. Bankers attracting enormous deposits insured by the Federal Savings and Loan Insurance Incorporation (FSLIC). Those same bankers then lending as much as five-times these enormous sums to very questionable real estate developers, home builders, limited partnerships, and a whole host of other nefarious lenders. It was the American taxpayer who ended up with the final bill, estimated today at $500 Billion, payable over the next thirty-years.

Federal Funds [see also Federal Reserve System in the Dictionary Section]:

What they say it means: Federal Funds are created through the deposit of funds by Commercial Banks to the Federal Reserve Banks to satisfy "The Fed's" current "reserve requirements." Banks may lend Federal Funds to each other on an overnight basis and may also transfer Federal Funds among themselves or on behalf of customers on a same day basis. The Federal Reserve uses Federal Funds that are deposited by its member Commercial Banks for the purchase of government securities (in its "Open Market Operations") and to settle transaction where there is no "float" involved.

What Federal Funds really mean: Here again we have the United States Government engaged in activities contrary to the "free market" aspect of capitalism. By controlling the "reserve requirements" of its member commercial banks, and through its Open Market Operations, The Fed controls the money supply which in turn effects directly the cost of borrowing money, and thus the velocity of the nation's economic activity. This, as stated previously, is in addition to its direct control over the absolute cost-of-money through its control over the Discount Rate.

Federal Savings & Loans Insurance Corporation (FSLIC):

What they use to say it meant: A Federal Agency that had been establish in 1934 to insure the deposits in member Savings & Loans and Thrifts Institutions. After the "lootings" of the S&Ls during the 1980s, the FSLIC became defunct and bankrupt. The Agency was disbanded pursuant to the landmark Congressional legislation known as the Financial Institution Reform, Recovery, and Enforcement Act of 1989, an Act that, in years to come, may possibly be hailed as one of the biggest federal legislative "cover-up deals" in U.S. history.

What it really meant: The agency FSLIC had been so completely "looted," that it was no longer in the interest of the Congress or the Executive Branches of Government to continue reminding the American Taxpayer of its existence, and thus it was given a quick legislative burial in 1989.

Financial Institutions Reform, Recovery, and Enforcement Act of 1989 (FIRREA):

What they say it means: Congressional legislation that reformed and re-regulated the S&L Industry, putting the S&Ls and Thrifts back into their original role of providing home mortgages to America's home buyers. The legislation signed into law on August 7, 1989, effectively reversed the GARN-ST. GERMAIN Bill of 1982 that deregulated these same S&Ls and Thrift Institutions allowing their "lootings" during the decade of 1980s.

What it really means: Hopefully it will give the S&Ls a second chance in assisting most Americans to economically finance their home purchases. On the bleak side, it may be nothing more than new legislation designed to again set the U.S. Taxpayer up as an insurer for a second "looting" as soon as the present S&L $500 billion Bailout becomes a faded memory. (See FSLIC above.)

Forward Contracts:

What they say it means: A forward contract represents a "completed transaction" (the buyer is obligated to buy, and the purchaser is obligated to sell) in a commodity, security, currency, or other financial instrument at a "negotiated agreed rate" (a price specified "now") with delivery and settlement at a "specified future date." Because the forward contract is "completed," it may be used as a "cover" (hedge) for a "Futures Contract," whereas an "Option Contract" cannot be used as a "cover" because the owner has the choice of "completing," or "not completing" the contract.

What Forward Contracts really mean: First there was a missile, then there was an anti-missile, and then there was an anti-missile-missile-missile, and so forth. Or in gambling lingo, a hedge, on a hedge, to cover a loss or lock-in a gain. First there was a Spot Contract (cash on the spot for the commodity on the day of the sale), then a Futures Contract, and then there was a Forward Contract (See Futures Contract in Glossary below). With so many of America's creative minds (I think there are still some left on Wall Street) engaged in so much of this "creative" Wall Street "wagering," you can almost "bet-the-form" that there will be new instruments and contracts invented to heighten the excitement long before you yourself can develop the skills to get in there and compete — better to devote your life's talents to a worthier pursuit, there being too much of it already wasted on the "Street."

Futures Contracts:

What they say it means: A financial instrument in the form of an agreement to purchase or sell a specific amount of a commodity, foreign currency, government security, or other financial instrument at a "specific price" on a stipulated "future" date regardless of the actual "market price" of that commodity on the "future date." Using the "open outcry" system, the "price" element of the agreement is established between the buyer and the seller on the floor of the Commodity Exchange. This financial agreement obligates the purchaser to purchase the underlying commodity, and the seller to sell it, unless the agreement is sold to another prior to the settlement date, which may occur if the contract holder desires to take a profit or cut a loss. Alternatively, the holder of a futures contract may also hedge his position through use of a "forward contract," thus cutting his losses, or locking in his profits while still retaining the original "futures contract" in his portfolio. (See Forward Contracts above)

What Futures Contracts really mean: Futures contracts are one of the most sophisticated forms of gambling in the United States. The Wall Street wagerer in this case is betting on both internal and external factors that might effect the "future market price" of the commodity he has agreed to sell or purchase at a specific future date. If the commodity price goes up (scarcity due to drought, flood, war, etc.) and the futures contract holder is the seller, he is obligated to purchase the commodity for delivery to the purchaser at the usually much higher "market price," thus losing money; if he is a buyer side of the "future contract," and the "market price" on the settlement date is higher than the future's contracted price, he takes delivery of the commodity at this below "market price," thus making a profit. The profit is the difference between the previously negotiated "future contract" commodity price and the "market price" that exists on the settlement date, multiplied by whatever the quantity was of the commodity contracted for.

Glass Steagall Act of 1933:

What they say it means: The Glass Steagall Act of 1933, prohibits commercial banks from owning or operating brokerage firms, i.e. those firms specifically engaged in the purchase and sale and "advice giving" to those persons who actually purchase stocks, bonds and other investment vehicles. The Glass Steagall Act also authorized deposit insurance for the commercial banking system known as FDIC. The Bush Administration and the American Banking Association blame Glass Steagall for their inability to compete with the scandal-ridden banks, and other financial institutions of Japan, as well as other international banking institutions operated in other competitor countries.

What it really means: The loan portfolios of the commercial banks which include such stellar assets as non-performing Third World debt obligations, non-performing commercial real estate loans, and non-performing building and construction loans after having been so poorly underwritten by the throngs of commercial bank lending officers — are now about to cause a complete collapse of the commercial banking sector. So now it's time to take down the wall (often referred to as the "fire-wall") and allow the banks to save themselves by entering the free "wheeling and dealing" world of Wall Street. That was where the Administration and your Congress were headed as the panic set in, all through late 1990, right up until now — the "proposals" still remain in Committee, awaiting the darkest of moonless nights for secret passage.

Now it's time for you to exercise your own suspicious minds! Can you somehow figure a way, if you were a major commercial banker, how you could use those federally insured deposits to work for you and your bank in the casinos of Wall Street; all one has to do is remember the escapades of Charles Keating III, former chairmen of the Lincoln S&L and American Continental Corporation, and the long line of his depositors who believed their life savings were insured as Mr. Keating and his gang convinced them to put their entire life savings in non-federally insured investment vehicles (kamikazes), unbeknownst to many of these savers, that these new investments where not federally insured deposits. Now think of all the millions of hard-working American depositors ready for all those "new toasters," to shift their insured deposits into some of those "financial kamikaze vehicles" those commercial bankers and Wall Streeters will be putting together — again remember the lines of angry Lincoln S&L depositors who wanted to lynch Keating as he was led into the federal courthouse for his arraignment in 1991 — multiply this by a million or so, and try to imagine ever again trying to achieve a sound American commercial banking system. The answer to the commercial banking mess is not attempted suicides but rather a redefining of their role in American Capitalism. We've got to work up from where we are now, not dig a deeper hole from which we'll all have to crawl out later. See Chapters Nineteen and Twenty for solutions to the present potential commercial banking crisis failing in America.

Ginnie Mae Pass-Throughs [The Business Side of Government Patronage]:

What they say it means: It's a data processing operation (a private business) that processes the monthly homeowner's payments on those "mortgage security backed by a pool of mortgages," guaranteed by the United States Government through the Government National Mortgage Associations, who after deducting a 1/2% service charge, forwards the homeowners payment of interest and principle to the institutional investors or individuals who purchased the homeowner's mortgage.

What it really means: A multi-million dollar data processing business, that if investigated would probably reveal some of the richest pass-throughs of "non-political-looking" political patronage. Think about the 1/2% (not a dollar or two, but 1/2%) on the billions of dollars in monthly mortgage payments! Perhaps you'd like to participate in the "ownership" of this operation, especially after the data processing operations are quietly transferred to the low-wage "sweat shops" of the Caribbean back-offices. (See Chapter Four)

Government National Mortgage Association [Ginnie Mae]

What they say it means: Ginnie Mae is the "government owned" equivalent of Fannie Mae. It is an agency of the U.S. Department of Housing and Urban Development (HUD). Ginnie Mae purchases mortgages from private lenders such as banks, S&Ls, and Thrifts, and thereafter packages them into securities called Ginnie Maes, and sells the resulting securities to investors. The agency guarantees the timely payment of both principle and interest to the investors of these securities (certificates). The general truism in the rhetoric here, and to which no competent economist in the world would disagree, is that the enormous growth of the secondary mortgage market that America enjoys today (as well as its Home Construction and Real Estate Industries) has been made possible by Ginnie Mae, Freddie Mac, Fannie Mae. The efforts of these three government or quasi-government agencies have increased the amount of money available for home mortgages and have provided a high yielding investment opportunity for America's conservative investors.

What it really means: In order to avoid redundancy, please refer back to the "What it really means:" Section of "Federal National Mortgage Association." With respect to the notion that Ginnie Maes, Freddie Macs and Fannie Maes represent opportunities for conservative investors, I suggest that these conservative investors also follow the national residential home foreclosure rate, the U.S. unemployment statistics released by the U.S. Department of Commerce, and the number of permanently "lost" American jobs each month. Note: Over four years ago, on July 1, 1992, the U.S. Senate approved legislation aimed at preventing "Massive Taxpayer Bailouts" of the two government-backed enterprises known as Fannie Mae and Freddie Mac. Between these two enterprises, the Federal Government (the U.S. Taxpayer) stands behind (guarantees) $900 billion worth of federally insured home mortgages. The Senate vote was 77 to 19. Let's hope these U.S. Senators can act this quickly on Medicare next year.

Insurance Company:

What they say it means: In economic and financial theory, the insurance company acts as a financial intermediary which takes in money (premiums) from the "many," to pay the catastrophic losses of the "few." In theory the insurance company is a holder of the "public trust" in that it is made the trustee of citizen's money today, to hold that money in secure investments, and finally return some of that money in the hopefully unlikely event the insured's risk matures. Some commentators have defined today's insurance companies as the ultimate "book-makers," as exemplified by the operations of Lloyd's of London, the insurer of last resort for the "low occurrence" risk, with the "gigantic loss" exposure; the business: Nothing more than "super premiums" — "super risks" — the insurers against earthquakes, hurricanes, riots, and volcanos — and in the case of Lloyd's of London, it's the "investor group" that assumes the "ultimate risk" for what has been termed the "ultimate reward." The "investor group" is betting that the earthquake won't occur, the insured seeks protection based on the fact that it might occur, and in order to avoid such catastrophic loss is willing to pay an enormous premium for what may seem to many as an unlikely risk of occurrence. Lloyd's of London announced in late June of 1992, that in 1989 its "investor groups" suffered their biggest losses in their 304 year history, $3.84 billion — hundreds of personal fortunes made in the past were totally lost for many!

As business has grown and the world's commerce expanded, so has the Insurance Industry. No longer is the concept for a few weak farmers pooling some portion of their funds to protect against the loss of a crop or a barn; today it's for hundreds of thousands of businessmen, consumers, and governments insuring everything from losses due to natural disasters to the negligence of their children in the backyard's of their homes. Life insurance, health, automobile, homeowner's, flood, general liability, umbrella coverages, workers' compensation, malpractice, the list goes on and on. Approximately 1.5 million Americans were employed in America's Insurance Industry in 1994, and this industry accounted for over $1 trillion of the $6.7 trillion U.S. Gross National Product (GNP) in 1994.

What it really means: The critical question with regard to insurance companies today revolves around their financial soundness. As stated previously, insurance companies are no longer comprised of small groups of individuals, farmers, or businesses pooling their funds to assure against a particular risk or catastrophe, but they are some of the largest financial institutions in America today. One only need to think of the Traveler's, the Aetna, The Hartford, or the Prudential, just to name a few in order to appreciate the diversity of business these insurance companies are involved with, the amount of economic resources they control, and the impact they might have on the American economy should anyone of them become insolvent. Very few Americans are aware that insurance companies have the majority of their assets invested in American real estate, and on Wall Street in corporate stock, bonds, federal, state and local municipal obligations, etc. Few Americans also are aware that insurance companies manage the assets of the majority of "pension funds" in the U.S. today, also investing these funds in the same investment portfolio previously stated. With the continuing collapse of the American real estate market, one could only imagine what would happen if there were a major crash in the stock market! And who amongst us hasn't heard of the failure of the Executive Life Insurance Company of California, and even the largest of these insurance institutions now refusing to pay certain large medical insurance claims submitted by persons who allegedly had paid premiums for such coverage. One of America's leading consultants and experts on the property & casualty insurance industry stated that the industry in 1992 had a $26 billion short-fall in its 1992 "loss reserves" — a scary number when one considers that 28.5% of all property & casualty insurance companies failed between 1969 and 1990, because of inadequate "loss reserves." This consultant is now employed full time by an off-shore subsidiary of a major American insurance company.

All of you reading this book have every reason in the world to be scared, but let me assure you, there is light at the end of this tunnel — it's set forth in Chapters Nineteen and Twenty of this book. If I didn't think there was light there, I wouldn't have undertaken the ordeal of writing this book.

Investment Banker:

What they say it means: It is important to understand that one will never find the office of the investment banker in his or her commercial bank or savings and loan. Investment banking has nothing to do with checking accounts or savings accounts, but only to do with those intermediary functions between the "issuer-of-securities" (stocks and bonds) and the "investing public." If the security issuer is a client of the investment banker, the investment banker's role commences with pre-underwriting counseling and continues long after the distribution of securities is completed and may even entail the investment banker being a member of the issuer's Board of Directors. To earn his keep, the investment banker prepares the SEC registration statement; consults on the issuance-pricing of the security; forms and manages other investment bankers into a so-called "syndicate" so that a broad-base of distribution for the issuer's securities is made available; and in some instances establishes a "selling group" that acts to maintain a minimum price of the securities issued during the offering period. Investment bankers also handle the distribution of large blocks of already issued securities through secondary offerings; function as finders in the private placement of certain securities; and create and maintain markets for securities already issued and distributed. Most investment bankers maintain broker-dealer operations, providing both wholesale and retail customers with investment-advisory-services and a whole host of other financial services.

What it really means: It is the dream of every MBA to enter the high-flying world of Investment Banking. It is here where the millions are made in the course of just a few hours. Investment bankers are also both the heart and soul of the Mergers & Acquisitions Gang. Names like Michael Milken, Dennis Levine, Ivan Boesky, and the infamous Drexel Burnham Lambert, household-names although short-lived, for much of the late 1970s and 1980s. Merrill Lynch and the former American Express-Shearson Lehman are examples of brokerage firms also having investment banking operations.

Junk Bonds:

What they say they mean: Those bonds, generally issued during the M&A holocaust of the 1970s and 1980s to acquire other companies, but which were also used to lure unwary investors from low-yield federally insured savings into these highly speculative high-interest paying bonds. Junk bonds, being extremely more volatile than "investment grade" bonds, are required to pay substantially higher rates of interest.

What they really are: A financial vehicle, sometimes referred to as a "kamikaze," where the lure of high yields generally blinds the investor as to the underlying value of the financial instrument itself, and the ability of its issuer to pay either its future interest payments or principal when do. The Junk Bond, for most, will always be remembered as the financial instrument, that among other things, allowed the so-called "Wizards of Wall Street" (the M&A Gangs) to fleece middle-income and fixed-income Americans who maintained their nominal standards-of-living by subsidizing their salaries or Social Security income with interest earned on savings.

Options Contracts:

What they say they mean: A financial instrument in the form of a contract evidencing the right, but not an obligation, to buy or sell generally stock, commodities, or stock indexes that is given an exchange for an agreed upon sum of money. An option buyer forfeits his money if he does not exercise his option within the specified period of time set by the Option Contract.

What it really means: Options include "puts," "calls," "straddles," and "spread eagles." Although options, in some form, have been around for as long as commerce itself, they became fanciful wagering devises in the U.S. in the mid-1970s. What many Americans not familiar with Wall Street do not realize, is that this so-called "investment" has little to do with reality. For example, there may exist a thousand Option Contracts where sellers have agreed to deliver a 100 million shares of stock in a company that only has one-million shares of stock outstanding. Obviously, if all of these options are exercised by the purchasers, all demanding the actual stock, all of the option sellers could not possible deliver all of the securities. To accommodate this difference between "fantasy" and "reality," option traders as do future contracts traders and forward contract traders settle differences in "pure cash." The underlying stock, commodity, etc. having very little meaning except for establishing gambling gains or losses. As a result of this difference between "fantasy" and "reality," some of the largest fortunes have been made and lost on Wall Street in the high-rolling gambling of Option Contracts, Futures Contracts, and Forward Contracts.

Monetary Policy:

What they say it means: Monetary Policy is a term generally used in juxtaposition to "fiscal policy" to describe the general principles by which The Fed is guided in its management of the U.S., and perhaps even certain elements of the world's economy. The Fed, through its four major tools of (1) Open Market Operations; (2) raising or lowering of the Discount Rate; (3) its use of "Moral Suasion" — threatening the nation's bankers with public disclosure of wrongdoings, violations of law, etc.; and (4) setting of the U.S. Commercial Banks' "reserve requirements," effects changes in the quantities of money and bank credit on the premise that control of these quantities is the prime way of maintaining a stable price level (minimal inflation) and modifying the "Business Cycle."

What it really means: If you've ever financed a home, it's The Fed's Monetary Policy that determined the interest rate you're paying on your mortgage; if you've ever purchased a car on credit, it's The Fed's Monetary Policy that determined the size of your monthly car payments.

The Fed's Monetary Policy is also determinative of what you earn on your savings, what your IRA earns in interest, and the cost of the money you may need to borrow if you should decide to start your own business. In fact, the price of almost everything you buy is in one way or another effected by The Fed's Monetary Policies, and if this is empirically true, how is it we still profess that American capitalism is a based on a "free market" economy?

To completely destroy this "free market myth" one need only add to the previous analysis, the fiscal and tax policies of either a Republican or Democratic Administration to determine which direction America's "wealth" is flowing, or will flow: If Republican, to the upper 2% of the nation's wealthiest Americans; if Democratic, to the lower 98%. How do you square this with "free markets" or "free" anything? Keep these premises in mind when reading Chapters Nineteen and Twenty of this book, when you start thinking they're going to be calling you some bad names if you're supportive of some "effective" government regulations and controls to take America back for yourself and your fellow countrymen.

Monetization of the National Debt:

What they say it means: A circumstance that exists when The Fed purchases government bonds, government bills, or government notes (see U.S. Treasury Bills, U.S. Treasury Notes, and U.S. Treasury Bonds) which result in an increase in the money supply.

What it really means: With an existing $5 trillion National Debt, and with an additional $300 billion expected to be added annually, it seems inevitable that "The Fed," in order to continue the "international myth" that America has the resources to repay this debt, will have to begin secretly "monetizing" this debt, as the more sophisticated international investors lose confidence in America's ability to repay the U.S. obligations they hold. When The Fed is forced into this circumstance, "money," as is true with any other commodity, will be in over-supply, and as a consequence be reduced in value. This is the equivalent to certain previous American Administrations of the 1800s, and early 1900s printing money to purchase goods required for war, etc. when there was limited or no funds available in the U.S. Treasury — the inflationary results were then disastrous, and will be the same, if or when it occurs again in America. There exists today no greater long-term threat to the American economy than this possible forced "monetization" of the National Debt.

Moral Suasion:

What they say it means: Sometimes rather very heavy-handed persuasion techniques used by The Fed to influence the present and future conduct of its member, or banks to force compliance with its general policies.

What it really means: A closed-door, strong-arm technique, bordering on extortion, used by The Fed on major commercial banking institutions to effect its most "secretive policies" — these secretive polices, if made known to the markets (Wall Street), or the American public might cause a run on the banks.

Open Market Operations:

What they say it means: Considered by many to be the most important overt weapon in The Fed's arsenal of weapons, Open Market Operations involves the purchase or sale of government bonds and bills of exchange by The Fed to either support the market price of government bonds, or to affect member bank reserves, and thus, their lending policy. It is the "securities department" of The Fed, also referred to as the "desk" that carries out the "buy" and "sell" instructions of The Federal Open Market Committee with respect to the aforementioned government instruments.

What it really means: Open Market Operations of The Fed is another example of the contradiction of American capitalism and its "free market" foundation. It also represents, as does The Fed's manipulation of the Discount Rate another element for the risk-takers (gamblers) of Wall Street to wager on.

Reserve Requirements:

What they say it means: One of the four tools used by The Fed to regulate the money supply and implement its Monetary Policies. Pursuant to rules of the Federal Reserve System, member commercial banks must keep, in either "cash" or other liquid assets, The Fed's then "prescribed percentage" (the "reserve requirement") of their depositors' "demand deposits" and "time deposits," deposited in one of The Fed's regional Federal Reserve Banks. The higher the reserve requirement set by "The Fed," the tighter the money supply; the lower the reserve requirement, the greater the money supply.

What it really means: Being usually the second most unnoticed of the four weapons in the arsenal of The Fed to control and manipulate the money supply, most Americans don't appreciate its importance. During the infamous 1990-1992 recession, which members of the former Bush Administration now concedes may very well have occurred, The Fed dramatically lowered the Reserve Requirements for its member banks. This was done for essentially two reasons: (1) To allow the banks to hopefully become more profitable by dramatically expanding the amount of money available for them to lend, and thus hopefully avoiding a commercial banking crisis; and (2) to allow the banks some leeway with respect to the enormous write-offs required by the collapse of their real estate portfolios, which itself had rendered five of America's ten major commercial banks "technically insolvent" in 1990. Thus, rather than just using the reserve requirement for the expansion of the money supply, The Fed also employed dramatically lower "reserve requirements" to stave-off collapse of America's Commercial Banking System. A complete abandonment of compliance with all federal law and federal banking regulation was also wisely employed so that the federal government might recapitalize America's Commercial banking system "subtly" through the quiet transfers of U.S. Treasury funds vis-à-vis the "favorable spread" it created between the "Federal Funds Rate" (interest charged the banks for the money borrowed) and the higher yielding U.S. Treasury Instrument (The National Debt Obligation) the banks invested in, which has secretly cost U.S. Taxpayers since 1990 alone, over $8 billion, without one word of protest from the U.S. Congress or White House — so much for American "representative government."

Savings & Loan Associations:

What they say it means: "Savings" to mean a depository financial institution the obtains the bulk of its deposits from American consumers, and "Loans" to mean those lending these same "consumer deposits" to other American consumers seeking home mortgage loans. Saving & Loan associations are either federally or state chartered and the depositors of such institutions are generally insured by either the federal government or the state that charters them. The Savings & Loan industry was given a legislative boost in 1932, by passage of the Federal Home Loan Bank Act which established supplemental lending resources for the state-chartered savings and loans, and in 1934 the Congress provided a second boost to this industry by creating the Federal Savings and Loan Insurance Corporation which provided federal insurance and guarantees for depositors of these institutions.

From 1934 until passage of the Garn-St. Germain Depository Institutions Act of 1982, a period of 48 years, the Savings & Loan industry in the United States puttered along making home loans available to home purchasers at reasonable rates. With onset of the "go-go" Reagan years, the altruistic efforts and endeavors of this industry were recognized to be both faulty and non-profitable as compared to America's Commercial Banks. Therefore, in order to shore-up the allegedly weak capital positions and historically low profitability of the S&Ls, saddled with old low-yielding fixed-rate mortgage loans, they were deregulated so that they and their "executive cadre" might also partake in all of the benefits of American capitalism. Eight years after this conversion to Mr. Reagan's pure American capitalism, and the influx of numerous American capitalistic entrepreneurs, including the son of our current President, the S&L Industry has not only taken its share of the American "pie," but has also tacked onto the American Taxpayer a bill that will probably exceed $500 billion over the next thirty-years.

What it really means: The lesson to be learned here is that the "looting" of America's banks, S&Ls, businesses, and manufacturing industries is most efficiently and best done under Presidential leadership, with the "advice and consent" of both the U.S. Senate & U.S. House of Representatives. Again, we can directly attribute this horrific condition to our present form of "representative government." See Chapter Twenty for my solutions of "taking-back" America.

Savings Insurance Fund (SAIF):

What they say it means: The Savings Insurance Fund (SAIF) and the Bank Insurance Fund (BIF) were new funds mandated by FIRREA in 1989 to insure depositors' money at Savings & Loans, replacing the former FSLIC.

What it was really all about: A "name-change," a new "spin"; the FSLIC was as "hot as a pistol" in the minds of almost every American in the late 1980s, and the fact that the S&Ls it insured had been so ruthlessly looted, allegedly right under both Reagan's and Bush's noses (not to mention the good time Neil Bush had at his own little S&L, Silverado that cost the U.S. Taxpayer $1.5 billion) was no plus for George Bush's future political fortunes, nor was it a "plus" for any member of the Democrat controlled Congress — thus, a little political "battle damage control," an unusual bipartisan effort to control both parties' possible political losses.

Securities Investor Protection Corporation (SIPC):

What they say it means: The Securities Investor's Protection Corporation (SIPC) was established by Congress under the Securities Investors Protection Act of 1977. SIPC is a nonprofit quasi-government corporation that insures the securities and cash in all customers accounts of member brokerage firms against both the fraud and failure of those firms. Membership in SIPC is required of all brokers and dealers registered with the Securities and Exchange Commission (SEC), or with a national securities exchange. SIPC is to the Securities Industry, what FDIC is to the Banking Industry, and what FSLIC "was" to the Savings & Loan Industry. SIPC insures account holders against loses of up to an overall maximum of $500,000 per customer, $100,000 of which may be cash or cash equivalents. Loses that are due to market fluctuations in an investor's security portfolio are not insured or protected by SIPC. As with FDIC, SIPC is backed by the "full faith & credit" of the United States Government: the U.S. Taxpayer, should their be a "looting" of the Securities Industry.

What it really means: Your "representative government" has again signed your name as an unlimited guarantor, and this time it is to protect those parties who choose to gamble on Wall Street. The next thing you know, you'll find toll booths on all the access roads to Las Vegas and Atlantic City being manned by our Congressmen selling government insurance to cover gambling losses in Blackjack and Craps — stay tuned, there is certainly more to come as the 1996 Dow Jones approaches 6000.

COMPOSITE DICTIONARY

Certificate of Deposit (CDs): A debt instrument issued by a bank or other financial institutions that pays interest at a specified rate and is payable in a certain term. The term may extend for as short as a few weeks to several years. CDs start as low as $100 and can be as large as $500,000 or more. Interest rates are allegedly set by the competitive forces of the market place.

Commercial Paper: Commercial Paper are short term obligations (debt instruments) with maturities ranging from two to 270 days. These short term obligations are issued by banks, corporations, and other borrowers to investors with temporarily idle cash. These obligations are unsecured and are generally discounted, although some Commercial Paper is interest bearing. Commercial Paper can be issued directly by its issuer or through brokers. The rates on Commercial Paper are usually marginally lower than current bank rates and are both flexible and safe since they are generally issued by only top-rated corporations and are always nearly backed by bank lines of credit. Both Moody's and Standard & Poor's assign ratings to Commercial Paper. (See Commercial Paper in Glossary Section.)

Credit Unions: A not-for-profit financial institution formed usually by the employees of a company, a religious group, a labor union, and more often by government employees. Credit Unions operate as cooperatives and offer a full range of financial services and may pay higher rates on deposits and charge lower rates on loans than commercial banks. Credit Unions are regulated by the Federal Credit Union Administration, who also insure depositors against losses similar to FDIC.

Demand Deposits: A commercial bank account which, without prior notice to the bank, can be drawn on by check, cash withdrawn by automatic teller machine, or by transfer to another account using the telephone, or in some cases a properly hooked-up computer. Demand deposits are the largest component of the U.S. money supply. Demand deposits are also the principle medium through which the Federal Reserve implements its monetary policy tool known as the commercial bank's "reserve requirements."

Discount Window: The term used to describe that functional area of the Federal Reserve from which banks borrow money at the Discount Rate.

Banks are discouraged from this borrowing privilege except when they are short on reserves.

Dow Jones Averages: More precisely known as the "Dow Jones Industrial Average" and the "Dow Jones Transportation Average," these two averages revolve around the theory that a "major trend" in the stock market must be confirmed by a similar movement in the "Dow Jones Industrial Average" and the "Dow Jones Transportation Average." According to the theory, a significant trend in the stock market is not confirmed until both of these indexes reach new highs or lows, and if one fails to rise ultimately with the other the market will fall back to its former trading level. Trends in the Dow Jones Averages are also said to be leading indicators as to which direction the overall economy is moving; as the Dow Jones Averages rise, it is believed the economy is improving, and as they decline long-term, it is believed that the economy in the future will also decline. There are 30 stocks that comprise the Dow Jones Industrial Average; these stocks include AT&T, IBM, Philip Morris, and Coca Cola amongst others. Component of the Dow Jones Transportation Average includes such companies as AMR Corporations (the parent of American Airlines), Burlington-Northern, Delta Airlines, and Federal Express, among others.

Eurocurrencies: A foreign currency owned by corporations and national governments that is deposited in banks (Eurobanks) defined as banks away from either the depositing corporations or governments home country, and where the currency itself is considered foreign in the Eurobank in which it is deposited. Transactions of this type become very common when one country has broken off political or trade relations with another, but where merchants nevertheless still continue trade using third country intermediaries. Eurocurrency is also used frequently to minimize "currency exchange losses" in international commerce and trade.

Eurodollar Bonds & Eurobonds: Obligations that pay interest and principal in Eurodollars, (U.S. dollars held outside of the United States). Eurodollar bonds are different from Eurobonds in that Eurobonds although sometimes denominated into U.S. dollars may be denominated in other currencies and sold to investors outside the country whose currency is used; whereas Eurodollar bonds are always denominated in U.S. dollars and always pay interest in U.S. dollars. Eurodollar bonds are not required to be registered with the SEC, and therefore may generally be sold at lower than the comparable U.S. Interest rate at the time of its original sale.

Eurodollar Certificate of Deposits: Certificates of Deposit primarily issued by European banks with interest and principal paid in U.S. dollars. Eurodollar CDs usually have a minimum denomination of $100,000 and maturities of less than two-years.

Eurodollars: U.S. currency held primarily by European banks and primarily used for settling international transactions.

Financial Institutions: Financial Institutions are broken into two groups, Depository Institutions and Nondepository Institutions; and there are also financial institutions performing both depository and nondepository functions such as the large brokerage firms (i.e. Merrill Lynch, American Express-Shearson Lehman, etc.). Depository financial institutions include Commercial Banks, S&Ls, Savings Banks and Credit Unions. Nondepository financial institutions include Insurance Companies, Pension Plans, and Mutual Funds. The term "institutional buyer" or "institutional seller" as used on Wall Street refers to insurance companies, pension funds, mutual funds, etc.

Federal Reserve System ("The Fed."): The Federal Reserve System was established by the Federal Reserve Act of 1913. The purpose of the Act was to regulate the U.S. monetary and banking systems. The Federal Reserve System is commonly referred to as: "The Fed." The Fed is comprised of twelve regional Federal Reserve Banks, twenty-four branches, and all National Banks, and State Banks that have chosen to become members of the Federal Reserve System. National Banks are stockholders of the Federal Reserve Bank in their region. The Fed's main functions are to regulate the national money supply, set reserve requirements for member banks, supervise the printing of currency at the mint, act as a clearing house for the transfer of funds throughout the banking system, and examine and regulate member banks to make sure they meet various Federal Reserve Board requirements. The Fed is considered an independent entity (not under the direct control of any one of the three branches of federal government), although the President of the United States appoints all Governing Board Members, including its Chairman (presently Alan Greenspan), such board members also require confirmation by the U.S. Senate. Governors to the Fed are appointed for terms of fourteen-years, which creates the fiction that they are free of political influence.

Financial Intermediaries: A term that includes such entities as the New York Stock Exchange, the American Stock Exchange, the Over The Counter (OTC) Exchange, as well as all other U.S. regional stock and bond market exchanges, all commodities markets, options markets, and foreign exchange markets.

Financial Supermarket: The prefix here "super" refers not to size but variety, and the term "market" is used here in the context of retailing (i.e. a grocery store). The term financial supermarket is applied to those companies that offer a wide variety of financial services such as brokering real estate, offering insurance, banking services, and securities brokerage services, thus serving a wide variety of their customers' needs or demands.

Fiscal Policy: A term coined in the 1930s to define the comprehensive government planning of budgets and their overall effect on the economy and particularly on the cyclical problems of growth and recessions, as well as depressions (the "business cycle"). Fiscal Policy emphasizes those activities commonly referred to as the "taxing-levers" and the "spending-levers" of government, and is contrasted to "monetary policy" which emphasizes control over the quantities of money and bank credit through the tools of Moral Suasion, Open Market Operations, the Discount Rate, and changing the commercial banks' reserve requirements. Both the tools of "fiscal policy" and "monetary policy" are used by the U.S. Government today to attain growth and lessen the pains of the alleged "business cycle."

Fixed Exchange Rates [Currencies]: An agreement between two or more countries that their governments will exchange each other's currency at a set rate of exchange; and a system which existed until the early 1970s, when a Floating Exchange Rate System was adopted by all those countries formally bound by the "fixed exchanged rates" of the Bretton Woods Agreement of 1944.

Floating Exchange Rates [Currencies]: The determination of the rate of exchange of one country's currency for that of another country's by market forces rather than the fixed exchange rates that had been agreed upon by countries in 1944, and known as the Bretton Woods Agreement. It is also worthy of note, that it was the Bretton Woods Agreement which established the International Bank for Reconstruction and Development and the IMF (International Monetary Fund).

Hedge: A strategy used to offset investment risk; the perfect hedge being the one that eliminates the complete possibility of future gain or loss. Buying a put option on a stock or selling a call option on a stock are a means of hedging against the decline of that stock's price. Selling "short" is another widely used hedging method. Commercial firms wishing to assure the price they will receive, or pay for a commodity will hedge their position by buying and selling simultaneously in the "futures markets," and in international transactions, to protect against exchange rate fluctuations, buy and sell currencies in the "currency markets," and "currency futures markets."

Index Options: Index options are "puts" and "calls" on indexes of stocks that are traded on the New York, American, and Chicago Boards of Exchanges, among others. The index option allows investors to trade in a particular market without having to buy "all" the stocks individually. For example, someone who believed that the Dow Jones was about to fall could buy a "put" on the Dow Jones Index instead of having to sell "short" the equivalent shares of the thirty companies comprising the "Dow."

Inverted Yield Curve (Negative Yield Curve): An unusual condition in the financial markets where short-term interest rates are higher than long-term interest rates. Usually, lenders expect to receive a higher yield when lending their money for greater periods of time, because of the inherent risk of the time factor itself; thus when the yield on short-term instruments are lower than longer-term instruments (the norm) there exists a "positive yield curve." The "inverted yield curve" occurs when the demand for short-term credit is so excessive that it drives up short-term interest rates, while long-term rates move-up less slowly, indicating generally that "borrowers" are not willing to commit themselves to the usual requirement of having to pay the normal long-term higher interest rates for long-term borrowings. Thus the "inverted yield curve." I need not comment on the effect this has on PP&E investment in the U.S., especially given, or perhaps even caused by, the high cost of labor in the U.S.

An "inverted yield curve" is usually a sign of an unhealthy economy, characterized by high inflation as well as low levels of confidence. With astronomical high labor costs, even when their exists a normal yield curve, or historically low short-term interest rates, both IRR and ROI analysis will deny any U.S. capital investment in PP&E, if comparable labor rate differences compensate or minimize the "cost of money" factors. Thus, The Fed's monetary policy of continuing lower interest rates even to zero will fail, so long as the labor rate differential between such countries as Mexico and the U.S. remain what will be seen as even a greater "truism" as "Fast-Track" progresses at a faster clip and tariffs are eliminated. See Chapter Nineteen if you want a solution to America's dive into joining the Third World as an equal partner in poverty.

Munis: See Municipal Bonds.

Municipal Bonds: Bonds issued by cities, counties, and local authorities which are free of federal income tax and generally state and local tax. Today Munis can be purchased whole or in pieces known as "unit investment trusts" (tax-free mutual funds).

Lloyd's of London: An insurance mart in London at which individual underwriters gather to quote rates and write insurance on the widest variety of risks. Back on June 25, 1992, David Coleridge, Chairman of Lloyd's, reported the worst loss in Lloyd's 304 year history. The loss amounted to $3.84 billion for the year 1989. At that time, this was the latest reporting year for which Lloyd's has final data. Coleridge blamed an unprecedented slew of disasters including Hurricane Hugo and the San Francisco Earthquake. Coleridge was also quick to point out that some of the same characteristics that effected 1989 were also present in 1990. Coleridge said, "Premium rates were at a low ebb while catastrophes continued to occur on an unprecedented scale." A large number, but nòt all investors in Lloyd's have pledged their entire wealth to become members of this unique insurance underwriter. With the all of the disasters of the 1990s i.e. the Earthquakes in Los Angeles of 1992, and the L.A. riots that occurred also in the same year, Hurricane Andrew, the 100 Year Flood in 1994, etc., etc., it seems relatively certain that many of these investors who made fortunes with Lloyds in the past, may very well find themselves homeless in the near future.

Money Market Deposit Accounts: These accounts are market sensitive bank accounts that are insured by FDIC if they are deposited in member banks, and which draw interest at a lesser rate than regular savings accounts. Today, Money Market Deposit Accounts are usually used by most persons as regular checking accounts. The funds are generally liquid and are available to depositors at any time without any penalty.

Money Supply: The total amount of money in the economy, consisting primarily of (a) Currency in circulation, and (b) deposits in the nation's Savings and Checking Accounts. Since the early 1980s the Money Supply has been broken into four classifications; M-1, M-2, M-3, and L. M-1, M-2, and M-3 representing money and what is referred to as near money; L representing longer term liquid funds such as Treasury Bills, Commercial Paper, Eurodollar Holdings of United States residence, etc. M-1, M-2, and M-3 may be viewed as three concurrent circles, M-3 being a largest circle including M-2 and M-1; M-2 being the second largest circle, including the smallest M-1 circle. The M-1 circles includes the most liquid of all money and money instruments. The M-2 circle includes lesser liquid money instruments, but includes everything classified in M-1. M-3 includes everything in M-1 and M-2 and time deposits in excess of $100,000 and "term purchase agreements." And now that you've got some idea of the three major components of the "money supply," it's time for you to get a feel for its "velocity" — how fast the "money" moves around in these three circles, and between them, is as important, or more so, than how much "money" is actually in them! A couple of quick examples in the interrogatory form: Do you think "velocity" of "money movement" will increase if the new car dealer in town sells 100 cars this week as opposed to 10 cars the week before? If unemployment rises from 6% to 7%, do you think the "velocity" of "money movement" will increase or decrease? If you said the 100 car sales would result in an increase, and the rise from 6% to 7% in unemployment a decrease in "velocity," you're ready for Economics 201.

Mutual Funds: Mutual Funds are funds generally operated by an investment company that raise money from investors (shareholders) and invest in stock, bonds, options, commodities, or money market securities. The primary benefit of these funds is to offer investors the advantage of diversification and professional management. For these services the investor is charged a management fee, typically one percent or less of the assets per year. There are also closed-end mutual funds, which have only a limited number of shares outstanding and create no new ones; there are also no-load funds offered by open-end investment companies that impose no sales charge (no-load) on its investors (shareholders). Mutual fund shares are purchased directly from the no-load fund company, rather than purchased through brokers, as is done in the purchase of "load funds."

It is estimated that there are approximately 3,200 mutual funds operating in the United States today. That represents more than three times the number of stocks traded on the New York and American Stock Exchanges combined. There is approximately $1.5 trillion of total assets in these 3,200 funds. Some of America's major corporations are owners and managers of these mutual funds; IBM has more than a billion dollars in three funds; General Electric has six funds; and other companies such as Amway, Dominion Resources, the parent company of Virginia Power Company; and Bechtel Corp., operate mutual funds.

Mutual Funds are regulated by the Securities and Exchange Commission, but are not insured by any Federal Government agency, quasi-government agency or by any other explicit or implicit government guarantees, as is sometime the case with certain private financial corporate institutions (i.e. Fannie Mae, Ginnie Mae, FDIC, etc.).

As the interest rates on federally insured Certificate of Deposit and other federally insured savings declined in the early 1990s, billions of dollars found their way into these federally uninsured Mutual Funds, primarily because many of these investors are dependent on their savings income to maintain their already nominal standard-of-living. We all have to be concerned, that if the stock market should lose between a third and a half of its value as predicted by many "Bears" on Wall Street today, that these investors who had previously been in Certificate of Deposits and other federally insured savings programs would essentially be "wiped out." I leave the analysis and the evaluation of the results of such a situation to the common sense of the reader.

National Association of Insurance Commissioners [NAIC]: The NAIC is an unofficial, but influential organization of all fifty state Insurance Commissioners. It was this association that standardized the annual financial reporting requirements of America's Insurance Companies and those insurance companies outside of the U.S. that did business in the U.S. These annual financial reporting statements, which account in detail for the conditions and operations of each insurance company are reviewed by the State Insurance Department of each state in which the insurer is admitted to do business. Although it is obvious the NAIC can't be responsible for major fluctuations in the stock or bond markets, it does regulate the types of investments that insurance companies can make in these markets. This is done individually through each state statutory scheme, but it is the NAIC that has been responsible for the national uniformity of all state schemes. The invisible regulatory arm of the NAIC is probably the most important factor for whatever soundness may still exist in the insurance industry.

The National Associations of Securities Dealers (NASD): The organization of Stock Brokerage Firms dealing in the "Over-The-Counter" (OTC) market. The NASD operates under the supervision of the SEC, and has five basic purposes: (1) To standardize practices amongst member firms; (2) establish high moral and ethical standards in securities trading; (3) provide a representative body to deal with the government and investors on matters of common interest; (4) establish and enforce fair an equitable rules of security trading; and (5) establish a body to discipline and enforce any rules or regulations pursuant to the first four objectives above.

NASDAQ (National Association of Securities Dealers Automated Quotations): The computerized system of the NASD that provides brokers and dealers with price quotations for securities traded Over-The-Counter (OTC) market. NASDAQ quotes are published in the business section of most major newspapers.

National System of Trading: A system that was developed to minimize arbitrage amongst the various stock and bond markets of the United States. This trading system facilitates the simultaneous listing of all prices for stock and bonds that are traded on the New York Stock Exchange and all regional Exchanges, thus allowing all buyers and sellers to achieve the best price by executing their trades on the exchange at the most favorable national price at the time.

Office of Thrift Supervision (OTS): The OTS was created by landmark Congressional legislation entitled the Financial Institutions Reform, Recovery and Enforcement Act of 1989 (FIRREA), a bill designed to reform the nation's S&L Industry after the "lootings" of the 1980s. The use of such powerful words as "reform," recovery," and "enforcement" were very pleasing to just about every American in 1989. It has been heard in some corners that it was this law that gave Administrative Law Judge Daniel J. Davidson the backbone to rule on December 17, 1990, that the Office of Thrift Supervision (OTS) issue a formal "cease-and-desist" order against the President's son Neil Bush. The Judge's order not only barred Neil from the kinds of conflicts-of-interest deals he participated in at Silverado (a looted S&L that will cost U.S. Taxpayers close to $1 billion Dollars) but would saddle Neil with a list of "no's no's," if he should ever again occupy a position of authority at any federally insured bank or another S&L. Now with Neil practically blackballed from the lucrative Banking Industry in America, can you see the necessity of Senior Bush's lame-duck efforts in 1993 of rushing NAFTA "Fast-Track?"

O.P.M.: [See definition below entitled "Other People's Money."]

Option: The right to buy or sell property in the future that is granted in exchange for certain consideration (i.e. an agreed-upon sum of money), where the right to which, if not exercised after a specified time period expires, and the option buyer, the one giving consideration, forfeits the consideration. Option traders can write either "covered options," in which they own the underlying security, commodity, or future; or the riskier "naked options," for which they do not own the underlying security, commodity or future.

Option Call: A call option is one that permits its holder, who has previously paid a fee for the option, to call a certain commodity or security at a stated fixed price in a stated quantity within a stated period of time. The broker is paid to bring the buyer and seller together; the buyer of the "call right" usually expects the price of the commodity or security to rise so he can sell it for a profit; thus, if the price on the commodity or security falls the option will not be exercised.

Option Put: An option permitting its holder to sell a certain security or commodity at a stated fixed price, at a stated quantity, and within a stated period of time. The "put option" is purchased for a fee paid the one who agrees to accept the commodities or securities, if they are offered. The buyer of the "option put" expects the price of the commodity to fall so that he can deliver the commodity or security (the "Put") at a profit. If the price rises, the option is not exercised. The reverse transaction is called a "Call."

Option Straddles: A combination of a "call" and a "put" permitting the "call" and the "put" to be exercised at the same price, for the same goods, which is the then market price. A "Straddle" is essentially a gambling strategy by the option holder whereby he may exercise each option whether it be a "put" or "call," separately for profit, although the combination of "call" and "put" options are usually bought and sold as a unit. The strategy is effected by purchasing an equal number of "put" options and "call" options on the same underlying stock, stock index or commodity future at the same "strike price" and maturity date. The "strike price" is the dollar price per unit price of the underlying stock, stock index or commodity future, at which, during the life of an option, a "call" option buyer can purchase the underlying stock or a "put" option buyer can sell the stock. The "strike price" is also known as "exercise price." Since option buyers must put up only a small amount of money known as the "premium" to control a large amount of the stock, commodity, etc., options trading provides a great deal of leverage and can prove immensely profitable. Straddle positions are generally held by only the most sophisticated of traders who have the expertise to combine various "call" and "put" options for serious profits, and sometimes significant losses. (See also Option Spread)

Option Spread: A combination of a "call" and a "put," so that the purchaser of this "spread" has the option to demand delivery from, or make delivery to the seller of the security, commodity etc. The "put" and the "call" are for different prices. If they are for the same price, this option contract would be a "straddle."

Other People's Money (O.P.M.): A term believed to have been coined by the Investment Bankers of Wall Street as applied to the money they raised from investors (other people's money) for those Captains of Industry and Architects of American Capitalism who chose not to use their own money in projects, ventures, acquisitions, and other endeavors they wished to pursue. Today it is used as a general term by the vast majority of Americans as the most efficient and effective means of entering into, or staying in the ranks of the middle-class, or moving to the next class above.

Securities and Commodities Exchanges and Markets: A term used to define all of the organized national exchanges where options, contracts, and securities are traded by members for their own account and for the accounts of their customers. All Security and Stock Exchanges in the U.S. are registered with, and regulated by the Securities and Exchange Commission (SEC); and all Commodities Exchanges are registered with, and regulated by the Commodity Futures Trading Commission. In the situation where "options" are also traded on a securities or stock exchange, as opposed to a commodity exchange, the activity is regulated by the SEC.

There are nine stock exchanges in the United States that deal in securities (the trading of stocks, bonds, right, warrants, and options on individual stocks), and four of which the New York Stock Exchange, the American Stock Exchange, the Regional Philadelphia Stock Exchange, and the Pacific Stock Exchange also all list and trade "option contracts" on stocks and commodity futures, U.S. Treasury securities, foreign currencies, currency indexes, stock indexes, and stock index futures.

The Chicago Board Options Exchange (CBOE), was the first exchange to deal in "listed options." Initially the CBOE dealt exclusively in "calls," but later added "puts." An essential difference that should be noted is that exchange-traded options differ from those traded "off" the exchanges in that the "strike price" and "expiration dates" of listed options are standardized giving them the characteristic of fungibility (i.e. interchangeability).

The U.S. futures market is represented by thirteen leading commodity exchanges. The principal commodities markets include the Chicago Board of Trade, the Chicago Mercantile Exchange, the New York Mercantile Exchange, New York Cocoa Exchange, the New York Commodity Exchange, the New York Coffee and Sugar Exchange, and the New York Produce Exchange. The commodities which traders speculate as to future prices (called futures) include wheat, live steers, soy beans, soy bean oil and meal, pork, oats, corn, rye, pork bellies, potatoes, platinum, cocoa, cotton, wool, frozen orange juice, lead, cooper, tin, zinc, silver, coffee, cotton seed oil, sugar, mercury, rice, and silver coins.

It is the Spot Market where commodities (the actual goods) are sold for cash and delivered immediately. The Spot Market is conducted through over-the-telephone trading, rather than on the floor of an organized Commodity Exchange. The Spot Market is also referred to as the "actual market," the "cash market," or the "physical market."

Short Selling: A legalized gambling technique where a seller sells the promise to deliver in the future at a set price a specific security, and where the actual sale is completed by the delivery of cash, rather than by the security itself. Short Sales are executed because the seller anticipates a decline in the price of the security. Regular "short sales" (those where the client has no position in the security, meaning he owns nothing of what he's selling) are made to profit from a price decline alone. "Short sales" against the "box" (where the client has an offsetting long position meaning that he owns units of that security) are made to avoid a loss and to postpone the tax consequences of a long sale to a subsequent tax year. The federal government, in order to protect itself against such postponement of taxes, has legislated certain laws enforced by the Internal Revenue Service that require minimum holding periods before such postponements of taxes, resulting from "short sales," can be exploited.

Spot Market: The market where the sale of goods such as corn, wheat or any other commodity is sold for cash and immediate delivery, as opposed to a futures market where contracts for the "future delivery" of the commodity are bought and sold at the current days "contract market price."

Spread: The term "spread" has many meanings amongst America's Financial Institutions. In the securities industry it can mean the difference between the bid and offer price for a security; or the difference between the high and low price of a particular stock over a given period of time; or in listed options trading, the difference in price in the purchase and sale of options of the same class; or the difference between yields on various fixed-income securities. "Spreads," as it relates to foreign exchange arbitrage refers to the larger-than-normal difference in currency exchange rates between two markets. The term "Spreading" as used in options trading refers to the circumstance where a customer buys options of the same class in an endeavor to profit from price change movements in the underlying stock. Spreads generally limit profits, but also limit the risk of loss. In the spectrum of options there are also "Bear Spreads," "Bull Spreads," "Calendar Spreads," and "Vertical Spreads."

Thrifts: Also known as Thrift Institutions, this is a generic name for both savings banks and savings & loan associations (S&Ls).

Time Deposit: A Savings Account or Certificate of Deposit held in a Financial Institution for a fixed term, with the understanding that the depositor may make withdrawals only by giving advance notice or suffer some form of agreed upon penalty. Savings Accounts and Passbook Accounts are generally regarded as available funds Even though each bank is authorized to require thirty days notice of withdrawal. Certificates of

Deposit, generally require the payment of a penalty for early termination. Banking and other financial institutions are free to negotiate any maturity term on a "time deposit" or Certificate of Deposit, so long as the term is at least thirty days. Negotiation of interest rates are also permissible, but don't run over to your bank with this idea, unless you're in the $1 million CD investor category.

Pursuant to the Depository Institutions Deregulation Monetary Control Act of 1980, NOW accounts (Negotiable Order of Withdrawal accounts) were created, state usury rates for home mortgages in excess of $25,000 were nullified, and territorial restrictions on mortgage lending were eliminated. Under separate legislation passbook savings accounts were deregulated in April 1986.

Treasury Bills [U.S.] [also known as T Bills]: Any U.S. Treasury debt obligation with a maturity of one year or less issued at a discount from face value. The U.S. Treasury auctions ninety-one-day and one-hundred-and-eighty-day Treasury Bills weekly, and fifty-two-week Bills once every four weeks. U.S. Treasury Bills are issued in minimum denominations of ten-thousand dollars, with five-thousand dollar increments above ten-thousand dollars. Treasury Bills are the primary instrument used by The Fed in its Open Market Operations to regulate the money supply.

Treasury Bonds [U.S.]: U.S. Treasury debt obligations with maturities of ten-years or longer issued in minimum denominations of one-thousand dollars.

Treasury Notes [U.S.]: U.S. Treasury debt obligations with maturities of between one to ten-years. Denominations range from one-thousand to several millions of dollars. Treasury Notes are sold by cash subscription in exchange for outstanding or maturing other government issues, or they may also be sold at auction.

Triple Witching Day: Similar to the concept of a full eclipse of the sun, the triple witching day is the unusual day that occurs when coincidentally all future contracts, forward contracts, and listed options contracts must be settled. This day often has an impact on both the stock and bond markets, because large amounts cash is taken from the stock and bond markets to conclude the transactions in the future and option contract markets, and just as often, no discernible effect is seen on either the stock or bond markets if there is no major amounts of cash needed to close out these options and future contracts. Cash is generally needed when the commodity or other gambling factor of the option or future contract has dramatically changed from the date of the initial entry into the contract as a result of some event (i.e. a flood that destroyed the corn crop, etc. which changes the price of corn on the settlement date of the option or futures contract).

15

Social Security, Education and National **Health** Insurance

Many of you are probably asking why I chose to put Social Security, Education, and National Health Insurance together in one chapter, when they are three distinct problems facing America by most political analysts, the media, and our elected politicians?

The answer is simple. All three of these issues represent much of the foundation upon which America will ultimately stand or *fall*. Unless we are able to resolve our differences on education, entitlement benefits, and health insurance as a nation, there can be no meaningful economic or political solution to America's other pressing problems.

The issues concerning Social Security, Medicare, Medicaid, and our education system ultimately effect all of us. Those receiving benefits now, those paying for it now, and those of us who will be in need of it when we reach retirement age will all be drastically impacted before the turn of the century. Unless we are intent on adopting the pre-westernization Eskimo "family value" of putting the elderly out to sea in "kayaks," there will soon have to be an adequate and very "real" economic solution to the Social Security problem. If not, I suspect the generation of children raised in the 1980s will most certainly resort to some means of *euthanasia* for those of us who are members of the so-called "baby-boom-generation," and I don't expect it to be as dignified or civilized a "final solution" as employed by the Eskimos.

There remains but a short fifteen years before the *first* of the "baby-boomers" will start filing for Social Security retirement benefits. By then it will be too late to adequately train and educate those Generation Xers (those people born in 1966 and after) that follow these "baby-boomers," to not only support *themselves*, but also to enable them to also contribute enough to Social Security to keep "kayaks" from becoming America's number one growth industry. In this light, the "quality" of American education should become more critical to "baby-boomers" than ever before. But what is "quality" education? If we aren't able to define it, or where we lost it, we certainly won't ever be able to achieve it.

Here is where we have to stop burying our heads in the sand and stop being embarrassed over our mistakes of the past.

Quality education is certainly not new to America. It has been revered as one of the most important economic and social cornerstones of America since 1642, when the first law in the Americas was passed requiring the building of free public elementary schools and the establishment of free public high schools to teach **The Three R's**: reading, writing, and arithmetic. By the year 1870, America already had in place, a well developed free public elementary, high school, and private university system. The need for "quality" education in America was not a concept born in the 1980s, but a concept that was necessarily *reborn* in America as a result of the past thirty-year decline in the "quality" of American education and family values.

Part of America's decline in "quality" education is directly traceable to a lot of "bad," and very naive American collective choices. One of these "bad" choices concerned "vocational" or "technical training" after WW II. Even my mother in her simplistic analysis of "quality" education as it concerned her eight children concluded that some of us might very well only suited to be the ones on the "factory lines" or even collecting America's garbage. "After all," she would say, "somebody's got to do it, and it's an honest living." And for over 100 years, as millions of immigrants arrived, the U.S. had recognized this need for "technical" and "vocational" training. As such, these pragmatic aspects of education were as much emphasized as that of the "general liberal arts education." This pragmatic thinking dominated most of the 19th Century formation of many of America's post-elementary free public educational institutions.

It wasn't until the mid-20th Century (circa, 1950) that the dilemma of educators regarding the dichotomy between education and vocational training surfaced as a major issue. The general liberal arts education and its intellectual pursuit were prestigious. Vocational and technical education and training, and its related manual-work and blue-collar stigmas, were looked upon with ridicule.

Another "new age" educational philosophy that became widespread in the 20th Century was "coeducation," a philosophical concept introduced to assure educational gender equality. In 1953, similar principles were also employed as a matter of law to eradicate racial educational segregation in <u>Brown vs. The Board of Education.</u> Proved in this case, this the **"separate but equal"** doctrine was shown statistically to result in not just "separate," but "financially unequal" schools, and thus all U.S. schools were mandated by the U.S. Supreme Court to desegregate. By the mid-1960s, America's poor and the majority of its middle-class were allegedly both racially and gender integrated in allegedly "equal" schools.

Since these alleged "equalizations" and "integrations" have occurred, we are all well aware something has dramatically failed in America's entire system of education. But we are reluctant to openly admit to the world that this failure is founded in our own impetuous, often thoughtless, and always irrational spur-of-the-moment social experiments. What the vast number of Americans still refuse to do as adults, has been forced upon its children for the past forty-years with the inevitable loss of what we cavalierly describe as "quality" education.

How many Afro-Americans and native Americans have to tell white Americans that forced integration has robbed them of their "cultural values" and "ethnic" and "racial identities?" How many men and women in America would not have been better educated today in separate, but truly equal schools? And how many black families would have remained intact, if there had not been this attack on the whole of black culture by the then nine *great white fathers* of the U.S. Supreme Court? None of these nine *great white fathers* or any of those who followed them, ever integrating their children or grandchildren into America's integrated schools?

The answer rings clear. And especially clear if read in the context of the political and economic solutions presented in the last two chapters of this book. In America we have made many mistakes with respect to educating our children: the integration of males and females as a means of allegedly attaining equality of education; and the forced integration of Afro-Americans, without regard or respect for the differences and richness in cultures that would ultimately be destroyed. The "solutions" to these aspects of America's education problem are already taking place and supported by 80% or more of all Americans, even though those "solutions" go against our liberal grains and democratic sensitivities of choice and freedom. Eighty percent of parents today want their children to attend private schools made up of students of the same religious, racial, or ethnic culture as their own. Denying this only camouflages and delays the real "solution" to "quality" education. The first step to remove the "sexual" and "racial" turmoil from the "education" process.

America needs a national policy of requiring the return to "neighborhood schools" and "neighborhood cultures" with *all* school funding originating from the federal government, and not local real estate taxes as a necessary step to assure *equal teaching and infrastructure facilities* for every school in America. It will be in the diversity, preservation, and learned respect of different cultures that America will find its future in excellence and education. Offering the choice between coeducational and non-coeducational facilities to all American parents for their children is a second step. Non-co-educational schooling should be mandated through grades K to 12 by the year 2000. Lastly, the creation of "special" schools with "special" curricula to satisfy those student's needs of superior and lesser abilities, with greater or lesser ambition, and all schools would be continually academically modified to match the future and ever-changing job needs of America, whether it be in the professions, the trades, the sciences, or the vocations.

Social Security

Social Security as we know it in the United States today is derived from the Social Security Act of 1935 and subsequent amendments. By no means was the United States the first country to enact this type of social legislation. Germany, the early leader, established the first Sickness Insurance Law in 1883. Germany again led the way in 1889, adopting compulsory old-age insurance. Social legislation began in Great Britain in 1887 with the passage of Workmen's Compensation Legislation and compulsory health insurance was added in 1911, the forerunner to Great Britain's extensive social security legislation enacted after World War I. Even ahead of the U.S. were the French, who in 1928 enacted compulsory sickness, maternity, disability, old-age, and survivorship insurance.

Not only were we behind Germany, Great Britain, and France, but we also followed behind Uruguay, who adopted an old-age, disability, and survivors insurance statute in 1919, and Japan, who adopted a sickness insurance law in 1922.

Thus, no matter how much we pride ourselves on being "The Nation" who's the first to care about its own people, it is obvious that other nations surprisingly have thought about these same ideas and enacted them into law long before America had even its first social program in 1935. It is generally recognized that Germany, France, Great Britain, along with several other European nations have more efficient and effective social security programs than the U.S. today.

Workers Covered Under U.S. Social Security

Year	No. of Workers Actually Covered	% of Workers Covered of the Total Labor Force
1940	26,800,000	57.7%
1950	48,500,000	78.8%
1960	59,000,000	88.0%
1970	105,700,000	90.0%
1980	137,400,000	90.7%
1990	161,200,000	93.0%
1995	167,900,000	97.0%

The schedule immediately above indicates the number of U.S. citizens covered by Social Security and the percentage that they represented of the total work force during the past six decades. The schedule is somewhat misleading because it does not indicate that there are perhaps as many as 100 million other Americans in 1990, who are covered by "survivor" benefits also provided by the Social Security Administration.

For those of you who only know Social Security as a payroll deduction appearing on your weekly or biweekly payroll stub, a brief description of how this system works is offered below.

How The Social Security System Works

It's not like a regular pension fund that looks to the growth of its paid-in contributions through investments to make future payments to plan retirees. Currently, Social Security is wholly reliant on taxing working Americans for retired Americans. In other words, the money you're paying now will *not* be there when you retire, but it will be the money paid by those Americans and the vibrant economy you leave behind that will assure your retirement benefits. The caveat of the 1990s coming from a few politicians leaving government, the media, and a couple of retired Social Security administrators is: Have no expectations of Social Security benefits, and you'll have no disappointments. This may very well be the best attitude for not only the Generation Xers to adopt, but also for the "baby-boom" generation to adopt, if this problem is allowed to become congressional business as usual. The "baby-boomer" generation are still sufficiently empowered to demand the necessary reforms required of both government and the economy as a whole to restore this nation's infrastructure to pay adequate wages to both them and the Generation Xers so that the nation can afford Social Security for their generations and all future American generations. If you want to preview some of these solutions, advance to Chapters Nineteen and Twenty, but return here afterwards so you understand why those solutions have to be implemented.

The actual cashflows of Social Security are simple. If you first understand that all past contributions that were to be set aside and retained in the Social Security Trust Fund have already been spent by your "representative government;" that the only thing that remains in the place of these moneys in this Trust Fund are the IOUs put in place of these moneys by your "representative government;" and that these IOUs are guaranteed by the full faith and credit of your government: that is its taxpayers (that's you). It is all rather simple.

Today, the IRS collects the prescribed Social Security payroll (FICA) taxes (7.65% of all your wages; 6.2% for Social Security, and 1.45% for Medicare). The prescribed tax for Medicare is similarly collected by the IRS for the Social Security Administration, though accounted for separately. Both you and your employer make these tax contributions in equal amounts. Your contributions are deducted from your gross pay along with your federal withholding tax. Both your contributions and your employer's contributions for Medicare are put into the Hospital Insurance Fund from which the program's benefits and administrative expenses are paid. Federal general revenues are used to finance Medicare benefits for those people who are not covered under regular Social Security or Railroad Retirement.

Those self-employed Americans pay 15.3 % of their earnings to satisfy the FICA and Medicare tax requirement vis-à-vis the same conduit system. As noted previously, the FICA taxes, in theory, were to be put into a Trust Fund where they were to remain until they were needed. Today these FICA taxes are paid out virtually immediately for :

1. Retirement benefits for America's retired workers.

2. Survivors benefits for survivors of deceased workers.

3. Disability benefits for permanently injured workers and their dependent family members.

4. Public assistance costs required by state governments in order to provide assistance to its citizens.

In addition to primary Medicare coverage, there is the federally regulated Supplementary Medical Plan (Supplemental B - Coverage) run by the private sector in which all Medicare-covered Americans are eligible (over age 65) to participate in by paying a minimal premium ($46.10 per month in 1996, but only if applied for within the statutory time frames) to cover those health-care services not covered under primary Medicare. Those of you in the "baby-boom" generation can be certain that more than 70% of the benefits now covered under Medicare-Part A, will be transferred to Medicare-Part B, with an exponential increase in premiums in relation to the health-care services that will be covered, unless you and your "co-baby-boomers become involved in the economical and political reforms that are needed for the benefit of all Americans.

Also administered by the Social Security, are federal moneys that are contributed to state governments for their Unemployment Insurance Funds pursuant to the Social Security Act of 1935. Because the 1935 Act prescribes minimum state standards, there exists a degree of uniformity in unemployment insurance benefits throughout the United States. Prior to passage of the 1935 Act, only four states had unemployment insurance. As a result of the 1935 Act, by the end of 1937 all states had passed such laws.

In addition to state unemployment insurance funding, the Social Security Act also provides public assistance and federal grants to states to develop health and welfare services for mothers and children, particularly crippled children. The so-called "public assistance moneys" offered under Social Security cover only the aged, dependent children, the blind, and the permanently and totally disabled. These public assistance moneys are paid under the Social Security Act's public assistance section. Here again each state is required to meet certain federal standards to participate in these programs.

Lastly, it should be noted that there are other federal and state retirement programs for employees who are not covered under the Social Security Act of 1935. Two of these programs are the Railroad Retirement and Unemployment Act of 1937 and the Civil Service Retirement system established in 1920, which is financed with Congressional appropriations as needed, and a tax on federal employees' wages which are allegedly also set aside in a trust fund for later retirement payouts.

The 1983 Crisis In The Social Security System

In 1983, President Reagan signed into law several significant tax provisions designed to restore the solvency of a then rapidly financially deteriorating Social Security System. For some individuals, certain Social Security benefits became subject to income taxation, representing a significant departure from previous federal law and policy.

As a result of the aforementioned impending insolvency in Social Security, Reagan signed the 1983 tax provisions, whereby beginning in January, 1984 up to one-half of the Social Security benefits paid retirees would be included in taxable income for those retired taxpayers whose incomes exceed $25,000, if single, and $32,000 if married and filing jointly.

Previously tax-exempt interest income was also included in the formula for determining the taxable income base for these newly taxed Social Security recipients. The 1983 amendments also "advanced" the dates on which Social Security tax increases were to take effect. The Social Security tax rates for the self-employed were revised to equal the combined employer-employee rate. The 1983 law dictated such substantial annual increases in the Social Security tax that it virtually wiped out much of the minimal tax benefits that were derived by the poor and middle-classes from Reagan's later legislated 1986 tax rate cuts.

The Financial State of Social Security Today

The Social Security system will be in deep trouble, some say as early as 2002, while others say not until the year 2014, when current projected Social Security tax revenues based on the present and projected American workforce will no longer cover the projected benefits required to be paid out. Thus, if the projections hold true, and Social Security taxes are not substantially increased, the benefits could begin stopping for everyone in 2014.

Now, for all of you 39 million Americans already receiving Social Security retirement benefits, you can comfortably say: "Who cares, I'll be long dead by then!" And I point out to the other readers of this book, these present recipients are correct in their assessment based on present life-expectancy tables. In 2014 most of these 39 million Americans will be dead, the youngest of them who will have survived to 2014 will be no less than 83 years old. So the attitude prevails amongst the 39 million voters now receiving retirement benefits: "Let the next generation worry about it, I've worried enough, and paid enough!"

It's not as simple a "solution" for those of you who really believe the fund will be there for "you" until 2014. It won't be, if the federal government keeps up present levels of spending and tax revenues keep declining. It's simply a matter of numbers and priorities. With the projected requirement of tax revenues needed to finance the growing National Debt, maintain national defense, pay the salaries of federal employees and the other costs of "government," etc., Social Security may very well be gone before the year 2014. When it comes to "no" money and individual survival, not even a full majority of the American electorate will be able to save what our elected representatives have called the "sacred cow" of the 1980s and 1990s.

"Why?" you ask, as you now become a little nervous at the suggestion that your monthly Social Security check and the Medicare that you rely on won't be there for you when it becomes your turn to retire. This is a real possibility, if we don't start making things work in this country.

You see all of those billions of dollars (almost a billion dollars a week) our federal government has been collecting is already being invested. Yes, invested to finance our National Debt and annual federal deficits (See Chapter One — Numbers Can Be Scary - Section A)

It is going on already today. The current $250 billion surplus that the Social Security Administration says should grow to $12 Trillion by 2030 is being invested in some interest-bearing U.S. Treasury Instruments, and the rest in government IOUs stored on a government computer in U.S. Senator Robert (Pork-barrel) Byrd's town of Parkersburg, W. Virginia.

So you say, "So what, it's the U.S. Government, they'll pay it; they always have in the past!"

Here again, the answer is simple. With the present $5 trillion National Debt that will grow at a rate of between $250 and $400 Billion each year, and the hidden off-balance sheet debts of probably another $3 trillion for the future foreseeable S&L, Pension Fund Guaranty Corporation (PBGC), SIPC and *a whole host of other possible other bailouts*, and the other $15 trillion of off-balance sheet obligations, all moneys that will either have to be "borrowed" or "printed,"to pay these various obligations. It won't be long if you recall reading the first Chapter of this book that the "interest" on this debt will be so large the federal government will not have sufficient U.S., Taxpayer revenue to pay the "interest" on the National Debt. Government projected "interest expense" for fiscal 1996 is already anticipated to exceed $318 billion.

As long as the federal government can continue borrow as it has in the past, there will be "no problem"; but as soon as the unlimited borrowing is "restricted" (i.e. a protracted world recession, or even depression, where U.S. tax revenues fall even more sharply), I need not tell you where the "cuts" will be.

I think we can all conclude that the "only" protection that *present* and *future* Social Security recipients can rely upon for their future benefits is an economically strong America; an America where there is an unemployment rate of 3% or less and where worker's wages are equal to both the task of supporting the current spending requirements of the Social Security program, and the needs of their families. This formula requires that there be available adequate American jobs, both in number and wage quality for all American workers.

One need only remember that there will be **no** Social Security, **no** Education, and **no** Medicare, and no National Health Insurance if there is **no** government; and there is **no** government, if there are **no** taxpayers to pay for it. Therefore, you may also conclude that every time you hear of another major American corporate downsizing eliminating those very jobs that employ those current and future Americans who are needed to foot the bill for Social Security, Medicare, and all other federal spending programs, that another nail has been driven into the coffin of America. It was announced on July 3, 1996, by the U.S. Department of Commerce that American corporate downsizings in 1996 were ahead of 1995s downsizings by 34%!

Now, if you're really upset about everything you've just read, why not ask your Senators or Congressmen to become a part of your Social Security system, and voluntarily sacrifice their own bloated retirement Congressional programs and life-long health insurance programs? I'll bet most of you didn't know that such liberals as Congresswoman Pat Schroeder (D-CO) now sits with $3.6 million in her congressional retirement program, resulting from her "public service" since 1964. Also members of the "congressional millionaires" and federal pensioners club are Robert Dole and his wife who are "double-dipping," both having been very *high-paid public servants*; the selfless liberal, and now convicted felon, public servant, Dan Rostenkowski (D-IL), and the poor-man's Senator Robert Byrd; (D-W.VA). These are just a few! There are hundreds more in the U.S. Senate and House of Representatives who remain under this cloak of secrecy having millions of dollars in congressional pensions awaiting them, as they have packed Social Security with federal IOUs, to be paid with your future taxes and your children's future taxes.

If your stomach is beginning to churn, why not send a letter asking your Congressman or Congresswoman, and Senators to relinquish their "princely retirement benefits" and their "royal medical insurance benefits" and voluntarily join you and the rest of us in the Social Security Program that they have borrowed into bankruptcy for their pork-barrel spending? Or, maybe we should all, as dutiful Americans, just simply accept Mike Royko's anecdote of *"everything's okay so long as their bellies' are full,"* and neither disturb our own digestive tracts, nor the digestive tracts of our alleged "public servants." If this is your attitude now, you'll be in real trouble when you get to Chapters 19 and 20 of this book.

National Health Insurance — Luxury or Necessity?

The two most critical reasons for creating a National Health Insurance Program are to assure:

1. All citizens have both continued and equal access to a minimal level of health care treatment, and

2. Cost containment over the present runaway private health care system.

The only way these two objectives can be met is through a national system of health care centrally administrated, possibly through six or eight regional locations, by the immediate consolidation of the insurance industry presently in place in America. With all of the *under-employed* workers in every region in the United States, currently flipping hamburgers or delivering pizzas, it should not be difficult to find sufficient quality personnel in each region to jump-start a National Health Insurance-Health Care System, and at a very fair wage rate. You ask: "But what of the cost of this privately run National Health Insurance-Health Care program?" "We can barely afford Social Security and Medicare. How could we ever manage the cost of a total National Health Care program?"

The answer is not as complex as America's Insurance Industry or America's medical profession or the present Administration would have you believe. Nor does it include all of the complexities introduced by Hillary's study group back in 1993. In fact, it is rather simple idea. But first re-read Chapter Eight so that you will have a clear understanding of how some of the conclusions presented here were reached.

The first argument favoring a National Health Insurance system is "cost," the very argument its opponents use against it. Americans in 1996 will spend approximately $810 billion for health-care. That's more per capita than any other country in the world. Yet there are now, as reported in July, 1996, 41 million Americans, 24.0% of our population without health-care-coverage. We were told by the former Bush Administration, and the 1994-1996 Republican Congress, that the U.S. <u>could not</u> afford the additional cost of providing health-care-coverage for then 37 million uninsured Americans and now there are 41 million Americans uninsured — yet contrasting Mr. Bush's sterile argument are our "less wealthy" Canadian neighbors who can afford to cover 100% of their population.

The primary cause of out-of-control "spiraling costs" in this industry is its hypnotic "infatuation" with the concept "profit maximization" brought to the medical profession and health-care (the hospitals and the 1980s medical and surgicenters) industry by their CPAs, their MBA financial planners, and their lawyers. I assure you their 1950 accountants and bookkeepers were satisfied with merely "counting their doctor's beans," whereas the new high-powered financial wizards who emerged in the late 1960s, and continued to sprout through the 1980s, were only interested "procreation of those beans." And what better industry for these financial wizards to invade! A ready made "monopoly" (we all require health-care) that had only been mildly exploited for thousands of years.

Once the "financial wizards" exposed the enormous and endless "gold-mines" the health-care professionals were sitting on and the means to "exploit" them, "greed" soon set in and smothered all morality, decency, and in many instances integrity in the medical profession (See Chapter Eight) and the health-care industry.

The four most fertile areas of focus for "profit maximization" identified in the early 1970s were:

1. Doctors
2. Hospitals
3. Prescription Drugs
4. Health Care Insurers

It is in these four areas that perhaps as much as 30% to 40% of America's Basic Health Care costs could be reduced.

The Doctors

In the past, no one would have agreed more than I that it would have been difficult at best to achieve "cost control" over this Reagan-Bush Health Care "laissez-faire" 1980s stronghold. Imagine trying to get the majority this nation's 670,000 physicians and America's other health care professionals to put America before their pocketbooks, especially after you read Chapter Eight of this book. But the good news is, it can be done for them. And this can be accomplished through a comprehensive single-payer National Health Insurance program using such technology as the Internet and its World Wide Web.

With a national monitoring program, as opposed to each state regulating the Insurance Industry and medical profession within its own borders, national standards would govern. All physicians and other health care providers and professionals would be licensed, regulated, and disciplined, and do all of their billings through a centralized organization on a regional basis run by the now existing, but modified Medical Insurance Industry. Some regulation by federal government law enforcement, and strict penalties would also be necessary, given the nature of the past greed in this sector. The central licensing and central billing process alone would eliminate much of the fraud and medical malpractice in the U.S. Can you imagine Medicare or medical insurance auditors seeing each of America's doctor's billings in one place, on one computer screen or ledger sheet of paper? Talk about setting off a burglar alarm every fifteen or twenty seconds in America! There is nothing like a little "sunshine" on some of the greed (billing practices) of some of our less scrupulous medical professionals and medical care providers to restrain there greed.

Fraud is rampant in the Health Care Industry. One volunteer at a local hospice confided in me that this hospice, which was being continually praised by all of the citizens of the county for its good work, was ripping off Medicare to the tune of $2700 a month by merely placing an oxygen tank and a bedpan in a Medicare individual's home who they certified was dying and under their care. This was not an isolated incident, he had seen a computer run of the billing to Medicare, and thereafter, found it very difficult to face all of the alleged *do-gooders* who were being praised for their selfless work with the dying.

The next area to be attacked in our reformation of the U.S. Health Care Industry are the medical schools that are out of the reach to those persons who have both the academic qualifications and the altruistic ingredients that place the care of human beings above the accumulation of wealth. This candidate identification process should begin as early as the beginning of middle-school (sixth to eighth grade) so that those persons, so inclined to become physicians, can change the direction of their education's so that the process of completing medical school can be started as early as the first year of High School.

The medical profession will most probably embrace this new system of early identification of future doctors, especially since the astronomical growth of their worst predators, the managed care corporations, the HMOs, the PPOs, etc. have now begun to enslave each of them under their own web of voracious greed, each of these now enslaved physicians begging to be relieved of their *watch* and be replaced by a younger generation of what will hopefully not be mere greed clones of the past. How refreshing for Americans to have, as a future objective, a sufficient number of physicians dedicated to the pure art of medicine and not to the past inefficiencies that occurred as a result of the competition for the lucrative patient base of the upper class (i.e. having two practically unused MRI centers two hundred feet apart on the upper east side of Manhattan).

In the previous paragraph, I do not suggest or imply this new breed of "early bred" physicians will be under-paid or work for slave-wages; quite to the contrary, as later suggested in Chapter Twenty, physicians would be paid commensurate with their skills and abilities, and not on the "profit-maximization-only-disease" of the 1970s, 1980s, and 1990s transmitted from their "financial wizards," and otherwise unemployable financial managers of those same decades.

Hospitals

Re-distribution of the nation's hospital resources and control over their "profit maximization" demanded by the wasteful and greedy corporations that now run them, as well as a the introduction of a new system whereby future hospitals and new "preventive medicine clinics" are allocated to geographic locations based on population densities, as opposed to per capita wealth of the neighborhood, will greatly <u>decrease</u> the cost of hospitalized health care.

A national system of regionally operated "open" clinics to provide "prevention care" through highly trained health care technicians will be another important step in getting the basic health care crisis and its related costs to this nation resolved. Much of the personnel for these suggested solutions are already in place, but are being used inefficiently, and only for the enrichment of the physician who employs them. You've seen some of these "health care technicians" at work already earning $6 to $9 an hour. Or haven't you noticed that in the past twenty years, much of the "diagnostic work" is not done by your physician, but the medical assistants who also happen to be the personnel you've seen operate the medical testing equipment in your physician's office or private clinic. None of the suggestions made here, make the physician obsolete, but it does afford the physician maximum time to interpret the "diagnostic data" collected and keep up with the changing technology of medicine.

Neither will much of this be any different in the proposed "prevention medicine clinics," that are proposed to replace the clinics of these private practitioners. More importantly for those 41 million Americans without health insurance, and the rest with health insurance, these "clinics" will provide mandatory free preventive care in the areas of:

1. Prenatal and postnatal care for all child bearing women in America,

2. Annual physical examinations for all children, adolescents, and adults; and

3. Appropriate education of our younger population in the education of personal hygiene and disease prevention.

It is in these three areas of illness prevention that perhaps as much as an additional 20% to 30% of America's long-term health care costs could be reduced and be used to pay for the improvement of America's health care, and the conversion to the system of delivery and control suggested in this chapter.

You may ask: Who will build these clinics? The answer is before your eyes: Most already exist. They are the hospitals, the surgicenters, the medical centers, the private clinics, and all of the other facilities that you see built up around the nation's hospitals. Again, if you think today's medical profession won't welcome this change with all of the HMOs, PPOs, and the 800 lb.-corporate-health-care-gorillas currently choking their chickens, even you'll be surprised. In July of 1996, the plastic surgeon sector had the highest unemployment rate amongst all doctors. Coincidentally, it is those 800 lb.-corporate-health-care-gorillas, who have eliminated this treatment code from their schedule of insured benefits. Never folks, has America and its medicine men been more receptive to change for the benefit of Americans than today!

Prescription Drugs

The cost of prescription drugs can also be controlled if a limit were set on the profits which may be earned by existing and newly patented drugs in the marketplace. Essentially the argument that these enormous mark-ups and resulting profits on existing and newly patented drugs are necessary to inspire research and development must be dispelled. The media has long ago exposed this myth noting that most of America's research and development does not occur in the laboratories of America's Pharmaceutical MNCs. But rather in America's laboratories of the National Institute of Health, the Universities of America funded in great part by your tax dollars or alumni contributions, and even NASA. Now consider this: What should you be paying for all of this research and development that actually went into the present drug?

Many of those research scientists who have worked in America's Pharmaceutical Industry, concur that it is shameful to see so much time wasted as companies and university research centers racing each other to find "the cure" for a particular disease, rarely, if ever, sharing important research information that may have resulted in a quicker "cure," for so many of America's and the world's suffering. The sole reason for the "secrecy;" the vast windfall of profit for the company who patents the drug first. The drug price is then set at what ever the market of those suffering and in need of the cure will bear!

The Health Care Insurance Industry

I can already hear the Health Care Insurance Industry's screams of "regulation" and "Big Government!" And to this I respond, "There's nothing as "big," except perhaps that 800 lb. gorilla we spoke of before, than the morass of forms, glitches, and bureaucracy of America's private health care insurance industry. It is estimated that as much as 20% of America's cost of health care ($120 billion to $160 billion) is caused by the industry's failure to adopt a singular "standard claim form" and singular "central payer system."

If a fully computerized Internet On-line National Health Care group as previously suggested replaced all of the present hundreds of "claim forms" and "payers" in the health-care-insurance industry with one singular "claim form" and one "centralized payer;" and controlled and implemented with strict federal fraud penalties for physician and hospital billing abuses; and had as its primary objective for increasing the number of physicians by seeking them out amongst America's poor and minorities, to be trained in America's soon to be up-graded public school system; and if there were implemented a national system of "prevention medicine clinics" as set forth previously — who of you would argue that present health care costs would not be substantially reduced and subsequently controlled thereafter.

How do we get all of this implemented in a reasonable period of time, or at least before the bottom falls out? Getting rid of the U.S. Congress is not the answer, but getting them to agree to the political reforms set forth in Chapter Twenty of this book is surely the first step. Perhaps with all of your axes, rather than the axes of the *special interest groups* hanging over their continued employment, their attentions and efforts might be re-directed toward their fellow American citizen's *well being and their health care needs*, rather than the prioritized interests of their wealthiest *special interest groups*, and the feared sacrifices they might have to endure if the political playing field was even mildly leveled. These folks in the congress should not be making the decisions for what you need and have demanded; their job is to implement it and thereafter make it work efficiently and keep it cost effective. If they can't do the job, the solutions in Chapter Twenty will tell you how you can get someone into the congress that can do the job! We are not without solutions.

Getting back to health care: The only argument I've heard against National Health Care Program is its impact on America's *top-two-percenters*, who would <u>not</u> have the same level of care they now enjoy, and which only they can now afford under America's present health care system. Their argument is "rationed medicine." As you might have expected, their argument, as usual, is designed to create "imagined fear" in America's remaining middle-class that "this same level of care" will not be available to them. They never say this diminished "level of care" only applies if their "illusory" middle-class propaganda targets achieve ***top-two-percenter*** status.

The solutions suggested above are the best I've heard, but if you know of a better solution to provide health care to those 41 million Americans not presently covered, or another means to correct the abuses of the health care industry past, present, and future than the suggestions provided above, kindly address your suggestions directly to President Bill Clinton, with copy to me C/O The Junior Man, 283 Wellington K, West Palm Beach, FL 33417.

- AUTHOR'S REVERSE "SPIN" GLOSSARY -

- "WHAT THEY SAY IT MEANS" & "WHAT IT REALLY MEANS" -

Medicare:

What they say it means: In 1965 the Congress legislated The Health Insurance for the Aged Act (Medicare). The Act became effective July 1, 1965, and payments and benefits began on January 1, 1966. As much as a "gold mine" that it has been for the medical profession, the American Medical Association (AMA) and the Health Care Insurance Industry successfully argued up until the time of the Medicare Bill passage that a federal health program was not a solution to financing adequate health care for the aged. As many of you might note, it sounds feebly familiar to the same arguments made by the same groups today, regarding a National Health Insurance Program. However, the AMA was correct then in its original assessment. The rising cost of Medicare has been staggering. In 1980, it cost the American taxpayer $35.6 Billion dollars. By 1990 the cost rose to just over $103 Billion dollars, accounting for 8.5% of all 1990 federal government expenditures. And the cost of Medicare can only increase as the baby-boomers (those born in the five-years following WW II) begin to enter their golden years beginning in the year 2010. At age 65, every U.S. citizen is eligible to receive hospital benefits under Medicare.

Medicare hospital benefits for those persons over 65 today are financed by compulsory hospital insurance contributions from those persons currently working under the Social Security Act. This is a group of Americans whose numbers are declining and will continue to do so, thus further burdening those who are left and required to remain in America's workforce under a "system" most Americans agree is already financially out of control and which will be of little benefit to them when they reach their "golden years."

What it really means: Medicare has been the gateway to entrepreneurial America for many American citizens who chose to enter the booming health care industry in the 1970s and 1980s. So many have entered this sector, it's no wonder that it has become the fastest rising cost sector in the United States during the past twenty years. In some years costs have risen at rates twice the national rate of inflation. By 1977, the level of fraud in Medicare had gotten so out-of-hand that the Congress was forced to amend the original Medicare Act. The amendment was entitled: "MEDICARE-MEDICAID Anti-Fraud and Abuse Amendments." The Medicare-Medicaid Anti-Fraud and Abuse Amendments initially had sent shivers up the spines of many defrauding insurance companies, hospitals, physicians, and others in the health care industry. But such fear wasn't long-lived, as evidenced by the gold-mine it is today for so many unscrupulous physicians, hospital, and other health care providers. Not a week goes by where a major newspaper doesn't carry a story about some multi-million-dollar Medicare fraud somewhere in the country. A $3 Billion Medicare-Medicaid fraud pulled off by several new Russian immigrants was reported in California in early 1992. In early July 1992, retiring Department of Health and Human Services Inspector General Richard Kusserow was so incensed by the "lootings," that even he complained publicly regarding the use of outside contractors to handle Medicare claims. He stated unequivocally that, "The use of outside contractors to handle Medicare claims was an inherent conflict of interest and amounts to thievery." He went on to say that this thievery was costing the federal government at least $100 million dollars a year and concluded that these outside contractors doing the "looting" should be honest about what they were doing, and at least apply to the government for a license to "steal."

Health and Human Services Secretary Louis Sullivan, when asked to comment on Kusserow's remarks stated that he didn't believe companies were stealing from the government. He would not go so far as to put it those terms.

Kusserow had also stated that the federal government could save over $250 million dollars a year by modernizing its data processing of paperwork and by giving sharper screening to the claims it receives from hospitals, physicians, and other health care facilities.

Medicaid:

What they say it means: Medicaid, a close relative of Medicare, is a joint federal-state welfare program available in virtually every state that provides medical benefits for low-income Americans, including the aged. The general qualification are set by the state in each states definition of "low-income."

What it really means: The frauds here operate in the same manner as those of Medicare, only here the nation's health care providers are less afraid to commit criminal acts since most states are extremely lax in investigating fraud in this area for fear of having to incarcerate most of the physicians in their respective states. See also "What it really means:" section above under Medicare.

Social Security - Both in Theory and Practice:

What they say it means: In theory, the concept holds that in the absence of government legislation many people would fail to provide for the financial consequences of old age, illness, injury, or retirement. Through government legislation, a base or floor for financial subsistence, to insure a minimum standard-of-living, is provided through mandatory savings (Social Security taxation). Up until the mid-1970s, there was virtually no argument over the necessity for either Social Security or Medicare. With the increase in life expectancy and, thus, the number of people receiving benefits, as well as, the enormous abuses inflicted on the system by both those in their retirement years and those in the health care sector, and also the enormous number of people who were projected to be entering these "entitlement programs" because of the extended mortality tables, the very foundation of the system came into question. As bad as all this may sound, the good news is approximately 30% of the Federal Government's income came from payments made into Social Security, Medicare, and other unemployment and retirement taxes. In actual dollars this approximated $373.3 Billion in fiscal year 1995. Outlays for these services during this same period came to $433.8 Billion, reflecting a mere deficit of just $70 Billion, not that much when you think of the almost $3 trillion in deficits rung up during the Bush & Reagan years, and $1 trillion so far (6/96) in the Clinton years. The bad news is that the "cost" of Social Security and Medicare, seems to grow with the increases in Social Security taxes. No matter what the government tells you, the Social Security taxes collected today may never be put into a "fund" to be available for future recipients. The IOUs put into the Social Security "funds" today are only as good as the "future" generations of American's desire and ability to pay them off. Frankly, knowing my own kid, I ain't holding my breath. As surely as the population of the aged increases, the number of these IOU's will dramatically grow. Regardless of any growth in the population in the elderly, based upon the dramatically increasing and uncontrolled cost of health care in the United States, these costs will grow even more rapidly than any source of government income. This forecast does not include the effect of the COLAs built in to these various social programs.

What it really means: Unless control is established over the runaway underlying costs of these social programs, the United States Government will be bankrupt by the year 2000, no matter how the Congress or the President juggle the numbers. The reality of the federal government getting control over these social programs before it goes bankrupt is practically "zero." Why? Because the largest consistent voting block in this nation are those persons in the age group 55 and older; a group that has consistently threatened through its voting power to defeat any incumbent who would even so much as mention reform in this area. If we accept this as fact, the only solution is to create an adequate economy, workforce, and taxpayer base to meet the challenge of this American financial reality. As a matter of financial necessity, America must implement a National Health Insurance and Cost Control Commission, just as the majority of state's in the past were, also out of necessity, required to create Public Utility Commissions and State Insurance Commissions to insure adequate regulation over those areas of the economy that were "unfairly advantaged" even in a "free market" economic system of capitalism.

COMPOSITE DICTIONARY

COLA: [see Cost Of Living Adjustment]

Cost Of Living Adjustment (COLA): The automatic increasing of a government benefit or entitlement to keep pace with inflation. COLAs are synonymous with the term Structural Inflation.

Federal Unemployment Tax Act (FUTA): A federal excise tax on every employer, presently at 6.2% on the first $7,000 of wages paid each of his or her employees, during each calendar year. FUTA taxes are placed in special trust funds administered by the various state unemployment agencies. Most states also have an unemployment excise tax on employers and in some cases employees that parallels the federal unemployment tax. Once the funds in the special trust funds have been exhausted (i.e. because of long recessions, etc.) the federal government, on an emergency basis, may make emergency appropriations to add to these special trust funds so that unemployment benefits may be continued to be paid out.

Social Security Tax (FICA): Social Security was enacted pursuant to the Federal Insurance Contributions Act (1939), and it is for this reason that the Social Security tax is also known as the FICA, although the Act itself is commonly referred to as the Social Security Act. Pursuant to the Act the Social Security Administration (SSA), under the direction of the Commissioner of Social Security, administers a national program of contributory social insurance whereby employees', employers', and self-employed persons' mandatory contributions are pooled in special trust funds.

When a worker's earnings cease or are reduced because of retirement, death, or disability, monthly cash benefits are paid by the Social Security

Administration (SSA) to replace part of the earnings the worker, or his or her family has lost. In addition to these benefit payments, the SSA also administers cash assistance program such as Aid to Families with Dependent Children (AFDC) and Supplementary Security Income (SSI).

Social Security also administers the federal Medicare program and the federal segment of Medicaid. In fiscal year 1994, the Federal Government spent 32% of its total outlays for these programs; this amounted to approximately $370.9 billion. Since 1991, $53,400 of every worker's wages were subject to the Social Security Tax. In addition, wages up to $125,000 were subject to Medicare Tax withholding. A taxpayer who crossed the $53,400-Social-Security and $125,000-Medicare thresholds paid $3,310.80 FICA taxes and $1,812.50 Medicare withholding taxes His or her employer was required to match these funds with respect to its share of payments to the Social Security Fund. For those persons self-employed the Social Security Tax currently amounts to 15.3% of the first $53,400 of moneys earned in 1991, and an additional tax of 2.9% must be paid by each person self-employed for Medicare. The total tax imposed on the self-employed individual who earns $125,000 per year, for Social Security and Medicare, is $10,246.60. This does not include any of the federal income taxes, state, or local income taxes that are, or may be required.

Workers Compensation: Workers Compensation, although technically not a tax, is a state-required insurance to be purchased by employers to cover risks under the Workers Compensation laws of each particular state. Such insurance is usually mandated by the state law, unless the employer is self-insured, requiring the employer to meet very strict standards with respect to financial resources. It is estimated that Workers Compensation laws have resulted nationwide in approximately $3 billion dollars of false and fictitious claims per year since 1991.

16 ‖ Racism

&
Ethnic Hatred

Either Europe Makes Space for Islam, or It Courts Disaster

Under this headline, on June 19, 1992, it was reported by <u>Firmas Press Agency</u> writer Carlos Alberto Montaner:

Before cutting his victim's throat, the Serbian soldier explained the reason for the execution: "These guys don't belong in Europe!" And in a flash, very professionally, he cut the Bosnian from ear to ear with icy indifference.

The dead man was a Muslim scarcely 20 years old, a militia man with no military experience. He didn't even have time to cry out. It was a very bloody death accompanied by violent stomach upheavals.

Just weeks before, the Serbians and Croatians, two other primary Yugoslavic ethnic groups were killing each other with the same ferocity, and for the same reason: Ethnic Hatred! After years of seeming ethnic harmony, or at least peaceful coexistence, under the strong arm of the former Soviet Union, other historic ethnic rivalries seemed to explode in almost every nook and cranny of these alleged new democracies of the former Soviet Union. Christians fighting Christians, Christians fighting Muslims, and Georgians fighting Russians, just to name a few.

It is not limited to these new eastern Europe nations. Ethnic hatred seems predisposed genetically between Turks and Armenians, Kurds and Iraqis, Turks and Kurds, Jews and Palestinians, Irish Catholics and Irish Protestants, India's Hindus and Pakistan's Muslims, and over half the tribes in the nations of Africa . And what ethnic groups other than

American Poles, haven't been degrading Poles for the better part of the last three decades?

Ghettoism, ethnic hate and violence, religious intolerance and bigotry, prejudice and discrimination. These are the underlying causes of events that make up half the news in the world. As you may not have already realized, all of the aforementioned ethnic conflicts are between different ethnic groups within the "white" race.

Racism, ethnocentrism, bigotry, *rightfully or wrongfully*, unfortunately seems almost a part of human nature, as if after thousands of years its existence, that it has possibly become a distinct gene in the long strand of each ethnic or racial groups' DNA. Even today, race and ethnicticty seem to be an indispensable part of one's self-esteem, ego, and sense of belonging. For example: On Columbus Day in America, is anyone surprised to see the buttons "Italian — And Proud Of It!" or on St. Patrick's Day, "There's the Irish, and the others who wish they were?" And in this regard, is it any wonder why African-Americans were so adamant in their demand for an African-American Holiday: Martin Luther King Day? It is hard to reconcile that only fifty years ago America was a nation of almost strict cultural pluralism.

So what is this **American Melting Pot** of cultures and ethnic differences that so many sociologists, anthropologists, and legal scholars have written of so often? Integration, inter-ethnic marriage, inter-racial marriage, and those "other things" that are so frequently seen on America talk-show TV! Has it become prominent in your neighborhood yet? Here again the realities of America seem very different from what we see on T.V. Yet who of you is not emotionally uplifted whenever one of our prominent T.V. talk show host hugs some fifty year old crying white "redneck" woman who confesses and openly repents on national television for being an "unknowing" subliminal racist for the past fifty years; this same repentant woman, who, three years later, attempts suicide when her daughter, or granddaughter, brings home *someone of color*, or someone not quite within the correct ethnic parameters expected.

I do not speak of these matters without having had first-hand experience. As the product of a multi-ethnic marriage, my mother was European Jewish, and my father, Irish Roman Catholic, I can unequivocally state that although my parents were tolerant of each other during their forty-four year marriage, neither was pleased, nor were their respective families pleased, when any one of my parent's eight offspring dated or married someone not of that parent's particular religion.

My mother literally glowed at her children's Jewish Weddings, and my father reveled in his victories, especially in his grandchildren's Baptisms and First Communions. He remained mildly anti-Semitic until his death in 1985, and my mother continues to believe that Jews remain the "chosen people" right up until today. Not even the "second coming" before her very eyes would change this.

Notwithstanding the inner family prejudice, to Jews I was a "goy," and to Christians, a "kike." Interestingly enough, with the accumulation of some wealth, prestige, and success, my external acceptability, at least superficially, over time did seem to improve. I had also learned very early, never to volunteer information on the subject unless absolutely necessary. Even after nearly fifty-years, I am still very conscious of suppressing my Irish Roman Catholic heritage when amongst Jews, or my Jewish heritage when amongst Christians.

I also point out that there still remains the same reaction from those Christians who suspect me of being a Jew, and Jews who suspect me of being a Christian. It usually arises in the context of their revealing their bigotry to me in confidence, generally in the context of a "prejudice" they believe may have been the cause of their own misfortune. It generally begins with: "You know he was nothing but a (ethnic slur)! It is usually realized the moment after the "slur" is voiced, they haven't "cleared" me ethnically. Then comes the *questioning look,* with the remarkably even-handed tone of voice: **"What religion are you"** . . . I usually answer: *"Me? . . I'm just a chameleon."* No longer interested in reversing the mighty underground or overt rivers of "racism" and "ethnocentric hate" that will always continue to flow overpoweringly in their same direction, I now quickly become whatever it is that my client prefers me to be. I would either recite a reassuring quick "Hail Mary," or if it was one of my Jewish brethren, I would drop in a few of the Yiddish words so natural to me, having been brought up primarily by my *Yiddish-speaking* Jewish grandmother.

Personal experiences aside, what is the real state of racism, religious bigotry, and ethnic hate in the United States? For those of you in your forties, I ask, has there been any change in your lifetimes? Except for minor flare-ups that seem to coincide with fluctuations in the economy, the answers is probably an unequivocal: "No." The good news is most Americans superficially accept racism, religious bigotry, and ethnic hatred for what it is and conduct their lives, careers, and community affairs: "business as usual." The bad news is that both America's political parties (in need of issues and votes) and those Americans having their standards-of-living diminished and now in need of a scapegoat seem to be reverting back to open acts of racism — and even as this book is being revised, hate crimes of all types appear to be dramatically rising in the U.S., and around the world in direct correlation to the decline in each nation's standard-of-living.

It should be obvious to all Americans, whether Christian, Jewish, Muslim, black, white, Asian, or native American that racism and ethnocentrism is not going away. The last forty years of integration and affirmative action has resulted in greater racism and hate that existed prior to 1954. More important, these unnatural, forced government social engineering policies have taken their toll on the American Family which had always depended on the community perimeter that protected its churches and cultural mores to sustain the spiritual and cultural quality-of-life that the majority of American Families had enjoyed over the first two hundred years of our nation's existence.

The end of cultural pluralism, i.e. Italians in Italian community neighborhoods, Irish in Irish community neighborhoods, etc., ended in the early 1950s. As stated above, this change was due to government's interference with America's delicate social order, which when looked at in historical perspective, will be said to be one of the primary causes for the destruction of one of America's fundamental foundations; as witnessed by the social decadence of the 1980s and 1990s when these ethnic communities for all practical purposes became extinct. It is this same **big government meddler** that today seeks to solve the problems for which they themselves unwittingly sowed the seeds back in the early 1950s: the problems of crime; destruction of the family and family values; drug addiction; single-parent families; unwed teenage mothers; and the failure to eradicate racism. As a result, seldom is heard about *the American Melting Pot* from our enlightened political, religious, and intellectual leaders of today, the catch-all replacement term *The Inner City* now being in vogue which reflects one of the primary effects of the cooking that went on in the *American Melting Pot*.

Black Racism v. White Racism

Probably the most unifying element of America's multi-ethnic white race is *Afrophobia,* a term I coin here to explain the growing American and international white racial attitudes that seem to have again been becoming more cohesive since the 1980s.

Afrophobia is not a white fear of black people, but the growing fear of white people that they will eventually become extinct, not by war, famine, or diseases, but merely because of their failure to procreate in sufficient competitive numbers, then, as a matter of simple arithmetic, black folks will be the "last guys on the block." I like to think of it as being similar to winning or losing an American "dance marathon;" the last couple to still be standing, gets the prize. Unfortunately, in this race marathon it will only be a booby-prize.

Before you dismiss all merit to this theory, I invoke Ross Perot's, "Now wait a second! Just hold on and follow this for a minute."

Based upon projections of the U.S. Census Bureau by the year 2020, the white race will be a minority in America, representing approximately 47% of the population. With this "minority status" in an alleged "democracy" also comes the erosion of the former majority's power; power that has been enjoyed by the white race in America since Columbus discovered the new world in 1492. This alleged majority power being a continuing *power* that is portrayed in history to have been enjoyed by the white race since its alleged beginnings in the Garden of Eden. This conversion of American whites to minority status by 2020, ought to give the Republicans something to think about, especially with their position on

Affirmative Action! As one of my black male clients smugly remarked to me recently: "All any **white boy** has to do is put on <u>**Cops**</u> to really put America's future in perspective."

It's time now to focus on America's racial statical reality. First, are African-Americans any better-off today than they were fifty-years ago? If this question is answered in the context of employment data, the number of African-American fatherless families; the number of black males not reaching the age of twenty-five; the number of African-Americans on drugs; the number of African-Americans in poverty; the number of African-Americans in prison; or simply the number of unwed teenage black mothers: The answer is an unequivocal. **No!** For these reasons, I can understand the message of Louis Farrakan, and not be offended. I think the last fifty years of legislative and judicial intervention directed toward forced integration of minorities, whether African-American, Korean, Chinese, or poor-whites, has created more catastrophic problems for these minority groups, and has done more to divide America than all the divisive efforts of the Klu Klux Klan, David Duke, George Bush, Ronald Reagan, and America's two political parties combined.

I often wonder, with the exception of the two black Supreme Court Justices Thurgood Marshall, and Clarence Thomas, how many children and grandchildren of our Supreme Court Justices, or our white Senators and Congressman attend integrated **public schools**? How many of these same altruists have moved to racially integrated neighborhoods, or have invited low-cost housing in or around their five acre estates. I often think these statistics would be more enlightening to the American people than their voting records or judicial dicta, as the case may be.

Now, given the democracy we claim we have, suppose, **we the people**, as a matter of law, require every person seeking elected office or political appointment to reside amongst the "poorest" segment of his or her constituency, along with his or her family, during their tenure in office and during their candidacy.

Then suppose, that **we the people**, further required our elected officials' children, as well, as their political appointees' children to attend the **inner city schools** in these "poorest" of areas of their constituencies or in the Washington D.C. public school system. Let's see if then all of these alleged **public servants** might not quickly come up with some real creative solutions to the **inner city** and **racial** problems at hand, that would be more consistent with the needs and desires of the people who put them in office.

This is one area where no one can fault the President or First Lady of either the Democrats or Republicans. During my last visit to Washington D.C. in 1990, my family was twice assaulted within view of the White House; and the hotel we stayed at just three blocks from the same White House was surrounded by both gunfire and police car sirens for the better part of the two nights we remained. No hypocrisy here! Not when the President and First Lady reside most of their tenure in office in the center of one of America's major, and ***most violent inner cities***, Washington D.C. I guess you're thinking: "Yeah, so would I live in the White House, if I had a couple hundred secret service men, along with a hundred or so security guards, working for me too with someone else paying for them!"

Some Popular Myths Concerning American Racism & Bigotry

U.S. Black & White Racial Makeup-1900-Projections Through 2050

YEAR	% BLACK	% WHITE	% OTHER
1900	11.6%	87.9%	.5%
1950	10.0%	89.3%	.7%
1995	12.8%	82.9%	4.5%
2025	14.2%	77.3%	8.5%
2050	15.7%	72.8%	11.4%

Given the above projections those racist white Americans should have less concern, and black Americans, more concern. White extinction, and even white minority, with an Afro-American majority is not likely in the next century. But, projections are only projections, and they don't necessarily reflect what will actually happen. From my own observations, approximately 35% all T.V. actors on prime time television are Afro-American. Watching both local and national news, excluding the three anchors on the three major network's, I counted 106 appearances by Afro-Americans and 93 appearances by white Americans. There isn't any statistical conclusion that can be drawn from any of this except that my own *perception* may very well be flawed by subliminal prejudices. Carrying this simple empiricism one step further, with the exception of a few American small rural towns, I am sure that most of you, both black and white, can attest, that the state counties in which the majority of you live, seem to be well mixed between black and white Americans. Therefore, I uncertain whether the U.S. Census Bureaus statistical data is a myth, or whether my empirical observations are somehow skewed. Obviously, some you will say or think that I'm a racist creating hallucinatory racist population myths. In any event, there seems to be certain agendas in place in America that seem to have as there objective the further racial divisiveness of the species, Boobus Americanus. And judging from the state of racial relations in America today, these certain agendas appear to be going forward with lock-step precision. More about solutions to America's racial problems in the last three chapters of this book.

OTHER POPULAR MYTHS

I.   Racism will not survive the Twenty-First Century.

II.   In America, everyone gets an equal chance.

III. American elected officials and appointees would themselves gladly live in racially mixed neighborhoods and have their children attend racially mixed inner city schools, if they could only find a dwelling for rent or purchase.

The Realities Of American Racism & Bigotry

I.   Racism may or may not survive the Twenty-First Century, but if it does, it's rather unlikely it will be white racism.

II.   In response to Myth II above, the very American cliché that seems to fit best is: "What goes around, comes around."

III. If you have any doubt regarding Myth III above, write your local Congressman and U.S. Senators and ask if they're living in "integrated neighborhoods" in either Washington D.C. or back in their home states.

COMPOSITE DICTIONARY

Anti-Semitism: The ethnically motivated acts of discriminating against, being hostile toward, possessing either hatred or "negative" attitudes of, or acting out violence ranging from the typical "hate crimes" against Jewish owned property to genocide against those of the Jewish religion or of Jewish ancestry.

Bigotry: Behavior or beliefs issuing from a person's obstinate or intolerant attitude towards others generally as a result as his or her devotion to his or her own church, party, belief, or opinion. In a broad sense of the term, the practice of some groups to identify certain people based upon their religious beliefs or convictions.

Color: As used in today's politically correct parlance, this term refers to the spectrum of skin colors other than that possessed by the "white" race.

Creed: A "categorization" word that groups persons based on their religious beliefs into "creeds"; or identifies the individual by the religious beliefs he or she adheres to.

Ethnic Origin: Generally, the geographic location from which a particular stock of persons come from, who generally have the same religious affiliation, common traits and customs, and who generally identify themselves as part of that "stock" based on the aforementioned factors.

Hate Crimes: Actions derived from intense hostility usually derived from fear, anger, or a sense of past or present injury coupled with a habitual emotional attitude of distaste and ill-will that is directed towards either a particular racial, religious, ethnic, or other minority group. No one is punished for merely having bigoted thoughts or for bigoted speech; "hate crime" legislation is focused on punishing those persons who are prompted to demonstrate their bigotry or hate in some form of criminal conduct. Then and only then does the state seek a stepped-up penalty for the assault, vandalism, trespass, or other "hate" motivated crime. Generally before the "stepped-up" penalty can be imposed, the state must prove beyond a reasonable doubt that the crime was "hate" or "bias" motivated.

Nonsectarian: A term generally used to identify the absence of any influence of "religion" as it pertains to any organization, charity, group, association, or function in American society.

Pluralism: The theory that all groups in society participate in the decision-making process and that their views are used to arrive at one policy. Pluralism was once said to be one of the foundations of American democracy.

Prejudice: A bias or fore-judgment, or a preconceived opinion leaning towards one side of a cause for some reason other than a conviction of its justice. There are numerous theories as to the cause of prejudice: (1) It's genetic; (2) It's something that arises without genetic predisposition, through the socialization process of the individual vis-à-vis his or her family and social relationships; (3) It derives solely from economic conditions; (4) It's merely a function of one's own self-esteem and the self-esteem one takes in being a part of a particular group other than the one that its prejudice focuses on; or (5) It's a mix-and-match of all of the reasons given in (1) through (4), some explanations given more weight than others depending on who is defining the term.

Race: A sub-set of human beings belonging to the same color stock, with common physical characteristics — and whose physical traits are transmissible by descent and sufficient to characterize it as a racially distinct sub-set of the human species. Race is often denominated in terms of the five colors: Black, brown, red, white, and yellow.

Racism: The belief by an individual or a group of individuals that race is the primary determinant of human traits and capacities, and that racial differences account for what they perceive as the alleged superiority of their particular racial group.

Red Neck: A term generally applied to bigoted American white people of the lower-middle and poor-class that live in the states south of New York. New Yorkers, and the other geographic members of the white upper-middle-class, and the *top-two-percenters* of the "same thinking, are called "closet bigots or racists." Originally this term referred to white southern conservatives from rural areas.

Skinheads: A worldwide self-proclaimed white supremacist group that believes all other persons of color or of the Jewish religion are racially inferior. Male members of this group generally have their heads cleanly shaven.

Slavery: The condition of a person who is wholly subject to the will of another; one who has no freedom of action, but whose person and services are wholly under the control of another who has absolute power over his or her life, fortune and liberty, as a right of possession. A slave may be sold and disposed of, his services and industry are the property of his master, and his status precludes him from being able to freely do anything, have anything, or acquire anything, but what his master so desires. The Thirteenth Amendment of the U.S. Constitution outlawed overt slavery in the United States.

White Supremacist: Persons of the white race who believe they are genetically, intellectually, and spiritually superior to all persons of color.

Willie Horton: The center piece of George Bush's election campaign in 1988. Willie Horton was the African-American who had been released from prison in Governor Michael Dukakis's State of Massachusetts under a program of early release. Willie Horton proceeded to commit murder immediately after his release pursuant to Massachusetts early release program. George Bush utilized this incident to demonstrate Dukakis's alleged softness on crime. This one, fifteen-second political sound-bite is said to have influenced the vast majority of white voters who had been still undecided up until that time.

17 | American Morality
Family Values, Drugs
and Pornography

There are probably a million theories as to why the **American family** and **American morality** have declined so dramatically over the last thirty years. Probably twenty million Americans, **believe it or not**, *are pleased with this decline* since it results in their keeping their jobs, the creation of new jobs, and possibly making enormous profits in both the "drug and porn" industries.

There are many reasons for the decline of American morality. Some blame it solely on television. Others blame it on television, combined with an array of other events of the 1960s; the shocking assassination of President John F. Kennedy in 1963, the explosion of the **Women's Liberation Movement** in the mid-1960s, and the advent of the birth control pill that fueled the beginning of America's 1960's *sexual revolution*.

There are others who argue that the decline in America's family and America's morals lies in America's past immigration policies and over-population of the wrong racial, religious, and ethnic groups. Others emphasize America's irreversible change from an agrarian society to a predominantly urban and suburban society. This "change" resulted in the *family unit* <u>no</u> longer being economically justified; children were no longer a necessary part of the family's economic scheme of survival. Children became merely the object of the marketing MBAs that began to emerge in the mid-1950s. Children, especially those born in the late 1960s, and thereafter, bore the full mark of these marketing MBAs, vis-à-vis the very potent Saturday morning boob-tube advertising blitz. By the 1980s this conditioning became more important to America's children and the American economy, than the Sunday School religious teaching programs that inevitably took a distant second place to the hundreds of thousands of arcade games depicting evil and violence that were now available on cartridges in the home. *Fun* and *self-indulgence* became the only games in town for the majority of American children as early as the late 1970s, and persist today. This generation of children, some now twenty-five became known to many of their parents as the *GET ME* or *GIMME GENERATION*. Every utterance from their mouths begins with a "get me that", or "gimme this!" It wasn't long before America's unemployed children under 12 became one of America's most powerful and financially influential consumer groups: $9.6 billion in consumer spending alone in 1995 for this infant group of consumers. This $9.6 billion does not include the cost to feed them, to clothe them, to educate them, or to purchase the other necessities needed for their survival such as medical care and summer vacations.

Before we get into the overt and unchecked manifestations of the decline of American morality and the decline of the American family, let's first examine some of the contrasting relationships and expectations that predominated in most American families *prior* to the emergence of the 1960s which were for many, the same as prior to the beginning of World War II.

There was the pre-1950s economic necessity of child labor on the farm. Prior to the modern industrialization of American farming, the American farmer was always faced with the question of who would work the "farm." Children were of great value during this pre-modernization period for two reasons. First, they contributed to the family's survival by performing many of the "chores" required by "farm life," thus justifying their need, both socially and economically. As late as the 1950s, it was commonly accepted that a "farm," to succeed in perpetuity, must raise crops, livestock, *as well as children*. Neither the "farms," nor the *family units* that ran them prior to WW II, could have survived without absolute adherence to this economic principle.

Secondly, in pre-modernization agrarian America, children facilitated the natural succession of both the "farm" and the "family" which provided assurance and security to themselves, their parents, and the nation. When each generation of adults reached an age when they were no longer able to contribute economically to the farm, there was the *family unit* still intact to provide both dignity and the necessary economic support until God's divine intervention to sever these elderly farmers from their fields.

Much of this agrarian-based"thinking," that children were correctly a part of the economic-contributing-side of the *family-unit*, followed farmers of both America and Europe into the cities, and in some cases, even into the suburbs of the 1960s. Remember, it wasn't until the late 1800s in Europe, and early 1930s in America, that government retirement programs, worker disability, and welfare programs displaced much of the economic need that was formerly satisfied by the notion of the *family-unit*, where children provided for the social and financial needs of their aging parents.

How can American *family values* ever be restored to America's *children*, if they are *not* given the dignity and self-respect of again being fully restored to the economic ecology of the American family: That is, made to feel that they too are contributing members to their families, and thus to society? How can we expect our nation's children to be *globally competitive* or of *moral worth* when such a vast majority of them, whether poor or rich, for their first eighteen years, are nurtured only in the values of self-indulgence and self-gratification?

THE DECLINE OF THE AMERICAN FATHER, HUSBAND, AND AS THE FAMILY PROVIDER AND PATRIARCH

Even with America's political and religious institutions propounding that the American Dream could only be fulfilled by the two-parent, two-child family, by the mid-1970s, poor and middle-class parents began to suspect the *old rules* of the game had changed, although most were unable to articulate this "change," or even identify its roots. The children, for the majority of these poor and middle-class American parents had become enormous T.V.-driven economic consumption burdens. Simultaneously, the ability to increase their earnings to accommodate these burdens seemed to be eroding as quickly as their children's interest in their last week's toys, their last month's designer clothes, and other luxury fad items that required these parents to purchase larger homes to have room for these out-dated consumer goods. The saying in the eighties of Boobus Americanus was: "My kid isn't spoiled, he just gets everything he wants." But the bottom was falling out under Boobus Americanus' *standard-of-living.* Boobus Americanus came to realize that the *family unit* was held in lesser-and-lesser value and their children, who had once been thought of as being the insurance policy for their old-age security, economic well-being, and perhaps to some, even immortality, now became viewed as the undesirable consequence of their sexual promiscuity or their poor choice of a proper mating partner.

Another important institution arose during the early 1970s and continues up until today, this phenomenon is known as *American Male Bashing.* All American males came under attack in the social milieu, in the home, and in the workplace. Women workers, and women in general, as a direct result of the Women's Liberation Movement, rightfully wanted equal pay for equal work, an end to sexual harassment in the workplace, an end to sexual discrimination in hiring and promotion, and the end of mental and physical abuse in the home, directed against them and their children by the American male.

Between 1965 and 1990, millions of new women entered the already-fragile American labor market, which was under attack by the M&A Gangs, the free-traders, and the Republican party. As a direct result of all of these factors, the average hourly wage-rate of the American male dropped between 20 and 25%.

By the early 1980s, the vast majority of American fathers, in both the poor and middle-classes, who had managed to stick-it-out through the early 1980s on religious and moral principles alone, were unknowingly being set up for the final *coup de grace* (i.e. the final execution) by the Reagan and Bush Administrations. The remaining $14.80 an hour industrial jobs, that facilitated many of them "hanging-in" through the early and mid-1980s, and which had been geometrically disappearing during this period already, under Reagan and Bush began to disappear exponentially. Most of these jobs would be gone forever by the mid-1990s. With the loss of their $14.80-an-hour jobs and, thus, their self-esteem, these now-displaced American fathers and family men joined the ranks of the unemployed. Many went on to become homeless or part of the American prison population.

The situation during this period was further exasperated by the federal government, targeting family welfare and other state-aid primarily to single-parent families, further causing those same unemployed fathers and patriarchs to become more disillusioned and depressed. They became economic drains on their families since their presence in the home resulted in reduced public assistance, if they continued on as members of the *family unit.*

For those fathers who remained a part of the *family unit* past the 1980s, although seriously weakened and betrayed by their representative government, it was now the time for the final *coup de grace!* The loaded Reagan/Bush gun was passed to Clinton to finish off a vast majority of the surviving of these poor and middle-class Americans fathers. The Democratic Party President of Hope, Bill Clinton, signed both the NAFTA and GATT, despite his **promise** to carefully study the effects of these two treaties on the American worker and American jobs. Obviously this was just a little more of his political rhetoric that went along with his other empty 1992 illusory campaign oratory denouncing the demise of the *American family*, and the demise of the American father's importance as the *primary breadwinner* of the American family. He simply joined his Republican predecessors and pulled the trigger on the NAFTA and GATT gun that they had left him in the closet of the White House. It was finally Clinton, who put the final bullets into the heads of the remaining American fathers still in *family units*, as he signed into law the very Reagan/ Bush NAFTA and GATT Trade Treaties, that would finally close off all hope for this generation of American fathers to remain in, or again become a part of the traditional American *family unit.* So died the last remnants of the *American Dream* that had remained somewhat alive in the first half of the 1990s.

Now that the 1990s have more than half-unfolded, it is obvious to most of you that America is continuing its rapid downward moral and economic spiral, no matter how many new jobs Mr. Clinton says his Administration is creating (10 million he claimed as of July 5, 1996). We all have to wonder what will be left by the year 2000, if anything, of the remaining *family units* of America's poor and middle-class that once comprised the vast majority of all American families; especially if we choose to do *nothing* socially, politically, and economically about it. If it is your choice to do *nothing*, there will certainly be *nothing* left for you, and possibly *nothing* left for even America's *top-two-percenters,* whose greed at various times has been self-smothering.

What is it that you could do to restore America's moral fabric and America's family values if it were your *watch*, and you were the President of the United States? The answer is: *Nothing,* unless there is a mandate from the most important *interest group* in America: and that's **you. All 260 million of you** who want to take America to where it is again *your* America and not the America now owned by America's *top-two-percenters*.

There is so much work to be done! As noted in Section O of Chapter One, at the end of 1995, only 20% of American families were intact as traditional *family units*. You may want to read below how effective American drug dealers have been in further destroying the American family unit. Nonetheless, the solution to reversing the decline of the American family unit is one of the most complex solutions facing Americans today. How do we incorporate three million unwed mothers, who are not even a part of the family units we've been talking about? How do we get the American male to again pay for the cow, when he's been getting the milk for free for over thirty years? How do we revive and re-inspire those same American males to embrace the concept of *self-respect*; when his employment outlook is hopeless, his genetic impulse to again be the *deer hunter* and *provider* for his family has, for the great majority of his species, disappeared? How do we reverse more than thirty years of continual male bashing that has him believing he is nothing more than a wife-beating, child-molesting, sex pervert, good-for-nothing, except for being able to slobber-down a six-pack of beer, seven nights a week?

Unfortunately, many young American females concur with this above analysis and have adjusted their own moral conduct and expectations downward, to stay in touch with the male members of their species, so perhaps the species. Perhaps the species itself will become extinct.

The first step, we as Americans, have to take to reverse the America's current downward spiral to deal a *death-blow* to America's *drug*, *porn*, and *violence* businesses that have expanded exponentially causing America's moral fabric to diminish to the point it is at now. How to accomplish this can be found either in your own common sense or in several chapters dedicated to the solutions of America's problems included in this book.

America's Make-Believe Drug Wars
Some User Facts About America's Illegal Drug Crisis

1. Approximately 1.2% of Americans (3 million) are hard-core cocaine addicts. It is estimated that there are an additional 800,000 American hard-core heroin addicts.

2. Although Americans represent only 5% of the world's population, Americans represent 50% of the world's hard-core drug consumers.

3. Although the Bush Administration in 1992 estimated that "casual" (non hard-core) drug users were down 40% in number (11.8 million from 18 million), emergency room treatment rates for "casual" cocaine users were up 10%, and for "casual" heroine users the treatment rate was up 13%. Between 1992 and 1996, the largest percentage increase in all illegal drug use has occurred in the age 10 to 16 year-old group.

The Battle Lines, The Business Lines & The Cocaine Lines

So, after thirty (30) years you're still wondering why the government hasn't won its war on drugs. One night on the late evening news you hear Congressmen Lewis Charles Rangel (D-N.Y.) say it's a $100-Billion-a-year business. A week later the former Bush Administration responded: "We're winning the drug war. Casual use of illegal drugs by middle-class America is down 40%."

For weeks afterwards, you don't hear a word about the government's war on illegal drugs. For sure, you think, they must have the problem under control. After all how could the news media let a $100-Billion problem go without coverage?

By the end of March, 1992, and up until three months before the 1992 elections, all media coverage of the "drug wars" ceased. No longer did you hear about any major drug busts. No longer did the DEA confiscate those huge shipments of between two and three metric tons of cocaine monthly in Miami. Nor was anyone dumping one-ton bales of cocaine from low flying airplanes off Ft. Lauderdale. The reports of such important events as the six-ton seizures of cocaine, in the past, as reported from Los Angeles all dried-up.

With this new lack of media information you were then certain the Bush Administration had positively won the war on drugs. Some of you were even interested enough then to think about the early 1992 disclaimers given at the end of every reported Drug-Bust, DEA, or local government news release. That disclaimer being that tons of cocaine were still coming across our borders with Mexico, in eighteen wheel trailer trucks, because neither the U.S. Congress, nor the Administration had provided sufficient funding to the DEA (Drug Enforcement Agency), the INS (Immigration and Naturalization Service), or the U.S. Boarder Patrol to pay for interception of these shipments. You weren't sure then whether it's just public relations so that the Drug Law Enforcement Officers could perpetuate their jobs, or whether the news was as bad as it sounded. The disclaimer generally went like this: "And this is only a small fraction of what enters the United States every month." And then, for almost six months before the 1992 election, there are no drug busts at all and no media coverage.

So, you sit back and ask yourself the same question, **"Is the government winning the war on drugs?"** You realize again this has been a thirty (30) year war, and you've finally got to ask yourself: "Does the government really *want to win* the war on drugs?"

If you've read Chapter One of this book, "Numbers Can Be Scary," and understand American Capitalism's roots in Malthusian Economic Theory, you should now be taking a whole new approach to this question. With your new understanding of Malthus, you too have come to the following awareness concerning illegal drugs.

America's controlled "war" or lack of any "real war" on the spread and use of illegal drugs serves to:

(a)   Maintain political, economic, and population control of the lower economic classes vis-à-vis fratricide, violent crime, and incarceration which is the end result of America's wide use of illegal drugs.

(b)   Maintain the lower, and now the middle-economic classes' dysfunctionalism, disorganization, and disorientation minimizing the risk that they may cohesively organize politically or economically.

"So okay," you say, "there's some kind of sinister Administration conspiracy going on, by either omission or commission. So what can anyone do about the illegal drug business in the country anyway? These drug addicts are just like alcoholics, and there's nothing you're going to do to stop them!"

Then you begin to fantasize. You ask yourself: "What would I do if I were the President of the United States?" You think on it long and hard. The word "war" keeps racing around your mind. You think of employing military force, perhaps some of those clean-cut boys who served in Desert Storm. Why not? They're trained in the basic concepts of law and order and, more importantly, "war." You call your local U.S. Congressman and two U.S. Senators from your state and tell them of your solution.

The response of your Congressman and two Senators are exactly the same. They tell you there is no precedent to use American Military Forces for domestic crimes, and that it would be a dangerous precedent to set. You're subtly reminded of Nazi-Germany's and Fascist-Italy's use of military force prior to, and during World War II. You are so strongly admonished regarding your suggestion that you feel not merely stupid, but sub-moronic, as the alleged *non-war on drugs* continues.

It's an hour later, and you again think about what you've been told by your Congressman and two Senators. Something is gnawing at you from the far reaches of what they have convinced you is your sub-moronic, subliminal mind. You recall the Los Angeles riots following the Rodney King verdict. You're certain that President Bush ordered Federal Troops to the outlying areas of Los Angeles in the event they might be needed to support California Governor Pete Wilson's already mobilized National Guard to restore "law and order."

You ask yourself, "How come the Governor and the President, and even the Mayor, who can mobilize the American Military for the purpose of quelling these riots and civil disorder, can't mobilize them to eradicate the crime and disorder created by the $100-Billion illegal drug business that has probably had an even greater detrimental impact on this same city of Los Angeles than the Rodney King riots?"

If it's true that the illegal drug business in the United States represents a $100-Billion Industry, which I have no doubt that it does, it remains no mystery to me why America's Military Forces will never be employed to eradicate this Industry. My inherent "American Capitalist" logic tells me that $100-Billion removed from the American economy during the Reagan-Bush or Clinton years, would have put the economy into severe recession long before the recession of 1990-1992. There would probably have been a major depression if a real war on drugs had ever been implemented and won, whether a recession or not..

After all, we're not just looking at $100-billion worth of drug sales. We're looking at the need of those drug-using-consumers to earn or acquire the money needed to purchase this $100 billion of drugs annually. Let's first look at this $100-billion from the "demand-side." Later, we'll again look at this $100-billion in illegal drug sales, and its overall impact on both the demand and supply sides of the U.S. economy.

Even during the "go-go" 1980's, the alleged record growth era of American capitalism, it was important where these drug users acquired the $100-Billion. Let's presume all the money to purchase these drugs came entirely from the "theft" of automobiles. Now let's do a *transactional analysis* of what happens under this hypothesis. These automobiles that are stolen are generally stolen for the purpose of being converted into re-salable "spare parts" by the thousands of "chop-shops" scattered all across America. For those of you who don't know, a "chop-shop" is an unlawful business that purchases relatively new "stolen cars" for their "parts" value. The sum of the recovered "parts" are generally valued at 120% of the original purchase price the car when new.

For the purpose of this *transactional analysis*, let's say the "chop-shop" owner pays $2,000 per stolen car. That requires 500,000 cars be stolen per year to get the $100- Billion needed for our theoretical illegal drug purchases. Remember, these cars have to be relatively "new," because the "chop-shop" can only sell relatively "new" parts. Thus we are looking at 500,000 theft-insured cars that are easily replaced with insurance proceeds. We, of course, all share the cost of these insurance proceeds in increased insurance premiums. "Some impact," you're saying "on the American Insurance Industry!" The best part of this transaction is the impact on the U.S. Automobile Industry, assuming only American-made cars were stolen. Say 500,000 American cars, at an average cost of $11,000 each, has entered the chop-shop. That's $5.5 billion in new, replacement car sales which has an enormous "trickle-down" impact on the whole American economy.

Let's not forget the 20,000 jobs that are created in the "chop-shop" industry, and the benefit for all Americans of having these 20,000 "chop-shop" mechanics spending their incomes for other goods and services produced or rendered by other Americans businesses. Think of all this "cashflow" through the U.S. banking system. Conversely, think what would happen if this "cashflow" were taken out of the U.S. banking system if America "legalized" the use of drugs. With the current downsizing of all major U.S. companies, including the banking industry, you certainly don't want to kick America in the can, by taking $100-billion out of its annual economic cash flow, and burden the already minimal job market with an additional 3 million junkies who are responsible for probably the creation of 5 million jobs resulting from their crimes. *Do you?*

Lastly, you don't have to be an expert on "durable" and "nondurable" goods to understand that the "nondurable" nature of "illegal drugs" makes them one of the fastest moving consumer commodities in the United States today. Thus, from an American Capitalistic viewpoint, "illegal" drugs are an (if not the most) important American commodity, especially if we expect to keep America's economic engine running fine-tuned for America's *top-two-percenters*.

Can you now understand all the brouhaha made over "legalizing" drug use in the United States? Any American with even a minimum education in American capitalism recognizes that if illegal drugs were made "legal," the "profit motive" that is so essential to its success and the fruits it brings to the American economy would quickly disappear. Continued growth opportunities in several prospering American and foreign businesses and industries (chop-shops, the Security Guard Industry, the Drug Rehabilitation Counseling Industry, the worldwide Automobile Industry, etc., etc.might very well be destroyed.). Legalization of drugs would also dramatically impact America's two fastest growing state-financed industries: Prison Facilities Management and Law Enforcement.

So Where Do We Go With Drug Wars From Here?

No where, if we intend to maintain the status quo of our present political and economic systems. You'll have a better appreciation of this after reading Chapters Nineteen and Twenty. If we, as Americans, do opt for an end to the present status quo as set forth above and in previous chapters, there is no doubt the drug wars in this country can be won.

How about this scenario for an alternate solution?

First, we all become altruistic, idealistic, and compassionate, and thus we are willing to provide other economic alternatives to the American sub-cultures that have developed primarily in America's "inner cities." This means job opportunity, economic stability, and the acknowledgment that these sub-cultures of the "inner cities" are entitled to an adequate standard-of-living; the opportunity for home ownership; and the opportunity to develop, operate and control the law enforcement functions within their own communities. This will obviously require a substantial initial investment in both training and money. Once up-and-running, the initial cost will be a fraction of the long-term cost of just maintaining these communities in their present condition.

Secondly, what if we accept that **drug addiction** is as much a part of American society as is **alcoholism?** What if for the benefit of those permanently addicted drug abusers, as well as, for the benefit of American society, drugs **were** legalized? This could be done in such a manner that the distribution to those permanently addicted is carefully controlled and monitored; sufficient to at least keep these addicted individuals functional and lawfully employed within American society. Many drug addicts would gladly sweep streets, if they were sufficiently supplied cocaine or heroin for free.

How else can we win the "drug war," except by eliminating its "illegal profits?" This will only be achieved through "legalizing" its trafficking, distrbutiion, and sale, and taxing it appropriately to those who now operate and control this $100-billion business without contributing one dime to the U.S. Treasury. Has anything else worked in the last 30 years?

Finally, we must break with the excuses of "precedence." America is at "war" within its own borders. To win this "war" requires a two-year commitment of a significant segment of America's Military Forces to clean-up the existing systems that facilitate illegal drug production, importation, trafficking, and sales. Why two full years? Because that's how long it will take to implement "legalization." An adequate system of controlled drug distribution and addict registration, which requires the implementation of the necessary political and economic reform to make such a properly-controlled and administered "legalized drug" system work.

American Pornography and Entertainment Violence

Next to illegal drugs, pornography in the United States is the second largest money maker in America's "amoral" business sector. This major American Business includes: topless bars; nude waitresses; topless bakeries; nude car-washes; thong-swim-suited hot-dog vendors; adult video stores; X, XX, and XXX rated movies; most television; and those expensive girlie magazines which substitute celluloid girlfriends to the American male in the place of the very best of real American women. Bet you didn't know there were so many new businesses in America? Notwithstanding, this comprises most of the vendors in the $80-100 billion American pornography industry.

You no longer even have to sneak out of the house to the sleazy part of town to purchase your "porn." Pay-TV and basic cable alike are already in your home for a couple of bucks an hour. If you don't need the hard-core trash, you need only to turn on your boob-tube, twenty-four hours a day, and over the public airwaves and the cable come programs, products, and services packaged directly or indirectly in "sex" to improve product sales and profitability; which also further debases your morality by giving you that quick dose of lust for no more than the cost of your cable, and for free if you are still using just a TV antenna.

Whether it's because times are hard, or meaningful jobs scarce, or because they're in it for the "thrill of it," we've condoned, and sometimes even cheered on many of our next door neighbors to "star" in and sell their own home produced "porn" videos in local video rental shops shamelessly in their own neighborhoods. Even more troublesome are the recent genre of gender-hate X, XX, and XXX movies. A rather stark example is American folk hero Clint Eastwood's Unforgiven. This celluloid piece of trash that was honored by numerous American Academy Awards, depicts women as a bunch of murdering, conspiring harlots, and depicts these women's male counterparts in heroic proportion, as promiscuous, sociopathic, cold-blooded killers. Given these qualities and attributes, they are then shown as being worthy of dominating society, as a direct result of having these rather anti-social and violent qualities.

One would hope that the Academy gave these numerous Oscars to Mr. Eastwood in return for his promise to never again subject America to such trash. Probably wishful thinking, at best!

We all know "sex" sells, and that "sexual perversion" super-sells! It always has, and it always will! It doesn't matter if you're 10, 30, or 100 years old. It's still "number one" on the "hot-list" of "attention grabbers" and the "marketers" of consumer products. This has been true since the beginning of the human experience. You just have to read the Bible to understand the longevity of *smut* in Judaic-Christian history.

Because of the enormous "selling power" associated with "sex" and "sexual perversion," society's historical preoccupation with it, and the inability of à usually small minority of its members to effectively control their sexual behavior, almost all societies have sought in one way or another to regulate sexual activity.

Given the moral and legal responsibility society imposes on its parents to support their children, it is not simply a matter of fairness, but necessity that society afford the opportunity to those same children who will become parents, to acquire the skills and social experience to both support their children and raise them in an environment of traditional *family values,* which include, amongst others: the need for sexual restraint, family unity, parental discipline, and those morals and attitudes that promote honesty, integrity, hard-work, and a drive for excellence, as opposed to our present condition, that encourages general lawlessness, promiscuity, and disdain for all of our moral and historical religious values. It is historically for this reason most regulation has been directed toward the protection of women and minors, generally those under the age of 18. The apparent historical reason for this was to allow needed time for "minors" to develop both "maturity" and "learned responsibility" that would then hopefully converge with the ultimate consequence of sexuality, bearing children, and parenthood.

Most academicians agree that women of all ages have also been singled-out by the law-makers for protection because: (1) they are significantly less violent and less sexually aggressive than men, (2) they are generally physically weaker than men, (3) they are (or were) less likely to act out their sexual drives and fantasies than men, and (4) they are the mothers, daughters, and sisters of men who have been historically charged with crafting such laws (i.e. statutory rape, rape, sexual assault, sexual battery, incest, child sexual abuse, child pornography, etc.).

Now, if you rewind your memory back to 1960 and fast-forward it to today, you would have to concede that the pendulum of sexual morality, as it pertains to minors, has completely swung to the far relaxed-end of the scale. Today, it is not uncommon to hear many members of our society advocating children of ever-tender-ages being encouraged to enjoy their sexuality; all in the context of America's allegedly new era of sexual freedom for the sake of simple biological pleasure.

Although all of the laws noted in the second paragraph above remain intact, or have been expanded in most jurisdictions, sex crimes against American women and American children have continued to explode out of control over the past thirty years. This is not merely the phenomenon of finally hearing the tree fall in the forest.

With this national explosion of amorality and immorality over the past thirty years, one almost has to wonder if this emergence of sexual immorality wasn't a *joint* conspiracy of U.S. government and business. One only has to look at our government's continuing abdication of its obligation not to undermine America's standards of morality, and American business' growing reliance and economic dependence on selling more and more inferior products disguised in "sexuality" to develop an earnest belief in this conspiracy theory.

Again, as Americans, we have to collectively determine what our "social" and "family values" are to be in this most critical area of American social morality. Based on what we've seen for the last thirty years, we can no longer abdicate the responsibility to control pornography to our present government, the self-appointed pundits of the media, America's sex counselors, or the "porn" segment of American industry. Here again the jury is in! Will we ever have the fortitude to clean out all of these "rat nests" before the turn of this century, or even before the turn of the next century? Or should we wait until this smut has finally smothered us all to death?.

Fully aware that we Americans are playing with a "stacked deck" (i.e. the overwhelming majority of Americans believe that some form of "censorship" is necessary to control America's massive "pornography" industry), also want to keep their present sexual addictions. I only offer an inexpensive, probably over-simplified means to achieve this limited "censorship" objective necessary to put **some** control over America's pornography and violence industries.

I suggest each state create an elected censorship board comprised of fifteen citizens with the following simple attributes and qualifications:

1. The individual must be a female parent of a female child between the ages of six and sixteen.

2. The individual must be free of any criminal convictions, illegal drug use, or a history of child abuse or neglect.

3. The individual cannot be employed in any area of law, entertainment, or mass media.

It would be the duty of this state-wide elected board to review all network and cable T.V. productions, movie productions, pictorial magazine publications, and any other visual or audio means of conveying sexually explicit materials or unacceptable portrayals of violence in their jurisdictions. Members of the board would meet in committees of three to decide by majority vote whether or not the material is pornographic. If the material were deemed pornographic there would exist the right of the producer of the product to modify his or her product and unlimited number of appeals to the board as a whole. In this circumstance, the appealing producer of the material would be required to pay all of the expenses incurred by the board for these appeals. I leave you with one final thought on this subject, as Mr. Clinton would say: "We can do better." These four words need to be taken to heart especially to the entertainment and media segments of our society.

The Destruction of The American Family
Media Focus on
The American Father

Back in 1992, when media was focused on the American father, I took special note of two of their pieces knowing I would someday write a book about America. Both media pieces focus on the once traditional financial cornerstone of the American *family unit*, the "father."

The first piece was done in early May 1992 by Diane Sawyer of ABC's <u>Prime Time</u>, entitled **"Deadbeat Dads."** These "dads" were not from America's impoverished classes or the inner city, were from "model" middle-class suburban communities. These men were college educated Caucasian males who had not fulfilled their roles as fathers for over a decade.

Featured as one of the "deadbeats," was a father, who two years earlier had abandoned his wife, thirteen-year old son and eleven-year old daughter, without any warning. He simply left without notice or explanation moving to a different city and assuming a new life.

The <u>Prime Time</u> investigators had tracked him down to find out why he'd abandoned his "model" family. The son and daughter featured on <u>Prime Time</u> were now about fifteen and thirteen, respectively. Obviously psychologically distressed, they too wanted to know why their "model" father had just picked-up and left, leaving them to fend for themselves with only their mother. Both children had intense anger with respect to what had happened to them, especially the son who felt personally betrayed since the abandonment had occurred just prior to his entering his teenage years; a period when most boys feel the greatest need for their father.

When <u>Prime Time</u> finally caught up with this *deadbeat dad,* the interview was structured in a manner that kept confidential from him that his two children would be simultaneously viewing <u>Prime Time's</u> interview of him in a van just a few yards from his new residence. The children apparently had agreed to do their segment of this <u>Prime Time</u> story only if they would be allowed the opportunity to confront their father when and if found by <u>Prime Time</u> investigators.

The *deadbeat dad* was finally tracked down and, as agreed between <u>Prime Time</u> and his two children, he was not made aware that his two children would be receiving simultaneous telecast of the interview as it was being taped. As his children watched secretly from the <u>Prime Time</u> van, the interview proceeded. Needless to say for any American, especially any American male the interview was, at best, painful.

"Why did you abandon your family?" the interviewer questioned. In so many words, the man responded, "I could no longer support them. I couldn't give them the things they needed to make it in this world. My son was soon going to be entering college. I couldn't afford his tuition. I didn't want to fail my family."

The second media piece was done by Paul Taylor, a writer for the Washington Post who covers various social-welfare issues. On this occasion he addressed this same "deadbeat" father phenomenon, but his *deadbeat dads* were from the impoverished classes of the "inner cities."

First Taylor quotes a startling statement from Louis Sullivan, the former Secretary of Health and Human Services. Sullivan stated: "We are raising a generation of young males who measure their manhood by the caliber of their gun and by the number of children they have fathered —a generation for whom the camaraderie of a gang has replaced the love of a family."

Taylor expands upon Sullivan's statement in defense of the "young males" to whom Sullivan had referred with a remarkably short, but insightful analysis. He writes: "The causes are broad and mutually reinforcing. The erosion of good-paying, low-skilled entry-level jobs; the evolution of the social welfare state; the sexual revolution; the movement of woman into the work force, and the increasing gender role convergence in modern culture all have conspired to make it more difficult to pull off what anthropologists believe is a critical task for any civilized society — to harness the male into the role of husband and father."

Taylor concludes his article with the following paragraph, "Unless society also learns how to re-value marriage and re-stigmatize broken relations between mothers and fathers, none of the rest will matter much. The empirical evidence is in: when marriage atrophies, so does fatherhood. And so does society."

Even before reading the bare-bones of the two *media* pieces above, if you are, or were ever an American "father," you knew before they ended, how it would turn out. If you have never been a "father" in

America, you certainly don't have to qualify as a "rocket scientist," a "brain surgeon," or a "renowned anthropologist" to recognize the series of "storm surges" that have decimated the traditional role of America's poor and middle-class "father." You would only have had to seen one TV show depicting today's alleged typical American family and run your adding machine tape to know the cost of rearing a family. In the minds of over 50% of America's fathers, they just became "failures," whether they lost their jobs entirely, or had their 1970 average $16.02 per hour work-wage reduced to $6.00 per hour, and thus were unable to meet the growing financial needs of their families in the 1980s and 1990s.

The Calculated Failure Of America's Moral Leadership

The term "morality" covers many things. It's family values, honor, honesty, integrity, self-control. It is respect for others and their property. It is the state of our collective "consciences," our ethics, and our laws and how they are administered and adhered to.

A society's state of "morality" is the measure of its resolve or "collective conscience" to deal with and manage both the *individual's* and its *communal self-indulgence,* the excesses of which always become detrimental to the "society" as a whole.

In America, "moral decadence" has become the *accepted norm,* for the majority of its citizens. With this state of "moral decadence" we've also lost our sense of "community" and our sense of "nation." Although some of you haven't yet realized it, we've all been betrayed by our political, religious, and professional leaders — as they focused on their individual wealth and *personal self-indulgences*, as opposed to nation's wealth, welfare, and well-being.

No longer does it seem relevant to our political and professional leaders, the media, and many of our Sunday morning preachers that our ancestors and founding fathers created this nation to escape the oppression and poverty of Europe and elsewhere for a better, freer way of life in America. No longer do these historic foundations of American democracy and the American Dream seem remotely relevant to our leaders.

Since 1989, all we have heard from our President and Congress is how we are going to suffer future hardships:

1. How we are going to have to reduce our standard-of-living;
2. How we (as if we were the ones who profited) are going to have to pay $500 billion looting of America's S&Ls;
3. How we can no longer globally compete, as our *representative government* permitted the destruction of our industrial infrastructure by the M&A gangs while telling us that these industries were nothing

more than a yoke on the neck of American global competitiveness; and

4. How we are going to have to pay-off a $5 trillion National Debt for both the President's and the Congress' reckless spending and pandering during the past sixteen years.

Ask yourself: With the exception of a little selective election year "lip service," who was the last American President . . . . To be "outraged" over the state of America's morality? . . . . To be "outraged" over America's cities and suburbs being destroyed by illegal drugs and crime? . . . To be "outraged" over the "lootings" of America's S&Ls, or America's industrial infrastructure? You certainly didn't hear any one of our last three Presidents screaming their outrage on these matters from the so-called *bully-pulpit. Did you?*

Compounding the failure of "moral" leadership by Presidents Clinton, Bush, and Reagan was the opposing political party's simultaneous widespread corruption within the U.S. Congress; the betrayal of the vast majority of American workers by American business; and the betrayal of so many of America's Televangelists, such as Jim Baker and Jimmy Swaggart, disguising themselves as spiritual and moral leaders.

One can only imagine what our *founding fathers* would have thought if they could observe the nation they founded today. Their noble notions of protecting "political" free speech, now used to subvert all American morality and promote all forms of perversion, pornography, and immorality. One can only imagine, if given this same environment as we live in today, whether Paul Revere would have gotten on his horse in the middle of the night to warn us that the British were coming to deprive us of the alleged freedoms we now enjoy. Frankly, I don't think Paul, given the circumstances of today, would have ever gotten on his horse, that is if it wasn't stolen from him first and sent off to a "glue shop."

The Myths Of American Government, Business, Media, Family & Morality

I. Our founding fathers, when they created the Bill of Rights, intended that freedom of political speech should be applied to all speech, even in a pictorial format.

II. American political and business institutions would like to see an end to drug trafficking and the drug business in the United States.

III. The majority of America's political, governmental, academic, and religious institutions are dedicated to re-establishing the moral fabric of America.

IV. America's political and governmental institutions are concerned with the preservation of the American family and its values.

V. The Donahues, Sallys, and the Geraldos, are interested in educating Americans with respect to new values, new breakthroughs in medicine, new breakthroughs in psychology and psychiatry, and in making America a better place to live.

The Realities of American Government, Business, Media, Family & Morality

I. It is nonsense to believe that our **founding fathers** intended that freedom of speech be applied to pornography and the related $60-120 billion pornography business. I for one, cannot imagine it was their intent to override almost 6,000 years of Judaic Christian principles in order that a few of our "top-two-percenters" could live the **high-life**.

II. The political and business institutions of America rely on the drug business almost as much as they do on Americans paying taxes. The sale of illegal drugs in the United State today is estimated to be a $100-Billion a year business, accounting for almost 1,000,000 better-paying American jobs, not including the derivative law enforcement jobs needed to keep this illegal drug industry from running over the U.S. Congress. Obviously there are not enough McDonalds, Burger Kings, or Dunkin' Donuts around to absorb the majority of these unskilled 1,000,000 people into their ranks. It is also important to recognize that no other consumer product in America today has the turnover with respect to both cashflow and profitability as do illegal drugs. If illegal drugs were eliminated from the U.S. stream of commerce, the U.S. economy would probably go into a *super-crash*. For this reason most politicians and the business community would not want to see an end to the illegal drug industry. If you're having trouble grasping this, think of it in terms of $100-Billion in fewer sales of yachts, extravagant homes, Mercedes Benzes, Cadillacs, expensive jewelry, etc., that would not be purchased by those currently earning their wages in this business. This applies to the global economy as well. Countries such as Colombia, Mexico, and Thailand, amongst others, would suffer severe economic hardship if illegal drugs were ended, or legalized.

III. The majority of America's political, governmental, academic, and religious institutions are not in the business of attempting to re-establish the moral fabric of America. Just as any other American enterprise, they're in the business of making money. Except for a

IV. Family values are contrary to the objectives of today's political and governmental leaders. First ask: Could illegal drugs flourish in a nation of strong family values? Then ask: If all of America's law enforcement officers were freed-up from drug-related crime, might their attention be turned to white-collar crime, and political corruption at the federal, state, and local levels?

V. The Donahues, Sallys, and the Geraldos are only interested in ratings. Ratings mean more money. And more money is something this group seems to have and an endless appetite for.

COMPOSITE DICTIONARY

Morality: A personal characteristic which subscribes to the law of conscience. It incorporates the aggregate of those rules and principles of ethics which relate to right and wrong conduct and prescribes the standards to which the actions of men and women should conform in their dealings with each other, and others. It is also deemed to be the "conformity" to ideals of "right" human conduct or "virtue," as well as the beneficial quality or power of those things that most men and women of ordinary being find spiritually pleasing and comforting. Courage, chastity, charity, truth, integrity, and righteousness are the primary attributes of "morality."

Mores: The fixed morally-binding customs of a particular group or culture that includes its moral attitudes, habits, and manners.

Political Correctness: The latest of philosophical bullying techniques found on American College and University Campuses that generally finds favor amongst those who have too little work, too much free time, and believe they bring something new to the "intellectual arena." "Political correctness" is taking offense at any reference that appears to diminish the importance of any minority religious, ethnic, or racial group, unless it diminishes the role of the American male descendant of the European male Caucasian, and simultaneously identifies this species as being the sole cause of all of America's racial, political, and economic problems.

Pro-Choice: Those who favor a woman's choice to have, or not to have, an abortion.

Pro-Life: Those who do **not** favor abortion.

18 | The American Democracy Dilemma:

Whose Government is it Anyway?

You're not a Corporate CEO, CFO, CIO, COO, or UFO. Neither are you a doctor, lawyer, or CPA. You've never had a taste for "public service," and you've never been a Congressman, the President, or appointed to a high level government position. Lastly, you're not one of those like my deceased client George, from New Purchase N.Y., who died in 1989 with a net worth in excess of $340 million, and whose glory was discussed in Chapter Ten.

You're the typical insecure American who comes home after a hard 10-hour work day. Right after you forget your promise to **never do it again**, you turn on the ten o'clock news. After a few minutes of careful attention you ask: "What the hell is going on in this country?"

Who are you, and how do you fit into all of this **mess** the **news media** slams into your face every day? Perhaps you have four or more years of higher education, or maybe you're a mixture of experience and some education, or some special skills that are still in demand somewhere in American Business or Industry. You partially own (the bank owns 80% of it) a three bedroom-two-and-a-half bath home, that you, your spouse, and your bank purchased for $90,000, ten years ago. You have a year-old Oldsmobile, a quarter of which you own and a four-year old Toyota with only twelve payments to go. You've done all that was expected to enjoy the American Dream. You worked hard while at school, worked hard while at work, played by the rules, and everyone else - especially those in the "inner city" and the "homeless" - thinks that you've made it; that you are living the American Dream!

But that's not what's going through your mind. There are those two continual gnawing and haunting questions: "What the hell is going on with this country's jobs, morality, and government? Will I be the "one" out of a job next week? Will it be me next month seeking room and board under one of those already overcrowded I-95 off-ramps?"

All you hear about is the coming recession, or possibly even a depression, the S&L bailouts that won't ever be paid-off, corporate downsizings, congressional scandals, presidential scandals, and unrelenting violent crime. You don't even feel safe outside your home anymore, much less in your car, or where you work. You've even given up going out after dark. The same haunting questions keep stalking you over and over. You try to figure out an answer, but you don't even know where to begin: "Is it too much government? Or is it just part of the luggage that comes with "freedom?" Is it big business, or is it welfare recipients who just won't work?

And with all the fifteen second sound bites, you can no longer distinguish between Republican and Democrat, right or wrong, left or right, much less black or white.

You've had eight years of Ronald Reagan, four years of George Bush, and four years of Bill Clinton, and as much time to think about it. There are a lot of things you now know for sure. The first is, you no longer feel secure "at all" about your job — you're told day-in and day-out the whole world has changed in just the past sixteen years — that you're now a part of this enormous **global economy**; it's a whole new ball game, a so-called, whole *New World Order*, and *you've got to adjust*, if you have any expectation at all of just holding-on to your ten-year-old home that now needs a new roof, your 1992 Toyota, and the few pieces of thread-bare furniture you were going to replace when your three kids had gone off to college.

Your second awesome realization is your new sense of insecurity. It's not just job insecurity, but it's the loss of your hard earned standard-of-living. In fact, it's as though the "inner city" you have observed for most of your life seems to be coming out to encircle you: Drugs, guns, and gangs in your kid's school, a dozen muggings in a week in the local mall, and neighborhood bank robberies. You and your spouse seem to be spending so much time setting your car alarms, house alarm, and reviewing your burglary insurance coverage, that there seems to be little time to do anything else.

Finally, you don't have a sense that anything is going to get better. You no longer have any faith in your company; your pension plan, if you still have one at all; or your medical insurance. Even though in denial, you know that if any "major illness" should strike, you'll be dropped like a hot cake with your whole family, and off to the "poorhouse," if there's still some room. With the complexity of your and the nation's problems, you have an overwhelming sense of paralysis and confusion. You try to avoid the six o'clock news and the morning paper. You continually feel disillusioned, dazed, and completely impotent, not only getting started on a solution, but just trying to figure out how this *enormous mess* came about. You think about all of those *local militia* boys, hundreds of them every day, in Arizona, Colorado, Minnesota, and elsewhere estranging themselves from the U.S. government. You wonder if there isn't a good reason, or two, for you now joining up in your own local group?

You sit and think. It was almost four years ago. To avoid thinking about it, you had put yourself into what psychiatrists call, *denial* ; a *denial* you had hoped would last long enough, so that when you awoke, everything would have just gone away. It was that same night in early June, 1992, that you had inadvertently flicked-on Ted Koppel's <u>Nightline</u>. It was that same night, a few hours after Koppel's broadcast that you tuned-out of America and its <u>lunacy</u>. Suddenly you are shot back to where you were in 1992. Your *walls of denial* are crumbling in around you. After twenty years, your wife just got downsized out of AT&T, and you, yourself, haven't worked in six months. You again remember that awful night in June of 1992! There on your 25" Sony in living-color, and as big as life, sat six members of the U.S. Senate, all with somber faces as they commenced serious discussion in one of Ted Koppel's *"A Conversation With So-and-So"* programs. Your first reaction had been, "Oh my God! Three Democratic Senators and three Republican Senators. Someone must have shot the President!"

You quickly turned up the volume so you wouldn't miss a word. You carefully studied the faces of Senator John Danforth (R-MO), Hank Brown (R-CO), Sam Nunn (D-GA), Carl Levin (D-MI), Bob Graham (D-FL), and Bill Cohen (R-ME). One word, more than any other seemed to ring clear. It was the word *"Sacrifice."*

Your worst fears were realized as the conversation continued. You were told that you were going to have to give up your expectations of any improved standard-of-living. America had entered a new era. If we were ever going to get past the *partying binge* of the 1980s, we had all shamelessly enjoyed, we were all going to have to make *"significant sacrifices."*

You remember having scratched your head and thinking, "What the hell *party* are they talking about?" You had then searched back over the past twelve years, and you still couldn't figure out what *party* they were talking about. Perhaps, it was either the Republican or Democratic *Party* they were referring to. But after some more careful listening, you had begun to catch on. They were talking about these horrific things called the National Debt and "runaway" Deficit. Although you heard just the other day that the 1996 National Debt was up to $5 trillion, you seem to remember having heard the number $4 trillion, and something about a $400 billion deficit. This was what Senator Danforth told you had over-spent and had borrowed in 1992, as a citizen of the United States to keep-everything a-float for another year.

You had again scratched your head, and remembered thinking out-loud: "What the hell are they talking about? I haven't been able to get ahead of my car payments and I still owe $180,000 on my house. For God's sake, I haven't even been able to afford a vacation in the past three years, and I still have a $6500 balance on my MasterCard!"

You remember how Senator Danforth appeared to be more upset than the others. He had even declared: "It was the responsibility of the three candidates running for President of the United States and every member running for the Congress to discuss directly with the people, both the Federal Deficit and the National Debt facing our country."

Danforth had gone on to insist that in the 1992 election, it was the duty of the American people to provide a "mandate" for "government action;" a "mandate" he insisted would require *shared sacrifices* amongst all Americans.

Another of the six Senators had chimed in that both the Congress and the media have ignored, or trivialized, both the Debt and the Deficit issue by suggesting that it could have been corrected by merely attacking waste, fraud, and abuse. A third Senator verified your worst thoughts and, almost as if rehearsed, he looked squarely into the eye of the camera and reconfirmed to you that the meaningful Deficit reductions that were being discussed that night could only be accomplished through the *shared-sacrifice* of all the American people. To tell **the people** anything but this, would constitute *gross deception*. The harshness of the words *gross deception* had sent shivers rippling up and down your spine. *"Gross deception"* by George Bush or your government? Never! Especially, not after America's great victory in Desert Storm! No sir!

You further recall that for the next twenty minutes the six Senators continued their relentless attack on the little bit of what was then left of your already diminished standard-of-living. You had been carefully studying their faces as they each spoke. It had seemed to you that they had actually been peering into your living room with the intent to take away, not only the few artifacts you collected on that vacation to Washington D.C. four years before, but also your furniture and your other personal belongings.

Noticing that your Timex wrist watch had been in full view, you had slowly dropped your arm out-of-sight to the side of the chair. You had again begun to wonder: "Where were these guys for the last twelve years? Weren't they supposed to be watching what the hell was going on? What the hell were they being paid for anyway?"

Your next recollection was the mundane voice of Senator Danforth again breaking your train of thought on that night in June, 1992. He was demanding that everyone of the three presidential candidates spend one hour alone, not in debate, but explaining how he intends to deal with your "runaway" National Deficit and National Debt. Another voice had interrupted. You heard the names of Senators Rudman and Wirth. They were to be assigned the task of cross examining each presidential candidate as to his specific program to reduce the Deficit and National Debt. Then all six of the Senators had nodded agreement. *My God, you think, they've made this thing a bipartisan issue — all six of these*

Senators agreeing that none of the three presidential candidates could essentially be trusted to tell the truth. Koppel then offered three hours of free ABC prime time TV for what might very well be the media event of the decade, and without commercial break! You remember being **scared to death** as you suspected that there must be some very bad news on the horizon if Koppel and ABC were giving away a whole bunch of prime time!

The walls of your safe-haven *denial* have now almost completely crumbled down to floor-level. You remember having suddenly looked up at the clock that had sat on top of your 25" Sony television in 1992. You remember the time you had seen. You had been surprised! It' was 3:30 A.M. For almost three-and-a-half hours you had pondering the latest bit of bad news that you, yourself had finally kaleidoscoped into your own *fifteen-second-sound-bite, and buried in your own crypt of denial.*

In denial or not, you had come to one conclusion: You just weren't going to vote for any of the three presidential candidates, or anyone else running in the 1992 elections; or in any election thereafter. "How stupid, do they really think I am?" you remember thinking. "They want me to vote for one of those three crooks to give them a "mandate" to take away whatever they didn't steal from me in the past twelve years." You had turned off your 25" Sony, muttering, "They've got a snowball's chance in hell of me doing that!"

Well, don't feel abandoned and alone. In 1992, there were 255 million Americans, 250 million of them were in your boat. Now there are 266 million Americans; 260 million of them, just like you, are now out of the boat and in the water, and many without so much as a life-preserver in sight. In the name of this now *sinking flotilla of former middle-class Americans,* I welcome you to *The Ronald Reagan and George Bush Legacy.* In the name of this **sinking flotilla** I also urge you *not to quit*, at least not until you've at least tried to put into place in the America that can still belong to you, some of this book's economic, social, and political solutions that appear in the next two chapters.

After having read eighteen chapters of this book, you should now have a "handle," or perhaps a "lasso" around almost all the things that are, and have gone wrong with America, as well as, most of the reasons why. To quote from the (gratefully) soon-to-be-former U.S. Senator, Bill Bradley (D-NJ): If you choose to "waffle-wiggle-and-waiver" at this juncture, not only will your worst nightmares come true, but they'll be even more **catastrophically horrible** than you might have imagined, even in your worst of *tortured* moments.

It's Election Year 1992

It was Jerry Brown, Ross Perot, and Bill Clinton Against George Bush. Jerry was hoping to win on a write in 1-800-ballot!

Jerry **(Moonbeam)** Brown, the former governor of California wanted to toss the entire Congress, along with its staff, out on the street, and thus put American government back into the hands of the American people. Just the same thing 255 million other Americans wanted to do. Unfortunately, only 4 million of them were sufficiently desperate to want **Moonbeam** at the helm. So Jerry, still screaming and squawking his 800 number, faded into the California sunset to get prepared for another shot in 1996.

Ross Perot wanted to run it from the "inside" of the beltway instead of having to view it from the "outside" sitting on his $3 billion perch in Texas. He promised us all a business-like approach to "sweeping out the barn" (the Congress), mixed with his Naval Academy-modified-Texas style. He'd sprinkle this with a lot of "love" and "compassion" for America's middle-class, if we'd all just get him on the 50 states' ballots and then vote him in charge. We all knew George Bush had Ross by the "whatchamacallits." I mean no one, especially from Texas, gets as rich as Ross doing so much government "contract work" without a whole cemetery of skeletons in their closet. Well, in 1992, George had a few of his Republican gangsters shake-up a few of Ross's "bones." The kitchen got a little too hot for Ross, and he took the easy way out. He just up and quit, and then came back three months later, when his own FBI-like files were loaded with enough blackmail material to keep George Bush and his ruthless Republican gangsters in line; too late for them re-load, after having totally committed themselves to knocking-off Clinton.

The Democrats, led by Messrs. Clinton and Gore, said we needed something they had read about called *re-inventing government* (You now wonder what happened to all of that *re-inventing government stuff* and wonder if we'll have to re-invent it again in 1996.). They felt we also needed a Congress and the executive branch both controlled by the Democrats to end the grid-lock of the last 12 years. In return, Messrs. Clinton and Gore would then give us their somewhat vague but *promised solutions* based on three cornerstones. These solutions would be mixed with somewhat *more* of the same "love" and "compassion" Ross had talked about, while spending $50 billion that neither we nor the U.S. Treasury had in its coffers, to put all the Democrats at the state & local levels back to work and a *twenty-year plan* for a complete re-tooling of America's school system to make the next generation of Americans more competitive. The same dilemma was still there, though. Who had $50 billion, and who was going to wait twenty years, with personal bankruptcies and home foreclosures, rising at record levels back in 1992? Even you, Boobus Americanus, suspected that in twenty years there might not be a United States!

The Real Problem Begins With What They Say American Democracy Means & What It Really Means.

Even this **Boobus Americanus** (the author) has, since 1990, figured out both the Democrats, **who say they will**; and the Republicans, **who say the won't**; are incapable of solving any of America's problems, even if given the billions-and-billions to spend on education, or tax break for America's "top-two-percenters."

Neither would it matter whether it was the Republicans or the Democrats who gathered the nerve to legislate the "Eminent Domain Tax" (toyed-with in Chapter One) on the existing wealth of everyone in this country with a million dollars or more. Not that I am discounting, nor am unfavorable to such a tax. However the revenues generated from such a tax, although able to pay-down about three-quarters of the U.S. National Debt, wouldn't create "one" new job. It would just put us back to about 1979 in job potential, and we'd still have all the other off-balance sheet "debts" mentioned, and still not create "one" new American job. Given this rather contrary conclusion, I'm certain a lot of the nervous American millionaires and billionaires reading this book are now thinking: "Then, how about a little tax on the middle-class?" Sorry folks, that can't be done. The Boobus Americanus middle-class is already over-taxed, significantly **unemployed** or **underemployed,** and is in serious jeopardy of losing whatever else is left. This kind of policy thinking could ultimately lead to an armed insurrection, whether it be Democrats **or** Republicans at the helm. Remember independent Gov. Lowell Weicker almost getting lynched in 1991, when he first proposed an income tax for Connecticut?

So what is the confusion in America, about this thing we call **American Democracy**? Those very two words, **American Democracy,** we want the rest of the nations of the world to emulate. You know what I'm talking about! You hear reference to it every night on the news. "Russia's new **democracy** is threatened if Yeltsin isn't elected!" Weren't you told over the last 50 years up until 1989, that communism was the greatest threat to our **American democracy**? How many millions of Americans have died for democracy in WW I, WW II, Korea, Vietnam, Lebanon, Desert Storm, and Bosnia? The four words, **To Save American Democracy**, have been the **battle-cry** and the alleged basis for American sacrifice in every war in which American fighting men and women participated. The only two things more sacred to Americans, than **American Democracy**, are Jesus and God!

As embarrassed as I am to admit it, I too, have for all of my life, been enamored of those two words, **American Democracy**, for all of my life, as was my father, and his father before him; as were you, and your parents, and their parents before them.

What is this **American Democracy** that we defend so vigorously, and for which so many of our fellow Americans have so willingly sacrificed their lives? Here lies the twist: **American Democracy** is a **loaded** and **bundled** term. The words **American Democracy** have come to include, as if a marketing-gimmick, all of our God-given inalienable rights, so sacred and precious to us, as Americans. Who of you doesn't believe *your constitutional rights, your civil rights, and your fundamental human rights*, that encompass those other sacred words *freedom* and *liberty*, aren't the very thing we call *American Democracy*? And maybe today it does mean all of these things. Unfortunately, the words *American Democracy* are also absolutely synonymous with *American representative government.* It is this *representative government* of ours that, for the past 220 years, has cleverly woven all of your aforementioned rights, liberties, and freedoms into the one tapestry we all subscribe to today as our *American Democracy*. After 220 years of constant indoctrination, everyone of us should understand why it so very difficult for Americans to think of *American Democracy* as being anything else but this sacred basket *God-given rights, liberties, and freedoms*. After 220 years, it will be very difficult for any of us to separate out these *God-given rights, liberties, and freedoms* from what has become the invisible yoke of our American form of *representative government.*

What I am suggesting is that we, as Americans, unbundle our rights, freedoms, and liberties from this *loaded term: American Democracy*. I suggest we limit the meaning of *American Democracy* to define the interplay or quantum mechanics of *American Capitalism* that operates within *American Representative Government*, or *American Representative Government* that operates within *American Capitalism*.

To many of you this sounds as confusing as the old riddle of which came first, the chicken, or the egg. Perhaps the inter-play of American Capitalism and American Representative Government is perfectly analogous to the theoretical physics of quantum mechanics: the instantaneous conversion of *matter* to *energy*, and *energy* to *matter*, that one is never sure which he is dealing with energy or matter. This is a mystery that plagues theoretical physicists, as much as the difference or non-difference between American Capitalism and American Representative Government plagues theoretical economists and political scientists. Nonetheless, there is no mystery concerning any of this to God, who keeps the historical records on all of these matters that seem to have perplexed all human minds, since the beginning of time.

It is this failure, or perhaps indifference, of Americans to view *American Representative Government* and *American Capitalism* as "one" singular system with two dynamically inter-changing states of being, that surreptitiously operates, *at the direction of the "few," by the "few," and for the benefit of the "few."* It is a singular system which has evolved to the point where it operates above the *rule of the majority*, and where it has been allowed to rape, plunder, and pillage America into social decadence and moral decay over the past thirty years. It is our alleged *American Democracy* to which I refer.

Americans must demand that the next Administration and the next Congress put American Capitalism back to work for them by restoring to all the American people the absolute *obligation* of their *American government* to have *American capitalism* benefit *all Americans*; especially if that government premises its right to exist on the principle of being *"a government of the people, by the people, and for the people."* For this to happen, will require Americans to truly participate in the major decisions and direction of American government, as later described in Chapter Twenty of this book. If all Americans are to have an American government that is morally and ethically independent enough to regulate the inherent abuses of some of its citizens, *Americans must be politically empowered to immediately, peacefully, and directly remove those of their representatives, who fail in either their duty, loyalty, honesty, or their integrity owed to all Americans, rich or poor.* This is needed in order to curb those citizens who think it's their birthright to have *all* the nation's (and world's) resources concentrated under their personal and private control. This assumed government-condoned birthright has resulted in the amassing of numerous personal fortunes that are larger than the present treasuries of the vast majority of our fifty states, and the treasuries of most of the world's nations, to the detriment of 98% of America's other citizens.

What little now remains of America's middle-class' standard-of-living is sufficient evidence that the allocation and aggregation of the nation's and world's resources (and wealth) in the hands of a few very rich individuals is certainly not an efficient or fair means of allocating the nation's or world's resources. It is of benefit to only the very rich themselves. This becomes more evident as the nation's and the world's resources shrink at their current alarming rate. Contrary to what Messrs. Reagan and Bush, and the rest of the Republican Party would have liked us to think, the facts themselves are self-evident to anyone not afflicted with either a mental or physical infirmity. There is little, if anything, in America left to "loot," especially the pocketbook of America's middle-class.

The solution of the former Bush Administration and the current Republican platform to solve America's economic problems should result in each and every one of us in the middle- and lower-classes being near frightened to death. Their solution: A new capital gains tax preference to further enable those who have already misappropriated the bulk of the nation's and world's resources, to endeavor further into this ignoble effort. Continuing NAFTA will only cause the continued acceleration of the depletion of America's Jobs, America's tax base, and America's only means to pay off its "National" and other off-balance sheet "Debts." These policies compounded with four more years of rhetoric on family values, abortion, job quotas, and "phantom" drug wars, by either Clinton or Dole will result in there being nothing left for the bottom 98% of

Americans. Many Americans have already noticed that the spigot of Republican Party Trickle-Down-Economics was completely turned off long ago, and that the Democrats are incapable of figuring out how to get one turned-on!

It is time for Americans to realize that it is not the "American Dream" to which we aspire, but it is the "American Promise" to which we are entitled. It was the "Promise" that we would all benefit from American technology and accumulation of wealth. It was the "Promise" that we would all have an improved standard-of-living as our nation grew and prospered. It was the "Promise," even apart from our inalienable Constitutional Rights, that our moral principles and shared values of honesty, integrity, and family would endure as we enjoyed the fruits of our system of free enterprise and capitalism. For these ideals and values, many ordinary Americans have freely offered the sacrifice of their lives, when necessary, in the service of our country, believing very deeply in these principles.

The Merger Of Government, People, And American Capitalism

It is now time for a modified form of American "representative government" (see Chapter Twenty) to merge with American Capitalism to form the American Democracy that we all, as Americans, have earned and have been promised. It is now time for a truly American nation to evolve that serves the "will" of the majority, and not the very wealthy American "top-two-percenters," their "special interests," or their "representatives" who now sit in the White House and both chambers of the Congress.

What is This "True" American Nation With Its Modified Representative Form of Government?

Well, the description and definitions are not sufficiently explicit in any of the "political science" books I've researched, nor in any of the dictionaries I've reviewed. I do know, as do millions of you, that present-day America is **not** the "democracy" defined by Abraham Lincoln in his Gettysburg Address: America is *not* a democracy *"of the people, by the people, and for the people."* Nor is America the "democracy" that was understood by American Soldiers, Sailors, Marines, Coast Guardsmen, and Air Force who fought, served, and too often died in World War I, II, Korea, Vietnam, and Desert Storm. Nor is it the "democracy" the children in our schools are taught. Nor is it the "democracy" we celebrate with "goose bumps" on the 4th of July, Veteran's Day, Memorial Day, and even give occasional tribute to on Thanksgiving Day; primarily reserved for Thanksgiving to God for our bounty as Americans.

So you ask: "Yeah, I know what you mean, but what's missing?"

The answer to this question lies in the undoing of the subtle, but unfettered evolution of America's "new aristocracy," the "top-two-percenter" and their "special interest groups." The "majority rule" and the "democratic right of self-determination" that we as Americans cherished did not just slip through the cracks, but were bought away through the greed and inevitable corruption of our "elected representatives." They were bought by an "aristocracy" astronomically more wealthy, sinister, powerful, consolidated and, for the first time, "global" in their endeavors than any of their predecessors. They were bought by an "aristocracy" more willing to align with the "aristocracies" that have emerged in Mexico, Europe, South America and Asia, than with the very Americans who inadvertently gave them their legitimacy, power, and approval through their tax dollars, their labors, and their blood shed on battlefields all over the world. Americans gave "approval" trustingly based on this same "aristocracy's" deceitful exploitation of America's concept of "freedom;" concealed in the words, **American Democracy**, which was solely moved to the right to serve their own "economic" objectives and the calculated demise of the American standard-of-living and the American dream. It was in this false womb of "freedom" that America's "aristocracy" sowed its seeds. The "seeds" left to grow would inevitably crowd out the few flowers that are left in America's ever-diminishing garden of true democracy where "representatives" of the people serve all the people, and not just America's "top-two-percenters."

Perhaps now we can understand why in 1991, when 68% of us favored a National Health Insurance Program, our "elected representatives" simply said, "No." Even if such a program had been patronizingly passed by the U.S. Congress in 1991, it would have been vetoed by former President George Bush, who, from the moment of his inauguration, neither voted the "majority will" of the people, nor felt any obligation to do so. Instead, as one of the "top-two-percenters," Mr. Bush was either too busy playing golf or fishing in Kennibunkport, or running off to Europe or Japan to discuss issues of "free-trade" which the majority of us believed, even back then, would neither benefit us as individuals, nor the country as a whole.

With the first protest vote of 1992 (dumping George for Bill), and the second subsequent protest vote in 1994 (dumping the Democrat majorities in both the House and Senate for Republican majorities), wouldn't you think that both of these parties would recognize that they are as welcome in the depositories of the nation's leadership, as the rest of us would welcome AIDS? Yet nothing changed in the past four years with regard to anything being done in Washington D.C. for the benefit of us, the American people even with two major protest votes. Let's not forget that it was the special interest groups who directed our elected representatives to put the sword to any kind of health care reform or

National Health Care Insurance. It wasn't that Hillary was leading the group that got Newt Gingrich all excited, but rather the **special interest groups** that pushed the right buttons to deprive us of any kind of national health insurance. Remember those 30-second-sound-bites of grandma and grandpa telling us how Hillary and her national health care program would bury us financially. Now do any of you really believe that grandpa and grandma who starred in these 30-second-sound-bites knew one thing about either the concepts or consequences of Hillary's program? Do any of you believe Hillary had any idea about the concepts and consequences of the national health care program she envisioned? For sure, the American "top-two-percenters" who reap the profits in America's Insurance Industry knew the concepts and the consequences of Hillary's national health care program. Putting a little Andy Rooney twist on all of this, how effective would these 30-second-sound-bites have been if they had starred George and Barbara Bush? Let's not forget that George and Barbara Bush are already covered by a national health care program paid for by you and me, that we are estopped from participating in. A last Andy Rooney twist: Why not have Elizabeth and Bob Dole, who are also both covered by this same national health care plan, make a 30-second-sound-bite denouncing a national health care program for you and me? Do you think this would give him the necessary votes from us to put him in the White House? The answer I leave to you and the vote you cast in this year's presidential election!

During the past twenty-five years, most Americans have ended-up confused, frustrated, and sometimes even angered over what they believed was a breaking-down of their "democratic" government and the subtle, but continual, diminution of their standard-of-living. In almost complete contradiction to this American malaise, there appeared to be no noticeable loss of certain of our Constitutional rights. In most parts of the country, you can now even get away with rape, murder, and child pornography, with most of Boobus Americanus still believing this to be a further extension of America's already illusive democracy. Obviously, if you are one of America's "top-two-percenters" none of these rules, values, or laws necessarily apply to you. One need only point out the benefit of having sufficient money to allow you to even commit murder and have better than a 50/50 chance of getting away with it if you've got the right team of well-paid lawyers.

So we travel round-and-round on the merry-go-round of confusion. We seek answers and try to understand why America seems no longer to be the "heart" of democracy or the "soul" of hopes and dreams.

Many of the would-be *answers* can be found in some very arrogant, and sometimes offensive premises, foundations, and concepts of our present system of American "representative government; a cynic's assumptions."

Below are underlying premises of our 220-year-old "representative" government to which will give you the **answers** to which I have referred above:

1) The people as a "whole" are **"stupid"** and are, therefore, incapable of making broad- based social, economic, and political decisions.

2) The "Two Party System" assures the **appearance** that "majority rule" prevails, but in essence assures that only an elite minority prevails in the political and economic control of the nation. Think about how a bill becomes a law, and how Congressional Committees and Sub-Committees work. Remember how you get legislation to a vote, and that even if the majority in both Houses decide to make the bill a law. It still faces the hurdle of the President's veto which, if exercised, then requires a two-thirds majority of both the House and Senate to be over-ridden; the second major cause of alleged American Government grid-lock.

3) The "Separation of Powers Doctrine" is another alleged gimmick supposedly used to assure Americans that their "majority ruled democracy" is protected (i.e. the "balance-of-power doctrine"). Its real effect has been to "grid-lock" true American democracy for almost 220 years to a much greater degree than it has ever preserved it. It's sort of like the rather altruistic, but nonsensical argument that, as Americans, we should rather see a hundred guilty men go free than one be erroneously convicted. So look who's running the "streets" and "institutions" of America today. No need to tell you again which convicted felon ran the U.S. Congressional House Ways and Means Committee, the most influential and powerful committee in the U.S. House of Representatives, prior to the 1994 Republican contract with America. Do you think we are any better off with the group that's running American government since 1994?

No book discussing any aspect of the inner workings of the alleged American Democracy would be complete if it didn't say something about the American Civil Liberties Union (or ACLU, as it is more commonly known). This **"lot"** has been around almost 100 years. I say **"lot"** because this self-professed, self-appointed privately-funded group of lawyers have allegedly been in there protecting all of us against the wrongs of big government, as well as, protecting "all" of our civil rights. These are **not** elected crusaders that you and I have requested to represent us in the fight against government wrong-doing, or to defend all of our other alleged constitutional "rights" they always seem to be popping-up to defend. Most of these "rights" are directly, in one way or another related to pornography, immorality, and/or vice. Have you ever wondered who it is that funds this mini-government of legal thugs that use our courts, that our tax dollars pay for, for their own selected agendas? I suggest that you demand that your President and Congress legislate a requirement that the ACLU and other groups like it, be required to furnish the American people with a complete list of their financial donors so that we may all see who it is that is attempting to shape and manipulate our business, our government, our law, our judicial system, and, most important, our **national immorality.**

New Technology and Antiquated Doctrines

Most of you should take umbrage at anyone who attempts to insult your intelligence by arguing in this decade of the 1990s, that the **Separation of Powers Doctrine** and the **Two Party System** are necessary to safeguard the component **American "representative government"** and **American Capitalism,** which I have shown are controlled by America's "top-two-percenters." Up until the 1950s, there might have been some strong, and even reasonable enough argument for these antiquated foundational principles of our alleged Democratic government. With America's and the world's "globalization" through mass media, instantaneous mass-communication, and jet air travel, these "divide and conquer" doctrines are of significantly less relevance in protecting our "rights" and "freedoms," compared with the need for all of our citizens to participate in a true "democracy" with a truly "majority ruled" government of the people, by the people, and for the people which modern technology makes possible today. See Chapter Twenty.

Critics of "greater" direct citizen involvement in government, as suggested in Chapter Twenty, will argue that Americans are truly not interested in the **small details** of the Federal Budget, or the complexities of such things as the Internal Revenue Code, or the details concerning the "secret deals" put together behind closed-doors of both the U.S. House of Representative and U.S. Senate as too complex for us to handle.

And to this I respond: Nonsense!

Since when is a $1.5 trillion federal spending budget a "small detail," especially when $1.1 trillion is coming out of our pockets and we're being forced to sign IOUs of between $250 and $400 billion each year? These are broad issues that could be presented in a referendum format. What *better* place to determine the percentage of federal expenditures on such things as education, defense, and the expenditures necessary to rebuild our nation's cities and infrastructure? If the nation is ever to see a fair and equitable system of taxation, where better to have it ultimately decided than by a referendum of the people, free of all "special interest groups?"

What Are the Chances For Change?

Today, we see a "mad exodus" from both the U.S. Senate and House of Representatives. Many outsiders say it's because of the House "Bank" and "Post Office" scandals. A few of those bailing-out say it's because of their despair over all the years of government grid-lock. A few courageous quitters even say it's because of their frustration with the corrupt system of government itself. For most, I believe their leaving is prompted by absolute "fear;" that Boobus Americanus might wake up and discover their lucrative and calculated aiding-and-abetting of America's "top-two-percenters" that occurred during the past sixteen years, and which amounts to the worst "looting" of America in its 220 year history.

So does the other "drum beat" continue from those Senators and Congressmen who are unafraid to remain in Washington D.C., as were Louis XVI and Marie Antoinette were unafraid or too "greedy" to leave France in the late 1780s. Their arrogance and their disrespect for their constituents, believing Americans will accept the "sacrifices" dictated from their malfeasance of office, a lower standard-of-living, and the 1990s buzz-word "shared sacrifice" so that they might continue to be enriched as we learn basic Third-World survival techniques. They tell us there can no longer be expectations of secure employment, nor can we continue to provide for our elderly, nor for our poor, nor for America's children, many of whom have already been living in poverty for twenty or more years. Their "drum beat" repeats over-and-over until your brains feel like mush, and then you begin to wonder who really won the Cold War after all?

It's almost as if they're telling you, that it was you who sat in the halls of the U.S. Senate and House of Representatives and ran up a $5 trillion National Debt; you, who allowed the $500 billion looting of America's Savings & Loans Institutions; you, who looked the other way as American Industries were "looted" by the M&A Gangs of Wall Street; you, who was paid in excess of $125,000 a year to serve the "special interest groups" that this "representative" bunch of crooks now also indirectly blames, as part of their already "the devil made me do it" defense.

The question for all of us now is: Are we going to allow the vultures one more "four-year" pass at our bones, or are we going to take America back and send the majority of these "crooks" and "incompetents," either to the "jails," or the "unemployment lines" where they deservedly belong?

For those of you who still haven't got it, I've put together a short summary in a format you've become used to from previous chapters. It says nothing more than before, but its presented in a manner that will hopefully eliminate any confusion, or misunderstanding as to where this book is coming from.

The Myths Of American Democracy

I. A cornerstone premise of American democracy dictates that the American "economy," American "business," and American "government" must remain separate and apart, and that the nation functions more optimally when this objective is achieved.

II. American "representative government" is a government "of the people, by the people, and for the people," and has been for the past 220 years.

The Realities Of American Democracy

I. A "democratic" government of the people, by the people, and for the people, can only be a government where the "economy," the "people," its "businesses," and its "representatives" are all dedicated to the development, growth, and well-being of all its people. There is **no other purpose** of "democratic" government, or any other kind of government.

II. If you believe Myth II above, you are either one of the "top-two-percenters," or haven't read this book. American government from its very inception has been a well managed, but "beneficial conspiracy" designed to invisibly channel the energies of the "majority" into productive "wealth" for a small, but very real American "aristocracy;" which for 220 years has allowed sufficient "limited" entry into its ranks to maintain a law-and-ordered society.

This American system of democracy worked well so long as there were "limitations" (i.e. certain government regulations) placed on the "aristocracy." It is when those "limitations" were allowed to erode vis-à-vis the inherent greed of those of our elected officials occupying the White House, supported by a corrupt, no less aristocratic Congress, that the "beneficial conspiracy" designed to originally foster the image of American "democracy," working for all Americans, also began to fail. The scales are now so out of balance, that America itself has begun to self-destruct. If you don't believe this, you haven't been to one of America's major cities in the last ten years.

19

American Economic
Solutions Without Sacrifice

*How Do You Create Thirty Million
New Quality Manufacturing Jobs?*

The Most Important "Question" Facing Americans Today!

Totally stressed out, burned-out, working two jobs, and not sure which job, if either, you'll have next week, you just don't have the time or inclination to tackle another of the numerous major crises plaguing America today. You're not the one getting paid $136,000 a year to worry about this "question" that somehow still terrorizes you, and the other 260 million poor and middle-class Americans always teetering on the brink of unemployment, since the beginning of the 1990s.

The author's proposed "solution" to this "question" at the end of this chapter hopefully will not terrorize the other 6 million Americans, who make up America's *top-two-percenters*. To begin our analysis, we'll first examine the "solutions" to this "question" proposed by the Republicans. Then we'll examine the "solutions" proposed by the Democrats, who appear to many us, just a bunch of wolves dressed in sheep's clothing, who are really Republicans, or at least, Republican wannabees.

The Republican Solution

You've heard their solution for sixteen straight years. Global "free trade," based on quadrupling American export of goods and services that will create 30 million new high-tech, high-skill, high-paying American jobs. The Republican formula for the creation of these 30 million new jobs is solved on the basis of former President Bush's formula: Each $1 Billion in Added American Exports = 20,000 New American Jobs. Thus, from the known export data of today American exports must more than "quadruple" to $2 trillion annually, from their present record $487 billion to achieve this goal.

Now, one has to ask: If Americans aren't buying American goods, how is it that the Republicans are expecting non-Americans to buy American goods? The answer is simple. They won't. At least not *our* "goods!" What our foreign trading partners are buying are our machine tools, our computer technology, all of our best military equipment, and all of our trade secrets, patents, and other "know-how," and in some instances, just out-and-out stealing vis-à-vis that new game in town called, *industrial espionage*.

And you thought Americans were the smartest people in the world! After this transfer of all American technology and "know how" to our foreign trading partners, what is it then that the Republicans hope to trade? Obviously, they have already transferred six million of America's high-tech, high-paying jobs to these foreign trading partners of ours, and frankly, I see little else of value in America that our foreign trading partners would want to buy from us.

One has to again wonder if our brain-trust in Washington D.C. ever heard of the mammoth and costly defense Coca Cola employs just to protect the secrets of its syrup formula? This is just an American syrup, not even America's National Security!

The Republican's economic job creation program is coupled with lower government spending, promised lower deficits, promised reduced National Debt, and ultimately a balanced budget that will make the American working middle-class allegedly more competitive. Now you've got to scratch your head a couple of times to get this one. I'm certain you believe this propaganda, as much as did George Bush, our last Republican President. Remember Mr. Bush's 1993 proposed Federal Budget requesting a record $1.515 trillion in spending? Let's also not forget that it was former Republican President, George Bush, who strapped America with his personal Air Force One Luxury 747 Airliner, at a cost of $435 million, with an additional cost of $40,000 per flight, per day. It must be giving him ulcers, thinking of Bill and Hillary now flying around in this Republican city of flying luxury.

Also a key element in creating these 30 million new American jobs is the Republican promise not to tax the wealthy class, whether it be income taxation, excise taxation, or otherwise. Instead they promise to provide this wealthy constituency of Americans with much needed tax cuts for new investments in both the U.S. and global private sectors of the billions-upon-billions of dollars being saved and thus allegedly creating the supposed plethora of jobs for every American who really wants to work at $4.35 per hour; a wage which is at least ten times above the global average of Third World Nations.

The arguments advanced by most adversaries against the above Republican proposed "laissez-faire, global free-trade" approach to "job creation" are:

1. Sixteen years of this approach has already resulted in the creation of 100 individual multi-billion dollar fortunes (America's new 100

Billionaires) with little if any investment in America's Industrial Infrastructure.

2. Twenty-three million of the previously created new jobs in the U.S. during both Mr. Bush's and Mr. Reagan's Administrations were mostly all minimum-wage and minimum-skill with little, if any, potential growth, promotion, or advancement, and generally were in the "flipping burgers," "delivering pizzas," or in the "cleaning bed pans" service sectors of the economy. The 6 million jobs lost over this same 12-year period were high-wage ($16.02 per hour), high-skilled manufacturing jobs that were exported overseas. Although Mr. Clinton took credit for the creation of ten million new jobs in his July 5, 1996 economic speech, neither he nor his economic advisors were able to describe the nature of these jobs, except to say that they were primarily in the service sector with a small percentage being in the manufacturing sector.

3. The only "investment" result that has occurred from the creation of America's "Super Wealth Class" was the aforementioned export of approximately 6 million of America's best paying middle-class jobs to American owned re-located factories in Third World countries unencumbered by the very laws the U.S. Congress imposed on American Industry to preserve both America's and the world's environment.

Four things make the Republican solution still acceptable to some Americans. First, second, and third are the beliefs that it will result in "no new taxes," "no new welfare programs," and a faint hope that these "still faithful" Americans can still somehow break into that elite group of the *top-two-percenters.* The fourth, and most important Republican "ace" is America's desire to return to a system of lawful "school segregation," under the "family value" code-word that says it's a parent's right to choose the school for their children, and have it funded by the federal government.

The Democratic Solution To Job Creation

The only difference in the Republican theory and the Clinton Democratic theory is Clinton's fear to go forward without some minimal modicum of government regulation, whereas the Republicans desire absolutely *no* government regulation of America's banks, businesses, industries, financial markets, and all other commercial institutions in the private sector; fervently arguing that this is the only environment that will facilitate the creation of these allegedly 30 million new jobs.

In 1992, Mr. Clinton promised he would create his 30 million new American jobs with money coming from the *top-two-percenters* and from the illusive "Peace Dividend" resulting from America's 1989, still questionable, Cold War victory. Mr. Clinton also promised a new Investment Tax Credit (ITC); mostly in the form of the 1963 Kennedy Investment Tax Credit, where the expense of such Tax Credit is paid for by the savings generated by the cutting of one-hundred-thousand federal employees.

You have to ask how Mr. Clinton's putting 100,000 Bush Administration Federal appointees, who coincidentally comprise America's most unskilled, unmotivated, and unimaginative arrogant bureaucrats, into an already over-burdened unemployment sector help the U.S. unemployment problem?

How Do You Create Thirty Million Quality American Jobs?

This question must be answered in both historical and economic perspective. Such factors as the availability of resources, world and national political structure, business and individual profit motives, consumer psychology, and a vast array of other factors all play a part. We are even going to have to understand a little bit about the so-called "business cycle" theory of economics to get a handle on all of the factors that might finally get you back to feeling secure about your own job, or if you're unemployed, secure about ever finding a job again.

There is, of course, the simplest of analyses, much of which is echoed in the Clinton solution: "The Economic Water Wheel Theory;"i.e., pump a lot of money into the economy ($50-$200 billion of U.S. Taxpayer money to build new roads, bridges, and a new transportation infrastructure), thus creating 100,000 new jobs and 100,000 new consumers. As the $50-$200 billion passes through the hands of these re-employed American workers, American Business and Industry anticipating new demand created by the $50-$200 billion in new wages, will begin to produce goods and services. In turn, America's Industries and Businesses newly hired workers become themselves new consumers, creating further demand for more and more American products and services.

The final result of all these newly employed Americans is that they are now able to pay new billions-and-billions in taxes to pay for those new roads, bridges, and transportation structures that got it all started, and also begin to payoff the $5 trillion National Debt.

And so turns the "Water Wheel of Job and Wealth Creation," becoming in theory ever bigger and bigger and benefiting all of the nation's citizens, more and more, as time goes on.

Unfortunately, the unregulated "Economic Water Wheel Theory" works efficiently only in closed economies, where all persons participating generally have a common "communal goal." The economics of the native American Indian Village, prior to their disruption by Christopher Columbus being a good example of "Water Wheel" economics efficiently at work. In the global economy today, $50-$200 billion of additional government spending on the industrial infrastructure will result in new roads, bridges, etc., and ultimately the wages earned from these government expenditures will not go into the American economy, but will be spent at the Walmarts, K-Marts, and even the fancier retail stores, who import their products from low wage Third World Nations. It is this sort of *leakage* of money out of the American economy that will result in the failure of Clinton's fiscal spending policy to create these 30 billion new American jobs.

To better understand this phenomenon, I again return to my analysis of the native American Indian Village. Remember these were small, self-contained communes that were not subjected to artificial (man-made) Federal Reserve Board recessions or depressions. The Indian village economy functioned in a "barter" environment, with adequate resources available and close-by to satisfy the village's generally *restrained* consumer needs and limited tastes, rather than America's voracious appetite for consumption and fickle tastes. There existed minimal government, no communal debt (National Debt), no financial institutions, nor each year the need to construct 1.1 million new homes, produce 10 million cars, consume 6.3 billion barrels of oil, amongst other of the indulgences demanded by the 266 million voracious consumers in America today.

At this juncture, I point out to you that the "Water Wheel Theory" is nothing more than Keynesian, or Fiscal Policy Economics. You may rest assured that much of the "solution" in creating 30 million American manufacturing jobs will depend on similar restricted economic flows as described in those Indian villages above. This "solution" to the present dilemma of American manufacturing job creation will "not" be resolved until we can first determine the following:

1. Where is the first burst of "water" to come from; the initial $50-$200 billion that was suggested by Mr. Clinton.

2. Will this first $50-$200 billion will be enough to get the "wheel" started or sustain its turning for any appreciable period of time to allow the creation of high-paying American manufacturing jobs? and

3. How will we keep most of the "water" from flowing into some already overflowing ponds, lakes, and oceans (metaphors for the *top-two-percenters*, the American MNCs, and our corrupt federal, state and local governments)?

To understand how we are going to accomplish this, we should first examine how job creation occurred in America during its four most significant economic periods: the pre-industrialization period 1750-1870; the period known as the American Industrial Revolution 1870-1918; the period known as the American Boom, Bust, and War period 1919-1945; and the post-WW II period 1945-1970.

But first, we will review America's experience with the so-called "Business Cycle" that preceded America's four most significant economic periods of job creation so you can have a better feel for the difficulties, hurdles, and consequences that may befall us, if we don't all get together and start rowing in the same direction.

Before you get further into this chapter, I strongly recommend you read through the Glossary and Dictionary sections at this chapter's end. As in most previous chapters, the Glossary Section has been formatted to take the "spin" off of many of the terms and concepts that originate in Washington D.C. and America academia. You'll also find many of the terms and concepts discussed below given new dimension if you follow my advice. Whatever you decide, at least read the "Business Cycle" entry in the Glossary Section before reading the subsection below.

America's Historic Business Cycles

Now that you are familiar with the basic concept of the Business Cycle (I presume you've just read it in the Glossary Section), you are probably curious as to how many of these "cycles" (ups and downs) occurred prior to our alleged already over-heating 1996 economy. Since 1750 (remember we only declared ourselves independent from England on July 4, 1776) there have been forty-three (43) recessions or depressions including the recession of 1990-1992 over this 246 year period.

Thus, America averages a recession or depression (a down turn) in the economy every 5.2 years. Historically, excluding the recession of 1990-1992, there were only eight major recessions or depressions that widely effected the entire U.S. during this 246 year period; one about every thirty years.

It is also noteworthy that 7 recessions, none of them major, of America's 43 recessions or depressions occurred during the post-war period 1946-1970. All were short lived, but each subsequent recession grew larger in intensity than its predecessor, as the 1960s, 1970s, and 1980s rolled by.

Different from past eras, the focus of the true visionaries of America's *top-two-percenters* was now on a "global" conquest. They pursued greater "global" conquests than ever previously conceived before, in either world history, or in America's relatively recent past.

The *top-two-percenters'* first test was the contrived "oil shortage" recession of 1972-1974. Their first test was simple: Would Boobus

Americanus, who then comprised the vast majority of America's middle-class, revolt if he had to wait six hours in line in his gas-guzzling automobile to get his weekly ration of three gallons of gasoline? Then came the second test, the contrived recession of 1980-1982, which set the final ground work for the final sprouting of those seeds sown by America's *merchants of greed* in 1974, and which came to full blossom with the election of Ronald Reagan and the steering of American Capitalism into the far right corner of Thomas Robert Malthus.

For the ten years, 1980-1990, the gardens of America's *top-two-percenters* grew unbridled. Looting went unhampered. Immorality was rampant. And then came the 1990-1992 recession. A recession very different from all of its predecessors. A "well designed" and "controlled recession," orchestrated by your government through Alan Greenspan, Chairman of the Federal Reserve Board, the U.S. Congress and the *top-two-percenters.* Control through the "invisible economic yoke" on the poor and America's ever-diminishing middle-class. There was no sacrifice or pain during this 1990-1992 recession for America's *top-two-percenters* or for those who represent us in American government. What was this "invisible economic yoke?" It has many components that touch each and every part of your daily life. It's the home mortgage interest rate that the bank demands of you, when you want to buy a new home. It's the new interest rate that you receive in the mail with regard to the existing balances on your credit cards and other lines of credit. It's the interest rate that you have to pay to finance the purchase of a new or used car. It is also the interest that is paid to you by your savings bank, or the interest rate that's available on the CD you finally put enough money together to buy. Who controls this "invisible economic yoke?" The same Alan Greenspan that was previously named. You might think that this "invisible economic yoke" is some kind of a well kept secret or government conspiracy. It's not! Alan Greenspan testifies on C-Span before certain committees of the U.S. House of Representatives and U.S. Senate regularly (i.e. the Humphrey-Hawkins Hearings) with regard to this "invisible economic yoke." Many of you have viewed these hearings, but either didn't know what these hearings were about, or found Mr. Greenspan so boring, that you just had to switch back to Sally Jesse Raphael. It is Chairman Greenspan's job to keep inflation under control. Inflation, for those of you who do not know, is the worst enemy of, and greatest cause of alarm for America's *top-two-percenters*. Alan Greenspan over the past twelve years as Chairman of the Fed has clearly shown he has no interest in the effects of inflation on the poor or middle-class America. It is middle-class America who is the "National Debtor" and it is the *top-two-percenter* who is the "National Creditor."

To really understand inflation, you have to know that inflation is good for debtors and bad for creditors, the reason being that debtors and creditors, during periods of inflation, lose *purchasing power* of their money. Therefore, at the end of a period of inflation, debts that were owed at the beginning of the period of inflation, are paid back by the debtor to the creditor with what are referred to as *cheaper dollars*. Now if you were a Sam Walton sitting with $26 billion and there was a two year period of inflation of 10% each year, your $26 billion, although still $26 billion two years later, would only be worth $20.8 billion in *purchasing power*. And if a bunch of debtors owed Sam $10 billion at the beginning of this same two year period of inflation, they would effectively be paying him back the same $10 billion of principal (and of course the interest), but the $10 billion principal would be paid back in *cheap dollars*, or dollars worth only $8 billion in actual *purchasing power* at the end of our theoretical two year period of 10% inflation.

Obviously, there is more to inflation than just debtors and creditors. The price of all goods for everyone generally rises in periods of inflation. Even middle-class money, savings, and other cash equivalents are lessened in value during these inflationary periods, but obviously losing $5.2 billion, as did Sam Walton in our theoretical model, would have been much more painful to him, than you losing 20% of the *purchasing power* of your $5000 in savings, or so would have thought Sam Walton.

Over the past twelve years, Alan Greenspan has done a stellar job at the helm of the Fed. Inflation has been under control for almost his entire tenure as Chairman. But what are the effects of the "invisible economic yoke" on you?

When Mr. Greenspan increases interest rates, the cost of borrowing increases. Dramatic increases by Mr. Greenspan in interest rates causes dramatic increases in the cost of borrowing. It is this increase in this cost of borrowing that results in marginal home builders, manufacturers, and retailers having to either decrease, or cease operations. As a result, jobs are lost. As a result of jobs being lost, there is less money in the economy to be spent, and therefore less demand for consumer goods. As demand declines for goods, prices fall, and when prices fall, inflation (the phenomena of rising prices of goods) decreases, and continues to decrease until it either disappears, becomes deflationary, or Alan Greenspan decides that the poor and middle-class have been in a recession too long, a recession that may very well now be effecting America's *top-two-percenters* more than the erosion of their wealth than the inflation itself during this imaginary two year period of inflation I've just described. It is axiomatic for Republicans that an annual rate of 5% or more inflation is much more painful to the *top-two-percenters* than a 25% unemployment rate is to the *bottom ninety-eight percenters*. The only more painful experience imaginable for America's *top-two-percenters* in the 1990s would be simultaneously cutting them off from their allies in the cheap global labor market, where wages range between $.08 and $.80 an hour, and getting rid of both NAFTA and GATT, thereby forcing them to again share the wealth of America by requiring them to employ American workers with fair wages.

If this is all still mysterious to you, and if you still don't understand why America's middle-class standard-of-living is diminishing daily, the events of July 5, 1996 might clear up some of your confusion. It was on this day that the Clinton Administration announced that the unemployment rate had dropped to 5.3%, its lowest level in ten years. Almost simultaneously with this announcement came the news that American wages increased $.09 per hour in the second quarter of 1996, this also being the highest increase in wages in the past five years. On this good news, the stock market went into a free-fall and dropped 114.88 points in five hours, the free-fall being curtailed only because the market was scheduled to, and did close at 1 p.m., July 5th being a part of the July 4th four-day weekend.

As soon as this economic news of July 5, 1996 was released, every economic guru on the financial news network questioned the ability of Alan Greenspan to continue as Chairman of the Fed. The inability of the Clinton Administration to bury both the news of this record hourly wage increase and record decrease in the unemployment rate was viewed by many of the *top-two-percenters* as not merely treacherous, but bordering on a traitorous attack on American Capitalism.

Now, folks, let's look at this $.09 an hour increase in wages. If you work 60 hours a week, you're looking at $5.40 a week in additional gross pay. After federal income tax withholding, Social Security, and Medicare Withholding you're down to less than $4.25 net money into your pocket for the entire work week. That's less than half the price of a movie and box of popcorn, and look at the anguish it caused the *top-two-percenters*. The bad news was that this $.09 really never flowed into any of the pockets of America's poor or middle-class, but was actually an average that was skewed by the enormous wage increases that filled the pockets of the 100 or so top executives of American corporations. This same $.09 an hour increase, *you can safely bet the farm on,* will be a major reason for the Republicans in the Congress to again attempt to defeat an increase in the minimum wage, this very legislation, coincidentally, scheduled for debate before the U.S. Senate the week of July 8, 1996.

It is America's *top-two-percenters'* political and economic "control" over the 1990-1992 recession that has kept it off its traditional financially-destructive path that would have allowed its usual signals to be readily observable. We do not see the results of this recession manifested in America's financial markets, nor in the tightening of money, nor in rising interest rates, nor in new high lending volumes (these occurred in the 1980s). We only occasionally hear murmurings of a potential commercial bank failure. Occasionally, we hear whispers of a potential "financial" collapse of American Government itself. These "whispers" do not hold back America's elected representatives' reckless spending and borrowings, recession or no recession, which increase America's ever expanding and explosive National Debt and exasperate geometrically the possibility of an American, if not a global, "economic supercrash."

Never before have all of the following ominous economic warnings been present, either in America, or in any other industrial nation in the world in any previous pre-depression period:

- The U.S. National Debt reaching gargantuan highs of $5 trillion.

- American Consumer Debt reaching monumental highs of over $1 trillion.

- State and Local Governments' Debt reaching historical highs of $853.9 billion, with a declining tax base to draw revenues from.

- American Home Mortgage Debt reaching colossal highs—exceeding $2.3 trillion from a meager $292 billion in 1970. Also relevant is the 1989 to present continuing decline in real estate values underlying these mortgages.

- An American Industrial Infrastructure that lies in decay and decadence.

- A nation and world linked in global economic interdependencies, especially dependent on the manufacturing economies of Japan and Germany.

- "Special Interests Groups" that totally dominate American political decisions and spending.

- An economy strapped by $400 billion in annual national entitlement programs, and a $300 billion annual interest charge on the U.S. National Debt.

- A new Freddie Kruger variable, *the underemployment factor,* now a hidden part of America's structural unemployment sector that resulted from the downsizing that began in the American manufacturing sector, and has, and will further spread to America's banking, retail, and other overpriced service industries (i.e. legal, accounting, brokerage).

- And most important, the national dilemma of an "America"with limited resources," "closed frontiers," and a disappearing middle-class, that had been previously relied on to pay America's bills.

Comparing America's Eight Major Previous Depressions

Notable are the six depressions of 1819, 1837, 1857, 1873, 1893, and 1929. Mixed in amongst the time frames of these six major depressions were the severe, but short-lived depressions of 1907 and 1921, which were minor downturns causing little social disturbance and minimal unemployment and bankruptcies. During these minor depressions there was also neither a serious decline in per capita income nor a wide spread loss of faith (or confidence) in the future of America or its economy.

The other six major depressions caused violent social disorder, prolonged and severe unemployment, severe deflation, extraordinarily high bankruptcy rates, and alarming falls in real per capita income. The second longest depression occurred between 1873 and 1878, and was preceded by the peaking of all American business indexes. Also preceding this depression was an almost 20% rise in the stock market, a new record level of foreign trade, and the most unfavorable balance of trade up till that time in U.S. history.

The period just prior to the 1873-1878 depression, and its unusual economic activity was fueled by the commercial banks slow, but continuous expansion of lending activities, which by June 1872 reached $872 million. The legal reserve requirement in 1873 was 25%, which during a period when deposits were uninsured, was insufficient to meet the 1873 run on the banks.

The 1873 depression first began when the stock market began to sag and out-of-town banks began to withdraw their deposits from local banks. The major banks in New York were forced to call in loans creating a money shortage which further triggered numerous failures amongst America's brokerage firms, as a result of their inability to finance their own customers' margin accounts . The whole roof fell in on September 18th, when the firm of Jay Cook who had over-extended itself in financing the construction of American railroads was forced to close its doors, thus setting off the panic that broke out in full fury and lasted for five years.

The most severe depression occurred between 1929 and 1938. The 1929 depression was preceded by the steady decline in real wages, a build up of business inventories of approximately $1.5 billion, a precipitous decline in foreign trade which had peaked in mid-1929, a decline in construction expenditures that had begun in 1928, and a decline in investment spending which had occurred beginning in mid-1928. On October 29, 1929, the stock market crashed, introducing the panic phase of this depression, and so began America's severest crisis that would include a record number of bank failures, bankruptcies, and real estate foreclosures. In 1932, foreclosures ran at the rate of one thousand a day. Consumer debt sank from $179.6 billion in 1929 to $144.2 billion in

1932. With little else to invest in, life insurance companies increased their holdings of real estate from $500 million to $2 billion during this same period.

It was the 1929-1938 Depression that witnessed the first major federal government intervention under President Herbert Hoover in the economy. In an attempt to relieve the death-like grip of the depression on America, President Hoover (1928-1932) moved to:

- Expand business activity by cheap money policies instituted through the Federal Reserve System.

- Restore public confidence through a balanced federal budget.

- Shore-up and "jump-start" the economy through direct government loans to insurance companies, banks, and railroads.

- Stem the deterioration of foreign economies by placing moratoriums on international debt payments **held** by Americans.

- Provide aid to state and local governments to relieve unemployment.

- Create relatively broad federal public work programs to attempt to revitalize the nation's work force.

During the 1929 depression, unemployment rates averaged 16%, peaking in 1933 at 24.9%. Gross Domestic Product declined at a rate of almost 10% a year during this period. Americans, including a few of the *top-two-percenters,* were thrown completely into poverty, and it was not uncommon for children to starve to death in remote poorer regions of the country.

1974-1975 Recession: To many Americans, the 1974-1975 recession was considered to be the worst downturn in the business cycle since the Great Depression of 1929. This recession was directly attributed to then President Ford's economists Messrs. Simon, Burns, and Greenspan (the same Alan Greenspan who heads the Federal Reserve today), who, in their desire to slowdown the inflation being caused by the great "oil embargo" of 1974-1975, elected to create, perhaps the first truly "government controlled" recession. Interest rates were artificially raised, money supply was contracted, and unemployment was allowed to rise to 8.5% by the end of 1975.

It was also during this 1970s period in American economic history, that America and the world saw a mutation develop within the theory of the "Business Cycle." It wasn't only the failure of Messrs. Simon's,

Burns', and Greenspan's economic policies to bring inflation under control, but for the first time "inflation" and "recession" existed simultaneously.

1980-1982 Recession: Deemed to be even worse than the 1974-75 recession by some of our younger Americans, who were too young to remember the 1974-75 recession, was the 1980-82 recession (also known as the Jimmy Carter Recession). This 1980-1982 Recession was preceded by a five-year period where unemployment hovered between 6.1 and 7.1%. By 1979, with interest rates already at 15.75%, the recession was poised to erupt. By 1981, interest rates hit a record 21%, inflation was running in double-digits, and unemployment was at up to 7.6%.

Most notably, it was the beginning of the 1980-82 recession that resulted in the defeat of President Jimmy Carter, and gave us President Ronald Reagan, who for his eight-year tenure as president presided over a dismal 7.7% average unemployment rate, but reduced inflation and interest rates by over seven percentage points, or 50% on average. It was also during Mr. Reagan's eight year tenure that the looting of America's S&Ls, the destruction of the American Industrial Infrastructure commenced in earnest, and the exportation of approximately 6 million American manufacturing jobs to oppressed labor markets in Third World countries began.

Pre-1870 Job Creation In America

Prior to 1877, the year that America entered into its Industrial Revolution, America's small cities and towns functioned economically similar to the pre-Columbus "American Indian Village." These small towns and cities surrounded by large agrarian (farm) communities bartered services and goods needed by the farmers in exchange for the farmer's excess produce.

A different sort of "money" was used during this period, as the means of exchange in the bartering process. It was usually valuable in its own right; being generally silver or gold coinage. If the money was not in either of these precious metals, it was initially represented by limited "bank notes" drawn on a local bank that was little more than a local vault where citizens sought protection for their actual gold and silver bullion holdings that backed these bank notes.

By 1862, the small local banks had grown to over 1600 in number with no less than 7000 varieties of coins and paper currencies. Deemed to be "chaotic," the paper currency was generally not trusted. The National Bank Acts of 1863 and 1864 ordered all of these individual state and local bank currencies replaced with singular "National Bank Notes."

Two other important items of note: The United States, prior to 1861, never had an income tax. The first income tax was levied in that year; placing a 3% tax on incomes above $800. In 1861, also for the first time the U.S. Treasury printed money (non-interest bearing legal tender); having previously issued only silver and gold coins, and interest bearing Treasury Notes. The first income tax was short-lived, and it wasn't until 1913 that the income tax that we know today first came into existence.

Another important factor of American life during the 18th and 19th centuries was that most Americans were also closely involved in the political process at the local level and usually knew their elected "representatives" personally. And more importantly, in the economic sector, up until the American Industrial Revolution in 1877, most Americans relied on themselves to produce the majority of goods and/or services they needed as opposed to being reliant on others for those goods and services, and the related "government regulation" to protect them from what was believed to be inherently the unlawful and dishonest practices inherent in mass commerce.

To answer the question "How were jobs created in pre-1870 America?" is to simply say they weren't created. They more or less existed in abundance because of America's farm economy. Those who chose to escape the "farm" could work in the small industries of the east, or could seek their fortunes in the west. Citizens had no Social Security numbers, no income taxes, and few if any people were reliant on a "government" controlled economic system for either their employment, their standard-of-living, or for that matter, their survival.

Job Creation During America's Industrial Revolution (1877-1917)

In 1870, 53% of the nation's labor force was still engaged in agriculture. By 1927, less than 27% of the nation's work force was employed in agriculture, even though the population of America had grown from 39 million to 106 million during this period, reflecting an increase of 67 million more people needing to be fed. It is mind-boggling to most observers that in just 57 years, half the number of people were needed to work the farm, and yet these same farms, in just 57 years, were producing triple the amount of food, for triple of the amount of people, then populating America.

It was also during this period known as the American Industrial Revolution, that a three-way economic, social and political divide and first class struggle took place in America. American "farmers" joined such agrarian political movements as the Granger Movement, joining against the banking, railroad, and industrial monopolies that had formed in the East for cheaper money. American "factory workers" of the industrial east joined labor unions in record numbers to combat the Robber Baron American "industrialists," who had formed into America's "politically powerful" wealthy big-business class.

Also significant during this same period was the closing of America's continental western frontier. North Dakota, South Dakota, Montana, Washington, Idaho, Wyoming, Utah, Oklahoma, New Mexico and Arizona all attained statehood between 1870 and 1912.

The complete closing of America's western frontier by 1912 defined the limits of America's natural resources, for the first time in America's history. This closing also heralded for the first time, limits on the once thought to be unlimited expansion of individual Americans westward. By 1912, the death bell of Horace Greeley's 1855 advice that "all those of youth and ambition, without family or friends, seek their fortunes in America's west," had been rung. With the end of westward expansion, America became physically smaller, and certainly began to become more and more crowded from this point forward.

How were jobs created during the period of America's Industrial Revolution in 1877-1918? It was "Big Business" and "Big Industry" and its endless need for factory workers — factory workers, working for slave-wages, 60-80 hours a week, and without any job benefits whatsoever. This was the era of the Robber Barons, who coincidentally are the same American Industrialists revered by many of us today. J.P. Morgan, John D. Rockefeller, Andrew Carnegie and a host of others, who are remembered as the namesakes of the foundations, museums, concert halls, historic landmarks, public parks, and the giant corporations they established and managed during this period.

Also during the 1877-1918 period of America's industrialization, more than 25 Million American immigrants were literally sucked-up by the employment demands the American Industrial Revolution's factories, plants, and sweat shops: 7-day, 70-hour-work-weeks. Wave after wave of immigrants came willing to work and to compete for lower and lower wages. There were also the demands for labor to build America's railroads, bridges, factories, and roadways needed to accommodate the transportation of raw materials to America's new plants and factories growing in the mid-west, and transportation for the return of those finished goods to America's ever growing ranks of demanding consumer; the "demands" of whom would continue to peak up until America's entry into World War I in 1917.

How were jobs created in this period? Unfortunately, most economists agree, by the very "greed" of the Robber Barons we simultaneously admire and despise. Pure "greed" put to work in a nation unfettered by resource or land limitations. Needless to say, it is doubtful whether there are any Americans today who would accept employment in the "sweat shops" and "factories," directly or indirectly, created by the Morgans, the Rockefellers, the Carnegies, or any of the other "Captains of Industry" responsible for America's Industrial Revolution.

Since 1918, the American work place, along with its "work ethics" and "work attitudes" have dramatically changed. We are no longer a nation of "green horns" or new immigrants. We watch too much television to be satisfied with merely a leaking roof over our heads, one pair of shoes, or just enough food to keep from starving. It's simply un-American to betray what we have come to believe is our birthright as Americans: The right to work for a decent wage in a decent job with decent job benefits. Unfortunately, this birthright is not recognized by the present ambitions of America's *top-two-percenters,* who firmly believe that the "horse" has too long ago been left out of the "barn;" that the American middle-class is so drugged-up, boozed-up, and screwed-up that it can never challenge the dominance of the new aristocracy created by these same *top-two-percenters*. If you middle-class folks out there continue to be observers and not participants, you too will find that you will never get the horse back in the barn and the ambitions of America's *top-two-percenters* will fully become realized.

It is now time for us to analyze how jobs were created during that period in American history from which America's first middle-class was conceived, and through which period it remained in gestation, until its actual birth in the years immediately following World War II.

Job Creation During America's Age of Economic Boom, Depression, and War (1919-1945)

In the past 75 years, the two most important events to shape America socially, politically, and economically were the Great Depression of 1929, and World War II that commenced on December 7, 1941, and ended with the surrender of Japan on August 14, 1945.

The period between 1919-1945 is most aptly described by most American historians and economists as the period of America's "Economic Boom, Depression, and War."

For most Americans, it was also the era of Franklin Delano Roosevelt, the only American President to be elected to four terms in office. Commonly called FDR, Franklin Delano Roosevelt is given the credit by most Americans today for such broad programs as Social Security, creation of the Tennessee Valley Authority (TVA), creation of the Securities and Exchange Commission (SEC), and although primarily a congressional initiative, the creation of the Federal Deposit Insurance Corporation (FDIC), and the Federal Deposit Savings & Loan Insurance Corporation (FDSLIC), which for the first time federally insured deposits of individuals in America's Commercial and Savings Banks and ended, what had been in the past, *panic runs,* also referred to as simply *panics,* on the banks by their depositors attempting to get their money, or what was left of it.

As much as today's Democrats revere Franklin Delano Roosevelt for saving the nation during its worst depression, he was never quite successful in lifting the yoke of the Great Depression off the back of America. It was the threat of Adolph Hitler's world domination, and the resultant industrial mobilization required by World War II that "created jobs" that got America out of its economic depression and put every American man and woman back to work.

Far from imposing a government dictated "social agenda" on America, FDR favored, what most of us would attribute today to Ronald Reagan, George Bush, and Bill Clinton. Voluntarism. And believe it or not, FDR supported the decentralization of the powers of the federal government during his first two Administrations. FDR, contrary to how most Republicans have attempted to re-define him, refrained from both large scale "deficit-spending" and avoided "tax policies" that would have resulted in the redistribution of either corporate or individual income or wealth. No better evidence supports this than the 1931 through 1938 eight-year total deficit-spending during FDR's Administration which aggregated less than $18.3 billion. This is less than 40% of the $50 billion Mr. Clinton wanted to spend in his first year of office, or less than 10% of the $200 billion he said he would spend over the next four years to create new American jobs and end the 1990-1992 recession.

America's Middle-Class: A Class Born Out of WW II

There was no true middle-class in America prior to World War II. Prior to WW II, the populace that was to become America's first middle-class were primarily first and second generation immigrants, struggling to earn and define their economic status and class under the *whip* of the great pre-WW II **Robber Barons,** the same **Robber Barons** who were given so much attention and glory in your high school History books.

Probably the most over-looked impact of World War II, in that same high school History book, was the creation of America's first true middle-class. It wasn't the labor unions, nor the early agrarian political movements, nor even FDR or his Democratic Party that wrestled a piece of the American "pie" from America's Wealthy-Class. It was solely a by-product of World War II. This most massive and horrific of all wars had spawned a whole new breed of Americans; a middle-class of Americans who would no longer be satisfied with the left over crumbs that fell to the floor from the plates of America's "Wealthy Class." At the end of 1945 this new breed of Americans numbered 16.3 million strong. These were Americans who had served their country in war for almost five years; men and women who risked, and knew others who died for the sake of American freedom. These veterans had come from both the city and farm, and had filled the ranks of the U.S. Military by the millions. They suffered for five years the horrors and terrors of war, firmly believing they had earned and were now entitled to a fair share of the American "pie." Certainly these 16.3 million Americans were not going to be denied by any of America's politicians or any of America's then *top-two-percenters* their right to their fair share of the American "pie" after risking their lives.

This middle-class demanded such post-war government programs as the GI Bill, V.A. home mortgage financing, and other government paid-for programs that made this generation that fought WW II, a cohesive and distinct economic class within America. And a grateful nation didn't deny its returning warriors the rewards they demanded: The opportunity to attend college under this GI Bill, affordable housing under new Veteran's Administration loan guarantees program, along with Veteran's work preferences and job protection, all of the foundations required by a genuine American middle-class. A middle-class that would later become the largest and wealthiest consumer group to ever populate the world.

In their wake, followed a series of American Presidents, who personally knew their sacrifice and accepted their trust — Truman, Eisenhower and Kennedy. Not even the former *Captains of Industry*, nor the *Robber Barons* had the power, or the stomach, to stop this mass of American humanity from achieving what it had affectionately dubbed , the *American Dream*.

Not even the "greed" of America's *top-two-percenters* could stand in the way of these masses of combat-hardened men and women. They were not to be denied. And so finally came the real promise of America, a genuine "middle-class," a real middle-class that would share in America's wealth, a real middle-class that would share in the hopes and dreams of America. And so America embarked on the period known by many of us, as the "Happy Days" of the 1950s.

Not that there weren't those lying-in-wait to re-establish the *pre-war order* who were desirous of taking what they continued to believe to be their's, and their's alone. But in those years immediately following the War, who would dare challenge these 16.3 million men and women who made up the core of America's new middle-class?

This new middle-class of 16.3 million WW II ex-warriors enjoyed 25 years of prosperity, and were already crossing the 50 year-in-age mark, before the pent-up fervor for the super-accumulation of wealth by the *top-two-percenters* dared to fertilize the latent "seeds" of their own voracious ambitions. Twenty-five years of prosperity, and the middle-class had been thrown-off its guard. They'd become complacent. Comfortable. "Fat And Soft Under Their Bellies," is how the "top-two-percenters" viewed these ex-warriors, and their offspring, by as early as 1974.

By 1966, America's *top-two-percenters* subtly began to move the pendulum back to the right, and by 1968, the majority of the middle-class believed it was again time for "change." A "change" calculated by *top-two-percenters* since the end of WW II, and a "change" dictated by the "top-two-percenters," who had for so many years been on the sidelines. The "middle-class," although then still strong economically, had never expanded its "economic gains" into real "political power." The often *exclusionary democracy* of the *top-two-percenters*, known as "representative government," had quietly survived any change or reform during the post-war period and remained completely intact, "lying in wait" for its opportunity to be reborn again in its full force and fury.

Perhaps it was the Vietnam War as many say, or the dwindling of both America's and the World's resources. Perhaps it was just the "bad feelings" created by government dictating "social change" through social programs that had to be paid for by that same middle-class that had emerged at the end of World War II and that was magnified by the first real post-war recession of 1972-1974.

For whatever reason, by late 1979, the majority of middle-class Americans wanted to "take back" what the *top-two-percenters* convinced them was being given away to the poor by a swollen bureaucracy of state and federal governments.

Even with a foul taste left in their mouths from the reign of Richard Nixon, America turned to Ronald Reagan. The underlying promise, no more "big government," no more "social change," and no more "taxes" spent on worthless social programs.

And for the next twelve years, the fiction of America's "melting pot" evolved into the 1990s "smoldering pot" of gender, racial, ethnic, and economic class distrust and hatred — continually fueled and flamed by the elimination of over 6 million American middle-class jobs being exported to emerging Third World competitors, the destruction of the American Industrial Complex by the M&A Gangs, the looting of the S&Ls by the "Reagan & Bush Robbers," and the "control" of American Government being bought by over 10,000 *special interest groups*, the majority of which were controlled by the *top-two-percenters* and their army of envious *knee-jerk wannabees.*

How were jobs created after WW II and before Richard Nixon?

Between 1945 and 1968, jobs were created as the country reaped the benefits sown by the creation of its true middle-class. Insatiable demand for automobiles, housing, and other goods and services fueled the American economy to almost the point of burn-out.

Job creation in the 1960-1975 period was again primarily a product of war, this time the 1963-1973 Vietnam War, one of the few "hot spots" of the Cold War. Oddly enough the U.S. National Debt over this ten year Vietnam war period only increased by $165 billion, thus making very questionable, the argument of the vast majority of the economists of then and today, that Americans were unable to finance an economy of both "guns and butter." Also it should be noted that the unemployment rate for each year during this period averaged just slightly less than 5.0%. (Author's note: Regardless of what the *top-two-percenters* tell you about my comments here, in no way do I condone creating a war to end a depression or recession, or achieve economic growth.)

Beginning in 1974 and continuing through 1992, America was faced with an average annual unemployment of 6.8% reaching a peak in 1982 of 9.7%. These unemployment statistics are the reason many Americans believe that America's recession, regardless of the government's changing of its definition of the phenomenon, truly began in 1974 and continues today. To put things in perspective, for those of you who do not remember, 1968-1974 was the Nixon Era that began with its hope of ending the Vietnam War and ended with the Watergate, that finally culminated in Nixon's resignation after two continuous paralyzing years of political turmoil in August 1974.

The period following Watergate, 1974 through 1981, was one of mediocre leadership and political turmoil. The two-year Ford Administration remained clouded by Watergate, and the Carter Administration, which never really began, had its scandalous "Burt Lance," and for the last 444 days of its "impotent" subsistence suffered under the humiliation of Iran's Ayatollah Khomeini. America, along with its middle-class had, by 1981, been brought to its knees, both politically, psychologically, and economically. The moment had come for the emergence of America's *top-two-percenters* as America's new aristocracy, who with their former California governor, and former star of B-Movies were poised to commence in earnest the looting of America's S&Ls and industrial infrastructure. It had all been quite calculated.

It could not have been better scripted even by the likes of Machiavelli! On the day Ronald Reagan was sworn in as the fortieth President of the United States, so was the Ayatollah's choke-hold on American self-esteem broken. The hostages were released and put on planes to Algeria to coincide with his inauguration speech. And so began the 1980s as we refer to them today. The Reagan Administration jubilantly joined with the linking of the freed 52 American hostages and the hope that the recession America had entered into 1980 would soon come to an end. The long awaited era of power for the *top-two-percenters* had finally come to fruition! The "lootings," the economic destruction, and the erosion of America's middle-class had begun. There were no viable alternatives left for the politically apathetic and impotent middle-class, who had gotten fat under their bellies! No longer were they consolidated by the victory of WW II, but divided by the calculated incessant subtle rhetoric of the *top-two-percenters.*

During the Reagan Administration (1981-1988) America's unemployment rate averaged 7.5%, having reached its peak in 1982, but, in all fairness to Reagan, the 9.7% peak unemployment rate of 1982 was due to the economic conditions that preceded his inauguration. In 1981, Reagan began the mission. Americans, again filled with hope, accepted any employment; employment in record numbers at sub-standard jobs waiting for the "promised" benefits of Reaganomics. This willingness to temporarily accept "any job" at "any wage," resulted in unemployment reaching its 6.2% low point in 1987.

By 1988, unemployment had again risen to 7.0%, a sharp decline in this unemployment rate occurred during the Bush Administration in 1989, when the unemployment rate allegedly dropped to 5.3%, but was adjusted the following month to 5.4%. Short-lived, the unemployment rate again gradually rose to 6.1% in 1990, to 6.5% in 1991, and to 7.8% in 1992. But most importantly, by 1992, the "transition" had been made. The middle-class was critically, and perhaps even fatally wounded. The "new global aristocracy" seemed firmly entrenched. Middle-class America still believed itself in a Reagan economic renaissance, although its standard-of-living had been reduced by 30%, its National Debt quadrupled, and its industrial infrastructure destroyed.

Job creation in the 1980-1990 decade, was the product of "borrowing." Even more important, these jobs were a product of the massive lootings in America, along with the massive federal government borrowings, endorsed by Reagan and Bush to allegedly win the "Cold War." Boobus Americanus fell right into line with Reagan's desire to conquer the "Evil Empire." Most Americans, who had visited Russia in the early 1980s, understood the USSR was already falling under its own economic weight, and the failure of Communism was inevitable.

A joke passing through some of the inner circles in New York during the Reagan 1986 Summit Meeting at Reykjavik with Gorbachev, was the question of who would be the first to unilaterally surrender to the other as it was observed that both of their economic systems were then in near collapse. The joke had it that as Reagan and Gorbachev chased each other around the negotiating table, neither of them was able to catch the other to hand-over the unilateral unconditional surrender document, and thus the Cold War was preserved until 1989. Since 1989, the vast majority of the old USSR has been in social, economic, and political turmoil. Ethnic cleansing is occurring in almost every former Soviet state and the level of lawlessness now even surpasses that of the United States.

The end of the Cold War in 1989 obviously greatly impacted America and every other nation in the world. No longer were the worlds two greatest adversaries seeking to dominate the other and everyone else. By 1993, after hearing four years of Bush's and Clinton's chatter alluding to the illusory *peace dividend*, many Americans wondered what the Cold War had really been about, and what it had actually cost in an almost surrealistic way. No longer able to unite Americans in the war against the evil empire, domestic issues now came to the forefront. For the first time, Americans, no longer in fear of nuclear destruction, focused on the drum beat coming from Washington D.C. that warned of America's own social, racial, economic holocausts awaiting them on the horizon.

With all of the spending by the Federal Government in defending against the Cold War, all of it only accounted for 15% of America's total employment, no doubt these jobs being its best "manufacturing jobs," but still only 15% of America's total employment.

So, how were the other 85% of jobs created or maintained during the Reagan decade of the 1980s? Through the largest borrowings in the history of America. Consumer debt more than doubled from $355 billion in 1980 to $735 billion in 1990; State and Local government debt also more than doubled from $335.6 billion in 1980 to $835 billion in 1990; the Federal Debt (National Debt) almost quadrupled from $907 billion to $3.34 trillion, and real estate residential mortgage debt, exclusive of $85 billion in home equity loans, nearly tripled from $950 billion in 1980 to $2.4 trillion in 1990. Since 1990 the National Debt has escalated to $4 trillion in 1992. This represented a "net" debt increase of $3.1 trillion in the 1980s decade into 1992, and a total debt outstanding of over $7.3 trillion in 1990, not including the S&L and PBIC, etc. bailouts that are not included in the "debt" figures.

Thus, to sustain the alleged growth of the 1980s decade took "aggregate borrowings" in excess of $4.7 trillion, or $470 billion each year. Think of this annual $470 billion in "borrowings" and the impact it had on the American economy over the 1980s, whenever you think of Mr. Clinton's $50 billion "spending" solution of 1992.

How Do We Now Create 30,000,000 New American Jobs In America?

Whether your economic bent is Keynesian (fiscal policy proponent), or you are a "monetarist" (a money supply proponent) there can be no question as to America's present *inability* to create 30 million quality new jobs through new government spending.

To create 30 million quality new American jobs, we must first completely dispel the notion that the "government" and the "economy" are two separate and distinct entities or systems. American Capitalism and American Government are one in the same, and if you do not buy this, you haven't read the first eighteen chapters of this book.

The second notion that must be completely dispelled is that all "government regulation" of business slows down economic growth. This is true of some regulations, and certainly they can be eliminated without a complete surrender to the desires of America's *top-two-percenters.* Government regulation of business, if enforced, merely keeps greedy men honest. Although the Bush Administration relied on a "few empty words" and a lot of "military marching music" to blacken the image of government regulation, as the world enters the Twenty-First Century, it is a whole new ball game for everyone. Neither slogans, lip service, or catchy fifteen-second sound bites will resolve America's problems, nor assist in creating America's much needed 30,000,000 high-wage new jobs.

The third thing we must completely dispel are the notions put forth by Messrs. Bush and Reagan. Supply-side economics, pure free-trade, and zero government regulation are as much a myth as a free-lunch. These theories are not only contrary to human nature and national security, but are contrary to good business and economic sense.

The "solution" presented in this chapter to creating 30 million new American jobs is conditioned and predicated on certain other political and social changes being implemented by America. These changes include:

1. The changes in America's present "representative" form of government as set forth in Chapter 20.

2. The implementation of a National Health Insurance Program so that cost control as previously stated may be achieved over this non-productive sector of the economy.

3. Enforcement of existing criminal and regulatory laws, and stiffening the criminal penalties of some of these laws, as suggested throughout this book and in Chapter 20.

4. Changes in the entire system of U.S. Federal, State and Local taxation in order to create an environment of accountability, fairness, and a reduction in the bureaucracy that feeds off this taxing phenomenon. (See Chapter 20 for suggestions on a new tax system to replace America's present archaic unfair and inefficient system of taxation.)

A major hurdle that will have to be crossed, will be when your elected representative tells you there is no precedence for many of the simple solutions presented in this book. Should this occur, first remind them of the $1.5 billion in federal loan guarantees approved by the Senate on December 19, 1979 to bail out the Chrysler Corporation. Remind them how the workers, the banks, and other with a stake in the company's future, to avoid a possible 700,000 worker layoffs which by anyone's estimate would have set-off a major recession or even a depression in the United States, asked for no precedence, before these allegedly necessary measures were taken.

Also, remind them that no "precedence," was required when the Bush Administration and Congress wanted to approve $10 billion in loan guarantees for the state of Israel in order that they might improve their economy sufficiently to allow the migration of one million Jews from Russia, even though the Berlin Wall had fallen three years before.

Certainly what was good for Chrysler in 1979, and good for Israel in 1992, and something that might create 30 million high-wage new jobs in America should not be set aside for lack of precedence. New circumstances compounded with new or old unresolved problems requires the implementation of new ideas and concepts, especially if there is nothing else available or on the horizon to correct these problems.

Now that we have the "precedence issue" tucked away, it's time to reach forward to a truly American solution to creating 30 million new quality American jobs.

Having been myself a good Republican for almost thirty years until 1992, but thereafter continuing to be a solid believer in America, and American Capitalism, I spent almost two full years thinking about the solution to this problem. In 1979, I had come up with this research & development tax credit idea and wrote to every member of the U.S. Congress about how it could result in America retaining its technological leadership in the world. In 1980 this idea became part of U.S. Tax Code. In 1985, I again wrote to every member of the U.S. Congress objecting to the Boucher bill which would have exempted CPAs and Lawyers from the penalties of Racketeer Influenced and Corrupt Organizations Act (RICO). The bill was defeated six weeks later in both the U.S. Senate and House of Representatives and almost every CPA and Lawyer I knew at the time didn't bother with me for months. Thinking I had made a difference twice before, I again wrote in July, 1991 with some of the ideas I had developed on an American Renaissance and the rebuilding of America's industrial infrastructure and how it all might be accomplished.

I kept, at the top of my mind, that the National Debt was approaching the $4.3 trillion mark. Thus I concluded, there could be little if any additional government spending, without threatening what little remains of America's credit-worthiness. While also trying to keep a hold on all the "problems" that I've set forth in previous chapters of this book, and after thinking about it during the whole month of May 1991, I sat in front of my computer for three days and drafted my initial solution in a letter to Congressman John Dingell (D-MICH), one of the few men in the Congress who still gets aroused about America's future.

And so I quote to you from this same "letter" which I also sent to every one of the fifty state Governors, to every member of the U.S. Senate and House of Representatives, to every major Presidential candidate running for office in 1992, to 68 American Labor Union Presidents, 46 newspapers, 16 news or and news related T.V. programs, and every consumer advocate group with offices in Washington D.C.

Some of the more intelligent, and outright belligerent responses received from America's elected leaders are in Appendix B, amongst other letters I received in response to other ideas or concerns elaborated on above.

Only one Union President, John Kirkland responded. And not one response was received from the media, except from the L.A. Times, who noted on a post card,: The "manuscript" was too long for publication.

As initially stated, this letter was directed to Congressmen John M. Dingell (D-Mich.) and was sent on June 27, 1991. A major excerpt from this letter appears below:

> "The solution of course, as I am sure you've suspected, is getting our own house in order. Making CAPITALISM again work for America. Regulating and protecting areas of American Industry that have been proven to be victims of prey, from within and without. Recognizing that there are limits and constraints needed for the good of society; recognizing that we can never again allow the greed and hypocrisy of the Reagan-Bush eras to enslave us as a nation again. An era of such monstrous arrogance, immorality, lawlessness, and greed that it almost destroyed the very thing it was pretending to save: CAPITALISM.
>
> And this requires rescuing the commercial banks that now teeter on the brink of collapse; nurturing the S&Ls back to health; and restoring the securities industry to one of true investment: investment in modern efficient American manufacturing facilities. This time around, let the Banks and Wall Street invest in productive American Plant, Property, and Equipment — PP&E — an almost forgotten American acronym. We still have some truly credit worthy borrowers that can almost turnkey this nation back into prosperity. The U.S. Fortune 500 Industrials. Especially those in the defense industry, many of them no longer with major defense contracts, and very little else to do. A re-tooling to consumer products that are now imported. The dying U.S. Automobile Industry — an aggressive re-tooling. Think about it. Consider the dramatically changing world without the Iron Curtain. Shiftless American resources with no national direction, and no national leadership. Think about why we can't kick off a new housing boom even with relatively low mortgage interest rates. What difference low interest rates to the consumer without a job, or a sense of future. Consumer

confidence — isn't that the real measure of economically successful capitalism? And isn't that what can be created with the existing resources at hand? Leadership and dreams. A real return to our national self-esteem. Compare it to the mobilization of our resources for the Gulf War, or W.W.II — but with real results. Think of the tax base of consumers that will be created. Better a trillion dollars in credit guarantees created by the full faith and credit of the United States for the sole purpose of rebuilding the PP&E of this nation than a couple of trillion dollars to forever work our way out of a "supercrash." A trillion dollars in properly legislated guarantees of the American people's money to get Americans back to work and prosperous — an America able to pay off the excesses of the last forty-five years, as opposed to the death of our nation. What better gamble have we? What better endeavor to embark upon? And who better to benefit by it, if not the American people, who will have to pay for it.

A regulated partnership of American government (the people), American Industry (the people), and American Banking and Wall Street (again the people) rebuilding America. With the work to be done, I suspect that we'd see full employment within six months. It's not hard to imagine an overflow of excess American capital and the technology of "building" and "rebuilding" not flowing around the world in a very short period of time. Not our industries and jobs, but our capital, our genuine peace-time technology, and our excess production — what better foreign aid? And God only knows if we can't do it here, we shouldn't be going deeper into the National Debt to show them how to "screw it up" over there. One has to openly wonder how Secretary Baker can travel the world keeping a straight face. Or how President Bush lies so sincerely. Can it be that they are in such "denial?" Or are we to presume it continues to be done in the name of our National Security?"

To effect the solution presented in the above excerpt from the June 27, 1991 letter to Congressmen John M. Dingell, I suggest the following:

1. Mr. Greenspan, and the Federal Reserve Bank, making available $1 trillion in loan money, at no more than 5% interest, immediately to America's Fortune 500 or perhaps Fortune

1000 American Industrial Companies that are deemed to be key industries to America's well being and National Security. These industries would include:

(a)   The U.S. Steel Industry

(b)   The U.S. and Automobile and Farm Equipment Manufacturing Industries.

(c)   U.S. Machine Tool and Heavy Manufacturing Equipment Industries.

(d)   U.S. Aircraft Manufacturing Industry.

(e)   U.S. Computer Chip and Computer Manufacturing Industries.

(f)   U.S. Durable Goods Manufacturing Industries.

(g)   U.S. Consumer Electronics Manufacturing Industries.

(h)   U.S. Textile and Clothing Manufacturing Industries.

Even with the borrowing mechanics in place, and the government on the hook as the guarantor for all of these loans, as every CEO, CFO, MBA and CPA in this country are well aware, there will be no American Fortune 1000 Company coming in to borrow money from U.S. Banks unless there are "profits" to be made. Even with a five percent (5%) interest rate on these federally guaranteed industrial infrastructure rebuilding loans, the self-serving Americans running America's MNCs won't be into borrow a dime to improve the lot of their fellow Americans.

To assure the necessary "profits" (also known as return-on-investment, ROI), part of America's "free trade myth" must be dispelled. This would be accomplished vis-à-vis a U.S. tariff structure that would assure a three percent (3%) ultimate U.S. unemployment rate by limiting the import of goods that compete with those aforementioned eight American industry produced goods. After reaching this 3% unemployment goal, and as long as it were maintained, all incremental trade would be free of tariffs.

A second very important element in the rebuilding of America is where this new plant and equipment will be located. And here we have capitalism working at its best: our new plants and factories will be located in close proximity to our existing labor forces. Those labor forces especially that have historically been in these industries before they were exported to foreign nations, and if those cities have been abandoned, to the cities where the highest rates of employment exist. Can there be any doubt that as a result of such re-location of American "capital," perhaps for the first time in both the history of America and the world, that "capitalism" will be made to work *for all the people* of this nation, rather than for just the mere few who occupy the top percent of the economic strata.

Now that you're all "revved-up," why not get on the phone right now with your Congressmen and your two Senators. Tell them you want a new America, an America where the wealth and its benefits are shared by all, as opposed to just a few. Flood their mailboxes with mail, feel free to fax them copies of the pages of this book, and ask them why they don't have on their agenda, a program to rebuild America for both your welfare and the nation's welfare? Ask them outright why "capitalism" can't be made to work for all Americans?

If you're still not convinced, read on. You're going to be asked again to call those of your elected representatives who "represent" the "special interest groups" of this country in lieu of you. You're going to demand the political reform of your government, that will for the first time truly enfranchise you and allow you to directly participate in your American government.

Now, if you took my advice and called your Congressman and Senators, let me dispel some of the "myths" they more than likely to tried to "spin" on you in order to assure their continued status quo.

Some Of The Myths You'll Hear

First they'll call you a "bad name" or two. First you'll be called a Protectionist! That's the equivalent of being called a "communist" six years ago. Well I'm not taken in by this "spin!" Not at all! I voluntarily spent three years in the U.S. Army, twenty-months in the far east thinking that's what Americans were supposed to be doing for other Americans, and nothing I've seen from those alleged Americans presently in Washington even has a glimmer of this notion. So if you're sensitive to "bad names," be warned, it won't be the first time this tactic has been used by those who would sell out the citizens of their country — take no offense.

Our Congress, and especially our President will then argue that the only way to expand America's economy, and the world's economy is to have the entire world free of all trade barriers. If you've read this book carefully, and have applied it to what you have read in your newspapers or heard on your TVS, you will know that this is in complete contradiction of:

1. The operations of the Federal Reserve Bank as it relates to money supply, the cost of money, and the manipulation of exchange rates with our international trading partners.

2. The contradictory system of taxation that presently exists in the United States and other countries throughout the world, that favor their "special interest" domestic industries (in the U.S., the tobacco industry and farm industries) so that these "special interest"industries have an advantage in trading in both the domestic and international marketplace.

3. The betrayal inherent in the most recently negotiated trade treaties: NAFTA or "Fast-Track" and GATT that was previously discussed in Chapter Thirteen.

And if your elected "representative" in Washington D.C. tells you that "protecting" eight key American Industries is detrimental to America's financial well-being, remember, these are the same bunch of "clowns" who:

1. Ran up an additional $4 trillion on the National Debt over the decade of the 1980s.

2. In 1992, voted themselves midnight raises to $130,000 per year with automatic future COLA increases, as America sank deeper and deeper in debt.

3. Allowed the looting of America's S&Ls, and

4. Watched, and perhaps even profited, as the M&A Gangs of Wall Street looted the nation's industrial infrastructure as almost 6,000,000 U.S. manufacturing jobs disappeared to factories overseas.

When America *abandons* Americans, what purpose does America serve for Americans? And when America no longer offers Americans the hope, the belief, the dream, and the opportunity to fulfill their reasonable ambitions; when America completely surrenders itself to the "greed" and "avarice" of a "few" at the sacrifice of the majority, then "America" itself is no more.

For many in our society, this condition has already become a horrifying reality — and for many others, it seems to be the only future left in America.

The time has now come for all of us to be counted — for all of us to get back to the hard work of making "America" what it was once thought to be, and can still be.

With all of the work that has to be done in this country and the world, there is certainly no need for any man or woman to be in need of work, or in want of employment. The recognition of this "condition" is the most redeeming characteristic of pre-Reagan-Bush American Capitalism. This is the same American Capitalism that came alive during WW II and rebuilt Europe under a simple concept called the Marshall Plan. This same American Capitalism can again come alive and take us all through the Twenty-First Century, with all of us rebuilding our standard-of-living, as well as, our hopes, and recovering the American Dream that so many of us believe has been forever lost.

America can be restored, and Americans can again look to the future with optimism — it lies before us as a nation if we take upon ourselves to do it together — to re-build America for ourselves and as a model for the rest of the world to follow.

- AUTHOR'S REVERSE "SPIN" GLOSSARY -

- "WHAT THEY SAY IT MEANS" & "WHAT IT REALLY MEANS" -

Business Cycles:

<u>What they say it means:</u> Upward or downward swings in the economy which occur over time (generally a full cycle being completed every 2 ½ years), with a major recession every 8 years, and a major depression every 30 to 50 years. The upward movements result in peaks called "prosperity" (upswing, expansion), and downward movements that result in "recessions" or "depressions" (downswings, troughs, or contractions). Most economists believe that the consequences of the "business cycle" are practically unavoidable in a capitalistic "free market" economy.

<u>What it really means:</u> The downswing in the business cycle occurs after a "minor looting" of the nation's wealth and generally results in a "recession." After a "major looting" of the nation, that almost completely destroys the economic system, a "depression" is generally what results. Upswings are then generally achieved through enormous government spending to refinance the rebuilding of the "looted" economy so that the cycle may begin again.

COMPOSITE DICTIONARY

Internal Rate on Return (IRR): IRR is a capital budgeting analysis tool to determine whether or not a capital project (i.e. real investment in PP&E, etc.) is acceptable for investment. The IRR essentially is a "discount rate" at which the present value of the future cash flows of the investment equals the cost of the investment. It is determined by a process of trial and error. When the net present value of the cost of investment and returns on investment equals zero, the rate of discount being used is the IRR. When the IRR is greater than the required return (also known as the "hurdle rate") the investment is deemed to be acceptable.

Many corporations use IRR as a means to determine whether or not a capital project will be implemented. As the various cost factors of the investment; i.e. labor, money, land, materials, etc. vary so does the IRR;

therefore the analysis remains dynamic until the actual capital budget expenditure is finally approved and committed to.

The other side to the equation obviously is the expectation and present value of the cash inflows (the revenues that the capital project will earn). If the IRR analysis shows that these revenues will not cover the cost of the capital budget expenditures pursuant to the IRR analysis, no investment in the capital project will be made.

Since "labor," being most expensive in the U.S., and substantially lower in Mexico and other countries, it's no wonder there are no new manufacturing industries being built in the United States. Applying the concept of IRR and ROI to a capital project in Mexico, free of environmental protection regulations and America's relatively astronomical labor costs, there can be no doubt that every capital budget project is economically better served by being moved by American Industrial Investors into Mexico. But is it simply a matter of economics and profits? That's the question answered in this Chapter of this book.

Key Industries: Those U.S. Industries that are of primary importance to both the nation's economy and the national security. For example, the "defense industry" is a key industry since it is crucial to maintaining the country's defense posture. The "automobile industry" is key since so many jobs are directly or indirectly dependent on it. Other industries which are deemed to be key or critical by the author and other Americans are: (1) The machine tool industry, (2) The consumer electronics industry, (3) The durable goods industry, (4) The aircraft manufacturing industry, (5) The computer & chip manufacturing industry, (6) The aerospace industry, (7) The textile industry, and (8) The steel industry.

Return on Investment (ROI): Also known as Return on Invested Capital, it means the amount, expressed as a percentage, that is earned on a company's total capital; in this instance, total capital refers to stock equity plus any long-term debt. ROI is calculated by dividing the "total capital" into corporate earnings that are unaffected by interest, taxes, and dividends. The ROI concept is also the primary tool used by major companies to evaluate purposed Capital Spending (PP&E) projects such as plant construction, research and development, and new business acquisition expenditures.

Secular Stagnation Theory: A rarely espoused theory that holds when an "economy" has reached "maturity" (the frontier is gone, important discoveries and technological advancements are lacking, and the rate of "population increase" is either stagnant or declining) that there must follow long periods of recession or depression, and only short interludes of prosperity. This cycle continues, unless there is some drastic change in government policy. Except for the "birth rate" factor, does this theory or term describe any "economy" you're familiar with?

Tax: "Pecuniary" (money) burden placed on individuals or property to support the government, the authority for such in a democracy being vested in the legislature by the people. A tax is not a voluntary payment, nor a donation, but an enforced contribution, exacted for the support of government, for the administration of the laws, and as a means of continuing in operation the various legitimate functions of the state. Taxes are generally said to include tolls, tributes, tillage, imposts, duties, customs, excises, subsidies, etc., the maturation of which results in a debt to the citizen, or a lien on his or her property or income.

Tax-Surtax: A surtax is an additional tax sometimes imposed on certain kinds of income, such as dividends from corporate stocks, interest from savings, royalties, etc. The surtax is generally calculated as a percentage of another tax which is due. For example, if one owed $50,000 in income taxes, the surtax, if it were applied at a rate of 10% would require the individual to pay an additional $5,000. Surtaxes are usually employed by governments when it is anticipated that revenue will fall dramatically during a particular tax period.

Tax-Value Added Tax (VAT): A consumption tax, usually stated in a form of a percentage, that is levied on the "value-added" to a product at each stage of its manufacturing cycle, as well as at the time of purchase by the ultimate consumer. The value-added tax has long been used by European Common Market countries as a major source of revenue. It is important to note, that the value-added tax does not tax the total value of a product at each stage of its manufacture, but only that part of the "value-added" at that stage of manufacture; thus the purchaser of a particular product, under a value-added tax system would only be paying a tax on that portion of the product that had not been taxed previously during its several stages of production and movement through its channels of distribution, whereas a sales tax, taxes the entire value of the product including the profit to the ultimate purchaser.

Tax-Accumulated Earnings: A tax imposed on the Accumulated Earnings of U.S. Corporations, when the corporation has accumulated the maximum amount of earnings it is allowed under law to retain. It is designed to force corporations to pay dividends because the tax is assessed against that part of retained earnings (now a part of "capital") which is not distributed as dividends, and which is not reasonably necessary for the maintenance and growth of the business. The government policy here is twofold: (1) To prevent large accumulations of unnecessary Corporate Wealth which might very well have a very chilling effect on government power itself, and (2) To force Corporations to pay out corporate dividends, which allows government a second opportunity to tax the Corporation's profits, this time through the dividend recipient, the stockholder.

Tax-Ad Valorem: A tax assessed on the "value" of goods and/or property; and <u>not</u> on their quantity, weight, or size.

Tax-Amusement: A tax imposed on tickets sold by places of amusement such as sporting arenas, circuses, concerts, etc., usually expressed as a percentage of the price of the ticket.

Tax-Capital Gain: A tax on the "gain" from the sale of an asset (synonymous with the term "capital asset," thus the use of the term "capital" when referring to the "gain" from its sale) sold at a profit. The U.S. does not have a special or preference tax rate for these so-called "capital gains." Presently, these "gains" are added to the individual's regular income and taxed at the individual's regular "income tax rate."

Tax-Capital Stock: A tax assessed as a percentage of par or assigned value of a corporation's capital stock.

Tax-Consumption: A tax imposed on the individual, as a consumer, for the consumption of goods and services. A "sales tax" is an example of a Consumption Tax.

Tax-Credit: A direct, dollar-for-dollar reduction of a taxpayer's tax liability (tax due), as distinguished from a tax deduction, which reduces a taxpayer's revenues to arrive at the taxpayer's taxable net income or profit. Essentially what this means is that if you have a tax bill of $1,000.00, that you arrived at after subtracting all of your "eligible deductions" and "personal exemptions" and have applied your "tax rate" to that taxable income you had just previously determined — to get to that $1000.00 tax bill — and you qualify for one of the enumerated "tax credits" allowed under the Internal Revenue Code, you may then subtract the prescribed "Tax Credit" amount based on your eligible "tax credit," dollar-for-dollar from your $1000.00 tax bill.

Tax Deferral: A term used to describe the delaying the taxation on certain income or gains derived from an investment (i.e. a house, a stock, a bond, IRA, pension plan, etc.) whose accumulated value or earnings in the form of appreciation or income are free from taxation until the taxpayer sells or otherwise triggers the taxation of the appreciation or income by some voluntary, or sometimes involuntary event or action, requiring that a tax be paid on part, or all of the gain.

Tax-Direct: A tax which is demanded from the precise person, who the taxing authority intended, or desired, should pay it. Examples of direct taxes are those taxes that exist upon a person's property, business, income, etc., and which are required to be paid by that one particular person owning the property, the business or earning the income.

Tax-Estate and Gift: The combining of the estate and gift tax is peculiar to the scheme of taxation in the U.S. An "estate tax" is the amount due the government generally based on the net value of one's property (wealth) at death. A "gift tax" is one generally levied on the donor of the gift by the federal government and most state governments when assets are transferred from one person to another during the donor's lifetime. In the U.S., where the Federal Estate Tax and Federal Gift Tax have been unified, one credit amount applies to the sum of the property given during one's lifetime and his or her other property remaining at death. Estate tax exemptions and deduction are numerous; and each U.S. citizen has a unified estate and gift tax credit of $600,000, which may be used, in whole or part, during his lifetime, or at the time of his or her death.

Tax-Excise: A tax on the sale or manufacture of a commodity usually considered an "unnecessary" or a "luxury" item. An example of U.S. excise taxes are the taxes placed on alcohol, tobacco, and telephone by the State and Federal Governments.

Tax-Federal Unemployment Tax Act (FUTA): A federal excise tax on every employer, presently at 6.2% on the first $7,000 of wages paid each of his or her employees, during each calendar year. FUTA taxes are placed in special trust funds administered by the various state unemployment agencies. Most states also have an unemployment excise tax on employers and in some cases employees that parallels the federal unemployment tax. Once the funds in the special trust funds have been exhausted (i.e. because of long recessions, etc.) the federal government, on an emergency basis, may make emergency appropriations to add to these special trust funds so that unemployment benefits may be continued to be paid out.

Tax-Floor: A tax that is assessed on all of the distilled spirits on "the floor of a warehouse." Contrary to its name, this tax generally covers all of the distilled spirits in the warehouse whether or not they are on the floor.

Tax-Franchise: A state imposed tax that is usually regressive and whose rate decreases as the tax base increases. This tax is generally imposed on state chartered corporations for the right to do business under its corporate name in the taxing state.

Tax-Graduated: A tax structured so that the rate increases as the value of the income or property increases.

Tax-Gross Receipts: A tax based on total sales rather than on net profits.

Tax-Head: A tax imposed on a per person basis, or per head basis.

Tax-Income: A tax based on the income earned by a person or business. Income taxes are the main source of revenue for the United States Federal Government and in many cases the main source of revenue for many states.

Tax-Indirect: Those taxes which are demanded from one person in the chain of commerce, in the expectation and intention that he or she shall indemnify himself or herself at the expense of another as the tax is passed forward with the service or product. Examples of "indirect taxes" are those that are levied on a commodity before it reaches the consumer, but is paid for by that consumer, not as a tax, but as part of the market price of the commodity. A "tariff" is an example of an indirect tax.

Tax-Inheritance: A tax based on the property value of a decedent, but imposed on those who acquire the property from the decedent. (See Tax-Estate)

Tax-Levy: The total sum to be raised by a tax through a bill, enactment, or measure of legislation of a lawful taxing authority.

Tax-Lien: A statutory obligation, existing in favor of the state or municipality, upon the lands of a person charged with taxes, binding the same either for taxes assessed upon the specific tract of land or in some jurisdictions, for all the taxes due from the individual, and which may be foreclosed for non-payment, by judgment of a court or a "forced" sale of the land by the tax authority.

Tax-Luxury: A tax on goods that are considered non-essential. The tax may be imposed on the manufacturer, on the seller, or on the purchaser of the luxury item.

Tax-Payroll: Any tax levied on wages or salaries, such as for Social Security (FICA), Medicare, disability insurance, and unemployment insurance.

Tax-Personal: A tax imposed on personal property, or a tax imposed without reference to property such as a poll tax.

Tax-Poll: A Poll-Tax is a tax of a specific sum levied upon each person within the jurisdiction of the taxing authority and within a certain class — i.e. as all males of a certain age etc. without reference to his property or lack of it. Poll-Taxes as a prerequisite to voting in federal elections was outlawed by the 24th Amendment to the U.S. Constitution; and as to state and local elections, Poll-Taxes were held long ago to be unconstitutional by the United States Supreme Court.

Tax-Progressive: A graduated tax which applies higher tax rates as the income increases. For example, a 30% tax on $30,000 of income, followed by a 40% tax on $40,000 of income would be one example of a progressive tax system.

Tax-Property: A commonly used term to describe the tax levied on the basis of value of either personal or real property owned by the taxpayer.

Tax-Proportional: Proportional Taxes are taxes that are structured in a ratio format so that each taxpayer pays his or her tax based upon his or her percentage of what they own or earn in relation to what is owned or earned in total by all taxpayers; and in the case of a "special tax," when that tax is apportioned according to the benefits received.

Tax-Public: A tax levied for some general public purpose or for the purposes of the general revenue, as distinguished from local municipal assessments of specific taxes on the value of property.

Tax-Real Estate: A tax assessed against the real property of a person or corporation based on the value of such property.

Tax-Regressive: A tax levied at rates which remain constant, or increase less rapidly than the increase of the tax base, thus usually bearing more heavily on poor taxpayers. State and local sales taxes are generally deemed to be regressive taxes, because no matter how much the individual's income rises the tax rate remains constant, but because of the nature of say an 8% sales tax, the effective rate for the poorer classes might result in an effective rate tax of 6% on their income, whereas, because you can only consume so much, the effective tax rate of the same sales tax on someone earning $5 million a year might result in an effective tax rate of less than 1%.

Tax-Sales: A tax imposed based on the value of the item sold. Sales taxes are a major source of revenue for most states and are generally imposed on the retail sale of certain items. Usually medicine and other "necessities" are exempt from this tax.

Tax-Severance: A tax levied on the mining or extraction of natural resource such as oil, minerals, or coal. The tax may be assessed either on the value or volume of the extracted product.

Tax-Specific: A tax imposed as a fixed sum on each article or item of property of a given class or kind, without regard to its value.

Tax-Stamp: A tax collected through the sale of stamps which must be affixed to certain documents such as deeds, stocks certificates, etc.

Tax-Stock Transfer: A tax levied by the Federal Government and by certain states on the transfer or sale of shares of stock.

Tax-Use Tax: A tax imposed on the use of certain goods which are not subject to a sales tax. This tax is commonly employed to discourage people from going out of state and purchasing good which are not subject to a sales tax in the state where the purchase occurs.

Tax-Withholding: A tax which is collected by the employer for the government by deducting it from the employee's wages. Federal and State Income Taxes, as well as Social Security and Medicare are examples of taxes withheld from employees.

20 | American Political Solutions with Public Servant Sacrifice

Can We Ever Get America Back On Track?

You wouldn't have continued reading this much, if you believed America hadn't fallen-off track for you somewhere during your lifetime. Whether it was in 1980, 1972, 1963, or whenever, you know America and the American Dream were derailed sometime during your lifetime. Many of you, like me, in the baby-boom generation date America's first slip-off the track with the assassination of President John F. Kennedy. Others blame the derailment on the Vietnam War, which officially began in 1964, and didn't end for America until 1973. Some Americans blame the America's decline on Richard Nixon, others on Ronald Reagan and George Bush, and still others on Bill Clinton. And everyone is probably correct to one degree or another. The real concern, for every American, is whether or not we can get America and the American Dream back on track before there are no tracks left. Take heart! It can be done as demonstrated by America's past heroic achievements. Remember the Marshall Plan and the rebuilding of all Europe right after WWII! More recently, remember the rise in the American spirit and the accomplishments of President John F. Kennedy in the early 1960s.

Most of the baby-boomers know this **One-Thousand Day Era** as the Kennedy "Camelot" years. A **One-Thousand Day Era** where a sense of rebirth, well being, hope, and opportunity were all directly injected into America's bloodstream. A **One-Thousand Day Era** where Americans were challenged to reach for the stars! It was during this **One-Thousand Day Era** that for the last time I remember feeling what was that *unique sense* of American hope, American opportunity, American compassion, and a sense of American future.

The Era itself is best summarized by one segment of President Kennedy's 1962 inaugural address, which reflected the hopes and dreams of all men and women, American or otherwise. Quite frequently, I reread this address and think the last segment worthwhile repeating here:

> In the long history of the world, only a few generations have been granted the role of defending freedom in its hour of maximum danger. I do not shrink from this responsibility, I welcome it — The energy, the faith, the devotion which we bring to this endeavor *will light our country and all who serve it . . . and the glow from that fire can truly light the world*. And so

my fellow Americans: *Ask not what your country can do for you . . . . Ask what you can do for your country?*

Within three months after this inauguration address, President Kennedy established the Peace Corps. Within two years the Peace Corp concept spread to twenty-three other countries. There was also a very *American* sense of leadership in the White House; a leadership that directed America towards investing in America. So was born the "investment tax credit." Less than six years after his death, on July 20, 1969, America fulfilled his promise to the nation and the world and America landed the first man on the moon.

More important, during this short Era there was a sense of a well defined *national priority*; a *national priority* directed at strengthening America's social and economic foundations; a *national priority* that reiterated the *opportunity* and *hope* for all Americans to achieve the past and future "promise" of America — the very essence of the American Dream.

Perhaps it was the eradication of so much **promise** in a single moment that set the stage for what America has become today. On November 22, 1963, the hope of not just America, but the world seemed to turn upside down. Media coverage from all over the world attests to this global phenomenon. A black woman in a remote part of Africa, cried uncontrollably after hearing of his death as she pointed to his picture prominently hung inside her hut. This sense of well-being was gone and it seems there has been no one to come forward since to restore what was lost in 1963.

Often since that day, I've wondered if November 22, 1963 might ultimately be viewed by historians as not just the day an American President was assassinated, but whether it was the day America's hopes and dreams were also fatally wounded and that the great, almost 200-year experiment with "democracy" might finally end. I have also more recently wondered if enough Americans of today will have the courage and fortitude to directly enter the political arena to restore what has been taken from us and change the fate which we seem almost inextricably destined to meet? I would not have written this book if I had not concluded the answer to this question would be resounding **YES!**

The two most important questions that squarely face us today are: First, can we put the American experiment in "democracy" back on a track designed for the Twenty-First Century? Second, can we pull America out of its present nose dive into Third-World economic status and restore it as the greatest industrial nation and democracy in the world?

As I have indicated in Chapter Nineteen, the "economics" are neither tricky nor difficult, but the *political* and *social* foundations upon which the "economic solutions" rely must be able to support the breadth and weight of its undertaking. **You, as an American, must participate.** It is *your future* and it should be *your decision* as to *what that future will be*. This can only be accomplished if your elected representatives are re-invented to implement what you demand, rather than these representatives deciding what you want or need, and then tying it up in gridlock. No longer should it be their decision whether you will have Medicare, a National Health Insurance Plan, or a $300 billion defense budget. In the Twenty-First Century, let these representatives *implement* the solutions you, as part of the majority of Americans, have demanded these elected representatives to enact. If these representatives can not, or will not, implement your demands, you will learn how to effectively deal with them later in this Chapter. It is therefore imperative that the following political and social suggestions be carefully reviewed by you, so that you can determine, finally, the kind of America you want to live in, be a part of, and work to change.

So How Do The Lower 260 Million Disenfranchised Americans Affect a Political Solution To America's Problems?

Some of America's middle-class direct political power will be accomplished through direct majority vote, and some by amendment to our Constitution so that it meets the needs of the upcoming Twenty-First Century. But above all, it will be done by the "majority will" of the people. A majority of the people, and not those "few" who have essentially taken control of our government in the past forty-five years. If American democracy has any "real substance" left whatsoever, this "putting-of-America-into-the-present" to achieve a "true" government "by the people, of the people, and for the people" will be both a peaceful and efficient transition, removing it once and hopefully forever from the *grips* of America's and the *world's new global aristocracy."*

1. Barriers To Overcome - American Citizen Apathy

Most Americas would rather hear about the escapades of Fergy, Diana, Donald Trump or Michael Jackson, than what's going on daily in the U.S. Congress or the decisions of the Clinton Administration that will ultimately deprive them of what little is left of their diminished standards-of-living.

The reasons for this are many, and complex. Keep in mind the complexities of America's financial institutions, the Two Party System, the Separation of Powers Doctrine, the "special interest groups," the concept of "representative government," the muddling effect of the "media," and all of the other complex hurdles discussed in previous chapters of this book. Keep in mind the "machine" and all its "parts" that are continuously interacting as described in Chapter Two. With all of these factors in mind, we are now ready for some of the more obvious "reasons" that divert America's *middle-class'* focus from the theft of their freedom and standard-of-living.

First, it's very difficult to focus on the thoughts, ideas, and other less noteworthy shenanigans of 535 members of the U.S. Congress who have made the system of government so complex over the past two hundred years. It is doubtful that more than 5% of the people have more than an *inkling* of what's really going on. Ask yourselves: "How can any citizen be expected to work a 60-hour work-week and have any time left to sort out even the "appropriations system" employed by the U.S. Congress?"

Second, compound the above with this same citizen's attempt to stay ahead of the mortgage payment; the car payment; the kids; the non-stop pumping of negativity, bad news, and immorality into his or her home every minute of every day, via T.V., cable, and countless and faceless radio stations. Add to this the bombardment of stress that is inherent in an unfettered *uniquely and politically evolved American capitalistic system* in search of making this same working-class citizen the most efficient profit-machine (defined, in reality, as *more and more Americans, working longer and longer hours,* for *less and less pay,* and *less and less employee benefits*), and what kind of answer should you expect? American workers have zero-time to understand American government, much less participate in any aspect of its processes. This is not for lack of interest, but simply for lack of time, stress overload, and, unfortunately, lack of interest in any of the individuals representing them in Washington, D.C., or at their state capitol.

This full-court press has caused America to become a time-bomb! Every where you go outside of the Washington, D.C. area, middle-class Americans are actually becoming angry and meeting in sub-groups to best decide how to change the thing they call The System! Notwithstanding the grumblings of a few million middle-class Americans, if a new American Political and Economic Order doesn't evolve; if the forgotten *promises* of the past are not fulfilled, the present government and economic system will inevitably itself financially self-destruct. The serious ticking of the time-bomb, begun during the *spending sprees* of Ronald Reagan and George Bush, which caused the build-up of America's $5 trillion National Debt, etc., is now waiting to explode under Bill Clinton; a fact that a few Americans, including you, are now acutely aware of and very much fear in fear of.

Not that many of our recently awakened Americans knows what's actually going on in our hallowed halls of government. It's the "sense" that one's job is no longer secure; that there are fewer and fewer quality jobs to be found. It is a growing conviction that there are some insidious forces, both in and out of government, that would permit the $500-billion "looting" of America's S&Ls, the $1-trillion "looting" of America's Industrial Infrastructure, the $100-billion "looting" of America's middle-class' pension funds while their government, through either self-imposed-impotence or even its actual aiding-and-abetting of these crimes, condoned this sixteen year conversion of America's middle-class to Third-World Nation status.

When the media and the *top-two-percenters* bring down the heat on you for seeking change, how are you going to respond? How are you going to deal with all of the "spin-doctoring," the "pseudo-intellectualism," the "labeling," and the "name-calling" that will spew from the "few" who profit from laissez-faire Capitalism, free-trade, the sale of drugs, pornography, and other trash vis-à-vis America's Cable vision and major TV networks, amongst other derelictions from which they profit?

Rest assured, those Americans seeking any kind of change suggested in this book will be branded by the Republicans as either a socialist, liberal, or even worse, a Communist. Democrats will brand you a militia member, a fascist, a right-wing-conservative, or even worse, a Neo-Nazi. Both parties will label you Protectionist, War-hawk, and Un-American. You might even be subject to some FBI scrutiny or ATF investigation, if you aren't targeted immediately as the example to be set for all the other so-called losers in the game of American Capitalism.

You'll hear the usual "spin:" What we have today is the *natural and inevitable result of American Capitalism* (i.e. the natural and welcome outcome of "the efficient allocation of resources"). Now I ask each and everyone of you reading this book: Was the "entrepreneurial allocation" of almost $23.8-billion by the late Sam Walton to his children and their children's children a part of this efficient allocation of America's resources?   Could the allocation of $1 billion or more to each newly created one-hundred American billionaires also be a further example of this sort of "efficient allocation of America's resources" our elected officials and economists have been *spin-doctoring* out over the past forty-five years?

I think the evidence is persuasive: One only needs to look at the crisis in the U.S. primary education system; the decay of the American Industrial Infrastructure; the collapse of America's Transportation Infrastructure; the raging inferno of America's drug-and- violent-crime scourge; and the lost hopes and dreams of not just a generation, but of a whole nation. This obviously doesn't speak well for the present system of *resource allocation* we've witnessed since the beginning of the Reagan Presidency. How is it, we can put a man on the moon, finance two World Wars, and support the entire U.S. Congress and Senate for over 200 years and never have had a National Debt that exceeded $980 billion until the election of Ronald Reagan as President? One can only imagine if he had been of the liberal persuasion, rather than a fiscal conservative!

If some or all of the above facts and historical hypocrisies don't wake you up from your deep apathetic sleep, you probably will be able to sleep yourself smoothly into what will certainly be yours and America's Third World standard-of-living.

2. Barriers To Overcome - Human Nature

You cannot legislate honesty, but you can legislate adequate punishment for dishonesty and malfeasance of office. And just as we have the "indifference curve" in economic theory, so it exists in justice. It is, and always will be, up to each individual to decide whether he or she wishes to risk the punishment for breaking the law. For example, if the punishment for murder was 30 days in jail, many of our citizens, some of them your own neighbors, would choose this crime to resolve many of their differences, perhaps even with you as some of them had.

It logically follows, that if the punishment for looting $5 trillion from the American Industrial Infrastructure, and looting $500 billion from America's S&Ls is a mere four-year vacation at "Club Fed" (with three years off for good behavior and an improved tennis game), there will be many more Michael Milkens, Ivan Boeskys, and Dennis Levines sprouting in America, rather than citizens who want to work on an honest and level playing field. When the very money stolen by the white-collar criminals can connect them directly to the most powerful forces in the judicial system, you should never expect to see "just" nor "adequate" punishment in America for anyone convicted of a major white-collar crime.

I ask you this: How many Milkens, Boeskys, or Levines (none of whom served one day in the military service of their country) would "loot" America in the future, if they knew the punishment would be forty years' hard labor in leg-irons, working by day to rebuild America's "inner cities, and spending each night resting in Rahway Prison amongst the general prison population?" As I put these words to paper, I not only hear the ACLU, but also America's entire legal profession screaming: "Cruel and unusual punishment! — "Violation of their Constitutional Rights, etc." If you think America's already failing criminal justice is *tangled up in its underwear*, wait till they start to test the constitutionality of any criminal law that is legislated to severely punish the Milkens, Boeskys, or Levines, or their own kind. They'll tie up present court calendars for another fifty years! They will avoid even the most remote chance of their or their future fellow clones ever being punished or deterred from the white-collar crimes that secretly destroy the very threads of American morality.

Now that you have reached this point in the book, if you're still of the mind-set that these lootings of America's wealth are just the "American Way," and that this is the way you want it to remain, I suggest you close this book and enjoy whatever may be left of America. But if you're one of those Americans who is not happy with what America has become, read on, so that you might see how to further change both American government and American Capitalism to benefit all Americans who are willing to work for an honest day's wages.

C. Barriers To Overcome -
The Obstacles Of Representative Government

The obstacles of "representative government" to which I refer, and which must be overcome, are the two primary principles or concepts underlying the foundation of "representative government" itself. The first principal of representative government" relies on the concept which is the *inability* of the citizen to be in constant and continual *communication* with his or her central government so that he may participate directly in its operations and decision-making processes.

The second principal of underlying "representative government" is the belief that the ordinary citizen (the masses to be governed) are just down-and-out *"stupid*," and therefore, are best served by superior elected representatives to make the current moral, political, social, and economic choices for these citizen *dopes*. You, the reader, can readily trace these same concepts back for yourselves to the Mycenaean period (circa.1200-

1400 B.C.). What should be most important to you, the reader, is that these "concepts" were conceived long before the inventions of the telegraph, the telephone, the television, the computer, and the Internet with its World Wide Web. Hopefully these "advances" were not contemplated or foreseen by our "founding fathers" back in the late 1700s. The only means of communication, even up until the late 1700s, between the *ordinary citizen* and his or her *central government,* was by horseback when anywhere from a week to several months were required to complete a single communication between two parties.

The second underlying principle can be traced back to the philosophers of ancient Greece who, long before our "founding fathers" believed that *we*, the common folk, the *ordinary citizen*, as a whole, were incapable of making broad-based moral social, economic, and political decisions. Yet, contrary to this possibly well-founded predicate conclusion, we *are* and have been intelligent enough to elect someone else to make these major decisions for us! Somehow the contradiction seems a little *oxymoronic*.

This second underlying principle is overtly contradicted by the actions of the U.S. Congress over the past 16 years. One need only observe the social, moral, economic, and financial bankruptcy of America in 1996 to conclude that "representative government" is certainly not capable of making these broad-based social, economic, and political decisions for America, even with all of the safeguards that were built into American government by the original U.S. Constitution, along with its first ten amendments (commonly called the "Bill of Rights") that were added to improve and expand those safeguards and our individual freedoms and liberty.

If you demand direct participation in the decision making process of your Federal, State, and Local Government, be prepared for the many critics who will argue that you as Americans, are not only *stupid,* but are truly not interested in details of the Federal Budget, or the complexity of the Internal Revenue Code, or the details concerning the bickering that goes on behind the closed doors of both the U.S. House of Representatives and the U.S. Senate, any more than you are concerned about what goes on behind the closed doors of your State Legislature or Town Hall. For this reason, the argument goes, they rely on the "checks and balances" of the President's veto power, etc., to assure that government (your representatives) remains in both political and financial control of "itself." To this you should respond: These "checks and balances" in aggregate have failed miserably. Just look at America's $5-Trillion National Debt, the number of drug addicts in the U.S., and all of the other horrifying facts set forth in Chapter One of this book. In 1996, all major polls found that less than 27% of all Americans have any trust in "government" at all. This trust is not merely to do the "right thing," but questions the singular and collective honesty and integrity of our elected officials. If crimes of both omission and commission were considered, probably none of these elected officials would have been given a modicum of credence regarding integrity or honesty by the American people.

If all else fails in your endeavor to accomplish the changes which you believe will make a better America for you and your fellow citizens, then agree with your elected representative and tell her or him that you are **not** interested in the finite details of every bill and amendment that consumes all of his or her time. Tell him or her that you are **only** interested in the **broad issues**, and that it is these **broad issues** that you want to have a "say" in. A "say" that can only be accomplished through true majority rule by use of both national and state referendums or plebiscites. For example, states which do not have constitutional protection for individual rights regarding abortion might want to vote on whether or not they should permit legalized abortions. What better place is there than a federal referendum to determine the broad allocation of federal expenditures on such things as foreign aid, the drug war, education, defense, and the expenditures necessary to rebuild our nation's cities and infrastructure?

If the nation is ever to see a fair and equitable system of taxation, where better to have it decided than in a "national referendum" by the people, free of all "special interest groups" which now include the very "representatives" who have and will continue to falsely represent you in your own federal and state government!

In the election years of 1992, 1994, and 1996, we saw a mad exodus from both the U.S. Senate and House of Representatives. Senators and Congressmen leaving "public service." Many because of scandal, but others because of what they called grid-lock (i.e. there's nothing left to loot or they were afraid to continue doing it before their C-Span audience), and others saying their sacrifice was just too great for the mere $136,000 a year they were earning! With good high-paying jobs as scarce as they are, even Boobus Americanus has to ask: Does this mass departure portend something more ominous than just the poor pay, the gridlock, or the fact that there maybe nothing left to loot?

If you still believe you are a citizen in a true democracy of the people, for the people, and by the people, why not call your U.S. Senators and Congressman? Test out this proposition on him or her! Ask them directly if they would surrender some of their "power" (granted to them, supposedly by you) by giving birth to either a state or national referendum format for direct majority vote on certain issues as suggested above. Ask them directly if they believe if you are "smart enough" or "experienced enough" to decide the major issues as they effect your future destiny. Don't forget to ask them when you will hear them speak-out on these issues and support legislation or Constitutional amendments to assist you, and all of us in taking-back our government. Isn't this the real "litmus test" of whether or not you are a member of Abraham Lincoln's "democracy," as opposed to the lesser form of government that exists today?

The Political Solutions

A. Downsizing Government

American Industry has gone through enormous downsizing in the past twenty-years, even though America's population has increased by over 30 million citizens during this same period.

What has not been proportionately "downsized," in any respect, are the elected representatives of the federal, state, and local governments.

To correct this problem of "oversized" government, one only has to answer the following questions:

1. Does it take the wisdom and counsel of one-hundred U.S. Senators to decide any issue critical to this nation? Could fifty U.S. Senators (one from each state) do the same job, and for that matter, for half the price?

2. Is there anything magic in having one member of the House of Representatives for each five-hundred-thousand people? Why not one representative for each 1.5 million persons, thus reducing the number and cost of this body by two-thirds. Remember, it is estimated that 90% of Americans don't even know the name of their district's congressional representative.

3. If we are all truly Americans, do we need a U.S. Senate and a House of Representatives packed full of "special interest group" representatives for each ethnic and racial group in this nation? This in itself is divisive.

4. As an American citizen who is subject to the nation's Social Security Retirement Program and Medicare, can you see any reason why all of our elected officials and all other government employees should have different special government retirement programs, and government-paid health insurance plans? Wouldn't it be more beneficial and fair for them to be subject to the same medical and retirement benefits you and I are entitled, e.g. Social Security and Medicare? Perhaps this would eliminate the stuffing of IOUs into the Social Security Trust Funds.

B. National & State Referendums (Plebiscites)

A System of National Referendums and State Referendums, as described previously, for important national and state issues: i.e. Abortion, National Health Insurance, National AIDS Testing, Rebuilding of America's Industrial Infrastructure, etc. *must* be implemented. From the state of America today, there is no doubt that the people might do as well, if not better than the Congress in deciding these very important national and state issues. Think about the benefit of bringing the people back into the political process. What better opportunity for Abraham Lincoln's democracy which he so eloquently described as a government "*of the people, by the people, and for the people*" to really work.

So you ask: "How could this ever be accomplished technically?" Recently AT&T and one of the major television news shows tied a major portion of the United States into a voting referendum on issues pertinent to all American citizens. This exercise demonstrated that the technology for national referendums using America's telephone communication systems has arrived. Every day in the U.S. House of Representatives and the U.S. Senate, electronic votes are cast on all aspects of legislation. This electronic referendum at the federal and state levels could be the most potent tool available to reduce the ill effects (i.e. control by special interest groups, bundling issues, etc.) of our present form of "representative government."

C. Recall: The Absolute Right to Fire Your Elected Representatives

Perhaps there is nothing more frightening to a politician than to have his elected term (i.e. power, salary, graft, and other perks) cut short, especially for incompetence, fraud, malfeasance, or inertia in office. There can also be no greater power retained by the people with respect to his or her elected representative than the right to recall these officials and make them stand again for re-election for any of the aforementioned reasons, or if they simply no longer have the confidence of their constituents. Here again, the petition process would work quite efficiently. A petition for recall signed by 20% of an elected official's constituents via the U.S. Super Communications Highway should automatically require that the elected official have to stand for re-election within thirty days after the petition has been certified by the local voting board of elections which certifies that 20% of the electorate electronically participated in the petition.

As part of its effort to gain a majority in both the U.S. Senate and U.S. House of Representatives, the Republican Party has advocated "term limitations." Even prior to 1994, I articulated that if the U.S. Senate and U.S. House of Representatives were controlled by the Republicans, there would be a quick end to all talk of term limitations. Guess what happened? That's right, the talk about term limitations has been put on the back burner. Guesswork aside, the notion of term limitations does deprive citizens of the very freedom provided by the voting process. The real solution is the "recall" procedure set forth above, simply because it allows the electorate to make the determination as frequently as they deem necessary to either re-elect or terminate their elected representative's term of office, as opposed to having to wait until the term automatically ends at the end of his or her two, four, or six years, regardless of how well or how poorly that representative has performed.

D. Elimination Of All Congressional And Legislature "Seniority Rules"

To understand how important it is to eliminate the seniority rules in both the U.S. Senate and House of Representatives with respect to committee assignments and chairmanship appointments, one need only look to the record of Senator Robert Byrd (D-W.V.), Chairman of the House Appropriations Committee to see how the wisdom and experience engendered in this process of seniority is abused. Senator Byrd, even above the objection of many other Senators, has channeled almost one-billion-dollars in special "pork-barrel" projects into his home state of West Virginia during his former tenure as the powerful Chairman of the House of Appropriations Committee. **Solution:** Majority vote within each chamber should determine committee assignments and chairmanships, with chairmen being limited in their authority to govern only the order and conduct of committee meetings. Committee chairmen should be limited to tenures based on annual re-election as set forth above.

E. Eliminating The Electoral College

The most obvious anachronism in the American political system is the "Electoral College," which delays the inauguration of the new President and which should have been eliminated probably as early as 1960 and replaced by a direct vote of the people. In an age of instantaneous communication, mass media, and jet transportation, it is also imperative that the transition period especially as it effects the U.S. Presidency and the Congress be shortened. Lame ducks generally don't serve the country well. Although it is argued that the period from election day in November to the inauguration of the new President on January 20th of the following year offers stability to government, it more importantly offers the incumbent the opportunity to violate the majority-will of the people during this "lame duck" period, especially since the "majority" are those people who may have just voted this elected official out of office. This occurs every four years for almost an additional two-and-a-half months in the highest elected office of this nation. It is also during this shortened "lame duck" period that all legislative activity and life-tenure appointments by the incumbents should be curtailed and be subject to ratification by the new President and Congress.

Besides assuring that the "people" will be properly represented by their newly elected representatives, a major benefit that could be derived from having the newly elected President and other newly elected representatives take office by December 1st of the year he or they are elected would be requiring that the presidential candidates make known, three months prior to election day, their cabinet choices and other appointments. These choices effect each and every citizen in this nation but, under our present system, remain very secretive until just prior to, or after the election process has been completed. Many a candidate will think twice about appointing obvious political hacks from his or her Party who are not qualified for those patronage appointments; thus giving more credence to "merit," than to past-political-favors being repaid.

F. Overhauling America's System Of Taxation

A "junking" of both the inherently unfair mind-crippling federal, state, and local tax codes (including taxes on residential real estate) is recommended; to be replaced by one simplified progressive tax, with distribution of tax revenues vis-à-vis a revenue sharing basis similar to the way New York State and New York City simplified their systems. No more sales taxes, no more loopholes, no chicanery, and no incentives to keep both the lawyers and CPAs, as well as, the massive federal and tax bureaucracies confused and in tax fraud conspiracy. This would apply to corporations and individuals alike. There would be no distinction among interest income, W-2 earnings, capital-gains, or dividends. There would be no deductions, no credits, and no exemptions. What a joy for the citizens and businesses of this country to know that they'll never have to spend weeks of wasted energy plotting and conspiring to defraud the government while simultaneously being enslaved to the charlatans of the legal and accounting professions.

What would I suggest to replace the myriad of taxes that now exist in this country? A Comprehensive Value Added Tax (See Definition section-Chapter Nineteen), and a simplified income tax. What is supposedly the toughest job in the world (the U.S. Presidency) only pays $200,000 a year. Let's not forget the scandalous salaries, bonuses, etc. paid to our nation's CEOs and their cohorts. An income tax on their greed might very well get some of them out of the "looting" business and back to work. In addition to a comprehensive value added tax, I also propose an income tax that would encourage honest endeavors but thwart the accumulation of enormous fortunes similar to those being created today and in the 1980s. I suggest a progressive income tax beginning with a "zero" tax on the first $100,000 of each individual's income, 25% tax on the second $100,000 of each individual's income, 50% tax on the third and <u>fourth</u> $100,000 of each individual's income, and 75% tax on all income above $400,000. Can there be any question with America back working and paying a fair tax, the National Debt, the S&L Bailout cost, the cost of National Health Insurance, as well as, all of the entitlement programs will finally get paid on a current basis? A working America equals an astronomically large tax base. Lower tax rates for all but the "top-two-percenters" lessens the need for the major welfare spending needs we have ourselves enabled by not creating sufficient jobs for all members of our society.

Changes in the entire system of U.S. federal, state, and local taxation will create an environment of simple accountability, fairness, and a reduction of the bureaucracy and its attendant hostility that now creates in America a system that is viewed as being unfair and wasteful by the vast majority of Americans.

G. Strengthening Securities Laws & Other Government Protections

Let's put some law enforcement teeth into the SEC for the benefit of the nation. Let's set some legal due diligence standards (honesty, ethics, etc.), along with implementation of some hefty fraud criminal liability statutes for both lawyers and accountants, as well as, investment bankers and commercial bankers. Trust me, you don't need the death penalty for this cowardly lot. Mandatory five-year increments of hard labor for each offense, and no more "Club Feds" will do the job. Get rid of the legal robbery and you'll naturally get rid of one of its offspring: Violent crime that results from the frustration of no opportunity.

In addition to tougher new criminal laws, both the legal and CPA professions should be regulated by the federal government. All attorneys and CPAs should be required to be licensed and disciplined by the federal government. Law firms should also be limited in size to no more than five partners and ten associates. CPA firms should have their audit fees set by the federal government since all public companies are required by the federal government to have annual audits performed by CPAs.

With the implementation of National Health Insurance Program in the U.S., there will be no need for the individual states to regulate the medical or dental professions since all physicians, dentists, and other professionally licensed health care professionals will be licensed and regulated pursuant to federal standards with all disciplinary actions and proceedings also under the purview of the federal government.

Now many of you are saying: "For someone who has suggested reducing government by a full 20%, this jerk is either a hypocrite or has lost his mind! Perhaps he has no concept of how much government will be necessary to regulate all of the aforementioned professions!"

To this I respond, look at the <u>inefficiencies</u> of all of the state regulators now regulating these professions. One way or the other, there can be no question that many <u>efficiencies</u> will be realized by making all of the regulatory systems uniform. A national system will also prevent the abuses that these professions have enjoyed in the past, i.e., the ability to lose themselves in the bureaucracy of a second state after committing malpractice in a first state.

With respect to all of America's professions, I suggest there be local civilian review boards (similar to those that review local police conduct) to act as arbiters in disputes that arise between the professional and local citizens and as a *check and balance* on possible future abuses that might arise in a federally regulated system. Currently there are secretive state disciplinary boards and professional association boards that discipline these groups.

H. Corporate Ownership Law

It is time that America made corporate management responsible to the owners or shareholders of their corporations, as opposed to management dictating their agendas to the owners of corporate America. I recommend such changes in the law that would facilitate stockholders: (1) being allowed unfettered access to all *corporate records* and the *books-of-account*, (2) having absolute approval rights for all increases in management salaries; and (3) having greater access to *shareholder records* to facilitate more efficient communication amongst the other owners of their corporation. Lastly, I would recommend that laws be strengthened to protect the "ownership rights" of shareholders, where they would have a choice of either retaining their stock in public companies as an "equal but protected minority," or would be guaranteed a buyout-price multiple of at least two times the fair-market value of their stock if corporate management chooses to arbitrarily relieve them of their shares in the corporation.

I. Reforming the American Judiciary System and Law Enforcement

Most Americans are unaware of how federal judges and some state judges are selected. As previously stated, federal judges are appointed, and the appointment process involves a process called "merit selection." I know of not one bar association in America today that doesn't endorse this "merit selection" process and for this reason alone, Americans should find the process "suspect." It almost seems a contradiction in terms to select an individual based on merit, who is selected based on his or her membership activity in a bar association, "political party affiliation," or political ideology.

I am not suggesting that judges become part of the Two Party System in terms of election process that exists already in some states today. Rather, I am suggesting that judges stand for election on a nonpartisan basis offering their credentials to the public at large, and that certain "free debate hours" be set aside on the various local cable television networks to facilitate each prospective judge giving an equal-time presentation as to why he or she believes he or she is fit to serve in his or her community, either in the local, state, or federal court. Under this nonpartisan election process there would no longer be the need for "life-tenure" for "judges" nonsense offered to allegedly assure their "political independence" from the party who appointed them.

This same process should be used to determine who will be the U.S. Attorney in each of the Federal Judicial Districts across the United States. Thus it is recommended each U.S. Attorney and judge be elected for four-year terms, and also be subject to the same recall procedure as set forth above in Section C.

Lastly, on a national basis, it is also important that people have a say in who is to serve as their Attorney General (presently a cabinet position, that deserves greater independence from the Executive branch), Director of IRS, and Commissioners of the SEC and CFTC, as well as the FBI, the FAA, FDA, FTC, FAA, and any other federal agency that has any sort of prosecution, law enforcement power or responsibility, or regulatory power. These political officials should be elected for four-year terms concurrent with that of the President, and should be subject to the recall procedure set forth above.

Everything that has been said regarding the people taking back control over law enforcement agencies at the federal level should also apply to the various state government counter-parts, if such organizational structures or procedures are not in place already.

J. Revamping the U.S. Supreme Court-Selection of Justices

As stated previously in this book, I would never suggest that the Supreme Court of the United States be denied its power of "judicial review." On the other hand, there are "issues" that should be solely within the province of the people; such as, abortion, National Health Insurance, the right to have referendums, recalls, and government downsizing amongst other issues. These should be beyond the purview of "judicial review." This differentiation should also be decided in the referendum or plebiscite process discussed previously.

The selection of Supreme Court Judges should also be changed to reflect a more nonpartisan, and a less personal selection process. Many of you may be unaware that when you file a law suit in your Federal District Court the judge who will sit on your case is selected randomly amongst those judges whose calendars are not completely filled. To effect a nonpartisan selection process of U.S. Supreme Court Justices, a similar random selection process should be implemented. Each state could submit three nominees from their highest state or federal appellate courts. These jurists could be selected from this pool of state judges or justices, with the approval of their Governor and two U.S. Senators. These three state nominees' names, along with the other states' nominees would be placed in one of those large screened rolling drums which would then facilitate the random selection by one American citizen in a nationally televised drawing of three candidates. Once drawn, the candidates would then appear before the U.S. Senate, not for the ridiculous hearings we now have, but for a required vote to be held within 30 days after the nationally televised drawing and following each candidate's one-hour opportunity to express why he or she is the most worthy for appointment to America's highest Court.

The most appealing aspect of selecting U.S. Supreme Court Justices in this manner is that the American people would never again be subjected to anything similar to the Clarence Thomas/Anita Hill hearings, and the rather despicable display put forth by then Senators Arlen Spector, Orrin Hatch, and Alan Simpson. Again, there would be free T.V. presentations of one hour's duration by each person drawn and submitted for final selection by the U.S. Senate. The actual vote of the Senate would also be televised, so that American voters might see how their Senators decided who was best qualified to exercise this ultimate judicial power in the United States.

K. "Special Interest Groups"

Even if all of the recommendations for bringing American government into the Twenty-First Century are implemented (i.e. down-sizing, recall, referendum, elimination of seniority, etc.), the "special interest groups" will still be there so long as money is allowed to be the predominant "force" in the political process of the United States. The only way to eliminate the influence these groups have on our elected officials is to make it illegal for all candidates running for office or holding office to accept money directly or indirectly from these groups. If there were stiff criminal penalties, "special interest group" activities would dissipate so rapidly there would be a "housing-glut" (which would probably be welcomed by most) in the suburbs of Washington, D.C. Perhaps these now- unemployed lobbyists would be forced to move into the inner city of Washington D.C. and create a rebirth there with some of the money that might still remain from those who they represented previously.

L. Drug Wars

I am a proponent of taking the "profit motive" out of the illegal drug business in the United States. I believe the only way this can be achieved is by the carefully controlled legalization of drugs, and the implementation of the severest of capital punishment we know of for those who choose to violate the drug laws that would be necessary to implement a controlled legalized drug program. Just as you have the chronic alcoholic and the chronic gambler in American society, you also have the chronic drug addict. We must once and for all accept that American society does include the chronic drug addict. Approximately 3 million (1.2%) of all Americans are estimated to be permanently drug addicted. If we are ever able to accept the fact that these 3 million members of our society have and will continue to choose a drug lifestyle over other healthier lifestyles, it should be obvious that the legalization of drugs in an extremely controlled environment is the only solution to this problem. If these 3 million permanently addicted drug addicts are properly controlled, I believe they can be productive members of society, given the chance.

Obviously, as both a lawyer and CPA, I have thought-out how to "control" the legalization of drugs in the United States. I do not see it as the insurmountable problem that our present politicians see it to be. Certain "others" would have us see it as insurmountable so that they might continue the make-believe-drug-war and make another $1.5 trillion in profits over the next thirty years as America continues it whirlpool-pace into criminal anarchy. The last 30 years of this "nonsense" should have been enough for all of us. Here again, the choice can be ours; i.e., referendum. If it be the will of the majority, there can be an end to the drug-crime-scourge that has been plaguing this nation for almost thirty years.

M. Education

American public schools have become a "live extension" of T.V. mid-day and evening soap-operas. I refer here to the romantic and sexual aspects of these shows, and their evening violence. If left unchanged, there is no solution short of putting a police officer in every classroom, if you want to restore order to this environment. This will neither improve the quality of the first twelve years of education for our children, nor will it improve their present spans-of-attention.

The simplest and only solution to the present dilemma in education is to separate the sexes (the boys and girls) in grades K through twelve, the period when they are most erratic due to hormonal changes.

In addition, our education system should become focused earlier with regard to directing our students into the careers that they desire and are capable of performing. Such capabilities can be determined through a system of national testing of ability, ambition, desire, as well as, through personal evaluation.

With great trepidation, I also put forth the notion that entrance into the different "trades," "professions," be more controlled and closely geared to the needs of society.

For example, if the nation projects it will need 200,000 additional physicians in the year 2010, 200,000 physician slots should be created and be available by 2005. All elementary school children should be made aware of the number of doctors that will be required so that they might begin their selection process this early. They can get a first taste of what the profession entails and have the opportunity to compete for and achieve this objective, or to opt out to another "trade" or "profession" more suitable to their needs, ambitions, abilities and personalities, and the needs of the society.

This type of early "election" and "selection" process should exist for all of the occupations America needs to prosper and survive — Auto mechanics, CPAs, nurses, teachers, construction workers, etc. If we are ever to become and remain competitive in this world, it will begin in efficient and focused elementary and high school systems. For those who wish to maintain the present status quo, I only ask: How do you square this against the results that have been attained in both American education and American competitiveness over the last thirty years?

Germane to the subject of education is the issue of parental "child support" which must be enforced federally through the Internal Revenue Service (IRS). Trust me, the only reason it hasn't been aggressively enforced through the IRS is because our alleged "family-value-oriented" politicians are afraid to alienate the large sectors of voters who are now not paying their "child support" obligations. Fortunately, since 1994, some strides have been made in this area by having those parents who do not pay child support lose their drivers licenses and their freedom should they be stopped by a police officer for any routine matter.

N. Pornography

It is estimated that the pornography business produces between $50 billion and $60 billion a year. With this much incentive, it will be difficult, at best, to have any of our elected "representatives" do anything to loosen the grip this "special interest group" has on America. Society will always have its "perverts." However, sex itself is so wonderful, I'm personally convinced it would be a sin against God to ban it. As with any other "pleasure commodity," in order to maintain its superior value (as in "family value"), sex requires regulation by society, as reviewed in Chapter Seventeen.

Since it is our mothers we trust most as Americans, I recommend that we again turn to this group to determine and lead us back to public morality (i.e. T.V., pictorial media, topless-this, bottomless-that, "thong" controversies, etc.). Since we have trusted our mothers in all instances to have primary responsibility for raising us, certainly we can trust them to determine what is best for the community in terms of morality. See

Chapter Seventeen, American Morality — Family, Drugs & Pornography for additional information on this suggested solution.

O. Financial Institutions

On the whole there is sufficient regulation, if properly employed, that now exists in both federal and state law to regulate America's Financial Institutions. The *problem* here is not legislating more regulation, but enforcing existing regulations and downsizing certain of America's financial or quasi-financial institutions.

The quasi-financial institutions to which I refer that require downsizing are those that are, or have become nothing more than high-priced gambling casinos. If you reread Chapters Four and Ten, especially the Definitions and Glossary Sections you will know precisely to which of these quasi-financial institutions I refer. As a matter of law these institutions should serve the purpose for which they were initially created for. They can be a genuine hedge against price fluctuations coincidental to the various commodities industries, as opposed to gambling mechanisms geared to merely weather conditions that effect imaginary crops, etc. I do not recommend their complete elimination, but I do recommend a substantial contraction in their activities and breadth of application, so that America's financial resources can again be channeled into more productive pursuits such as initial investment in American property, plant, & equipment and creating modern high-tech facilities that will again make the American worker the premier worker in the world in relation to his and her productivity.

P. Social Security

Once America has a National Health Insurance Program in place, and the abuses associated with Medicare and Medicaid are eliminated, these "entitlement programs" will be substantially reduced in cost, perhaps by almost $200-Billion.

The real dilemma facing America is the burden that Social Security places on future generations that will probably not benefit from it at all unless the American economy can be rebuilt as described in Chapter Nineteen. If America does adopt these economic solutions there will still have to be some modifications in the Social Security program.

First, the age limit for receiving benefits will have to be further increased to coincide with the increase in life expectancy in America, similar to the "indexing" now done with the federal income tax system to ward-off "bracket-creep" due to inflation. This also requires that the nation provide adequate employment for all those able-bodied persons who would have normally retired at age 65 and who were, as part of their future retirement program, relying on Social Security. Part-time 25- and

30-hour, 3 or 4 day, work-weeks would be a welcome challenge to many of our now idle elderly Americans. It just takes a little creativity, planning, and commitment by industry, government, and the American people.

Secondly, Social Security should not be a dividend check for many of our wealthiest citizens. I therefore recommend that Social Security retirement benefits be eliminated for all single citizens who earn over $50,000 a year from all sources, and for couples whose combined income from all sources is over $100,000 per year. Medicare benefits will not only not be reduced but these citizens will be covered, as will we all, by the National Health Insurance Program recommended previously.

Q. Government Regulation

The worst two words besides the "R" (Recession) and "D" (Depression) words to all Republicans, are the two words "government regulation." All of the failures during the Bush Administration were blamed on "government regulation." How many of you today, since the ValuJet Everglades plane crash June 12, 1996 would remove all "government regulation" over the airline industry? It's not "government regulation" but the inconsistent enforcement of these regulations and the payoffs made by those being regulated that is the problem. It is not difficult to find 50% of all former federal regulators in extremely well-paying jobs within the same industry that they regulated, after their tenure as a regulator has been completed. Now folks, this is just a payoff for a job *not* well done while working in that person's past regulatory position. Similarly, all American businessmen and America's corporations blame all of their failures on too much "government regulation." After all of this brainwashing by the Administration, even you the reader have wanted to toss away this book, as I have implied the need for certain "government regulation."

But before you condemn me as either being a "Socialist," "Communist," "Whistle blower," or just a "Liberal," let me share with you a quote from the great capitalistic economist Lord John Maynard Keynes, from his treatise, End of Laissez-Faire (1926):

> I think that Capitalism, wisely managed, can probably be made more efficient for attaining economic ends than any alternative system yet in sight, but in itself it is many ways extremely objectionable.

"Wisely Managed," are the key words used by Lord Keynes. Synonymous with "wisely governmentally regulated." Now when you hear the Republicans bashing "government regulations" even now, not just during the "glory days" of former Vice-President Dan Quayle, I admonish you not to forget how well deregulation of America's Airline Industry has worked (remember June 12, 1996), or how much more efficiency or profitability was recognized by America's S&Ls as they were deregulated in 1982. Has any of Reagan's or Bush's "deregulation" improved your lives or the lives of your family and friends? Has it really made America more competitive?

- AUTHOR'S REVERSE "SPIN" GLOSSARY -

- "WHAT THEY SAY IT MEANS" & "WHAT IT REALLY MEANS" -

General Revenue Sharing:
What they say it means: The Federal Government provides to the 50 states, and more than 35,000 cities, towns, counties, townships, Indian Tribes, and Alaska native villages under the State and Local Fiscal Assistance Act of 1972, unrestricted funds which can be used for any purpose.

What it really means: Before answering this question, one must ask why the Federal Government would tax the "public" and then return the Moneys to the state and cities and other groups, when the state and cities already have the necessary taxing power to do the same thing? Once this first phase of the analysis is complete, one can only suspect three things. (1) The "top-two-percenters" wanted to limit the "taxing powers" of both state & local governments, thus Revenue Sharing as the federal controlling mechanism (i.e. the federal government says what will be spent by controlling the "purse strings" of what they'll match. Therefore that becomes the first reign-in on what the state & local tax men can justify taxing the "top-two-percenters." (2) Revenue sharing is just another means of channeling taxpayer moneys back to the local party "hack" so that he or she might properly take care of his or her local "special interest groups." (3) One also becomes suspect of the traditional "pork barreling" that usually occurs in the Congress. The term pork barreling essentially means making government appropriations based on favoritism usually for public works projects. These projects are often of questionable merit and always of "special stink" in that they bring economic benefit to one legislative district, and are allocated as a favor to the particular legislator who is in need of bringing some "pork" home to his or her constituents. The powerful Democratic Senator from the State of West Virginia who also happens to be Chairman of the Senate Appropriations Committee unashamedly allocated $435- million worth of "pork-barrel" projects to his home state of West Virginia in 1992. Who could argue that W. Virginia wasn't in desperate need of the "jobs" this humongous "piece-of-pork" created? Certainly not this commentator. The only argument from this quarter is that the same number of "jobs," if not thousands more, could have been created - not at U.S. Taxpayer expense - if Mr. Byrd and the rest of our federal government were more creative and took the leadership role in creating "real jobs" in the private industrial sector as suggested in Chapter Nineteen.

Proposition 13 [California Moonbeams]:

What they say it means: Proposition 13, recently upheld by the U.S. Supreme Court, refers to a law mandated by the people of California through the process of a state-wide referendum (Proposition 13) requiring the state & local governments of California to limit real estate taxes on residential properties to those taxes in effect at the time when the residence is purchased, allowing for increases of 1% per year after purchase, if justified by necessary spending requirements. Thus as years pass, and residences sold, new purchasers are burdened with much higher real estate taxes than those people who have remained in residence for longer periods of time. The U.S. Supreme Court held that the Constitutional rights of those persons having to pay the higher tax assessments as a result of having acquired the property later did not violate any constitutional protections or rights of those later purchasers.

What it really means: Proposition 13 means that anyone in the state of California can go in and purchase a home, knowing what his or her maximum tax bill will be five or even twenty-five years down the road. No longer is the California homeowner the sitting-duck for the local school board and any other taxing jurisdiction that has authority to tax his residential real property. Proposition 13 demonstrates the "power" of citizens making decisions through referendums as to their own destiny. As such, Proposition 13 may be viewed as one of the great victories for democratic *freedom.*

The Two Party System:

What they say it means: A concept in political science theory employed for the majority of America's political existence that allows a "majority" instead of a mere "plurality" to prevail, supposedly in order to protect the "majority will" of the people.

What it really means: As many Americans recognize, America's Two Party System somehow robs us as a nation of people of the very "majority rule of the people" we are taught that it is to protect. How does this Two Party System "rob" us of "true majority rule?" It is the "bundling," as defined previously. All you have to do to test this hypothesis is ask: Do I favor tax increases for a national health program? If you answer yes, you are part of a 68% majority of America. Next, ask if you are a strong supporter of the death penalty? If you answer yes, you are in a 80% majority of America. It doesn't matter that 70 million Republicans and 60 million Democrats support the death penalty, or that 75 million Democrats and 55 million Republicans support a National Health Insurance Program. Both issues are of no consequence to America's "representative government," even though the numbers representing a clear majority are on one side of both issues.

COMPOSITE DICTIONARY

Gerrymandering: the drawing of boundaries for legislative districts by all of our local political hacks (state legislators) of the smoke-free political wards in such a way as to help their party control not only the state legislature, but assure election of their party's candidate to the U.S. House of Representatives. This is another of our alleged democratic linchpins that supposedly protects democracy, but actually robs the nation and its people of its democratic right of true majority rule by empowering the two political parties to select those who will represent their constituents of "special interests," and who will also enjoy the largest slices of the American "pie."

Recall: A power reserved by the people whereby there is a predetermined method for removal of officials in power before the end of his or her term of office generally by a vote of the people to be taken upon the filing of a petition signed by a required number of qualified voters. A "recall" procedure adopted uniformly throughout the United States might very well prove to be the best alternative to "term limitations."

Referendum: A referendum is the process of referring to the people for approval a proposed new constitution, constitutional amendment, or a law passed by the legislature, where the constitution of a particular state reserves the right of the people to approve or reject the law. Not all state constitutions provide for referendums. The term referendum is also loosely used to describe citizen "initiatives" that find their way to the ballot.

The Separation of Powers Doctrine. (See first the Definition Section- Chapter Two, Three Branches of Government) Now even if one of the two parties has as much as a 65% majority of both the U.S. Senate and the U.S. House of Representatives, but the Administration, the President, is of the other party then any majority under 65.9% of these "representatives" <u>fails</u> because of the President's Veto power. Thus the power of one person, the President of the United States, is singularly able to override even this last of the abstract notions of "majority rule."

EPILOGUE

THE BOOK OF PSALMS
BOOK FIVE
PSALM 149

P*RAISE the Lord!*

Sing to the Lord a new song,
  And His praise in the assembly
    of saints.

Let Israel rejoice in their
    Maker.
Let the children of Zion be
    joyful in their King.
Let them praise His name with
    the dance.
Let them sing praises to Him
    With the timbrel and harp.
For the Lord takes pleasure
    In His people.
He will beautify the humble
    with salvation.

Let the saints be joyful in
    Glory;
Let them sing aloud on their
    beds.
Let the high praises of God be
    in their mouths.
And a two-edged sword in
    their hand,
To execute vengeance on the
    nations,
And punishments on the
    peoples;

To bind their kings with
    chains,
And their nobles with fetters of
    iron;
To execute on them the written
    judgment—
This honor have all His
    Saints.

Praise the Lord!

APPENDIX A

SELECTED RESPONSE LETTERS TO THE AUTHOR FROM SELECTED

U.S. SENATORS

U.S. REPRESENTATIVES

&

STATE GOVERNORS

(SEE FOLLOWING PAGES 413-431 OF THIS APPENDIX SECTION)

STATE OF FLORIDA

ℬffice of the ℬovernor

THE CAPITOL
TALLAHASSEE, FLORIDA 32399-0001

LAWTON CHILES
GOVERNOR

July 12, 1991

Mr. Ronald A. Drum
931 Village Boulevard, Suite 907
West Palm Beach, Florida 33409

Dear Ronald:

Thank you for providing me with a copy of your recent letter to
Congressman Dingell. This information is very helpful, and I've
passed it on to my staff for their review.

Although these issues will be debated at the federal level, I
certainly have a keen interest in their outcome. They will have
a large impact on our financial future. Please be sure that I
will keep your views in mind as Congress takes up proposed
banking reforms.

With kind regards, I am

Sincerely,

LAWTON CHILES

LC/trs

WILLIAM DONALD SCHAE
GOVERN

ANNAPOLIS OFF
STATE HO
ANNAPOLIS, MARYLAND 2
(301) 974-3

BALTIMORE OFF
ROOM
301 WEST PRESTON STR
BALTIMORE, MARYLAND 21
(301) 225-4

WASHINGTON OFF
SUITE
444 NORTH CAPITOL STREET, N
WASHINGTON, DC. 20
(202) 638-2

TDD (301) 333-3

July 17, 1991

Mr. Ronald A. Drum
Attorney at Law
931 Village Boulevard
Suite 907
West Palm Beach, FL 33409

Dear Mr. Drum:

Thank you for writing me on July 4, 1991 enclosing your letter
of June 27, 1991 to Congressman John M. Dingell.

I read with interest your concerns about the state of the nation's
economy and morality and commend you for suggesting steps
that would lead to an "American Renaissance."

Please accept my appreciation for sharing with me correspondence
that contains so much food for thought.

Sincerely,

Governor

EXECUTIVE OFFICE
STATE OF MISSOURI

July 16, 1991

JHN ASHCROFT
GOVERNOR

P.O. BOX 720
JEFFERSON CITY, MO 65102

Mr. Ronald Anthony Drum
Attorney at Law
931 Village Boulevard, Suite 907
West Palm Beach, FL 33409

Dear Mr. Drum:

Thank you for your recent letter. I appreciate receiving it, and have taken the liberty of sharing the information with Marise Stewart, Director, Missouri State Office in Washington, D.C. I know she will be interested in reviewing it too. If you have additional materials of interest, please send them to her at:

> Missouri State Office
> Hall of the States
> 400 North Capitol
> Suite 374
> Washington, D.C. 20001

Again, thank you for sharing this information with me. If I or my staff may be of assistance to you in the future, please feel free to contact my office.

Sincerely,

John Ashcroft

GOVERNOR

State of North Dakota

OFFICE OF THE GOVERNOR

600 E. Boulevard-Ground Floor

BISMARCK, NORTH DAKOTA 58505-0001

(701) 224-2200

GEORGE A. SINNER
GOVERNOR

July 25, 1991

Ronald A. Drum, MBA, CPA
931 Village Boulevard, Suite 907
West Palm Beach, Florida 33409

Dear Mr. Drum:

Thank you for furnishing a copy of your letter addressed to Representative John M. Dingell. Your letter was most interesting, even though it made us focus on issues many people would just as soon avoid. I share some of your concerns and frustration over the growing social problems and the level of fraud and dishonesty so prevalent in today's environment.

The bills before Congress to reform the banking industry and deposit insurance fund will have a devastating impact on all of us, if not carefully crafted. In May of this year, Governor Sinner and Wisconsin Governor Tommy G. Thompson sent a joint letter to each member of the House and Senate Banking Committees outlining concerns over a number of provisions contained in the Treasury Bill, The Financial Institutions Safety and Consumer Choice Act of 1991. The letter dealt with issues of importance to our states and the need to preserve a sound financial industry by maintaining a state system of chartering and regulating.

Your warning about the effects of repealing the Glass-Steagell Act is well presented. Provided appropriate "fire walls" are not constructed to separate the banking and securities industry, the potential is ripe for added problems to emerge.

Your statements about the United States and the American consumer being all borrowed out are right on target. Unfortunately, the nation has built a standard for consumers to utilize buying power over time. We need to develop incentives that will encourage people to cultivate a savings habit once again.

Again, Mr. Drum, thank you for sharing your interesting letter.

Sincerely,

Lloyd B. Omdahl
Acting Governor

LBO:JSC:ksp

STATE OF COLORADO

Roy Romer
Governor

July 26, 1991

Ronald Anthony Drum
931 Village Blvd., Suite 907
West Palm Beach, FL 33409

Dear Mr. Drum:

Thank you for your letter regarding the financial condition of commercial banks in this nation. The information you provided was interesting, and I appreciate your taking the time to contact me.

I share your concern about the health of the banking system in this country. I have forwarded your letter to Barbara Walker, the Colorado State Bank Commissioner, for her input. If you have any further questions or concerns, please contact the Colorado Division of Banking directly at 303 W. Colfax Ave., Suite 650, Denver, CO 80204.

Again, thank you for writing.

Sincerely,

Roy Romer
Governor

RR: nat

cc: Barbara Walker, Colorado State Bank Commissioner

RICHARD A. GEPHARDT
3D DISTRICT, MISSOURI

MAJORITY LEADER
COMMITTEE ON THE BUDGET
PERMANENT SELECT
COMMITTEE ON INTELLIGENCE

Congress of the United States
House of Representatives
Washington, DC 20515

WASHINGTON OFFICE:
1432 LONGWORTH HOUSE OFFICE BUILD
WASHINGTON, DC 20515
PHONE (202) 225-2671

DISTRICT OFFICE
9959 GRAVOIS
ST. LOUIS, MO 63123
PHONE (314) 631-9959

August 22, 1991

Mr. Ronald Drum
931 Village Boulevard, Suite 907
West Palm Beach, FL 33409

Dear Mr. Drum:

Thank you for contacting me regarding my decision not to run for President in 1992.

A little more than two years ago, I took myself out of the 1992 Presidential contest when I announced my candidacy for Majority Leader. That decision was right when I made it, and I reaffirm it now.

In recent months I have been urged by people such as you to reconsider and to launch a second campaign for the Presidency.

The record of the Bush Administration makes your case compelling. Diminished opportunity for the next generation of Americans, declining investment in education and research and public works, the decay of tax policy into a spoils system for the rich, the immoral Republican strategy of racial division, underlying problems in our foreign policy, and the beating we take every day in foreign trade are issues which demand the strongest possible challenge by our party.

For two years I have conducted surveys on issues of concern to Americans. All of the information I have seen has persuaded me that George Bush's popularity is paper-thin -- that he can be defeated in 1992. But I am also convinced that my greatest contribution to that cause will be made, not as a Presidential candidate, but as Majority Leader, helping to shape, define, and advance the Democratic message.

I feel that it is best for my district and for the Democratic Party in Congress and across the country for me to remain as Majority Leader.

Even though I will not be a candidate for President in 1992, I am not withdrawing from the fight to make the Democratic Party stand for working families and the middle class. I will continue to campaign for Democratic ideals and to work for their realization in Congress.

Again, thank you for your kind words. I always welcome the opportunity to hear from you. Please stay in touch.

Yours very truly,

Richard A. Gephardt

Richard A. Gephardt
House Majority Leader

United States Senate
WASHINGTON, D.C. 20510

April 13, 1979

Mr. Ronald Drum
79 Village Rd.
Manhasset, New York 11030

Dear Mr. Drum:

Thank you very much for your recent letter. I
appreciate your taking the time to send me your
insights.

You can be sure that I will give careful attention to
the concerns you have raised.

Very truly yours,

Orrin G. Hatch
United States Senator

OGH/ucr

United States Senate

WASHINGTON, D.C. 20510

March 5, 1979

Mr. Ronald Drun
79 Village Road
Manhasset, New York 11030

Dear Mr. Drun:

Thanks so much for taking the time to provide me with a
copy of your letter to President Carter regarding technological advancement and America's economic future.

I value your thoughts and opinions, and I hope that you
will continue to keep in touch with me on other issues that
need my attention. I will be sure to carefully review any
other materials or information which you may care to send me
here in the Senate.

Sincerely,

Bill Bradley
United States Senator

EB/bk.

JESSE HELMS
NORTH CAROLINA

United States Senate
WASHINGTON, D.C. 20510

March 14, 1979

Mr. Ronald Drum
79 Village Road
Manhasset, New York   11030

Dear Mr. Drum:

Thank you for sending me a copy of your February 22 letter to President Jimmy Carter.

I appreciate your sharing these thoughts with me, and you may be assured that I, too, shall give them every consideration.

Many thanks for taking the time to write.

Kindest regards.

Sincerely,

Jesse Helms

JESSE HELMS:bsa

DEPARTMENT OF THE TREASURY

WASHINGTON, D.C. 20220

August 6, 1981

Mr. Ronald Drum
605 North Old Ranch Road
Arcadia, CA 91006

Dear Mr. Drum:

On behalf of President Reagan, thank
you for your letter. Because the Treasury
Department is responsible for tax policy,
your letter was referred to me. We have
noted your comments and appreciate your
taking the time to write.

Sincerely,

John F. Kelly
Public Liaison &
Consumer Affairs

ARGE ROUKEMA
5TH DISTRICT, NEW JERSEY

COMMITTEES:

NKING, FINANCE AND
URBAN AFFAIRS

UCATION AND LABOR

T COMMITTEE ON HUNGER
ANKING MINORITY MEMBER)

Congress of the United States
House of Representatives
Washington, DC 20515
December 31, 1985

WASHINGTON OFFICE:
303 CANNON HOUSE OFFICE BUILDING
WASHINGTON, DC 20515
(202) 225-4465

NEW JERSEY OFFICES:
555 ROUTE 17 SOUTH
RIDGEWOOD, NJ 07450
(201) 447-3900

58 TRINITY STREET
NEWTON, NJ 07860
(201) 579-3039

. Ronald Anthony Drum
torney at Law
0 Broadway - Suite 1515
w York, NY 10038

ear Mr. Drum:

Thank you for your recent letter concerning the Racketeer
fluenced and Corrupt Organizations Act (RICO). I regret that you do
t share my support for Congressman Boucher's bill to clarify RICO's
tented reach.

As you may know, Congressman Boucher's bill, H.R. 2943, would
end the RICO statute to allow civil actions to be brought under the
t only after a defendant is convicted of a criminal offense. I have
sponsored this important legislation because I believe it is
cessary to clarify the intent of Congress in enacting the original
CO law in 1970. This bill is presently before the House Judiciary
bcommittee on Criminal Justice, which held hearings during July,
ptember, and October. Let me assure you that I will make my
lleagues aware of your suggestion that the RICO statute contain a
od faith requirement rather than a prior conviction requirement, as
H.R. 2943.

Thank you again for taking the time to write. I hope you will
ntinue to give me the benefit of your thoughts on this and other
tters of mutual concern.

Sincerely,

Marge Roukema
Member of Congress

R:SL

THIS STATIONERY PRINTED ON PAPER MADE WITH RECYCLED FIBERS

TED WEISS
17th District
New York

Chairman
Subcommittee on
Intergovernmental
Relations and
Human Resources

2442 Rayburn Building
Washington, D.C. 20515
202/225-5635

Patricia S. Fleming
Administrative Assistant

Congress of the United States
House of Representatives

January 15, 1986

Committees:

Foreign Affairs

Government Operations

Children, Youth and Fa

National Commission
on Working Women

Executive Board Membe
Congressional Arts Cau

Secretary, New York Sta
Congressional Delegati

Mr. Ronald Drum
Attorney at Law
150 Broadway, Suite 1515
New York, N.Y. 10038

Dear Mr. Drum:

Thank you for writing me to express your opposition to H.R. 2943, a bill introduced by Congressman Boucher to amend the Racketeer Influenced and Corrupt Organizations Act (RICO).

H.R. 2943 was introduced last July, and referred to the Subcommittee on Criminal Justice of the House Judiciary Committee. Since then, three hearings have been held on the bill.

Many business groups and professional associations have expressed concern about what they regard as the wrongful use of the RICO statute. However, I have not yet been convinced that the approach taken by Congressman Boucher is the correct one. Please be assured that I will keep your views in mind if this bill comes before me on the House floor.

Thank you again for your letter. Please do not hesitate to contact me in the future on this or any other issue of mutual concern.

Sincerely,

TED WEISS
Member of Congress

TW:mlr

𝔘𝔫𝔦𝔱𝔢𝔡 𝔖𝔱𝔞𝔱𝔢𝔰 𝔖𝔢𝔫𝔞𝔱𝔢

WASHINGTON, D.C. 20510

January 13, 1986

Mr. Ronald Drum
150 Broadway, 1515
New York, New York   10038

Dear Mr. Drum:

Thank you for taking the time to share your concerns with me. I appreciate hearing from you.

During the current session of Congress, the Senate is considering a variety of issues crucial to the future of our country. Your comments are particularly valuable to me as we consider solutions to the pressing problems of this country. As my colleagues and I consider policy proposals -- on the floor of the Senate, during committee deliberation, and in the development of new initiatives -- I'll be sure to keep your concerns in mind.

Again, thanks for giving me the benefit of your views.

Sincerely,

Gary Hart

PATRICIA SCHROEDER
1ST DISTRICT, DENVER, COLORADO

WASHINGTON OFFICE:
2410 RAYBURN HOUSE OFFICE BUILDING
WASHINGTON, DC 20515
(202) 225-4431

DISTRICT OFFICE:
1800 EMERSON STREET
DENVER, CO 80218
(303) 866-1230

Congress of the United States
House of Representatives
Washington, DC 20515

ARMED SERVICES COMM
POST OFFICE AND CIV
SERVICE COMMITTE
JUDICIARY COMMITTE
SELECT COMMITTEE C
CHILDREN, YOUTH AN
FAMILIES
CONGRESSIONAL CAUCU
WOMEN'S ISSUES, CO-C

January 27, 1986

Ronald Anthony Drum
Attorney at Law
150 Broadway, Suite 1515
New York, NY 10038

Dear Mr. Drum:

Thank you for your letter on civil RICO.

H.R. 2943, a bill to amend the civil RICO provisions, has been referred
to the House Judiciary Subcommittee on Criminal Justice. It would limit
civil RICO actions to those cases where the defendant has already been
convicted of rackteering crime. A number of hearings have been held.
At least one more is scheduled in February.

It is true that civil RICO has been misused by some against legitimate
businesses. It is also true that civil RICO has evolved into something
different from what Congress originally intended.

On the other hand, some have argued that RICO has proved to be an important
consumer protection statute against white collar crimes. To require prior
criminal conviction would eliminate most of the civil RICO suits, thus making
RICO an ineffective deterrent against fraudulent behavior.

To be frank, I haven't made up my mind on the issue. For this reason, I
appreciate your sharing your opinion with me.

Sincerely,

Pat Schroeder
Member of Congress

PS/apz

United States Senate
WASHINGTON, D.C. 20510

February 14, 1986

Mr. Ronald A. Drum
150 Broadway, Suite 1515
New York, New York 10038

Dear Ronald:

Thank you for contacting me on issues of importance to you. I greatly appreciate having the benefit of your views. While I deeply value the input of my constituents from Iowa, letters from concerned citizens such as yourself from all over the country offer an additional perspective and enhance the legislative process.

I hope you will continue to keep me informed of your views on matters of importance to you.

Sincerely,

Tom Harkin
United States Senator

TH/gs

CHARLES A. HAYES
1ST DISTRICT, ILLINOIS

COMMITTEES:
EDUCATION AND LABOR
SMALL BUSINESS

Congress of the United States
House of Representatives
Washington, DC 20515

REPLY TO:
WASHINGTON OFFICE:
☐ 1028 LONGWORTH BUILDIN
WASHINGTON, DC 20515
(202) 225-4372

DISTRICT OFFICE:
☐ 7801 SOUTH COTTAGE GROVE
CHICAGO, IL 60619
(312) 783-6800

January 4, 1986

Ronald Anthony Drum
CPA, JD
Attorney at Law
150 Broadway, Suite 1515
New York, N.Y. 10032

Dear Mr. Drum:

I appreciate your taking the time to inform me of your views. Your ideas are thought-provoking and I shall certainly keep them in mind when called upon to vote in the House. I remain convinced that it is only through the assimilation of opinions and of citizens like you, Mr. Drum, that the House of Representatives can truly meet the real needs of the American people.

Please keep in contact with me on this or any other issue of public concern.

Sincerely,

CHARLES A. HAYES
Member of Congress

CAH/df

HAROLD E. FORD
9TH DISTRICT, TENNESSEE

COMMITTEES:
WAYS AND MEANS

CHAIRMAN
OMMITTEE ON PUBLIC ASSISTANCE
UNEMPLOYMENT COMPENSATION

LECT COMMITTEE ON AGING

RAYBURN HOUSE OFFICE BUILDING
WASHINGTON, DC 20515
(202) 225-3265

MEMPHIS OFFICES:

167 NORTH MAIN STREET
FEDERAL OFFICE BUILDING, SUITE 369
MEMPHIS, TN 38103
(901) 521-4131

MALLORY POST OFFICE
193 WEST MITCHELL ROAD
MEMPHIS, TN 38109
(901) 521-4141

ROBERT BOYD
ADMINISTRATIVE ASSISTANT

A.J. COOPER, JR.
TAX COUNSEL

Congress of the United States
House of Representatives
Washington, DC 20515
January 24, 1986

Ronald Anthony Drum, Esq.
150 Broadway Suite 1515
New York, New York 10038

Dear Mr. Drum:

Thank you very much for writing regarding H.R. 2943, the
Racketeer Influnced Corrupt Organizations Act (Civil RICO).

The rise of civil lawsuits under the "RICO" statute has
reached epidemic proportions. In the past several years
there have been at least 420 federal court decisions in
treble damage RICO cases. The current law crowds federal
courts with run-of-the-mill, costly and protracted litigation and subjects defendants to damaging accusations of
racketeering activity.

Fifteen years ago when Congress passed this legislation, its
original intent was to eradicate organized crime in the
United States. It was essentially a criminal statute aimed
at mobsters. But Congress also provided for persons hurt by
various kinds of fraud, to bring civil suits in federal
courts and receive treble damages if successful. As a
result, Congress inadvertently generated litigation that
bears no resemblance to the legislation's original intent.
Thus, reform by Congress is essential.

I will lend my support to legislation that will correct the
inherent defects in the current law. However, numerous
proposals have been suggested and I am currently reviewing
them before making a final decision as to which proposal I
will support.

Again, thank you for writing and please feel free to call if
you should have any questions.

Sincerely,

HAROLD FORD
Member of Congress

HF/dew

ALBERT G. BUSTAMANTE
23RD DISTRICT, TEXAS

CONGRESS OF THE UNITED STATES

HOUSE OF REPRESENTATIVES

January 21, 1986

Mr. Ronald A. Drum
Attorney At Law
150 Broadway
Suite 1515
New York, New York 10038

Dear Mr. Drum:

This acknowledges your letter of November 27th. Please
forgive this late response. As you know, the House
Judiciary Subcommittee held hearings on H.R.2943
throughout the latter part of 1985. Subcommittee staff
expects a House vote on this bill early in the 1986
session.

Be assured that as I consider the merits of H.R.2943
your views will be kept in mind. Again, your interest
in this issue is much appreciated.

Sincerely,

Albert G. Bustamante
Member of Congress

AGB:mep

Committee on

ARMED SERVICES

Subcommittees:
PROCUREMENT AND
MILITARY NUCLEAR
SYSTEMS

MILITARY PERSONNEL
AND COMPENSATION

SEAPOWER AND
STRATEGIC AND
CRITICAL MATERIALS

Committee on

**GOVERNMENT
OPERATIONS**

Subcommittees:

COMMERCE, CONSUMER
AND MONETARY AFFAIRS

ENVIRONMENT, ENERGY
AND NATURAL RESOURCES

Please reply to:

☐ **Washington Office:**

1116 Longworth House Office Building
Washington, D.C. 20515
(202) 225-4511

☐ **District Office:**

Federal Building
727 East Durango Street
Room 146-B
San Antonio, Texas 78206
(512) 229-6191

Federal Courthouse Building
Room 103
100 East Broadway
Del Rio, Texas 78841
(512) 774-6546

1300 Matamoros Street
Laredo, Texas 78040
(512) 724-7774

Uvalde County Courthouse
Uvalde, Texas 78801
(512) 278-5021

101 East Dimmit
West Annex
Crystal City, Texas 78839
(512) 374-5200

THIS STATIONERY PRINTED ON
PAPER MADE WITH RECYCLED FIB

WILLIAM V. ROTH, JR., DELAWARE, CHAIRMAN

'EVENS, ALASKA   THOMAS F. EAGLETON,
ES McC. MATHIAS, JR.,   MISSOURI
'LAND   LAWTON CHILES, FLORIDA
M S. COHEN, MAINE   SAM NUNN, GEORGIA
OURENBERGER, MINNESOTA   JOHN GLENN, OHIO
:N B. RUDMAN,   CARL LEVIN, MICHIGAN
HAMPSHIRE   ALBERT GORE, JR.,
:OCHRAN, MISSISSIPPI   TENNESSEE
    JOHN M. DUNCAN, STAFF DIRECTOR
MARGARET P. CRENSHAW, MINORITY STAFF DIRECTOR

SUBCOMMITTEE:
WILLIAM V. ROTH, JR., DELAWARE, CHAIRMAN
WARREN B. RUDMAN, NEW HAMPSHIRE, VICE CHAIRMAN
CHARLES McC. MATHIAS, JR.,   SAM NUNN, GEORGIA
    MARYLAND   LAWTON CHILES, FLORIDA
WILLIAM S. COHEN, MAINE   JOHN GLENN, OHIO
THAD COCHRAN, MISSISSIPPI   CARL LEVIN, MICHIGAN
TED STEVENS, ALASKA   ALBERT GORE, JR.,
                                TENNESSEE
    DANIEL F. RINZEL, CHIEF COUNSEL
ELEANORE J. HILL, CHIEF COUNSEL TO THE MINORITY

United States Senate

COMMITTEE ON
GOVERNMENTAL AFFAIRS
SENATE PERMANENT SUBCOMMITTEE
ON INVESTIGATIONS
WASHINGTON, DC 20510

January 24, 1986

Ronald Anthony Drum, Esquire
150 Broadway
Suite 1515
New York, New York 10038

Dear Mr. Drum:

Thank you for your recent letter expressing concern over proposed changes to the current RICO statute. I am aware of the important assistance, both criminally and civilly, which this law has provided law enforcement the last fifteen years in its fight against organized crime. However, I am also aware of some of the abuses that some plaintiffs have committed in applying the law to situations that it was not intended to cover.

I have been closely following the hearings that both the Senate and House Judiciary Committees have held concerning the various proposals, including Representative Boucher's, to amend the RICO statute. Through the committee process, I believe a final proposal will be passed that balances the need for effective law enforcement with protecting innocent businessmen from costly and needless litigation.

In closing, I want to thank you for your letter and interest in this problem. Please do not hesitate to contact me again about this or any other issue that may be of concern to you.

Sincerely,

Sam Nunn

APPENDIX B

Law School Dedication Speech Indiana University September 12, 1986.

by William H. Rehnquist*

The State of the Legal Profession**

I am not a legal educator, but I have been a member of the legal profession for thirty-four years. Every member of the profession has a vital interest in, and derives benefit from, the activities of the law schools of this nation. I would like to talk to you for a few minutes about the current state of the legal profession and why I think that subject should be of interest to law schools as well as to lawyers and clients.

During the past generation the manner in which law is practiced in the United Sates has changed dramatically in more than one way.

a) Within the last fifteen years alone, the number of lawyers in the United Sates has more than doubled, from fewer than 350,000 in 1970 to nearly 700,000 today. This increase is out of all proportion to the increase in the nation's population: in 1960 there was one lawyer for every 627 people in the country, whereas today there is one lawyer for every 354 people.

b) Lawyers on the average today make considerably more money, even after adjustment for inflation, than they did twenty-five years ago. A recent ABA Journal survey reports that the median income of lawyers responding to the survey is roughly $65,000. I suspect that the percentage of gross national product going to pay for legal services has likewise increased; current estimate suggest that law firms bill close to $40 billion a year. The latest headline-making development in this area is the decision of several leading New York law firms to substantially increase their associates' compensation, and to pay additional bonuses to those who had the misfortune to work for government lawyers' salaries as law clerks for one or two years.

c) The structure of the firms which engage in the practice of law has also changed dramatically. Today, according to the same ABA survey, the median law firm size is eight lawyers, and nearly one-quarter of the lawyers work in law firms that billed between $1 and $3 million in 1985. The number of firms with one hundred or more lawyers has increased from only four in 1960 to well over two hundred today. Indeed, in just the last *five* years, the number of firms with over two hundred lawyers has increased nearly four-fold, to about seventy. According to the recently adopted report of the American Bar Association commission on Professionalism, it is not uncommon to find firms of over three hundred lawyers, with offices not only in many states but in foreign countries as well. Twenty-five years ago, firms of that size and geographic diversity were simply unknown.

d) Young associates in large law firms today apparently work much harder, and under significantly different conditions, than they did twenty-five years ago. It is apparently common in some major New York firms to expect associates to bill in excess of two thousand hours per year, and the ratio of associates to partners in some large firms is increasing sharply. There is some speculation that the recent associate salary increases will be paralleled by increased expectations in terms of billing hours.

* Chief Justice of the United States Supreme Court

e) Institutional loyalty appears to be in decline. Partners in law firms have become increasingly "mobile," feeling much freer than they formerly did and having much greater opportunity than they formerly did, to shift from one firm to another and take revenue-producing clients with them.

These strike me as very significant developments that affect not only lawyers, but laws students who anticipate practicing law, clients of lawyers, and in some ways the public as a whole. There is nothing intrinsically good or bad about change, and generalized complaints that the profession is "losing its professionalism" may represent only nostalgic yearning for the "good old days" that people in my age range always seem to have. But is does appear that the organization of the profession is moving in a particular direction, and that academic institutions concerned with the profession - that is, law schools - should pay attention to and examine what is happening.

I think if similar developments occurred in the field of medicine they would be of considerable interest not merely to medical students but to members of medical faculties, and if they occurred in the field of business they would be of considerable interest not merely to business school students but to members of business school faculties. But for some reason the history of law school faculties is quite different; very, very rarely do they evince any interest in the sort of empirical studies that might shed light on the sorts of changes I have mentioned. Law school faculties have preferred to devote themselves, by and large, to criticism and analysis of legal doctrine as it is found in the opinions of appellate courts. This is undoubtedly a very worthwhile enterprise, and one which law faculties are peculiarly qualified to pursue. But one wonders whether some of the emphasis of law school study and research might not profitably be shifted to the broad area of how legal services are delivered, and surely the structure of the practice of law is a vital element in the delivery of those legal services.

A very informative symposium on the corporate law firm was recently conducted at Stanford University Law School. Professor Robert W. Gordon described the papers collected in the symposium this way:

"Together, they amount to a series of excited reports from explorers returning from journeys into the heart of a vast, mysterious, and almost unmapped interior of American society, its large metropolitan law firms . . . .

When one thinks about it for a moment, it seems astonishing that law firms should have for so long remained almost unexplored in legal scholarship. These are, after all, social institutions of some prominence. They have a significant place in the economy, billing some $38 billion annually . . .

Yet the legal academy from its inception has on the whole made a determined decision to remain aloof from the institutions where most of its students will spend their careers."

37 Standard L. Rev. 271, 272.

And if the "large metropolitan law firm" that was the subject of this symposium is *virtually terra incognita* the smaller firm in which most lawyers still practice is *totally terra incognita*.

My particular interest today is in suggesting a few questions - questions worth answering, I think - that I see raised by the changes in modern practice alluded to earlier.

First, there are several questions that spring from what, to the outside observer at least, look to be fairly substantial changes in the life of an associate in a relatively large firm. What are the consequences to the associate, to the profession, and to the public at large if the associate is expected to bill two thousand to twenty-one hundred hours per year? Does such an associate have time to be *anything but* an associate lawyer in that large firm? At the time I practiced law, there was always a public aspect to the profession, and most lawyers did not regard themselves as totally discharging their obligation by simply putting in a given number of hours that could be billed to clients. Whether it was "pro bono' work of some sort, or a more generalized discharge of community obligation by serving on zoning boards, charity boards, and the like, lawyers felt that they could contribute something to the community in which they lived, and that they as well as the community would benefit from that contribution. It seems to me that a law firm that requires an associate to bill in excess of two thousand hours per year, thereby sharply curtailing the productive expenditure of energy outside of work, is substantially more concerned with profit-maximization than were firms when I practiced. Indeed, one might argue that such a firm is treating the associate very much as a manufacturer would treat a purchase of one hundred tons of scrap metal: if you use anything less than the one hundred tons that you paid for, you simply are not running an efficient business.

How do associates react to this treatment? Is the instinct of the young lawyer faced with staggering hours to favor exhaustive and exhausting research over exercising the judgment necessary to decide whether ten more hours of research will really benefit a client?

What other consequences flow from the apparent move toward profit-maximization? One consequence appears to be an increasing degree of specialization, particularly in large firms. There seems to be little doubt on the part of those in practice that specialization both serves the client and succeeds in maximizing the firm's income. I suspect that it may have the additional effect of making the work of lawyers in these firms more like drudgery than similar work was twenty-five years ago. There is more than a little evidence that while associates are perfectly willing to take the increased pay that they receive from large firms, they do not find the work particularly satisfying. Let me caution that the evidence I have seen in this area is almost entirely "anecdotal," and in the absence of more systematic studies it cannot possibly be otherwise.

A second area worth studying is the apparent increase in ethical difficulties that has come, if not as a result of structural changes in the profession, at least at the same time as those changes. It is only natural, I suppose, that as the practice of law in large firms has become organized on more and more of a business basis, geared to the maximization of income, this practice should on occasion push towards the margins of ethical propriety. Ethical considerations, after all, are factors which counsel *against* maximization of income in the best Adam Smith tradition, and the stronger the pressure to maximize income the more difficult it is to avoid the ethical margins.

I served for a number of years during my practice in Arizona on what was called the "Administrative Committee," which heard complaints against practicing lawyers and recommended disciplinary action against them where appropriate. My impression from this service was that the typical respondent in a proceeding before our Committee was a solo practitioner who was struggling financially; he ended up using for his own purposes trust account money which belonged to his client.

Lawyers in the established firms in Phoenix managed to avoid getting into this trouble, not necessarily because they were more ethical, but because they did not feel a great deal of financial pressure. Indeed, the lawyers in the well established firms in Phoenix in the 1950s were probably rather complacent. Each had regular institutional clients who brought in sizable revenues to the firm each year. The associates were assured of being able to make their house payments, and the partners were assured of being able to pay their country club dues. People in these firms put in a good days' work, but they did not feel,[in] the words of the song, that "they owed their soul to the company store."

I am sure that from an economic point of view of fully exploiting available resources, the changes in the structure of firms in the twenty-five years I am talking about probably make a good deal of sense. More work is undoubtedly being done for the client, and logged to the client, by partners and associates in today's large firms than was done by similar firms twenty-five years ago. But while in business there is essentially one side to this equation - maximization of income - there is another side to it in the practice of law. The greater the pressure for maximization of income, the more likely some sort of ethical difficulties will be encountered - whether the firm consists of a solo practitioner or of several hundred lawyers.

Recent examples abound of big firms running into big trouble. A large Baltimore law firm is currently being sued by an agency of the state of Maryland changing that the firm represented conflicting interests in connection with the Old Court Savings and Loan Association, which played a large part in Maryland's recent savings and loan crisis. A large Miami law firm is being sued by the government of Venezuela, which alleges that the firm knew or should have known about fraud against the government by one of the firm's clients. Another nationwide law firm based in New York recently settled for $40 million a suit against it by former customers of a client of the firm. Of course, neither being sued nor settling a law suit necessarily indicates wrongdoing. But these incidents, among others, were sufficient to prompt a recent article in the respected magazine "Business Week" entitled "A question of Integrity at Blue Chip Law Firms: Once Unthinkable, Charges of Foul Play are Hitting Prestigious Partnerships."

If, as Professor Roger Cramton observed in a recent article, the word being passed around some big law firms is that "you only eat what you kill" it is only natural that lawyers practicing in these firms will be more conscious than ever of the need to bring in their share of revenues. It would not be surprising if this sort of pressure led to ethical difficulties. Similarly, if one is expected to bill more than two thousand hours a year, there are bound to be temptations to exaggerate the hours actually put in.

But as any lawyer knows, ethical violations do not necessarily require knowledge on the part of any one lawyer in the firm that the canons of ethics are being violated. Size alone can lead to ethical problems. A partner in one branch of the firm may be representing one client while another partner in another branch of the firm represents another client; if it turns out that these two clients have "conflicting interests," there may be an ethical violation even though neither partner actually knew that someone else in the firm was representing the conflicting interest. Despite the blessings of modern communications, it simply must be harder to keep track of the activities of a firm consisting of several hundred lawyers in several different cities than it would be of a significantly smaller, local organization. Obviously this fact alone does to counsel against expanding successful small organizations into successful large ones, but it again suggests that a law firm cannot treat the question of expansion precisely the way a business organization does. Careful study in this area could expose developing systemic ethical problems and begin the search for solutions.

The changes in the structure of the legal profession to which I have referred have a profound effect on lawyers, and therefore a very significant effect on law students who are being trained in law schools to practice law. They may well affect the cost of legal services, the concept of a reasonable fee when a court is making a determination as to what fee is reasonable, and many other matters connected with the law generally and the delivery of legal services in particular.

Perhaps one response to the curiosity which I have expressed is that so long as the clients are willing to pay the bills, and the insurance company is willing to insure, no outsider need question what is going on. I don't think that is an adequate answer. Even the most devoted advocate of the free market speaks in terms of an informed seller as well as an informed buyer. And yet the information we have about many of these developments is either nonexistent or largely anecdotal. Surely more information in this area would be of benefit to the profession at large and to society as a whole.

I would also add that while we may prefer the free market model for many forms of enterprise, the legal profession, always heavily regulated, has never been one of those enterprises. The profession of law is not like the manufacture of widgets in which the widget manufacturer presumably pays its own way: hires its own labor, furnishes its own plant, ships its own products. The education of almost every law student in the country is subsidized by the law school which the student attends. And the ultimate distinction between lawyers and non-lawyers, though many of them may not take advantage of it, is the ability to appear before a court and advocate the cause of a client. The courts of the United States are subsidized by United States taxpayers; the courts of the state of Indiana are subsidized by Indiana taxpayers. It is certainly not amiss to wish to have more information about the structure of a profession which relies so heavily on the use of publicly subsidized institutions for the conduct of its business.

I once asked a good friend of mine who is the dean of a law school why law professors didn't conduct more empirical studies of the profession and the way law actually effects people, and his reply was that legal academics were just not very good at dealing with empirical studies. It struck me later that this would have been an entirely appropriate remark for the dean of a seventeenth century medical school in Western Europe to have made; after all, Galen, the great Roman physician, had long ago explained largely as a matter of abstract inquiry how the body worked, and why on earth should someone like William Harvey bother himself with experiments on real human beings to see how blood circulates?

Practitioners of law have long lamented that law is getting to be "more and more like a business"; Louis D. Brandeis made that observation in 1905, and it has been made periodically since. If present complaints meant no more than that lawyers are more careful about keeping time sheets, using firm manpower, and the like, no eyebrows would be raised. But the practice of law has always been a subtle blend between a "calling" such as the ministry, where compensation is all but disregarded, and the selling of a product, where compensation is all important. The move over the past twenty-five years has been to increase the emphasis on compensation - to make the practice of law more like a business. Whether or.not it has "gone too far," I have neither the necessary information nor the necessary expertise to say. But I think that these changes over the past twenty-five years would be a very sensible subject for careful examination by law schools.

I like to think of the profession of law as a multi-legged stool - one leg is the practicing bar, another leg is the judiciary, another leg is the academic lawyers, another leg the government lawyers. No leg of the stool can support the profession by itself, and each leg is heavily interdependent on the others. The practicing bar has always been greatly concerned, and rightly so, with the quality of education given in the law schools. The judiciary is concerned with the quality of the practicing bar; the practicing bar, the government lawyers, and the academic lawyers are concerned with the quality of the judiciary. It seems to me entirely fit and proper that the law schools should concern themselves, perhaps more than they have in the past, with the structure of the practicing bar. But whether or not the academic lawyers at the Indiana University School of Law choose to follow my suggestions today, I have no doubt that they and the Law School will continue to flourish as they have in the past, in the finer and more spacious surroundings which we dedicate today.

APPENDIX C

- TABLE OF CONTENTS -

THE KEY PARTS OF THE AMERICAN MACHINE

I.   Federal Government:

    A. The Executive (The President)
       (1) The President's Cabinet
       (2) Federal Agencies (i.e. The IRS., etc.)
    B. The Legislature (The U.S. Congress)
    C. The Judiciary (The U.S. Supreme Court, Federal Appellate Courts, Federal District Courts & Miscellaneous Federal Courts i.e. Federal Bankruptcy Court, U.S. Tax Court, etc.)
    D. The Federal Reserve
    E. Special Interest Groups: the Lobbyist, the PACs, etc.
    F. The Democratic Party
    G. The Republican Party
    H. The Swing Independent Non-Party
    I. Ross Perot, Louis Farrakan, Jessie Jackson, & Pat Buchanan

II.   State Government:

    A. The Executive (Governor)
    B. The Legislature (State Assemblies & Senates)
    C. The State Judiciary (State Supreme & Appellate Court, Circuit Courts, County Courts, Criminal Courts, Traffic Courts, Justices of the Peace, etc.)
    D. Special Interest Groups: Lobbyists, PACs, etc.
    E. The Democratic Party
    F. The Republican Party
    G. The State Tax Collector

III. Local Government:

    A. County Government:
       (1) The County Commissioners
       (2) The Democratic Party
       (3) The Republican Party
       (4) The Property Tax Assessor
       (5) Special Interest Groups: Lobbyists, PACs, etc.
       (6) County Courts-See II.C. above.

B. City Government:
   (1) The Mayor
   (2) The City Council
   (3) The City Tax Collector
   (4) The Democratic Party
   (5) The Republican Party
   (6) Special Interest Groups: Lobbyists, PACs, etc.

IV. Financial Institutions:

   A. Commercial Banks
   B. Savings Banks:
      (1) S&Ls
      (2) Thrifts
      (3) Credit Unions
   C. Investment Bankers
   D. Wall Street Brokerage Houses
   E. Stock Markets (i.e. N.Y., Chicago):
      (1) The New York Stock Exchange
      (2) The American Stock Exchange
      (3) The National Association of Securities Dealers
          (NASDAQ)
   F. Bond Markets
   G. Commodity Exchanges
   H. Futures Markets
   I. Options Markets
   J. Insurance Industry
      (1) Life
      (2) Fire & Casualty
      (3) Health & Medical
   K. Pension Funds
   L. Illegal Drug Industry
   M. Merger & Acquisition Groups & Gangs
   N. Ford Motor Credit Corp., etc.
   O. Social Security, Medicare, and Medicaid
   P. Pawn Shops

V. Industrial -- Manufacturing Business:

   A. Mining, Metals, Lumber, Oil Drilling & Refining
   B. Factories -- Property Plant & Equipment:
      (1) Consumer Goods (Autos to Cosmetics)
      (2) Industrial Goods, Machinery, Equipment
      (3) Raw Material Processing, Chemicals, etc.
      (4) Assembly Operations & Plants
      (5) Pharmaceuticals
      (6) Electronics
      (7) Photographic
      (8) Computer Hardware
   C. Home Building & Construction
   D. Commercial Construction
   E. Aircraft Aerospace
   . Apparel

G. Printing
H. Food & Beverage

VI. <u>Retail Industry:</u>

A. Department Stores
B. Specialty Stores
C. QVC -- T.V. Buying
D. Mail Order
E. Auto Dealerships
F. Grocery Stores & Supermarkets
G. Convenience Stores
H. Discounters

VII. <u>Religions & Certain Charitable Businesses:</u>

A. The Salvation Army, United Way, etc.
B. Save Somebody, Inc.
C. Churches, Synagogues, Mosques & Storefront Missions

VIII. <u>American Service Industries:</u>

A. Dry Cleaners
B. Auto Repair
C. Accounting and Tax Services
D. Weight & Diet:
   (1) Gym
   (2) Diet Centers
   (3) Massage Centers
E. Unlicensed Psychological Counseling
F. Insurance Sales
G. Sanitation & Garbage Disposal
H. Telemarketing
I. External Data Entry
J. Consulting
K. Computer Software Development

IX. <u>The Educational Industry:</u>

A. Universities & Colleges
B. Public Schools
C. Private Schools
D. Day Care Centers

X. <u>Professions:</u>

A. Medical
B. Dental
C. Legal
D. CPA (Certified Public Accountant)
E. MBA (Master in Business Administration)
F. Engineering

G. Consulting
H. Teaching
I. Corporate Executives
J. Clergy
K. Banking Executives
L. Stock Brokers
M. Michael Jordan, et al.

XI. Import -- Export Industry:

A. Import Brokers
B. Export Brokers
C. Manufacturer's Representatives
D. Labor (American Jobs) Outsourcing Specialists

XII. The Media Industry:

A. Cable T.V.
B. Network T.V.
C. Tabloid T.V.
D. C-Span
E. Cable News Network (CNN)
F. Newspapers
G. Magazines
H. Video Stores
I. Movie Studios
J. Talk Radio
K. Publishing

XIII. Fun & Entertainment Industries:

A. Spectator Sports, Spectator Sports & More Spectator Sports - The New American Heroes
B. The Billiard Rooms & Pool Halls
C. The Disco Clubs
D. The Dance Halls
E. The Comedy Clubs
F. The State Fairs
G. The Amusement and Attraction Parks
H. Vacation & Resort Facilities and Centers
I. Escort Services
J. Movie Theaters
K. Gambling ($800 Billion Industry):
    (1) Bingo
    (2) Casino
    (3) Dog Racing
    (4) Horse Racing
    (5) Jai Alai
    (6) Lottery
    (7) Illegal Sports Gambling
L. Bars and Cocktail Lounges

XIV. **Smut , Drugs & Other Sundry Crimes**
($1.2 Trillion Industry):

    A. Pornography:
- (1) Magazines
- (2) Videos
- (3) Books
- (4) Nude Clubs

    B. Illegal Drugs:
- (1) Cocaine, Crack, and Crank
- (2) Heroin
- (3) Marijuana
- (4) LSD; Steroids; Uppers and Downers, etc.

    C. Prostitution
    D. Violent Crime - Armed Robbery, Kidnapping, etc.
    E. Non-Violent Crime - Government Corruption, Bank Fraud, Securities Fraud, etc.

XV. **The American People -- As of 1996:**

A. The Upper Class	(2%)
B The Gentry Middle Class	(8%)
C. The "Necessary" Middle Class	(12%)
D. The Slipping Lower Middle Class	(48%)
E. The Working Poor (Some Assistance)	(20%)
F. The Non-Working Poor (Welfare)	(8%)
G. The Homeless	(2%)

XVI. **Transportation Industry:**

    A. Small Package & Freight Delivery
    B. Railroad & Air Freight Delivery
    C. Airline Cargo & Passenger Service
    D. Trucking Industry
    E. U.S. Mail
    F. The Worldwide Internet

XVII. **Utilities Industries:**

    A. Gas
    B. Electric
    C. Nuclear
    D. Telephone

XVIII. **Agriculture:**

    A. The Family Run Farm
    B. The Industrial Farm
    C. Meat Packing Industry

APPENDIX D

N. The Business of Crime: Growing to be a Trillion Dollar Enterprise?

III. The Social Malaise:

A. Racism & Bigotry.
B. The Economic Middle-Class: Disintegration & Confrontation.
C. American Family Values:
   (1) Single Parent Families.
   (2) Teenage Pregnancy.
   (3) Drugs, Crime, & Self-Indulgence.
D. American Dreams, Fantasies, and Reality.
E. A National Health Insurance Crisis.
F. A Nation of Pessimists -- A Sense of Things Only Getting Worse.
   Can We Turn It Around?
G. The Media Madhouse.
H. Organized Religion in Crisis? Or No Religion at All?
I. What is Freedom Really? -- The Scope of Our Constitution and the "Bill of Rights."